SOCIOLOGY IN THE USSR

A Collection of Readings from Soviet Sources

Editor
STEPHEN P. DUNN

INTERNATIONAL ARTS AND SCIENCES PRESS, INC.
WHITE PLAINS, NEW YORK

INTERNATIONAL

ARTS

AND

SCIENCES

PRESS

901 North Broadway
White Plains, New York 10603

The material included in Sociology in the USSR first
appeared in Soviet Sociology and Soviet Anthropology
and Archeology, translation journals that are published
by International Arts and Sciences Press, Inc.

Library of Congress Catalog Card Number: 68-23895

Printed in the United States of America

Contents

EMPIRICAL METHODOLOGY AND TECHNIQUE

DEMOGRAPHY, ETHNOGEOGRAPHY, AND SOCIAL STATISTICS

EMPIRICAL STUDIES OF WORKER COMMUNITIES

RURAL SOCIOLOGY AND AGRICULTURE

RELIGION

LOCAL GOVERNMENT AND ADMINISTRATION

Preface

The articles in this collection have been drawn from the translation journals Soviet Sociology and Soviet Anthropology and Archeology, which began publication in 1962. The original Soviet sources are indicated on the first page of every article.

It is hoped that the collection will help fill the void in Western knowledge of the current state of Soviet sociology, a rapidly expanding field of study in the USSR.

Two important omissions require comment. First: I have not included any work on the sociology of labor because a forthcoming IASP translation of the Soviet book Man and His Work, edited by A. G. Zdravomyslov et. al., and based on a four-year study of work attitudes conducted by the Laboratory of Sociological Studies of Leningrad State University, supersedes everything published heretofore on this topic. Second: a critique of Western sociology has been omitted because, in order to reflect adequately the range of interests of Soviet scholars and the range of empirical information available, a special issue of Soviet Sociology is being prepared.

Stephen P. Dunn

Sociological Theory and Research

Voprosy istorii, 1960, No. 11

V. Iu. Krupianskaia

THE SUBJECT MATTER AND METHODOLOGY OF ETHNOGRAPHIC

STUDY OF THE SOVIET WORKING CLASS

The problem of the culture and mode of life of the working class is increasingly attracting the attention of Soviet researchers. In recent years considerable progress has been made in their study. This work is also proceeding actively in the people's democracies. (1) Nevertheless, it must be recognized that this field of ethnography continues to lag. Pre-Marxist, and particularly prerevolutionary Russian ethnography, did not set itself the task of studying the working class. It regarded the working class as a uniform mass without specific ethnic characteristics, and saw the peasantry as the sole bearer of national culture. As a consequence, a substantial portion of the population of a particular nationality, not engaged in agriculture or the fishing and hunting occupations, remained outside the purview of ethnographic study. This not only impoverished but distorted the general picture of the development of the folk way of life, the folk culture.

The weakness of the theoretical treatment of this most complex problem is undoubtedly also a consequence of the lack of necessary contact between ethnography and other humanistic disciplines, particularly history. Whereas historians, in studying the working class, place in the foreground such problems as the origin of the working class and its role in the production of material goods, as well as its role in political life as the advance detachment of the working people, ethnographers, taking these most important problems as their point of departure, raise a number of other questions. Working with vital, concrete material, centering their attention on man and his consciousness and raising most important questions with respect to the appearance of the new, Soviet family, the new societal way of life, ethnography is in a position substantially to enrich the understanding of the historical process. It can reveal more clearly the revolutionary transformative and creative role of the working class in building a communist society.

Naturally, this most complex subject matter can be elaborated more deeply and broadly if the efforts of historians and ethnographers are applied jointly.

Due to the vast scale and rates of growth of industry in the USSR, the leading role of the working class in the life of the entire country is constantly rising. It is absolutely clear that the study of any aspect of the culture and way of life of the people today is possible only if the role and significance of the working class in the history of society are revealed. Soviet scholarship has posed ethnographic study of the working class as one of the most important and pressing problems of the day.

The general trend of Soviet researches is characterized by an orientation toward contemporary problems, the study of the regularities of the development of the culture and way of life of the workers under the conditions of socialist reality. This flows from the very essence of Soviet science (ethnography in particular), which intimately relates theoretical problems to the practical work of building a communist society.

The principal objective of ethnographic studies of contemporary problems lies in detailed research into those vast and most complex processes that are occurring in the way of life of the present day as well as in other fields of life. The problem is to determine their direction and the factors that accelerate or retard the process of development. This type of problem cannot be resolved without clarifying the historical roots of contemporary phenomena. This produces a need for a deeper historical study — i.e., careful clarification of the manner in which the modes of life of workers took shape at particular stages in the development of society.

The first efforts of Soviet ethnographers to study the fundamental changes that have taken place in the way of life of workers in production, society and the family as a consequence of the triumph of socialism proved unsuccessful, because the problems posed were put and resolved without a historical approach to the phenomena under examination and without considering the historical conditions of formation of the mode of life. This was the nature of the studies of the USSR Academy of Sciences' Institute of Ethnography undertaken in 1950 with the object of studying various groups of workers in Moscow, Leningrad, the Moscow coal region,

and the Urals. In the ethnographic sense these studies went up a blind alley. The material collected did not make possible the solution of even a single scientific problem. Nor was it possible to elaborate a methodology of investigation. (2)

In 1951 the Institute of Ethnography conducted a special discussion on objectives and methodology of ethnographic study of workers. Its participants advanced, as an essential prerequisite to solution of the problem, a study of the history of the establishment of the hereditary working class, with determination of its territorial (national and regional) as well as social roots. Only under this condition is it possible to pose one of the most important problems in the study of the way of life of workers, the problem of the role of ethnic traditions (particularly the interpenetration of various national cultures) in the development of new forms of this mode of life. It was with these considerations in mind that the new program, underlying the studies now under way at the Institute of Ethnography of the USSR Academy of Sciences, was elaborated.

The Institute of Ethnography launched studies in the Middle Urals — one of the oldest of Russian industrial districts. (3) During the first stage of the work attention was centered on the old enterprises of Nizhnii Tagil: the former Nizhne-Tagil Metallurgical Works (founded in 1724) and the Vysokogorsk Iron Ore Mine (opened in 1721), which had repeatedly attracted the attention of scholars. (4) The choice of these enterprises makes it possible to study the socialist way of life of the present day with due consideration of the forms of culture and life of the workers which had developed historically in Nizhnii Tagil. The workers of these enterprises were not studied in isolation but in their interaction and intercourse with other strata of the population. This is important because only a comparative study makes possible a detailed demonstration of the specific mode of life of workers and guards us against an oversimplified and schematic approach to solution of the problem. (5)

In order to achieve a more precise clarification

of the processes occurring under the conditions of socialism, it is proposed in the immediate future to proceed to a study of the culture and way of life of workers of the Novo-Tagil Metallurgical Works, built in 1940. This plant, equipped with modern machinery, employs a large number of highly skilled workers. This will make it possible to more completely discover and shed light upon trends of development in one of the most progressive units of the working class.

Nizhnii Tagil is thus regarded as a unique sort of experiment station for long-term ethnographic studies.

Within the overall concept of comparative study of the way of life of workers and peasants, in 1954 the Institute of Ethnography of the USSR Academy of Sciences organized an expedition in the Kama and Viatka River valleys (within Sverdlovsk, Perm', and Kirov oblasts). One of the objectives of the expedition was to discover any distinctive features in the way of life of workers of the Urals. The survey showed that as early as the second half of the 19th century the way of life of Ural factory towns differed from that of the peasants in its tenor, in the broader cultural demands of the population, which may be traced in the principal aspects of material culture (housing, clothing, foodstuffs). The ethnographers also discovered the significant influence exercised by the way of life of workers upon the local peasantry, among whom urban culture forms (city dress, changes in dwellings, etc.) became widespread earlier than among peasants of the non-industrial districts of the country. (6)

The Nizhnii Tagil Regional Museum, which has become the organizer of local students of regional lore, including workers themselves, is playing a major role in study of the old way of life of the workers of that city and that of the population of the former mining district. (7)

An interesting undertaking was carried out in 1952-1953 by the Cheliabinsk State Teachers College in research into the way of life of workers of the Southern Urals. (8)

Thus, ethnographic study of the workers of the Urals has developed on a comparatively broad front. But this does not eliminate the general and immediate task of proceeding to planned and systematic study of the Soviet working class, taking in all major industrial areas of the country and leading branches of industry.

This undertaking would be resolved most successfully by the combined efforts of historians and ethnographers. Specifically, it would be important to suggest objects for joint study. Recently a number of special studies have appeared bearing on the formation of the labor force in various industrial districts. B. N. Vasil'ev's The Origins of the Textile Proletariat in Shuiskii Raion [Formirovanie tekstil'nogo proletariata v Shuiskom raione], 1949, which provides a detailed examination of the composition and process of formation of the core of the working class of this industrial center, is worthy of attention. It is desirable to combine historical investigations of this type with ethnographic studies. This makes for a deeper and more complete investigation of the history and features of the culture and way of life of the workers of given industrial districts.

Significant work has been done in the Ukraine in studying the workers' culture and way of life. The work there is conducted both in the form of studies of particular topics and of monographic studies of particular groups of the working class. (9) In 1953, the Institute of Art Research, Folklore, and Ethnography of the Academy of Sciences of the Ukrainian SSR undertook the study of the culture and way of life of workers of the Donbass. The State Historical Museum conducted research there at one time. (10) The result was the assembly of interesting materials, including data on the interrelationships in culture and mode of life between the Ukrainian and Russian peoples. (11) This work must be continued. It also provides comparative material for the researches in the Urals.

Study of the principal elements of material culture and of the social and family relationships of workers in various branches of industry made it possible for the investigators to provide a well-rounded picture of the culture and way of life of the Ukrainian workers in the general historico-ethnographic work The Ukrainians [Ukraintsy], which is being prepared for the press.

Ethnographic study of the working class is also being conducted in a number of other centers of research in our country. It is going on on a fairly large scale in Georgia, where elaboration of the problem began with the study of the way of life of workers of the older mining districts of the republic (the Chiaturi manganese industry, the Tkvibuli coal basin). As the work progressed, new enterprises which came into being during the first Five-Year Plans were included in the study (the Kasin Cement Works and the Zestafoni Feroalloys Plant), as well as the postwar Ordjonikidze Auto Works at Kutaissi and the Stalin Steel Mill at Rustavi, which came into operation after the war.

The selection of these enterprises was based on a principle by the Georgian researchers, who supposed that comparative study of industries whose personnel came into being under different socioeconomic conditions would make it possible to trace with the greatest clarity the process of establishment of the workers' culture and life and to discover its principal regularities.

The comparative data assembled (including detailed genealogies of workers' families) demonstrated that the working class in the manganese and coal industries of Georgia had been formed chiefly from the ranks of local peasantry. This is of definite significance for clarification of the paths followed in development of the culture of the workers of these most ancient districts of Georgia. Studies have shown that these industrial centers are characterized by a greater stability of the traditional forms of material culture and of certain aspects of family life than the new industrial centers. (12)

Work on the study of the culture and life of the workers is currently under way in Belorussia as well, where it is being conducted by the Institute of History of the Academy of Sciences of the Belorussian SSR (Ethnographic Sector) at a number of enterprises in Minsk. (13)

The range of problems involved in studying the mode of life of workers of those peoples of the USSR who had no industry of their own prior to the revolution is being elaborated in a number of other constituent and autonomous republics (Uzbekistan, Turkmenia, Kazakhstan, Kirgizia, Ossetia, etc.).

Of considerable interest are studies of the culture and mode of life of oil workers conducted in districts differing greatly with respect to the time and conditions of the development of the petroleum industry, in terms of nationality and in cultural traditions. Such researches are currently being conducted among Azerbaidjani workers in the oldest of oil districts, Baku, (14) in Borislav (West Ukraine) where the mode of life of the workers took shape under conditions of interpenetration of Ukrainian and Polish culture, and in Turkmenia where the petroleum industry came into being, for all practical purposes, in the Soviet period. This creates particularly favorable conditions for study of the way of life of the workers as it takes shape. The studies performed in Turkmenia (in the districts of Nebit-Dag and Kum-Dag and on Cheleken Peninsula) have already demonstrated the fundamental changes which have occurred in the mode of life of Turkmenian workers, who in the recent past were seminomadic herdsmen, agriculturalists and fishermen (on Cheleken). At the same time, a number of contradictory aspects have been found in the present way of life of the Turkmenian workers — a distinctive interweaving of the new, socialist characteristics of the culture side by side with manifestations of old traditions (clan-tribal, large-family, and religious). (15)

Generalization from these data will make it possible in the future not only to compile in each individual instance a specific picture of the paths of development of the working class of the various nationalities, but to discover ethnic peculiarities in the culture and mode of life of the workers of the various peoples of the USSR and at the same time to make a deeper study of the general laws of development of the workers' way of life under conditions of socialist reality.

Broad-scale study of the Soviet working class was substantially facilitated by the conference on this problem organized by the USSR Academy of Sciences' Institute of Ethnography in 1957.

Ethnographers are giving much attention to study of production unit personnel, inasmuch as the rapid rates of development of industry are resulting in significant changes in the composition of the working class, which is being supplemented constantly by people from other strata of the population. In our country supplementation of the working class is currently taking place to a considerable degree from the ranks of urban youth graduating from secondary school. The village remains one of the most important sources of recruitment into the working class. However, new recruits coming from the village of today differ qualitatively from those of this background in the prerevolutionary period. Under today's conditions, with the gradual erasure of the line of demarcation between town and country, the transformation of present-day life, both urban and rural, occurs in the process of the construction of communism. Surveys in various industrial centers have shown that the working youth of today coming from the collective farm village is at a general level of culture hardly inferior to that of urban youth.

However, does this eliminate the problem of study of traditions, i.e., consideration of views, habits, customs, tastes formed in a particular social medium, and of their influence upon the process of socialist reorganization of the way of life? An answer to this question requires, above all else, the accumulation of considerable factual data. What is needed is a differentiated study both of hereditary workers (local and incoming) and of first-generation workers emerging from other sections of the population.

In this connection, study of the influence of the production unit personnel and life in the factory upon the way of life, world outlook, and moral fiber of the young worker is urgently needed.

It is from this point of view that we are studying the problem. A number of problems appear that seem, at first glance, to be outside the scope of ethnography. But without consideration of these it is impossible to clarify how the new type of worker is coming into being and, in the final analysis, how the process of erasing the differences between physical and mental labor, a process inherent in the construction of communism, takes place.

One of these problems is study of all the changes that have occurred and are occurring

in the social and productive activities of workers — i.e., their conditions of labor. A clear picture is needed of the degree of mechanization and automation of production, the influence of this factor upon the cultural and technical level attained by the worker, upon the expansion of his horizons, his cultural requirements, etc. Detailed knowledge of the makeup of the personnel in terms of skills (and, in particular, of their schooling) is of major importance. Determination of the general level of culture of the workers is particularly important. This makes it possible to demonstrate the degree to which the working class may serve as the reservoir for the emergence of the Soviet intelligentsia (particularly its technical component) and the nature and rates of progress of this process in an environment of hereditary workers and in an environment of new additions to the working class.

Ethnographers are today also investigating relationships that come into being in a unit of production personnel in the process of work, and primarily all forms of socialist competition, inasmuch as this is one of the principal factors in the formation of communist consciousness. In this regard, much attention is given to the movement of "shock workers" and communist labor brigades. The job of the ethnographer is to investigate the influence of this remarkable movement of our day upon the social life of Soviet people, upon morals and the family. (16)

An extremely important problem is study of the family and family structure. This topic has always held a place of prominence in ethnographic studies. However, it becomes of absolutely primary significance in study of the laws of development of the socialist way of life. All-round study of the family makes it possible to demonstrate more deeply and completely the process of establishment of new modes of life and at the same time to reveal the sources that nourish vestiges of the old outlook and that are manifested in many aspects of family and social life. For this reason, the subject of the family involves posing a number of problems of considerable importance in the construction of communism: further improvement in the position of woman by freeing her from immersion in housework; the upbringing of the rising generation; the material conditions of the family's life as one of the most significant factors in rebuilding it in socialist fashion, and a number of others. Linked with this, in turn, is an interrelated group of questions requiring detailed study. They include family structure (forms, number of members, the nature of kin relationships), internal arrangements, the level of culture at which it stands, etc. A large group of problems are related to study of the material foundations of the family, particularly its budget. This question has as yet had little elaboration in our ethnographic research. Yet analysis of family budgets is also very much needed to assist in clarifying the appearance of the new Soviet family and the rise in its level of culture and material circumstances. Of extreme importance are questions about marriage and the moral foundations on which it rests (particularly clarification of the causes and circumstances of divorce).

The all-round study of the family and the process of its socialist reshaping poses the problem of researching the influence of Soviet legislation on marriage and the family upon family life. Also of considerable importance is research into vestiges of what is called "customary law" and clarification of the reactionary role of customary law in the family life of workers of many formerly backward peoples of the USSR. Studies in Turkmenia have shown that despite the fundamental changes in family life, certain customs related to clan and tribal traditions have been retained in the lives of Turkmen workers (for example, the custom under which the bride returns to her parents' home for a given period, the custom under which son-in-law and bride avoid older relatives, hidden forms of bride-purchase payments, etc.).

The question of the establishment of progressive ideology and of its influence upon all aspects of life and the formation of new customs are among the most important of all. Therefore, particularly careful study is given to all new phenomena which have become typical for the contemporary way of life of a worker's family.

Significant results have been obtained by investigations of the consequences of family custom (related to marriage, the birth of children, death), (17) as well as of religious customs and habits retained by part of the population.

Clarification of these questions is impossible without a study of the level of culture of the worker's family, of the fundamental changes which occurred in it as the consequence of socialist changes (formation of an intellectual subgroup within the family, the new culture of the worker associated with his job, involvement of women in social labor, the role of Communists and Komsomol members in family life, etc.). In so doing it is necessary to determine how one or another factor influences the day-to-day mode of life of the family, its culture and the appearance it presents to society. And as has already been said, this in turn acutely poses the question of the influence of the production unit and of life on the job upon the processes of transformation of family life.

In emphasizing the special importance of study of spiritual and social life, we do not in any way understate the need for investigation of material culture. There can be no question of the great importance of, for example, thorough knowledge of the types of settlements and houses for study of the social and family relationships of a family, its organization for purposes of earning a living and carrying on the work of the household, and its cultural level. There are some elements of material culture through which the role of ethnic traditions in the process of the shaping of new forms may be followed with precision. Thus, interesting results have been provided by A. I. Robakidze's study of the evolution of the home in the mountain districts of Georgia, where new houses were built fundamentally in accordance with the tradition of the old west Georgian home. However, this was not at all a mechanical reproduction of the old. On the contrary, the traditional forms of homes were changed to meet the needs of modern life. (18) Analogous phenomena were also observed in other industrial districts (Donbass, Nizhnii Tagil).

Study of these problems is possible only if

they are studied jointly in a manner that makes it possible to research phenomena in their interrelationship and mutual dependence. Therefore ethnographic study of workers is conducted primarily on the level of monographic investigations of the culture and mode of life of workers of individual enterprises, cities and industrial centers. The multi-faceted nature of the study also determines the technique. Reference to the data of related disciplines and independent elaboration by the ethnographer of certain historical and social problems are also often required. Problems in this category include study of the socioeconomic conditions of the territory, the conditions of labor of the workers, the history of the local working class movement, and the general status of culture.

Ethnographic study of the Soviet working class presupposes clarification of the composition of the labor force of the individual enterprises under study. It is also necessary to familiarize oneself, albeit only in general terms, with the history of formation of the proletariat of the entire industrial district. This makes possible, thereafter, a more profound study both of material culture and of the mode of life of the workers in its historical development as well as a broader posing of questions pertaining to mutual influence of workers and peasants in culture and mode of life. In elaborating this special problem, which requires extensive use of archives, collaboration between an ethnographer and a historian would be particularly fruitful. In studying the composition of the workers of today, ethnographers make extensive use of statistical data and engage in special surveys by means of questionnaires. For example, this was the experience in Nizhnii Tagil, where questionnaires of various types were employed. In order to acquire mass data on the nationality, regional, social and occupational composition of the workers, a questionnaire of simplified type, filled out by the workers themselves, was employed. It contained the following questions: surname, given name, patronymic, job rating, year of birth, nationality, native tongue, social stratum of origin, date and reason for arrival at Nizhnii Tagil, education, trade (number of skills the

worker possesses, and means by which he acquired his trade) and, finally, home address.

Generalization of the data in this questionnaire provides a rather clear picture of the composition of the working class of today and the level of culture and technical knowledge it possesses. At the same time this analysis helped shed light on the complex question of the role played by ethnic and other interwoven traditions, characteristic of the social group of origin, in the evolution of the socialist way of life.

The peculiarities in the manifestation of this process among the workers were determined by the specific features of the particular labor force: the differences in time of recruitment and the extreme complexity of national and regional origins. Thus, even in such an old industrial center as Nizhnii Tagil, the questionnaire survey showed that the enormous number of new workers came from approximately 100 regions, territories and nationality republics. Moreover, they consisted of comparatively small groups (from 2 to 5 to 20 to 40 or, in rare cases, up to 80) from each region. In addition, in the majority of cases, the spouses came from different regions.

Particularly complex is the ethnic composition of the working class of republics that previously had no industry of their own. Here a major role in establishment of the core of skilled personnel was played by the more experienced workers of other nationalities, particularly Russians and Ukrainians. [19] Work and struggle for national and social liberation side by side drew workers of various nationalities closer together. Specifically, there was an increase in the frequency of mixed marriages which, as ethnographic data indicate, play an important role in reorganizing the mode of life and overcoming its formerly ingrown nature. This is why a survey of the ethnic composition of the workers is of major significance. It makes for a more profound and more valid posing of the problem of ethnic interrelationships and interactions and of their role in the process of formation of new aspects of life.

In studying the culture and mode of life of workers, the major techniques are the usual ones of ethnographic research — direct observations. The basic unit for observation is the family. Particularly fruitful results have been provided by comparative study of several generations of a family, its material and intellectual culture. (20)

The method of direct questioning cannot now, for natural reasons, yield data going back earlier than the 80's of the past century. However, inasmuch as the ethnographer deals with living phenomena in which appearance of the new is accompanied by preservation of old elements (most frequently in changed form), retrospective study makes it possible to shed light upon earlier stages in the development of the family.

Much may also be provided by employment of archive data. This was demonstrated by the experience in Nizhnii Tagil, where an important source for study of the history of the evolution of the worker's family in this oldest of industrial centers was provided by poll-tax rolls of the 18th and particularly of the first half of the 19th centuries, providing a clear picture of the form and composition of the family in the pre-Reform period. Of major interest, too, are documents (of the first half of the 19th century) contained in this archive, describing the housing of the factory settlement. (21) This, in comparison with field research results, makes possible a thorough study of the types of homes and housing plot arrangements in Nizhnii Tagil and their process of evolution.

In studying the modern family, both on the collective farm and that of workers, ethnographers make use of special questionnaire surveys. They differ when applied to workers in that, because of the large numbers of factory personnel, they must naturally be only samplings. The method of sampling has to be carefully thought out. Samplings should be as complete as possible, with proper consideration of the relationship between native and newly arrived populations, for only thus will the statistical data be objective. The family information card provides information on the composition of the family, blood relationships, place of birth and nationality of members of the family living apart from the parents, as well as data on family budget and certain aspects of the material

way of life.

A family data card set up on the principle of correlation of data descriptive of the interrelationship among socioeconomic, cultural, and mode-of-life phenomena provides data not only for study of the family and its way of life but also for proper clarification of the nature and direction of those general changes occurring in the culture and mode of life of the entire population. Questionnaire surveys carried out at home, in workers' families, make it possible to accumulate a vast volume of vital, direct observations of the contemporary mode of life of the workers.

In addition to the family questionnaire, aimed principally at a study of current mode of life, a questionnaire has been worked out on the genealogy of the worker's family. It contains the following headings: birthplace, nationality, native tongue, social status and occupations of the parents of the family head (for whom the family card is being made out), his paternal and maternal grandparents and great-grandparents, data on the family economy and certain factors in the material culture. The questionnaire envisages clarification of the historical roots of a number of the most important mode-of-life phenomena, which are identified and recorded in their present form on the family card.

Conducting questionnaire surveys makes for a better-founded and more correct selection of individual families for further detailed study in the light of the problems discussed above. (22)

* * *

All the thoughts advanced here are, of course, most incomplete. Ethnographic study of the working class is still substantially in the stage of searchings, of initial experiments. No work along this line is being conducted at all in certain republics.

It must be observed that to this date no research institute, including the Institute of Ethnography of the USSR Academy of Sciences, has any substantial research staff of ethnographers for study of the working class. Monographic investigations of the largest and most complex objects of study are conducted in handicraft fashion, as it were, usually by the efforts of one or two persons, with the result that the work drags out over a period of years. In a number of cases important researches have remained unfinished. The need now exists to proceed everywhere to planned, systematic study of the culture and mode of life of the working class, to elaborate an overall, long-range plan embracing the basic industrial districts and the most important branches of industry in a given republic.

There is, to no less a degree, a need for exchange of opinions, observations and materials, and of all experience in the study of the given problem. Discussions, conferences, extensive publication of materials, and researches into the ethnography of the workers will doubtless promote a deeper theoretical elaboration of this most complex problem, and will help to find a more exact method of studying it.

Footnotes

1) See the monographs: Kladensko, Prague, 1959; Banicka dedina Zacarovce, Bratislava, 1956; the monograph Rosicko-Oslavansko (Brno) has been prepared for the press. For work under way in Poland, see communication by D. Dobrovol'skaia and V. Kvas'nevich, "Ethnograficheskie issledovaniia sovremennoi kul'tury pol'skogo naroda krakovskimi uchenymi," Sovetskaia etnografiia, 1959, No. 4.

2) Typical in this respect is the article of N. N. Cheboksarov, "Etnograficheskie izuchenie kul'tury i byta moskovskikh rabochikh," Sovetskaia etnografiia, 1950, No. 3.

3) The first results of this work were published in an article by V. Iu. Krupianskaia, "Opyt etnograficheskogo izucheniia ural'skikh rabochikh vtoroi poloviny XIX veka," Sovetskaia etnografiia, 1953, No. 1.

4) See series of articles published in the Zapiski istoriko-bytovogo otdela Gosudarstvennogo Russkogo muzeia, Leningrad, 1932. Also see Materialy Sredneural'skoi ekspeditsii 1949 g. Gosudarstvennogo Istoricheskogo muzeia, published in Istoriko-bytovye ekspeditsii 1949-1950 gg., Moscow, 1953, pp. 184-212.

5) The questionnaire surveys conducted in Nizhnii Tagil revealed, in particular, a most intimate connection in the past between the local working class population and the handicraftsmen. Many workers, particularly carpenters, cabinetmakers, blacksmiths and tinsmiths, sought additional income in self-employment over and above their work at the mill or ore mine. Many mill or mine workers sometimes quit those jobs completely, became self-employed or worked for wages for master craftsmen, and then later returned to the plant. It was a general rule that the young fellows in workers' families worked for wages for independent mechanics. All this testifies to the intimate ties between these groups in the population.

6) These data are being published in the Trudy russkoi etnograficheskoi ekspeditsii, publications of the Institute of Ethnography, USSR Academy of Sciences.

7) See T. K. Gus'kova, "Nekotorye etnograficheskie osobennosti naseleniia byvshego Nizhne-Tagil'skogo gornozavodskogo okruga v kontse XIX-nachale XX v.," Sovetskaia etnografiia, 1958, No. 2.

8) See V. E. Gusev, "Iz opyta etnograficheskogo izucheniia rabochikh starykh zavodov Iuzhnogo Urala," Uchenye zapiski Cheliabinskogo gosudarstvennogo pedagogicheskogo instituta, 1956, Vol. I, No. 1.

9) See V. T. Zinich, Sotsialisticheskii byt i kul'tura rabochikh g. Kieva, dissertation for the candidate's degree, Moscow, 1959; A. S. Kunitskii, Sotsialisticheskii byt rabochikh Voroshilovgradskogo zavoda imeni Oktiabr'skoi revoliutsii, dissertation for the candidate's degree, Kiev, 1953. D. I. Figol' is studying the houses of workers in L'vov; M. T. Lomova is investigating the culture and mode of life of the oil workers of Borislav.

10) See Istoriko-bytovye ekspeditsii 1951-1953 gg., Moscow, 1955.

11) Of interest in this connection is a work by N. P. Prikhod'ko, Rabochee zhilishche Donbassa v ego istoricheskom razvitii, dissertation; same author, "Zhitlo robitnikiv Donbasu," Narodna tvorchist' ta etnografiia, 1957, No. 1.

10

12) A. I. Robakidze, <u>Nekotorye storony byta rabochikh Chiaturskoi margantsevoi promy-shlennosti</u>, Tbilisi, 1953.

13) U. M. Ivanov, <u>Sovremenni byt i kul'tura rabochei sem'i g. Minska (na materialakh min-skikh predpriiatii: traktornogo zavoda, radioza-voda, fabriki 'Kommunarka' i zheleznodorozhnogo minskogo uzla)</u>, dissertation; same author, "Risi novogo v pobuti robitnikiv Radians'koi Belorusii," <u>Nardona tvorchist' ta etnografiia</u>, 1959, No. 1.

14) A. G. Trofimova, <u>Bakinskie rabochie-nef-tianiki</u>, dissertation, Moscow, 1954.

15) Sh. Annaklychev, <u>Byt rabochikh neftianikov Nebit-Daga i Kum-Daga</u>, dissertation, Moscow (1958; in press); same author, "Nekotorye storony byta rabochikh neftianikov Nebit-Daga," <u>Sovetskaia etnografiia</u>, 1959, No. 1. A study on the culture and way of life of the Turkmenian oil workers of Cheleken has also been prepared for publication.

16) Ethnographers who study communist labor brigades question not only shift chiefs and brigade leaders but as many of the participants as pos-sible. This makes for a clearer understanding of the nature of the movement as a whole and provides a clearer picture of competing teams. A family card is also filled out for each individ-ual questioned; it provides for information on details of family mode of life, human relation-ships in it, organization of family life, and its culture. This was specifically the procedure of the Nizhnii Tagil Expedition of the Ethnography Institute of the USSR Academy of Sciences in 1959.

17) A number of articles on this subject have appeared in <u>Narodna tvorchist' ta etnografiia</u>: V. T. Zinich, "Sovremennyi rabochii brak i svad'ba" (1957, No. 2); same author, "Pro deiaki gromads'ki sviata ta kollektivne dozvillia robitnikiv " (1958, No. 3); same author, "Novi risi v simeinomu pobuti robitnikiv" (1957, No. 3). See also articles by the Belorussian ethnographer U. M. Ivanov, "Suchasny shliub i viasellia u ra-bochyk," <u>Vestnik AN Belorusskoi SSR</u>, 1959, No. 2; and "Z gistoryi vyvuchennia bytu sa-vetskikh rabochykh," <u>ibid.</u>, 1959, No. 3.

18) See A. I. Robakidze, <u>op. cit.</u>

19) Interesting data on this problem will be found in the cited writings of Sh. Annaklychev and also in an article being prepared for the press by F. Arikov, "K voprosu formirovaniia uzbekskogo rabochego klassa (Po materialam zavodov sel'khozmashinostroeniia)."

20) See A. I. Robakidze, "K nekotorym vo-prosam etnograficheskogo izucheniia novogo byta," <u>Sovetskaia etnografiia</u>, 1952, No. 2.

21) The following documents are in the Nizhne Tagil Regional Studies Archive: <u>Kniga na vnesenie planov i fasadov obyvatel'skikh domov N.-Ta-gil'skogo zavoda 1834; Kniga po zapisi planov, vydavaemykh zavodskim zhiteliam na postroiku domov pri Nizhne-Tagil'skom zavode i prinadle-zhaschikh k nemu seleniiakh</u>, 1841, and others. An interesting attempt to reconstruct the type of urban and rural dwellings based on the data of the poll-tax rolls has been made by V. A. Alek-sandrov in his article "Russkoe zhilishche v Vostochnoi Sibiri v XVII-nachale XVIII veka," <u>Sovetskaia etnografiia</u>, 1960, No. 2.

22) On the use of questionnaire surveys, see T. A. Zhdanko, V. Iu. Krupianskaia, and L. N. Terent'eva, "Ob organizatsii i metodike polevykh etnograficheskikh issledovanii, <u>Sovetskaia etnografiia</u>, 1956, No. 3.

* * *

Sovetskaia etnografiia, 1964, No. 4

V. Iu. Krupianskaia and M. G. Rabinovich

THE ETHNOGRAPHY OF THE CITY AND THE INDUSTRIAL SETTLEMENT

Urban ethnography is an important branch of the science. The past century has seen a rapid growth of towns in most countries. Recent ethnic statistics give us the following figures for urban population: 75% in Australia and Oceania, 53% in the Americas, 52% in Europe outside the USSR, 50% in the Soviet Union, 20% in Asia outside the USSR, and 13% in Africa. (1) This process of urbanization, characteristic of the present day, is expressed not only in the growth of cities, but in a fundamental reorganization of the villages, a change in their social composition and entire way of life, and an intensification of the influence of urban modes of life in the countryside. The influence of urban culture upon that of the peoples as a whole is constantly increasing. Therefore it is impossible today to study the life of any people without consideration of the urban population, although this was typical of ethnography in the past. In recent decades, historians and ethnographers both in the Soviet Union and abroad have increasingly been engaging in urban-directed projects. Their major interest has been study of the working class, which is the prime population of cities and industrial towns, and study of the specifics of the formation of that class, its ethnographic features, and its influence upon the course of the historical process and the development of the culture of the given country.

Experience has demonstrated, however, that investigation of the culture and mode of life of the workers of any enterprise (or group of enterprises) inevitably becomes a study of the population center (city or industrial town) as a whole, inasmuch as the labor force of an enterprise does not dwell in isolation, but in constant and intimate communion with other strata of the population. Many ethnographers have turned directly to study of the urban mode of life, urban customs, holidays, and the like. (2) Yet ethnographic study of the city has but barely begun. Until recently, the city has primarily been an object of investigation by geographers, economists, sociologists, architects, historians, and archeologists.

If we recognize the dominant significance of the city in the life of modern peoples, at least since the coming of the capitalist era, we must abandon the classic treatment of the peasantry as the sole bearer of the national cultural tradition. Even in the past, during the feudal era, the urban population participated along with the rural in the shaping of nationalities and, later, of nations, and made no small contribution to the establishment and progress of national cultures. Such major areas of national culture as housing, clothing, particular forms of folklore, customs and rituals took shape to a considerable degree as a consequence of the interaction between the urban and rural population with respect to culture and mode of life.

The leading class of modern society — the working class — took shape and matured substantially in urban conditions. And although it was formed primarily at the expense of the peasantry driven off the land and moved to town, this process occurred under the strong influence of the urban population, with its mixed social composition and long-established material and intellectual culture and conditions of life. To determine the concrete conditions under which the contemporary urban culture came into being, a consecutive historical study of the town in various epochs is thus essential.

We know that the towns of the entire world have many common traits resulting from the fact that they developed as industrial, commercial, political, and cultural centers. At the same time, there are features characteristic of towns of particular economic and geographic zones, while cities in a particular country have distinctive ethnic characteristics, and others in it have regional features. There are also common characteristics of particular groups of towns resulting from their common histories. Finally, there are individual characteristics found only in particular cities. These common and distinctive features in the development of cities have been the object of investigation by scholars in various fields for several decades. (3)

In speaking of the study of cities, we also have in mind the study of towns of a type transitional from the rural to the urban or primary stage in the development of the city, i.e., the industrial settlement, for it is precisely this transitional type of industrial center that has played in the past and continues today to play an enormous

role in expanding the influence of large-scale machine industry on the life of the rural population. Lenin himself took note of this. (4) In recent years the problem of the reciprocal influences of town and village has been the subject matter of the largest single category of ethnographic investigations. (5)

Wherein lie the specific features of the ethnographic study of the city? It appears to us that, in studying so important a subject, ethnographers must direct their attention primarily to those aspects of its development which are associated with particular ethnic processes. It is particularly important to discover the ethnic environment in which the given town came into being, to trace the later sources of enlargement of its population and the ethnic processes occurring in the city: the interrelation between newcomers and the indigenous ethnic core of the population, in many cases the gradual assimilation of the newcomers, the mutual enrichment of cultures, and the founding of new forms of culture and daily life. The ethnic composition of the population of a town is always much more complex than that of a rural settlement. Sometimes the nucleus of the urban population has not even belonged to the same people on whose lands the town arose (for example, the German cities in the Baltic states). The foreign ethnic population arriving in towns has in many cases settled in compact groups, creating what amount to distinctive neighborhoods with identifiable ethnic characteristics, often even with special legal status. This could not but influence the way of life of the town as a whole. Cities that have not yet eliminated this boundary among various national groups provide particularly important data for study of processes of ethnic integration. (6)

Particular attention is deserved by study of the ethnic features of urban life and the changes occurring in them as a consequence of reciprocal influences in culture and everyday life. Such processes are characteristic, for example, of the oldest cities in the non-Russian Soviet republics (Central Asia and elsewhere), whose centuries-old culture was not simply equated with that of Russian urban culture as a consequence of the influence of the latter, but was transformed, retaining to a substantial degree the distinctive features of the traditional national way of life.

The process of social differentiation of the population occurred considerably more rapidly in the towns (under the conditions of both feudalism and capitalism) than in the villages. Here the ethnographer is interested in the establishment of the way of life of various social groups, the contribution each of these groups makes to the development of the national culture, and the degree to which integration of these groups is observed. In this regard, the role of the town as a cultural center is very great indeed.

Ethnographers are studying the material and intellectual culture of various strata of the urban population. The traditional culture is not retained equally by the entire population of a town. Ethnographic investigation must center primarily on all new manifestations in the mode of life of urban people, and on the influence of this new aspect upon the development of the people's culture. In studying the town as a population center, particular attention must be given to its social topography and to changes in the neighborhoods populated by various social groups during different periods in history. In particular, the problem of the city center and the outskirts, with their clearly opposite modes of life in times past, is most important.

An important component of the ethnographic study of the town is research into the basic and subordinate occupations of the population, and their relationships in cities of various types and in different periods of history. When examining the town in late stages of its development, the ethnographer studies the basic occupations of the population — industry and trade — primarily in terms of their influence upon everyday life (job-related habits and practices, and social structures in the organization of particular crafts and trades), as well as the features of household life associated with the occupations of various strata of the urban population. Ethnographers also study the social mode of life of cities: the reflections of their political life in holidays, forms of recreation, customs and morals. They also deal with various forms of art and the place of these in urban life, particularly musical habits.

Ethnographers give special attention to the family lives of urban people, particularly that which is distinctive of the worker's family, and those characteristic and typical features that differentiate it from the peasant family, with which the worker's family is genetically connected in the overwhelming majority of cases.

A most important problem in urban ethnography is determination of the area into which the workaday, commercial, and cultural connections of the town disseminate, and with which the city is often associated as the source of recruitment of its labor force. Study of the interrelations between town and city is, as we have already noted, one of the most important aspects of this problem.

The town is not only an economic and political center, but a center for the development of the country's cultural life. Here are concentrated its most advanced cultural personalities, institutions and values. This places a specific imprint upon the entire way of life of the urban population.

Ethnographic study of towns may provide material for monographic description of an individual city or group of towns, and for studies devoted to particular aspects of urban life, based on data drawn from one or several towns.

While the ethnographic features of towns of earlier epochs may be studied primarily on the basis of the work of historians and archeologists (with an ethnographic approach to the interpretation of these data), towns of the present and the recent past may be studied by the ethnographer through the standard techniques of ethnography (field research, questionnaire surveys, etc.). In studying the modern town, ethnographers find valuable data for shedding light on earlier stages of their development. In this regard, we find instructive the experience of Soviet scholars in investigating the cities of Central Asia, many of which had retained, until the October Revolution, the flavor of centers of feudal societies (Bukhara, for example) with their fortifications, craft quarters, and distinctive form of urban life, and with the clergy playing a tremendous role in the life of the people. (7) The employment of ethnographic material made it possible to penetrate into spheres of life inaccessible through written sources. In these ancient urban centers, the ethnographers studied living vestiges of feudalism, and are in a position to trace the socialist reorganization of the city in its entirety.

For Soviet ethnographers, the study of the modern socialist town is a task of the very greatest importance. In our multi-national country, this problem acquires special interest and uniqueness. But it is also exceedingly complicated. Backward tsarist Russia was only 13% urban in population, while in the Soviet Union the figure reached 50% in 1961. (8)

The rapid growth of cities is occurring not only on the basis of influx of people into towns already existing, but on the basis of the appearance of new cities and industrial towns in areas of industrial development. This is the reason for the great variety of types of urban settlements. Along with the old industrial centers, which have grown extraordinarily as a consequence of the further development of large-scale industry, there are a number of towns that previously had virtually no industry at all. In these towns, industrial growth is associated with a fundamental change in the social and ethnic composition of the population. This is true, for example, of many older towns in the former non-Russian borderlands, where industrialization did not occur until Soviet times. The new towns, built in recent years, often in formerly uninhabited places, have distinctive characteristics as far as the establishment of their populations is concerned. These have usually taken shape from a variety of nationalities and persons from many regions. As a typical example, we may cite the new town of Nebit-Dag, socialist in character, which arose in 1933 in the Turkmenian oil fields and contains persons of 50 different ethnic origins. Study of the ethnic composition of towns of this type makes it possible to form a judgment with respect to concrete manifestations of the process of mutual assimilation of population groups of various origins, and of the establishment of new forms of life under urban conditions.

The conditions of the processes presently occurring in the Soviet Union are determined primarily by the fact that the culture of the socialist town is lacking in class contradictions, and the role of conscious influences of social forces and the state is clearly manifested in its development.

From its very first steps, the socialist revolution exercised a decisive influence upon the nature of towns. Their social topography was the first scene of change. The Soviet government began by moving workers into the apartments of the bourgeoisie and then proceeded to large-scale housing construction for workers. The scope of this housing effort and the complete reconstruction of many towns had the consequence that the modern Soviet town lacks the "aristocratic" downtown areas and workers' outskirts of the past, not to speak of the slums in which the urban poor formerly lived. Nor do Soviet cities have the division into the "old" or "black" city inhabited by the indigenous nationality, and the "new" or "white" city populated by Russians.

The abolition of capitalist property in real estate has made it possible to effectuate a fundamental reorganization of the cities on a unified plan. The ethnographer is interested in this reconstruction not only in terms of the change in the people's housing conditions, but because of the establishment of an utterly new urban way of life, as a consequence of the establishment of streets and neighborhoods of an utterly new type — so-called microdistricts — with their service and cultural institutions. Of particular interest is the study of new urban construction in the republics where towns are appearing in conjunction with the development of particular branches of industry. Here, town planning is a major lever in eliminating negative manifestations of the old ethnic way of life associated with the former cultural backwardness of particular peoples (settlement in clan groups, the closed nature of the dwellings, with sharp division into male and female quarters, and so forth). As a consequence of their very planning, the population of such towns is more rapidly assimilated into new, USSR-wide forms of life. (9)

Changes in material culture (for example, in house furnishings, dress and foodstuffs) occur differently in the towns of the various republics. As already indicated, changes in national mode of life do not merely take the form of leveling, but are a consequence of the assimilation, interpenetration and creative reshaping of components of various cultures: those of the indigenous and newly arrived population, as well as of neighboring peoples. In studying these processes, the ethnographer is in a position to define those vital and valuable phenomena of the traditional culture, the development of which enriches the new, socialist culture. Ethnographers also extend practical assistance to various construction, manufacturing and commercial agencies in developing forms of production that will accord both with long-established customs and with the esthetic concepts of the modern townsman. (10) They also uncover negative phenomena of the old way of life, with which it is necessary to wage a persistent struggle.

A most important problem for Soviet ethnographers engaged in studying the mode of life of the modern town is the investigation of the process of erasure of the differences in culture and mode of life existing among various strata of the urban population, differences that manifested themselves so sharply earlier, in conjunction with the class division of society. Ethnographic investigations show that the modern urban family is characterized by having not only members of different occupations, but by the fact that it may contain persons engaged in physical labor and others engaged in mental labor. The sharp increase in the level of education and culture of the rank-and-file townsman has had the consequence that it is now often difficult to determine the social category in which a particular urban family should be classified, not only in terms of social composition, but above all in way of life and level of culture. Yet the urban family is still not entirely homogeneous in terms of culture and way of life. This is explained by many factors — the social origin of particular population groups, the length of time they have resided in the city, the type of occupation, income level, and so forth. It must be remembered that the problem of traditions cannot be disregarded, even in the urban medium — that is, the influence upon the way of life exercised by views, habits, morals, esthetic tastes and so forth that have come into being in partic-

ular social environments.

All this calls forth the need for a differentiated approach to study of the urban population, with consideration of its ethnic, social, and professional composition, and consequently the use of enormous quantities of statistical material as well as the conducting of special surveys.

The posing of this important problem is indissolubly involved with the comprehensive study of the urban family, its structure, mode of life, and level of culture. In particular, it requires that light be shed on the question of the establishment of an intellectual stratum within families. An enormous role in the process of reorganizing the way of life and establishing forms common to the USSR as a whole is provided by the nature of marriage ties — for example, the extent of what are termed mixed marriages in the ethnic and social sense. Directly related to this question is detailed study of modern methods of raising children, which play the major role in shaping the new generation, whose image ceases to display adherence to a particular social stratum.

Study of the family has a major independent significance, for it deals with an entire complex of problems directly associated with the practical business of building communism. This includes the introduction of public forms of satisfying the family's needs in terms of material goods and services and thereby emancipating the woman from immersion in housework, involvement of the housekeeping mother in socially useful labor and the influence of this factor upon the family's way of life, the upbringing of children, and so forth. These processes proceed more rapidly in the city than in the countryside, and the entire mode of life changes more intensively.

Nor do ethnographers ignore family rituals and the entire complex of customs associated with this. Study of this aspect of the family life of city folk demonstrates that the urban center plays the leading role in overcoming various vestiges of the past in family-and-marriage relationships and in developing rituals free of religion. In this area, the work of ethnographers may be integrated with the practical activities of state and civic institutions.

In the field of social life and in the establishment of new forms corresponding to the new stage in the development of Soviet society, the leading role of the city and, in particular, of the working class is clearly manifested. Serious attention is deserved by those forms of everyday social life in which combination of the governmental and volunteer principles are clearly to be seen. This applies to the unarmed public-order squads, comrades' courts [of fellow-employees or neighbors], street and house committees, etc. The new forms of organization of civic recreation also manifest the best traditions of the old national cultures. From this point of view, it is necessary to study carefully the civic holidays that have become most developed and acquired their particular ceremonial forms, especially in the cities. Finally, the form in which political undertakings are pursued, including elections of deputies to the soviets, constitutes a significant line in the new, socialist form of social life. Teaching the masses to appreciate the arts — in particular, the question of urban musical culture (study of the repertory of songs sung by the people, their sources and the channels through which they are added to) — takes on major significance. (11) All this is very important to clarify the tasks facing the professional arts today.

It is clear from the foregoing that the city is of great interest, as well as of great complexity, to the researcher as an object of ethnographic study. The broad range of problems and the variety of sources provide broad scope for creative thought. At the same time, the very variety of these problems demands that the approach to them be particularly careful. The very fact that the investigator is, in each instance, dealing with a population that is numerous and complex in occupational and ethnic composition and origin demands the development of differentiated methods of research. In certain cases the ethnographer studies the town as an entity, in others he singles out particular neighborhoods, while in still others he chooses social groups in its population. But on the whole, in ethnographic study of a town, it must be characterized as a complex social organism in all the multiplicity of the interactions of various groups in its population. The methods of studying the city will also vary

greatly, depending upon the problems to be solved, Clearly, a number of problems require contact with associated scientific disciplines, sociology in particular.

We have noted certain and, in our opinion, the most important aspects of the ethnographic study of the city. Naturally, the range of problems involved in such studies is considerably more extensive, and cannot be dealt with in a brief article. Discussion of this problem at a special symposium of the Seventh International Congress of Anthropology and Ethnography will certainly facilitate deeper treatment and further development of research techniques.

Footnotes

1) See Chislennost' i rasselenie narodov mira, Moscow, 1962, p. 20.

2) See, for example: W. E. Peuckert, Volkskünde des Proletariats, I, Frankfurt-am-Main, 1931; H. Kommenda, "Warum Stadtvolkskünde?", Konferenz für volkskündliche Kartographie in Linz an der Donau, 1959, pp. 58-65; for bibliographies of German works, see W. E. Peuckert and O. Lauffer, Volkskünde: Quellen und Forschungen seit 1930, Berne, 1951, pp. 43-44; also see R. and H. Lynd, Middletown, New York, 1929; same authors, Middletown in Transition, New York, 1937; M. Davie, Problems of City Life, New York, 1932; R. Dore, City Life in Japan, Berkeley and Los Angeles, 1958; K. Fojtik, "Výskum súčasneho života obyvatelstva měst a prùmyslových oblasti v německé spolkové republice," Český lid, 1964, No. 3, pp. 168-172.

3) See, for example, N. N. Baranskii, "Ob ekonomiko-geograficheskom izuchenii gorodov," Voprosy geografii, Book 2, Moscow, 1946; N. I. Lialikov, "O geograficheskom izuchenii goroda," Uch. zap. MGPI im. Lenina, Vol. IV, Geograficheskii fakul'tet, No. 1, Gorod i raion kak ob'ekty geograficheskogo izucheniia, 1949; N. Pirenne, Srednevekovye goroda Bel'gii, Moscow, 1937; D. Luzzato, Ekonomicheskaia istoriia Italii, Moscow, 1956; V. V. Stoklitskaia-Tereshkovich, Osnovnye problemy istorii srednevekovogo goroda X-XV vv., Moscow, 1960; Ia. A. Levitskii,

Goroda i gorodskoe remeslo v Anglii X-XII vekov, Moscow, 1960; L. E. Iofa, Goroda Urala, Moscow, 1951; O. A. Konstantinov, "Gorodskie poseleniia Urala," Voprosy geografii. Geografiia gorodov, Moscow, 1956.

4) "The muzhik isn't allowed into the factory: the factory goes to the muzhik," wrote Lenin (see V. I. Lenin, Razvitie kapitalizma v Rossii, Soch., 4th ed., Vol. 3, p. 459).

5) Interesting studies in this respect are being conducted in Poland and Czechoslovakia. See D. Dobrowolska, "Stúdium života a kultúry, robotníckej triedy v polskej vede," Slovensky národopis, 1957, Nos. 3-4. Also the following monographs in Czech: K. Fojtik and O. Sirovatka, Rosicko-Oslavansko, Prague, 1961; Kladensko, Život a kultura lidu v prúmyslové oblasti, Prague, 1959, and others. Analogous work is being done in the USSR. For example, there is the investigation begun by the Kazan Institute of Language, Literature and History, under the USSR Academy of Sciences, of the people of the exceedingly rich oil field found in southeast Tataria in 1940, and others.

6) See the publications of the International UN Conference on Science and Engineering, Section G (Social Problems and Urbanization), Geneva, 1963 (shelved in the Fundamental Social Science Library of the USSR Academy of Sciences). Also see O. Skalnikova, "Etnograficheskoe izuchenie peremen v bytu afrikanskogo goroda," SE, 1963, No. 5.

7) See O. A. Sukhareva, Pozdnefeodal'nyi gorod Bukhara kontsa XIX-nachala XX v., author's abstract of doctoral dissertation, Tashkent, 1962; same author, K istorii gorodov Bukharskogo khanstva (istoriko-etnograficheskie ocherki), Tashkent, 1958; A. Iu. Iakubovskii, "Glavnye voprosy izucheniia istorii razvitiia gorodov Srednei Azii," Trudy Tadzhiksogo filiala AN SSSR, Vol. XXIX, Stalinabad, 1951.

8) SSSR v tsifrakh v 1960 godu, Moscow, 1961, p. 65.

9) Interesting observations have been made by the Turkmenian ethnographer Sh. Annaklychev in studying the mode of life of the Turkmenian oil workers of Nebit-Dag. Thus, from the moment this town and the workers' settlement of Kum-Dag came into being, settlements arose spontaneously on their outskirts, in whose construction and mutual relations many old traditions were manifest. Most families of workers from tribal groups settled here in compact groups of fellow tribesmen, in which the previous clan organization was adhered to. On the other hand, within the town they scattered and lived in apartment houses and individual homes as neighbors not only of persons coming from different clan and tribal groups, but of other nationalities. This explains the high retention of certain backward traits in the culture and mode of life of the population specifically of the suburban settlements (see Sh. Annaklychev, "Nekotorye storony byta rabochikh-neftianikov Nebit-Daga," SE, 1959, No. 1).

10) The writings of Polish sociologists in this area merit attention. See, for example, the article by A. Matejko, "Wartóść użytkowa nowych mieskań w swietle doswiadezen ich meischańców," Zaludnienie i uzytkowanie mieszkan w nowych osiedlach, Warsaw, 1959.

11) The pioneering study of urban musical culture by a Soviet scholar was K. V. Chistov's survey of the present-day song repertoire of the small industrial town of Segezha in the Karelian ASSR: K. V. Chistov, "Literaturno-khudozhestvennaia kul'tura sotsialisticheskoi Segzhi," Izv. Karelo-Finskogo filiala AN SSSR, 1960, No. 2.

* * *

Voprosy filosofii, 1965, No. 5

V. N. Shubkin

YOUTH STARTS OUT IN LIFE*

The growth of the productive forces, the revolution in science and technology, and the vast changes in all spheres of the life of our society are the causes of high occupational and social mobility, and present diverse and rapidly changing demands upon our young people as they begin their working lives. It is a general rule that a new generation's start in life involves complicated and many-sided problems, touching upon a broad range of matters that include job placement, the family, education, character-building, personnel training, job training in schools, choice of occupation, etc.

Proper and prompt solution of these problems always yields both social and economic benefits. On the one hand, the possibility of errors, dissatisfaction, and disillusionment in the first steps taken by young people is reduced, and this leads to a decrease in various types of anti-social phenomena (drunkenness, crime, immorality, etc.). On the other hand, it makes for more rapid and

efficient involvement of young men and girls in the labor process. It reduces labor turnover and migration, makes for a higher rate of permanent settlement by young people in newly developed parts of the country, and improves the quality of selection and preparation of personnel for all branches of the economy, science, and culture. (1)

The social problems of youth are not solved automatically. In order to make it easier for young men and girls to begin independent life and in order to resolve successfully and promptly the contradictions arising in this process, there is a need for systematic scientific studies of the social problems of the young generation in socialist society.

Some of these problems are being studied by the Sociology Group of the Laboratory for Research in Mathematical Economics of Novosibirsk University. (2)

The program of our work embraces a rather broad range of socio-economic, sociological, and socio-psychological problems involved in the entry of the younger generation into independent life. Specifically, the following were studied: the social prestige and attractiveness of various occupations and types of work; objective and sub-

_____

*Based on data of a sociological study of problems of job placement and choice of occupation. The article is published for discussion purposes.

The author is from Novosibirsk.

18

jective factors influencing the education, aptitudes, choice of occupation, job placement, and course in life taken by various groups of young people; social, occupational, and territorial mobility in the choice of an occupation; effectiveness of the system of practical training in the schools; certain means of improving the process of planning for and training of skilled personnel, and improvement of the system of occupational guidance and orientation. The problem was also posed of determining, on the basis of these investigations, the degree to which it is possible to predict personal plans, job placement, and occupational, territorial and social shifts as a consequence of choice of occupation among the group of young people which makes this choice in essentially unregulated fashion. Such forecasting is essential if social planning and management of these processes are to be at all dependable. The breadth of the goals of this study was to a certain degree unavoidable. In order to assure objectivity of the analysis, it is necessary to take into consideration the maximum number of aspects of the process under study.

Novosibirsk Oblast was taken as the region for study. (3) The investigation covered graduates of full and incomplete secondary schools. Of all the groups of young people taking jobs, these groups are of particular interest to us not only because their choice of occupation is not predetermined but also because, with the development of our society, the school becomes an increasingly important source of skilled personnel for the labor force, science, and culture.

The study was conducted in three stages.

The first stage (1962) saw trial surveys of 300 secondary-school graduates in order to develop the technique for studying the questionnaires and determining a number of co-relations.

The second stage (1963) was that of a mass-scale survey covering all the secondary schools and 10% of the incomplete secondary schools of the oblast (all told, some 9,000 questionnaires were circulated).

The third stage (1964) was a complete repetition of the second-stage survey to determine variations in the information and to study the possibilities of scientific prediction of certain social processes.

Thanks to support by agencies of the Party and of public education, and with the active support of school principals and teachers, the planned program of research has by now been essentially carried out.

The data are now being processed at computer stations and in the computer of the Computer Center of the Siberian Division of the USSR Academy of Sciences. Although the analysis is not entirely complete, we consider it desirable to publish certain materials and conclusions resulting primarily from the second stage of the survey and, in particular, to deal in detail with the following questions: the specific character of the job placement of young people in the years immediately ahead, resulting from the "demographic echo" of the war; on-the-job training; certain social problems of education; and, finally, the attractiveness of various occupations to young men and girls graduating from school.

1. Job Placement of Young People

The young men and women we surveyed in 1963 are the final generation born during the war years. We know that all the warring countries witnessed a sharp drop in birthrate during the war. The more active the country's participation in the war, the more marked was this drop. On the other hand, the birthrate showed a sharp rise after the war.

At present we are witness to a kind of "demographic echo" of the war. It is expressed in a sharp, flood-like increase in the number of youths aged 17 and 18 going out into independent life. Thus, according to calculations conducted at the Laboratory for Research in Mathematical Economics of Novosibirsk University, the number of young men and girls in Novosibirsk 17 years of age will increase 60% in the years 1963-1965, and those 18 years old will increase 70%. Graduations from secondary schools will rise even more rapidly in these next few years. This may be seen from the single fact that the number of students graduating from the general educational schools of Novosibirsk Oblast will multiply several-fold in the next few years.

Contrary to what is the case in capitalist society, the possibility does objectively exist in socialist countries of solving the problems involved in the job placement of young people successfully and in planned fashion. But we must not rely upon spontaneity. If the attention of Party, Komsomol, and economic agencies is not drawn to these questions, if we do not study the personnel needs of the economy by skills, the structure of job and skill training, and the occupational aptitudes of youth, negative consequences may ensue.

Under our conditions, the problem of job placement has territorial, industrial, (a) and occupational aspects. If we bear in mind that labor resources are today distributed very unevenly over the territory of the USSR, we are justified in anticipating major differences in future problems of job placement for young people in different areas. In regions with excess labor resources, particularly Moldavia, the Western Ukraine, Western Belorussia, the Transcaucasus, and the Central Asian republics, job placement of young people has already been a rather complex task for a number of years. But even in certain eastern districts of the country which, as a rule, have experienced a labor shortage, certain problems in placing young people in jobs may occur in the years immediately ahead.

Calculations for Novosibirsk Oblast demonstrate that even in the distinctive conditions of 1963, when the number of graduates was considerably lower than will be the case in the next few years, and when the percentage of youth entering higher educational institutions and technical secondary schools [tekhnikums] was considerably higher than will be the case, approximately one-half of the secondary-school graduates went to work, primarily in industry. In the years immediately ahead, with identical (or approximately identical) rates of admission to higher educational institutions and tekhnikums, both the percentage and the actual number of young men and women who will have to go to work will increase sharply. It must be emphasized particularly that the sharp increase in the number of secondary-school graduates, as a result of the fact that the period reflecting the drop in birthrate during the war has been passed, will reach 100% in the years immediately ahead due to the reduction in the total period of schooling — i.e., the transition from eleven-year to ten-year schools. It is therefore obvious that job placement is becoming an important socio-economic problem of our society.

To what degree are we prepared to solve these problems? What has to be undertaken so as to deal with them most effectively in the forthcoming Five-Year Plan?

The problems of job placement of young people cannot be resolved in the new Five-Year Plan in isolation from the overall problems of utilization of labor resources.

At present this work is complicated by the fact that the years of the Stalin personality cult saw a serious weakening and abandonment of the "labor services" that had existed in our country. We are referring to the abolition of the People's Commissariat of Labor and of the research institutes and journals in the field, as well as the reduction in or complete abolition of social research (in demography, social psychology, social statistics, social hygiene, etc.), of studies of scientific organization of labor and management, and the absence or limited nature of information on the degree of employment and utilization of the labor force. (4) The neglected state of the "labor services" is still exercising an extremely negative effect upon improvement of man-hour output, the planning of public education, the training of skilled personnel, and job placement. Often, numerous complications are created for the young men and women entering upon independent life.

Moreover, some of our economic and scientific personnel are underestimating the significance of problems of job placement. Here we continue to see the influence of that peculiar "theory" of spontaneity or automatism, according to which the socialization of the means of production itself automatically guarantees full employment of the entire population. In point of fact, no such automatic solution is operative, for public ownership of the means of production creates no more than the objective prerequisites, the possibilities for resolution of these problems. As far as automation and technical progress in general are concerned, they lead and must lead — as a general rule, even under our conditions — to a reduction in the need for labor at the particular enterprise or in the particular industry. The fact that we are able to foresee such phenomena and, given the conditions of a planned economy, promptly redistribute and retrain personnel who become superfluous as the result of technological progress, automation, change in the structure of production, etc., is something else again. Therefore there is need for painstaking work, day in and day out, to bring to reality the advantages of the socialist mode of production, and particularly to provide systematically for full employment of the population.

Above all, it is necessary to have a complete, all-round picture of the utilization of the labor supply in the country as a whole, as well as regionally and by branch of the economy. It seems to us that effective utilization of labor resources requires not only a highly authoritative state institution such as a ministry of labor, but also interdepartmental, territorial offices and agencies for planned redistribution of the labor force. In the first place, such bodies could systematically inform the public about needs for personnel. Secondly, they could provide the required information to economic, project-drafting and industrial planning agencies with respect to the labor force available in a given raion, town, oblast, or territory. This would reduce the losses involved in seeking work in one's field, and would make it possible to decide problems of planning and economic development of a district with consideration of the labor resources at hand, their distribution, sex, age, occupation, qualifications, etc. At the same time it appears desirable to charge these institutions with the task of providing jobs for personnel dismissed as the result of introduction of new equipment, change in direction of emphasis, etc.

In our view, these territorial offices should also make long-range calculations of the needs for personnel by occupations. Experience shows that the oblast planning commissions, which now have the responsibility for this work, are actually essentially incapable of resolving these tasks be-

cause of their small size. Often they are not in a position even to collect requests from enterprises specifying their needs for labor, not to speak of monitoring and guiding this work.

Educational institutions to retrain and re-qualify personnel who have been laid off should also be concentrated under these territorial offices. At the same time it is essential to emphasize that the territorial offices must definitely be super-departmental and embrace the entire territory, all branches of the economy, and the entire population of the given region. Not infrequently, for example, the consequences of the building of enterprises or industrial complexes with respect to the labor force available to agriculture are not considered, with the result that the latter suffers. Therefore it is necessary to understand most clearly that there can be no positive results of work on the problem of the labor force without a multi-faceted approach.

It would be useful to take all these factors into consideration with respect to the utilization of labor resources, as the Five-Year Plan is confirmed. Because of the special acuteness of the problem of job placement of young people during the new Five-Year Plan, it seems desirable to provide, in that plan, a special section on job placement for young people. It would be desirable to examine the major indices of the Five-Year Plan both for the USSR as a whole and region by region, with this in mind. This is particularly important in conjunction with the elaboration of measures with respect to the geographical distribution of the economy and the utilization of capital investments.

2. Job Placement and Work Training in School

One of the important means of successful solution of the problem of job placement of young people during the new Five-Year Plan is the effective organization of work training in school. The system of polytechnical instruction, providing both for development of work habits and for training in skills needed by the economy, makes it possible to ease young people's entry into working life.

What role is work training in school now playing?

In Novosibirsk Oblast, only 11% of the secondary-school graduates of 1963 were working at the skills learned in school — i.e., the majority of graduates were not working at the trades learned in school. This means that the state is compelled to make further outlays to retrain boys and girls who have only just gained a skill: it must provide buildings, power, and transportation, machines, raw materials, wages, tools, etc. This does not even consider the cost in morale when retraining is required.

But could we say that the goal of work training — in the form it now takes in most schools — is being attained indirectly in that a love for labor is developed and the young people acquire work habits?

We know that one of the objectives of work training in school is to coordinate the personal strivings of youth with the interests of society. If, say, 90% of the graduates, after completing studies, will have to take jobs in industry, construction and agriculture, and 90% of the graduates actually intend to do so, no problems exist. But if only 10% want to take jobs, serious problems arise. It was the school reform in general, and the introduction of job training in particular, that were supposed to help solve this problem, according to recent proposals.

Analysis of the data of the mass-scale survey of Novosibirsk Oblast students on the eve of graduation from secondary school and after job placement shows that important differences exist between their personal plans and their actual jobs. For example, 80% of the graduates wished to continue with their schooling immediately upon graduation (see Table 1). These personal plans underwent significant modification due to external circumstances. Not 80%, but 44% of the graduates continued their education immediately after graduation (a very high percentage, explained by the small size of the 1963 graduating class).

We find a picture different from the foregoing in the personal plans of those graduates who associate their futures with work in the economy. Only 8% of the graduates planned to go to work right after graduation. However, 32% — and not 8% — actually did so. Moreover, as indicated above, the majority of graduates get jobs other than those for which they were trained in school. This shows that job training in school is not yet playing the role for which it was intended.

This can hardly be explained merely by inertia in the educational system. There must be more serious causes than this.

In the first place, many of the trades at which young people have to work after graduation provide very limited opportunities for creativity and often do not require a high level of general education. Yet our survey shows that the boys and girls place an extremely high value particularly upon the creative nature of work, and judge occupations by this standard above all others. Unfortunately, certain managerial and planning personnel hold that the provision of opportunities for creativity, growth, etc., concerns factors of third-rate importance. Therefore they are often not considered. However, these factors are not only means for increasing labor productivity and for reducing losses, but are also a necessary condition for transforming work into the primary felt need of life. That is why this social aspect is exceedingly important from the standpoint of the principal objectives of the further development of our society, when new enterprises and departments are planned, and when new equipment and new forms of organization of the labor force on the job are introduced. On the other hand, each stage in the development of society has its particular optimal distribution of the population by level of education. A low level of education is not the sole factor preventing a more rapid rise in the forces of production and in living standards. In our view, a premature transition to forms of education not called forth by the actual needs of the economy, science, and culture also inhibits growth of the productivity of social labor and a rise in the people's standard of living.

In the second place, the system of training in work skills in school took shape, in years past, in a largely spontaneous, unplanned fashion. The transition to trade schooling as part of general education requires the solution not only of educational but, above all, of socio-economic problems. One cannot seriously answer the question

Table 1

Personal Plans of Graduates and Their Actual Realization
(as % of total)*

| | Total | Of which | | | Total | Of which | |
		Boys	Girls			Boys	Girls
Planned to go to work	8	8	8	Actually went to work	32	26	35
Planned to work and study on the side	12	7	14	Actually worked, with study on the side	3	2	3
Planned to study	80	85	78	Actually became students	44	48	41
Total	100%	100%	100%	Total	100%**	100%	100%

* From data of complete survey of Nobosibirsk Oblast secondary schools in 1963.
** Totals in some columns fail to add up due to lack of "Others" row.

of how to teach without having solved the problem of what to teach, what trades the graduates should be trained for. To determine the trades in which instruction should be given, it is necessary, in the first place, to have information on personnel requirements for each trade, with due consideration for the future. However, no dependable data on these subjects existed. Nor was there any information on the occupational interests and aptitudes of the school population. The schools themselves had to determine the fields in which they would give job training, without considering either personnel needs or the aptitudes of the pupils. As a consequence, some graduates would like to find work in the skills they have learned, but cannot, while others, in turn, do not wish to work at the skills they were taught in school. An inevitable consequence is that there are too many people trained in certain skills and too few in others. Therefore, in working out the structure of education in work skills for the country, no matter how the question of job training is resolved (training through the general school system or through special trade schools), it is necessary to proceed from the personnel needs of the economy in the oblast and raion, skill by skill, and to take into consideration the aptitudes of the young people. (5) There is need for an optimal state plan for the distribution of educational institutions, training shops, and enterprises, independent of bureaucratic interests and based upon long-range needs for personnel by skills and the aptitudes of young people.

Thirdly, in the mid-1930's, all work in occupational counseling, orientation, and choice of occupations was brought to an end for all practical purposes. In the process of criticizing the supporters of child study ["pedologists," in Soviet parlance (b)], the baby was thrown out with the bathwater. In our view, this was a mistake. It is specifically in socialist society that systematic scientific study of the inclinations, aptitudes, and interests of schoolchildren becomes necessary and possible. Lacking this, we cannot make full use of the capacities and talents of each. This work must assist young men and women to find their natural calling, to select an occupation, work that would be needed by society and would give maximum satisfaction.

All this shows that improvement in job placement of young people, particularly under conditions of a sharp increase in the number of secondary-school graduates, requires the urgent development of measures not only of an educational but, above all, of a socio-economic nature, and demands a real reinforcement of the ties between the school and life.

24

3. Certain Social Problems of Education

Inasmuch as our goal is to create for young people of different social groups, and on a nation-wide scale, equal opportunities for education, we must constantly check and predict probable changes in this process. Calculations by the Sociological Group of the Laboratory for Research in Mathematical Economics of Novosibirsk University enable us to judge how demographic factors, particularly the decline in the birthrate, affect not only the numbers entering and graduating from school but the nature of dropout, the opportunities for young people to enter higher educational institutions and tekhnikums, and the paths in life taken by members of various social groups.

The decline in the birthrate due to the war had its first effect in reducing the number of children entering school. Thus, the number of first-graders in the schools of Novosibirsk Oblast dropped two-thirds from 1947 to 1953. This could not but have its effects upon the numbers of dropouts and upon the paths in life of various categories of young people.

In our view, the role of this factor may be seen most clearly with the aid of "educational pyra-

mids," which we have constructed on the pattern of the Christmas-tree diagrams widely employed by demographers.

Here, for example, are two pyramids (6) (see Table 2). The former illustrates the progress from the first through tenth grades of children who entered the first grade in Novosibirsk Oblast in 1947 (the generation born before the war). As we see, only 4,500 of 45,000 boys, or 10%, and only 7,100 of 41,000 girls, or 17%, completed the full 10 grades. Together, 13% of the entrants became secondary-school graduates.

The second pyramid illustrates progress from the first through the tenth (or eleventh) grade of children who entered the first grade in Novosibirsk Oblast schools in 1953 (the generation born during the war years), when the drop in birthrate had reached its maximum. As we see, about 20,000 boys entered the first grade, of whom 2,700 graduated from secondary school (ten-year and eleven-year graduating classes), while 4,700 girls, or 26% of the 17,800 entering, graduated. In all, 20% graduated.

Overall analysis of the "educational pyramids" shows that the decline in numbers of pupils due to the drop in the birthrate led to a reduction in

Table 2

"Educational Pyramids"

First-graders of 1947
(i.e., graduates of 1957)

First-graders of 1953
(graduates of 1963)

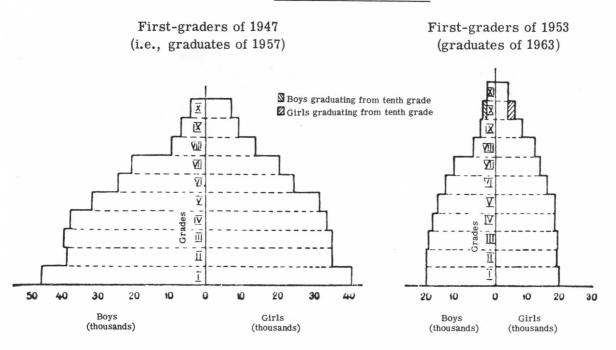

Boys graduating from tenth grade
Girls graduating from tenth grade

the number of dropouts and to an increase in the percentage of those graduating from school. At the same time, this necessarily had the effect of reducing the competition for admission to higher educational institutions and tekhnikums — i.e., it increased the percentage of admissions to such institutions out of the given group of first-grade entrants.

It is important to bear in mind that the opportunity to enter higher educational institutions depends significantly not only upon the demographic situation in the country, but also upon a number of social factors which, in our view, it is impermissible to ignore. The opportunities available today to young people living in large cities to enter higher educational institutions are considerably higher than in rural localities because the level of preparation in urban schools is, as a general rule, higher. Analysis also shows that their parents' educational level has a serious influence upon the children's interests and strivings (see our article, "Choice of Occupation Under Conditions of the Building of Communism" [Vybor professii v usloviiakh stroitel'stva kommunizma], Voprosy filosofii, 1964, No. 8). The standard of living, housing conditions, etc., have a major influence upon a child's grades, upon his occupational inclinations, and consequently upon

the opportunity to obtain an education. As a result of all this, the social structure of those entering first grade differs markedly from that of those who graduate and, even more, from that of students in higher educational institutions.

Here, for example, is the manner in which the social status of parents (7) affected the personal plans of graduates and their actual realization (according to the 10% sampling survey of secondary-school graduates of Novosibirsk Oblast in 1963) (see Table 3 below).

Table 3 shows that children of urban non-manual personnel showed the highest percentage actually able to continue beyond secondary school. Next come children of workers in industry and construction, while children of workers in the service industries and rural non-manual personnel are in third and fourth place, with fifth and sixth places occupied by children of workers in transport and communications and of people doing manual work in agriculture.

Thus, while we categorically oppose any broad interpretation of these selective data, we do have grounds for affirming that the paths through life taken by young people from various social groups today show significant divergences. Of every 100 secondary-school graduates coming from the families of collective-farm members and state-

Table 3

Social Status of Families, Personal Plans of Graduates, and Their Realization
(in %)

Occupational status of families	Percentage of children wishing:			Percentage of children succeeding:		
	to work	to work and study simultaneously	to study	to work	to work and study simultaneously	to study
Urban non-manual	2	5	93	15	3	82
Rural non-manual	11	13	76	42	-	58
Manual, in industry and construction	11	6	83	36	3	61
Manual, in transport and communications	-	18	82	55	-	45
Manual, in agriculture	10	14	76	90	-	10
Manual, in services	9	15	76	38	3	59
Others	12	38	50	63	12	25
Total	7	10	83	37	2	61

farm workers, only 10 continued to study after completion of secondary school and 90 went to work, while of every 100 graduates coming from the families of urban non-manual persons, 82 continued their studies and only 15 went to work.

Consideration of the factors influencing education provides a basis for the assumption that the sharp increase in the number of young people entering upon working lives during the new Five-Year Plan will give rise to a number of trends opposite to those observed at the time of decline in the numbers of youth consequent upon the decline in birthrate. If special measures are not taken promptly, there will be an increase in the number of dropouts from secondary school and a reduction in the percentage of those who will graduate. At the same time, it is clear that competition for admission to higher educational and semi-professional institutions will increase. The effectiveness of job training at school will increase, provided the conditions previously cited are adhered to.

It must be particularly emphasized that the increased competition for admission to higher educational institutions, combined with the rise in the number of secondary-school graduates, may lead to a diminution in the percentage of children of workers and peasants entering higher educational institutions. Therefore it is necessary to take measures in advance to counteract such trends. This is a rather complicated problem. On the one hand, we must strive to provide equal educational opportunities for all. On the other hand, due to differences in their families' material circumstances, in their parents' level of education, in their place of residence, in the geographical distribution of educational institutions, in the level of teaching, etc., young people of equal capacities — but differing in preparation — will actually differ in their opportunities to gain an education.

In considering this question, we must not forget that the principal means for overcoming social differences in the sphere of education is change in those objective conditions themselves. Efforts to establish preferential conditions for admission to higher educational institutions for particular social groups, regardless of level of preparation, not only will not help to solve the prob-

lem but, on the contrary, may reduce the general level of education, which would be equivalent to holding back the progress of science and technology.

This is the contradiction. It cannot be solved quickly, but it must be recognized, and specific steps to resolve it must be planned, in accordance with the level of development of the productive forces. At this time in particular, as measures are developed to cope with the sharp rise in the numbers of those 17 and 18 years of age, it is important that the new Five-Year Plan should not permit a decline in the chances for higher education of children of workers and peasants, particularly of rural youth.

4. Attractiveness of Occupations

There is also an occupational aspect to problems of job placement. There is no such thing as job placement in general. Job placement is something that only occurs in specific branches of the economy and in specific skills. In this respect it is important to know the attitude of youth toward different occupations and forms of work.

Our questionnaire to graduates asked them to evaluate, by degree of attractiveness, 70 occupations embracing the principal branches of the economy, science, and culture, on a ten-point scale (giving 10 points to the most attractive, 1 to the least, and intermediate values to others). The replies were analyzed by age-and-sex and by territorial considerations (the city of Novosibirsk, other large and small cities, raion centers, towns, and villages of the oblast. The findings of the overall survey make it possible to ascertain the attitude of various groups of young people toward occupations in various branches of the economy, science, and culture.

Let us illustrate the attitude of secondary-school youth toward various types of occupations that do not require higher education (see Table 4).

If we assume that the least attractive occupations are graded between 1.0 to 4.0 points, those of medium attractiveness from 4.0 to 7.0, and the most attractive from 7.0 to 10 points, then, as is evident from the table, the most important

Table 4

Unskilled and semi-skilled occupations	Evaluation of attractiveness, in points		
	Total	Boys	Girls
Industrial workers	4.26	4.35	4.20
Transport and communications workers	5.28	5.46	5.19
Construction workers	4.07	3.75	4.25
Service industry workers	2.63	2.34	2.79
Education, culture, and health jobs	4.82	3.46	5.52
Agriculture	3.75	3.73	3.76

occupations that do not require higher education are of average attractiveness to the secondary-school graduates. The greatest differences between girls and boys are in evaluating jobs in the spheres of culture, education, and public health, which girls rate at 5.52 against 3.46 for boys. The highest evaluation is given to transport jobs. The lowest goes to agriculture (3.75) and the service industries (2.63). The same trends show up in analysis of occupations requiring higher education.

If we analyze not the average point value of a group of occupations, but the evaluation of individual occupations, the lowest value is given to clerical work, work in housing and other urban services, and that of sales clerk, while the most popular occupations are those of pilot and radio technician. Among manual occupations, the most popular, among both boys and girls, is chemical worker (in the industrial classification); lumberjack is the least popular. In construction, work on erection is most popular, and painting least popular. In transport and communications, the job of diesel engineer is most popular, while that of a letter carrier, telephone operator, and telegrapher is least popular. In agriculture, the most popular jobs are those of equipment operators — tractor drivers and harvester-combine men — while work with livestock is least popular.

Of the occupations requiring the highest qualification, those which are most attractive to secondary-school graduates are those of radio technician and geologist, while the least popular is that of engineer for the foodstuffs and clothing industries. Among the rural occupations of high-est skill, agronomist rates highest, and veterinarian lowest.

The attitude of secondary-school graduates toward work in various fields of science is also of definite interest (see Table 5).

As we see, it is the physics and mathematics group that enjoys maximum prestige, followed by the natural sciences, with the humanities in last place. Boys gave their highest rating to physics (7.91), and girls to mathematics (8.20). Both sexes gave their lowest rating to biology. While the sexual differentials in attitude toward various types of work in the sphere of material production have a certain foundation in objective reality (because "male" and "female" occupations still exist), the attitudes toward certain sciences, and particularly the reasons for boys' low interest in biology (4.24) and in certain humanistic fields, require serious attention.

The low attractiveness of the mass-scale occupations in agriculture and the service industries is particularly deserving of close attention.

Let us first consider agriculture. In our opinion, despite the fact that the rise in man-hour output in agriculture is leading and will lead not only to a relative but to an absolute reduction in the number of people it employs, there are many parts of the country, Siberia in particular, where the problem of creating permanent staffs for agriculture now has, and will continue to have, first-rate significance. Without stable bodies of personnel who like their work, it is impossible to create efficient agriculture. Therefore the question of increasing the attractiveness of the agricultural occupations has great practical significance.

Table 5

Branch of science	Attractiveness, in points		
	Total	Boys	Girls
Mathematics	7.50	7.45	8.20
Physics	7.69	7.91	7.56
Geology	6.84	6.43	7.08
Chemistry	7.23	6.57	7.65
Biology	4.66	4.24	4.93
Medicine	7.32	6.28	7.89
History	6.17	5.57	6.49
Philosophy	6.05	5.42	6.39
Literature	5.75	4.78	6.27
Economics	5.52	4.89	5.88
Mathematical economics	6.33	5.79	6.62

The cause of the outflow of youth from agriculture resolves, in the final analysis, to the socio-economic differences between town and country, and to those in culture and conveniences of life; these differences are still quite great among us. Moreover, the rapid growth of industry, the building of new towns and the development of such parts of the country as Siberia, the development of the radio, movies, and television, and the penetration of urban standards of life to the countryside, have all also promoted the intensified flow of young people to the cities. (See Table 6.)

Urbanization also has a pronounced influence upon the attitudes of youth toward various occupations. Therefore the attractiveness of agricultural occupations differs in areas that differ in degree of urbanization.

Table 6, compiled from the data of a 10% sample, demonstrates very clearly that for young people living in the country and familiar with the conditions of farm work, these occupations are more attractive than for urban youth. Agricultural specialists are also held in higher esteem in rural localities. The farther one goes from the countryside, the more negative the attitude toward agricultural occupations, particularly among young people.

This indicates that one should not now count on any high percentage of youth — of those groups of young people who have already been touched by urbanization — remaining in agriculture. Therefore, appeals to urban youth to work permanently in the villages will hardly be effectual. As a consequence, in districts where there is a shortage of labor in agriculture, it is necessary to take all possible measures to retain rural

Table 6

Attractiveness of Agricultural Occupations in Areas of Varying Levels of Urbanization

	Evaluation in points			
	Villages	Raion seats and towns	Cities	Novosibirsk
Boys	4.70	3.97	3.16	2.76
Girls	4.33	3.81	3.78	3.35

youth itself there (naturally, we are talking not of administrative, but of socio-economic and other measures, and the like).

In this connection, it must be noted that the means of retaining young people in agriculture cannot be reduced to financial incentives. Very often we encounter here factors that are not merely economic, but social, political, and so forth. For example, in drafting rural youth into the army, we must recognize that we thereby often destroy the natural sex-and-age structure of the countryside (because a considerable proportion of these young men go into construction, industry, and the like, after their period in the service). As a result, few men remain in the villages. But the balance is restored because many girls also move to the cities one way or another. Moreover, their reasons for leaving for the towns are generally not based on material considerations, but merely on an effort to arrange their personal lives. And one cannot disregard this.

Thus, to increase the attractiveness of the agricultural occupations, it is necessary to solve major economic and social problems, to improve material incentives, and to take sociological [and] demographic factors into careful consideration. In addition, it would be useful, particularly in the rural schools, to put occupational counseling on a proper footing, especially with respect to advocating entry into agricultural occupations, and also to make wider use of the press, television, radio, and films toward this end.

The illusions to the effect that socialism is possible without commerce have now receded into the past. We know that while the percentage of those occupied in agriculture and industry may be ex-

pected to decline in the future, the numbers working in the sphere of service will increase both relatively and absolutely. Therefore it is exceedingly dangerous to underestimate the significance of this branch of the economy. However, underestimation of the service sphere, of occupations in trade, of clerking, and of technical work in this area is still seen. Some people in the movie industry, radio and the press have encouraged the establishment of a humorously contemptuous attitude toward the professions in the service field. Today we are not systematically and seriously presenting the humanistic nature of these occupations and their rising role in the building of communism, and are harvesting bitter fruit as a consequence.

These occupations, like farming, appear to be particularly unattractive to urban young people. (See Table 7.)

That the prestige of the service industries is higher among girls than boys is firmly established. But they rank lower among urban youth than rural.

Increasing the prestige of these occupations is one of the important tasks in our educational work. It is necessary to break down a series of rather firmly established false notions about the service industries. It must be demonstrated, persuasively and vividly, that to serve does not mean to demean oneself or to behave like a lackey, that commerce is a matter no less important than any other, that it does not involve thievery and skulduggery, and that without clerking, bookkeeping, stenography, the handling of funds, etc., it is impossible to manage the economy, develop science, culture, etc. Elevation of the authority

Table 7

Attractiveness of Occupations in Service Sphere in Urban and Rural Places

Occupations	Rural youth		Urban youth	
	boys	girls	boys	girls
Restaurant industry	2.96	3.44	2.55	3.1
Salespeople	2.52	3.16	2.02	2.66
Clerks	2.12	2.37	2.06	2.24

of the occupations in the service sphere is an exceedingly important economic and ideological undertaking.

* * *

Our research has shown that Soviet boys and girls stepping out into the workaday world face a considerable number of complicated problems. At the same time, experience shows that, under the conditions of socialist society, every opportunity exists for successful solution of the contradictions that arise and for overcoming difficulties. However, in order to act, one must know. Therefore one of the most pressing and most effective forms of aid to young people by workers in the social sciences is large-scale development of sociological investigations and the development of concrete proposals for the leading bodies of our society.

Editor's Notes

a) I.e., relating to various branches of the economy or of industry.

b) "Pedology" in Soviet usage referred to any study of child psychology in the psychological plane. This and any policies based on it were condemned by the Party as inconsistent with socialism.

Footnotes

1) For greater detail, see the article "O konkretnykh issledovaniiakh sotsial'nykh protsessov," in Kommunist, 1965, No. 3.

2) This work is being done by the Sociological Group of the Laboratory for Research in Mathematical Economics of Novosibirsk University, consisting of G. Kochetov, Iu. Karpov, L. Borisova, N. Moskalenko, N. Buzukova, Z. Baglai, V. Sennitskaia (with the participation of V. Artemov, N. Verbitskaia, Iu. Kovalenko, I. Kuznetsova, A. Pusep), under the guidance of the author. Computer programming was by F. Borodkin, V. Kolmogorov, R. Strelko, and L. Chernova. Students of the Department of Economic Cybernetics of Novosibirsk State University did the coding.

3) By the 1959 census, the region had a population of 2,298,000, of which 1,274,000 was urban and 1,024,000 was rural.

4) For example, see the article "O dvukh zabytykh oblastiakh sotsiologicheskikh issledovanii," Kommunist, 1963, No. 17, and 1964, No. 9.

5) Contemporary methods of optimal planning make it possible (given the necessary information) to develop models for the structure of job training in school that would simultaneously assure both the meeting of the needs of the economy for personnel by particular skills and the minimization of dissatisfaction in choice of an occupation. This problem is similar to that of linear programming for allocation of personnel and is therefore reducible to the common transport problem (see, for example, Kolichestvennye metody v sotsiologicheskikh issledovaniiakh, Novosibirsk University Press, 1964, Part II, Section 4).

6) In analyzing the data of the "educational pyramids," it must be borne in mind that they are plotted without consideration of population movements and do not include boys and girls who went on to study in tekhnikums, and in trade-and-technical schools and similar educational institutions.

7) In families with both father and mother, social status was determined from the father's occupation, but if there was no father, then by the mother's.

Nauchnye doklady vysshei shkoly,
filosofskie nauki, 1963, No. 4

A. G. Kharchev

ON SOME RESULTS OF A STUDY OF THE MOTIVES

FOR MARRIAGE (1)

The family is one of the most complex of social institutions. The fact that there are so many sides, so many aspects, to family relationships makes it possible for a large number of social factors to influence them. These range from the ratio between men and women in a country's population to the nature of the morality dominant in the given society. Most important among these factors is the economic system, which influences the status and development of the family as an institution both directly and through other aspects of social life: the position of women in society, the standard of living, government policy and law, social ideology and psychology, etc. Therefore, the triumph of socialism in the USSR led to a corresponding change in the field of marriage and family relationships and to the appearance of a new, socialist type of family. Socialization of property in the means of production resulted in a fundamental change in the nature of the very need for marriage: from an economic necessity it was transformed into a moral one.

As Friedrich Engels once observed, under the conditions of dominance of private property, the monogamous family "is based on the dominance of the husband, with the clearly-defined purpose of producing children whose descent from the father is not subject to doubt, and this unchallangeability of descent is essential because the children will, in the course of time, as direct descendants, come to possess the property of the father" (Marx and Engels, Selected Works [Izbr. proizv.], Vol. II, Gospolitizdat, 1955, p. 208). The same thing, essentially, although in less clear-cut form, is granted in a number of contemporary sociological publications in the West: "The family," we read, for example, in one of them, "not only distributes the wealth, but accumulates property of various types in the form of capital. For individual and social progress it is quite important that this accumulation proceed in a specific and orderly fashion from generation to generation" (Sociological Theory, New York, 1956, p. 274).

The freeing of family and marriage relationships from subordination to concerns of accumulation and transmission of private property by inheritance had inevitably to exert an influence upon the nature of those relationships and, above all, upon the motives for marriage. By motives we understand everything that impels people to marry, including both the major and "secondary" goals of marriage. For all their diversity, it is possible to reduce them to two forms:

1. Motives deriving from the essence of marriage, from the human desire for motherhood and fatherhood and intellectual, moral and esthetic strivings, of which the highest is love.

2. Motives alien to the essence of marriage, depriving it of significance in and for itself, and transforming the selection of the future mate into merely a means of achieving goals external to the marriage relationship itself (increase in wealth, the receipt of economic, political or administrative benefits and advantages, etc.).

Both groups of motives have been operative in all socio-economic systems starting with that of slavery. But a private-property economy provides a stimulus for the motives that deprive marriage of its real essence and therefore, as Marx once put it, "at a higher stage of development the principle of private property contradicts the principle of the family" (Marx and Engels, Works, [Soch.], Vol. I, p. 334). On the other hand, a socialist economy and the entire system of social relationships existing under socialism create the atmosphere "most favorable" to marriage for love and sharply reduce the opportunity for "marriage of convenience."

Suffice it to say that in the majority of bourgeois countries, despite all the efforts of the progressive strata of society, economic, political, legal and, in particular, moral-psychological discrimination against women persists, while in all socialist countries women are equal with men in the opportunity to get jobs, in payment for their work, in civil rights and in the eyes of society. At the end of 1960, women in the USSR numbered 53% of all employed persons with higher education and 63% of all with higher and secondary education in professional skills (The National Economy of the USSR in 1960.

Statistical Yearbook [Narodnoe khoziaistvo SSSR v 1960 godu. Statisticheskii ezhegodnik], Moscow, Gosstatizdat, 1961, pp. 661, 662). Thus, the socialist system eliminates the economic and social bases for the dominance of man in the family and thereby sharply accelerates the operation of the tendency, arising even under capitalism, to convert marriage into an equal and voluntary alliance of man and woman. (2) But on the other hand, we know that the changes toward socialism in the USSR took place under conditions of serious economic and social difficulties associated, in the first place, with civil war and devastation, then with World War II and the fascist occupation of a considerable portion of the country, and finally under conditions in which the threat of a new world war had not yet been eliminated.

As a result, despite the immense improvement in the material well-being of the people and in housing construction, (3) the standard of living in the USSR does not yet in all respects measure up to the opportunities inherent in socialism. Moreover, the death of millions of men at the front led to a great disproportion between the male and female populations in the USSR after World War II. According to the 1959 census, there were 20,700,000 more women than men in the country. And while today this applies primarily to people in the middle and older age groups (over 32), ten to fifteen years ago it was typical of a younger segment of the population. Naturally, all this influenced the thoughts, psychology and behavior of human beings, and complicated the struggle against the old property-holding, petty-bourgeois, anarchistic and other traditions in relationships between the sexes. Therefore one cannot regard the present status of marriage and the family in the USSR merely as a consequence of the socialist transformation of the economy and the social structure. In the sphere of personal and everyday life there is, along with the predominant progressive and socialist tendencies, still a good deal that is negative. However, this is not a product of socialism, but, as a general rule, of those extremely difficult historical conditions under which socialism was fated to develop.

This must be borne in mind both in considering marriage and family relationships in the USSR and in comparing them with the institution of marriage and the family in bourgeois lands.

* * *

In the USSR, special studies of motives and practices in marriage have been a rarity. The question was usually regarded as one of the problems to be dealt with in overall study of the family and family life (see S. Ia. Vol'fson, The Family and Marriage in Their Historical Development [Sem'ia i brak v ikh istoricheskom razvitii], Moscow, Sotsekgiz, 1937; N. A. Kisliakov, Family and Marriage Among the Tadzhiks [Sem'ia i brak u tadzhikov], Moscow and Leningrad, USSR Academy of Sciences, 1959; S. M. Abramzon, K. I. Antipina, G. P. Vasil'eva, E. I. Makhova, and D. Sulaimanov, The Way of Life of the Collective-Farm Peasantry of the Kirgiz Villages of Darkhan and Chichkan [Byt kolkhoznikov kirgizskikh selenii Darhan i Chichkan], Moscow, USSR Academy of Sciences, 1958; Viriatino Village in the Past and Today [Selo Viriatino v proshlom i nastoiashchem], Moscow, USSR Academy of Sciences, 1958; The Family and Family Life of the Collective Farmers of the Baltic Region [Sem'ia i semeinyi byt kolkhoznikov Pribaltiki], Moscow, USSR Academy of Sciences, 1962, and other works).

Inasmuch as data directly descriptive of the goals and intentions of persons entering into marriage are confined to their own opinions and value judgments, we have, in addition to studying these opinions, made an attempt to obtain some indirect evidence of an objective nature. The role of parents in marriage, the relation between the ages of bridegroom and bride, the duration of acquaintance before marriage, the rise in marriages across ethnic lines, etc., fall into this category.

With the object of shedding light on these matters we conducted, toward the end of 1962, a questionnaire survey of the persons getting married at the Leningrad City Registration Bureau (ZAGS), and also analyzed the data of these bureaus for the Uzbek SSR, the city of Kiev, the town of Tiumen', and Mga Raion of Leningrad Oblast.

It appears to us that the following circumstances testify to the representative nature of the data obtained in the Leningrad City Registration Bureau:

1) a majority (about 85%) of all marriages in which the ages of both parties do not exceed 30, and about half of all marriages in the city are registered there;

2) persons marrying for the second or subsequent times are not registered at that office. Thus, the very regulation governing this institution assures that the marriages studied are the most typical;

3) the structure of the population of Leningrad is a sort of "optimal model" of the structure of the country's urban population in its entirety (a high percentage of skilled industrial workers and of scientific and technical professionals, a large stratum of persons employed in culture and education and of students and a minimal proportion of persons not directly engaged in work for socialist society);

4) the study extended over a comparatively long period of time (two months). A total of 500 couples were questioned, and 300 more questionnaires were filled out as a check against the results obtained.

The persons queried consisted of 21% workers, 10% engineering and technical personnel, and 28% students, plus white-collar workers, physicians, and people in science, culture and education, the arts and military service.

The question pertaining directly to people's ideas as to the motives for marriage was formulated as follows: "What, in your opinion, is the prime condition for a lasting and happy marriage?" This formulation made it possible to transfer the "stress" from the factors that led to the choice of the particular individual (which might have been regarded as "interference in personal affairs") to the general moral bases of these factors. This, in our view, diminished somewhat the probability of untruthful answers.

Of all the couples who filled out the questionnaire, 76.2% regard the prime condition for a lasting and happy marriage to be love or love plus community of views, mutual confidence, sincerity, friendship, etc.; 13.2% regarded equity of rights and respect as primary; 4% named love and housing conditions; 1.6% — love and material well-being; 0.6% named the presence of children and 0.2% said "a realistic view of life." The remaining 4.2% gave no reply. Even if we assume that many of those who failed to reply held views similar to those who gave preference to material factors, the total number of such persons would still constitute only some 5% of those getting married. This ratio indicates that the moral approach to marriage has come to predominate in Soviet society.

However, the preference given to the moral approach should not be interpreted as indicating any inclination toward asceticism. Sample oral interviews showed that the people getting married understood the full importance of economic security in married life, but when the moral and material conditions for marriage were in conflict or not in harmony, the moral were given preference. This is particularly indicated by the answer to the following query in the questionnaire: "Where do you intend to live after you get married?" The present housing shortage often faces young people in love with the dilemma of postponing marriage and waiting till they get housing, or of marrying despite unfavorable material circumstances. Which choice is favored? 9.4% replied: "We hope to obtain a new place to live"; 7.6% intended to live in the groom's present quarters (without parents); 7.6% in the bride's, also without parents; 19.6% with the groom's parents; 16% with the bride's parents; 2% "part of the time with the groom's and part of the time with the wife's parents"; 15.6% intended to rent a room; 9.8% expected to remain in dormitories for the time being; one pair (0.2%) was leaving for Siberia after the marriage; the others answered "we don't know" (1.4%) or gave no answer. The decision to marry of that portion of the youth who do not enjoy normal living conditions is associated with its confidence that, in view of the fact that the USSR has the world's highest rates of public and cooperative housing construction they will be able to obtain an apartment in the relatively near future.

Summation of the findings on the role of parents in marriage yielded the following results.

Of 500 couples, 79.6% had asked their parents' agreement before deciding to marry and 77.8% obtained it, 1% "got it, but not at once," and in four cases (0.8%) the groom's parents objected. 13% did not ask the parents' agreement but informed them. In 3.4% of the cases "our parents don't yet know we're married"; two couples (0.4%) have no parents; and the remaining 18 couples (3.6%) did not respond to this question. Thus, the overwhelming majority of the marriages (78.8%) were concluded with the knowledge and agreement of the parents. As was demonstrated by sampling conversations with newlyweds after they had filled out the questionnaires, in all these cases the choice of partner was made by the person getting married; the parents merely gave their approval to the choice. Thus, parents have not been ousted from a part in the marriage of their children but their role has changed significantly as compared to the past.

The results of ethnographic study of marriage and family relationships in the USSR testify to the clear dominance of moral over material motives, both in choice of a partner and in the decision to marry.

Before the Revolution, marriage among the ruling classes, as well as among the peasantry and the urban petty bourgeoisie, jointly constituting the overwhelming majority of the population of the Russia of that day, was normally accompanied by the payment of a dowry or bride-price or other economic transactions. Today, all ethnographic expeditions observe that the institutions of dowry and bride-price are no longer mass phenomena. In cases in which marriage is still accompanied by monetary arrangements, this is usually condemned by public opinion. Such arrangements are sometimes even concluded by parents against the will of the young couple. Moreover, the dying-out of these institutions is characteristic not only for the central regions of the USSR but also for formerly backward ethnic borderlands, and even of areas that have become part of the Soviet Union comparatively recently. It is interesting to note that the new marriage customs at times even find expression in language: in Fergana Region of Uzbekistan the popular name for the ZAGS (Bureau for Registration of Documents of Civil Status) is "kholadim," which means, "I wish, I want" (see O. A. Sukhareva and M. A. Bikzhanova, Past and Present of the Village of Aikyran [Proshloe i nastoiashchee seleniia Aikyran], Tashkent, 1955, p. 195).

With respect to the role of parents in marriage, ethnographic studies modify somewhat the conclusions we have made on the basis of the Leningrad data, inasmuch as these studies deal with rural areas and districts with strong vestiges of patriarchal traditions. Thus the expedition headed by S. M. Abramzon found that in the Kirgiz village "by no means all marriages concluded by mutual agreement between the partners receive the approval of the parents on both sides, although in the majority of cases the parents did not stand in the way of the wishes of the young people. About half the marriages were concluded without obtaining the agreement of the parents of one of the parties, most frequently against the wishes of the girl's parents" (Abramzon et al, op. cit., p. 241). However, these cases of parental interference in choice of marriage partner are local in nature relative to the total number of marriages in the country, and are transient in terms of the direction of development of family and marriage relationships in the USSR.

To our question as to the circumstances of acquaintance that led to the marriage, we obtained the following replies: 9% of couples knew each other from childhood (lived in the same building or immediate neighborhood); 21% met at work; 17.5% at school; 27.2% at places of recreation (community center, dance, skating-rink, theater); 5.7% at house parties; 5% at summer vacation spots; 5.2% through mutual friends; 3.3% through relatives; 0.7% lived in the same dormitory; 1.6% met on the street and the other 3.8% in other places (streetcars, trains, hospitals, libraries, and at a mathematical elimination competition). Thus, about one-half the marriages are the result of acquaintances not associated either with place of residence, work or study. This relative independence of choice of marriage partner from occupational or residential localization is also to be seen in the countryside. But

here it is limited by the very conditions of rural life, which continues to be a "compact" phenomenon confined within each village. V. Iu. Krupianskaia reports, for example, that "as a result of the fact that population mobility is greater than before the Revolution, boys and girls working outside their home village very frequently get married where they are working. But we heard repeatedly that the youth continue to prefer to marry fellow-villagers" (Selo Viriatino ..., pp. 225-226). There are both positive and negative aspects to this tendency to expand the socio-geographic domain from which one's future life-partner is selected. To the degree to which it increases the possibility that the individual chosen will correspond more fully to the moral and esthetic ideals of the individual entering marriage, it certainly will improve the prospects of the marriage. But at the same time there is an increasing possibility of chance evaluation and decision in choosing a mate, inasmuch as the knowledge of a person one obtains through contact on the job or in daily life cannot always be replaced by some other form of verification. A person's internal nature often does not correspond to his outward appearance or even to his behavior in some comparatively brief period of time.

Soviet scholars have as yet made no attempts to study "stages of courtship." But it would seem that we have not lost much by this, for the conclusions Western sociology is coming to in this regard do not as yet go beyond trivial assertions to the effect that people first meet, become acquainted, date, and then these dates either break off or end in marriage. This sequence apparently is not affected by the societal differences in the modern world and therefore exists in all countries where patriarchal power of parents over children and men over women does not exist.

Of considerably greater sociological interest is the question of the length of acquaintance preceding marriage. Summation of the responses to this question enables the following conclusions to be drawn (data in %) in Table 1.

Although these figures hardly parallel the nature of the marriage and family relationships

Table 1

A few days	Under 3 mos.	3-6 mos.	6 mos. 1 year	1 to 2 years	2 to 3 years	3 to 5 years	5 to 8 years	Since child-hood	Total
0.7	2.9	9.3	5.6	23.0	25.6	14.8	9.1	9.0	100

that ensues, they are, however, the only objective source for our judgments in this field.

Judging by these data, most marriages (58.5%) are the result of comparatively long-term acquaintance (over two years) and this means, one must assume, of tested feelings and a serious, morally-motivated decision. This also applies, although certainly to a lesser degree, to marriages preceded by acquaintance of one to two years' duration (23%). Only in cases totalling less than one-fifth of all marriages (18.5%) may doubt arise that the individuals who have entered them have had the chance really to get to know each other and make sure of their feelings.

* * *

A study of the ages of persons entering upon marriage may be useful in determining the motives and essence of marriage in two respects: 1. The average age at marriage gives us an idea of the degree to which natural need in this respect is in accord with social conditions or is distorted by the latter. 2. The relation between age of the two parties provides some indication of the degree to which the marriage is free of utilitarian calculations and factors, for, as H. Bowman correctly observes, among the factors explaining "why young people marry older ones," "a powerful drive for economic security, money, heirs, social status, and prestige is far from the least important" (H. Bowman, Marriage for Moderns, New York, 1942, p. 166).

Different and often even contradictory trends are characteristic of different parts of the USSR, as far as average age at marriage is concerned. Thus, according to L. N. Terent'eva, "comparison of data on the age of persons marrying during the years of bourgeois dictatorship in Latvia and prior to that, as far back as before 1917, with those for two years after 1940 shows that

there was a rise in age of marriage during the first years after establishment of the Soviets. In later years, this age declined considerably, to 24-25 for men and 21-23 for women" (Sem'-ia i semeinyi byt..., p. 81).

Another picture may be seen in Uzbekistan. Here are data obtained from ZAGS documents for that republic over a twenty-year period (in %) (see Table 2).

Consequently, while this twenty-year period showed comparative stability of mean age at marriage for men (the only major fluctuation was in the immediate postwar year of 1946) this age rose steadily for girls. The number of marriages of girls 18 and under dropped by nearly two-thirds. At the same time there was a considerable rise in the percentage of marriages in which the bride was between 19 and 22, or over 26. True, this increase occurred to some degree as a result of the influx of Russians and Ukrainians after the war and was less typical of the indigenous people, but this only modifies our conclusion somewhat, without changing its essence.

Thus, we face two trends in change in the average age at marriage: a reduction in Latvia and a rise (among women) in Uzbekistan. What is the explanation in each case? In the pre-socialist Latvian countryside, marriage was governed first by the age at which a son came to own a farm or a portion of one, and secondly upon the accumulation of the dowry. Farm laborers usually postponed marriage, hoping first to accumulate some sum of money to buy land and tools. All this increased the number of late marriages and led to a rise in average age at marriage. Consequently, the reversal of the process indicates that these factors had ceased to be operative and that marriage has come to be governed not by factors external to it, but by the desires and personal choice of the individuals

Table 2

	Men	Woman	Men	Women	Men	Women
18 and under	2.2	35.0	4.0	16.8	2.4	12.8
19-22	19.0	27.7	16.4	37.7	19.4	36.3
23-26	31.1	17.1	19.0	19.0	28.2	15.3
27 and over	47.7	20.2	60.6	26.5	50.0	35.6
	100	100	100	100	100	100

entering into marriage themselves.

In Uzbekistan, on the other hand, before the changes to socialism, forced giving of under-age girls in marriage was widely practiced. As the table indicates, this tradition remained in substantial force in 1937. It goes without saying that as equality of rights for women took stronger root, along with their increasing economic independence and cultural advancement, this tradition could be expected to disappear gradually. One of the indicators of this is the regular reduction in the number of early marriages of girls and the gradual equalization of the marriage age of men and women.

Thus, these tendencies, despite the significant differences between them, actually constitute an expression of the same process: the liberation of marriage and the humanization of its motives.

In order to determine the approximate relationship between the ages of groom and bride in marriage in the USSR today, a selective study of marriage records was made at the registries in Kiev, Tiumen' and Mga Raion of Leningrad Oblast. In our opinion, the choice of these places meets the requirement that the sample be representative both geographically and in terms of the society. Kiev is one of the largest industrial and cultural centers in the country, and has the style of life characteristic of large cities. Tiumen' is a comparatively small regional center. Finally, Mga Raion was chosen as an ordinary (and in that respect typical) rural district.

All told, 600 cards were studied, 200 from each of these places. No special selection of the cards was made: all the marriages concluded during a given time interval were considered. (The length of the interval depended upon the number of marriages recorded by the given ZAGS per day.) It seems to us that such an approach assured the discovery of general trends considerably better than a special system of selection could have done, in that it preserved the relationship which had objectively taken shape among the various categories and types of marriages during a given period.

The study yielded the following results in Tables 3, 4 and 5.

It should be said in explanation of these tables that in cases in which the groom was younger than the bride, this difference usually did not exceed three or four years, and was usually one or two years.

The data on the relationship of ages at marriage permit us to identify certain trends in this field of marriage and family relationships, independent of or little dependent upon local conditions.

We note, in the first place, that in the overwhelming majority of marriages the difference in age between partners does not exceed six years (81% in Kiev, 84.5% in Tiumen', and 89% in Mga Raion).

Marriages in which the partners are of the same age or in which the age difference is minimal (not over three years) number over two-thirds of the total, and marriages in the top range of difference (twenty years and more) are virtually nonexistent because there are only isolated instances of these. Even marriages in which the husband is ten or more years older than the wife are comparatively rare, ranging

Table 3

Marriage Age Ratios in Kiev (1959, in %)

Age of bride	Ratio of ages of grooms to brides							
	Groom younger	Same ages	Groom older					Total
			1 - 3 years	4 - 6 years	7 - 9 years	10 - 12 years	13 years and more	
Under 20	1.0	1.0	1.0	2.5	—	—	—	5.5
20 - 24	8.0	9.5	22.5	8.5	5.5	2.0	—	56.0
25 - 28	3.0	0.5	4.0	1.5	0.5	0.5	0.5	10.5
29 - 32	2.0	1.0	2.0	1.5	0.5	—	—	7.0
33 and older	3.5	0.5	5.0	2.5	3.5	2.0	4.0	21.0
Total	17.5	12.5	34.5	16.5	10.0	4.5	4.5	100.0

Table 4

Marriage Age Ratios in Tiumen' (1959, in %)

Age of bride	Ratio of ages of grooms to brides							
	Groom younger	Same ages	Groom older					Total
			1 - 3 years	4 - 6 years	7 - 9 years	10 - 12 years	13 years and more	
Under 20	—	0.5	7.0	5.0	2.0	1.5	—	16.0
20 - 23	6.5	6.0	19.0	9.5	4.0	—	—	45.0
24 - 29	10.0	1.5	4.5	1.5	2.0	0.5	—	20.0
30 and older	6.0	2.5	3.0	2.0	1.5	3.0	1.0	19.0
Total	22.5	10.5	33.5	18.0	9.5	5.0	1.0	100.0

from only 4.5% (Mga District) to 9% (in Kiev).

Of no less interest is the fact that marriages in which the groom is younger than the bride are comparatively numerous. On the basis of a study of the statistics of natural population movement in 1924-1925, V. G. Peschanskii, a Soviet demographer of that day, concluded that there was a tendency for "men 25 years of age and older to take wives younger than themselves." But grooms of 18 or 19 married older women in one case out of three (Natural Movement of Population of USSR. 1923-1925 [Estestvennoe dvizhenie nase-leniia Soiuza SSSR. 1923-1925], Moscow, TsSU SSSR, 1928, pp. XXVII-XXVIII). Whereas the first of these two observations may be ascribed to the fact that physiological evaluation of the woman was the prime consideration, the latter was also often based on the economic advantages then to be gained by marrying spinsters and widows (a larger dowry, a peasant farm holding ready at hand, etc.), which were particularly important for grooms who had not yet established themselves, economically speaking.

Today, as we see, the situation has changed

Table 5

Marriage Age Ratios in Mga District (1959, in %)

Age of bride	Ratios of ages of grooms to brides							
	Groom younger	Same ages	Groom older					Total
			1 - 3 years	4 - 6 years	7 - 9 years	10 - 12 years	13 years and more	
Under 20	0.5	1.5	7.0	5.0	2.0	—	—	16.0
20 - 24	9.5	7.0	18.0	7.5	2.0	0.5	0.5	45.0
25 - 28	7.0	2.0	3.5	1.0	0.5	—	—	14.0
29 - 32	6.5	0.5	0.5	0.5	0.5	—	—	8.5
33 and older	6.0	0.5	3.0	2.0	1.5	1.5	2.0	16.5
Total	29.5	11.5	32.0	16.0	6.5	2.0	2.5	100.0

substantially. Marriages in which the woman is considerably older than the man and in which, as A.A. Luts has correctly noted, "economic considerations were self-evident" (Sem'ia i semeinyi byt..., p. 101) have virtually disappeared. Marriages in which the bride is one to three years older than the groom are much less apt to be associated with material considerations. Moreover, the fact that they are fairly common may be regarded as evidence of the change in the attitude toward women, and in the criteria of female beauty and of choice of a bride in the direction of increasing importance of intellectual, moral and esthetic factors in these criteria as against physiological ones.

Along with these common trends which, precisely because of their universality, are obviously due primarily to the economic and social system obtaining in the USSR, there are certain differences among the places studied. These differences have to do primarily with the ages at which women marry. Whereas in Kiev the number of women marrying early (20 or younger) is only 5.5% of the total, in Tiumen' and Mga Raion it is 16%. At the same time, the number of women marrying at 33 and older is 21% in Kiev, and only 16.5% in Mga District.

The former circumstance is obviously due to the fact that in small towns and in the villages there is a comparatively smaller percentage of students, a group that usually postpones marriage until the completion of education or, at least, until the senior years. At the same time, the countryside offers greater opportunities for newlyweds to find the things they need to set up housekeeping, housing above all.

With respect to the second circumstance, it may be explained both by the fact that in the countryside there is a considerably smaller number of second marriages than in the large cities and by the fact that the disproportion between the male and female populations which came into being in the USSR after the war has made itself felt to a much greater degree in the countryside than in the city.

The correlation between the ratio of ages at marriage and the motives for marriage, as well as the dependence of both these factors upon the economic and societal relationships dominant in society, are seen with particular clarity when data are analyzed not for one year but for a number of years separated by a comparatively lengthy historical period. Taking this into consideration, let us make an attempt to compare the data on the relationship of ages at marriage in 1920, when the socialist revolution in our country had just taken place; in 1940, when socialism had triumphed not only politically but economically, and in 1960, representing the present period in the development of Soviet society. These data are the result of selective study of marriage records in the Leningrad ZAGS archives. All told, 3,000 records were studied, 1,500 of them for the city of Leningrad (Kirov and Kuibyshev Raions) and 1,500 for Leningrad Oblast (Mga Raion). The results of the study are as follows in %):

ing majority could be regarded as equal marriages.

Thus, the present ratio of age at marriage in the USSR is certainly not accidental but a logical result of the progress and consolidation of socialist principles in the life of Soviet society. It testifies to the rising influence of these principles both upon the motives in choice of a mate and on the marriage itself.

Table 6

Year and place of marriage		Relationship of groom's and bride's age at marriage							
		Groom younger	Same age	Groom older older					Total
				1 – 3 years	4 – 6 years	7 – 9 years	10 – 12 years	13 years and more	
1920	City	12.5	6.5	25.5	24.0	16.0	8.0	7.5	100
	Country	13.0	4.5	23.5	22.5	17.0	6.0	13.5	100
1940	City	28.0	4.5	20.5	30.5	8.0	4.0	4.5	100
	Country	16.5	10.0	26.0	24.5	10.5	4.0	8.5	100
1960	City	33.5	6.5	28.0	18.5	8.5	3.0	2.0	100
	Country	30.5	10.5	32.0	16.0	6.0	2.5	2.5	100

These data indicate primarily that there has been a steady reduction, in the USSR, in the percentage of marriages with a large difference in age between the parties. The percentage in which the husband is older by 13 years and more dropped with particular sharpness. Marriage in which the husband was seven and more years older than the bride, which were 31.5% of all marriages in the city in 1920, and 36.5% in the countryside, were 16.5% and 23%, respectively, in 1940, and in 1960, only 13.5% and 11%. Simultaneously, we observe a regular increase in the number of marriages between equals, the age difference between the parties being minimal (not over three years). Further, it must be borne in mind that in 1920, in marriages in which the bride was older than the groom, the difference in age was considerably greater than in 1940 and 1960. Therefore the data on marriages in 1920 showed that most of them were unequal, while in 1940 and 1960 the overwhelm-

Naturally, the sociological data we have presented are not a sufficient basis for broad general conclusions encompassing the country as a whole. However, they do to some degree describe the trends presently operating in the USSR in the field of marriage and family relationships and, in particular, of motives for marriage.

To begin with, we observe that people see the chief value of marriage not in its material but in its moral consequences, and the fact that it serves as the social sanction for love. Marriage based upon the love and mutual respect of the partners is regarded for all practical purposes as the only morally acceptable form of marriage.

Entry into marriage is the result of the personal choice and personal decision of the future partners. This decision is based primarily upon individual feelings and experience, although in the majority of cases it is made with the knowledge and approval of the parents. Upon entering into marriage, people seek to assure themselves of the necessary minimum of material conditions for their lives together and it would appear that occasionally the choice of the future mate itself serves as a means of attaining this goal. However, even in these cases utilitarian calculation is not the sole stimulus to the conclusion of a marriage alliance but is primarily an "auxiliary" motive. This is indicated indirectly by such an objective fact as the tendency toward "equalization" of the ages of groom and bride at marriage. When material and moral aspirations conflict it is usually the latter that win out.

In the USSR, the moral prestige of the institution of marriage is particularly high. However, the number of divorces is still comparatively large. According to data of 1960, there were 12.1 marriages per 1,000 in the population, as against 8.5 in the USA, 7.5 in England (excluding Scotland and Northern Ireland), 7.0 in France, and 9.4 in West Germany. At the same time, the number of divorces, also per 1,000 population, were 1.3 in the USSR, 2.2 in the USA, 0.5 in England, 0.6 in France, and 0.8 in West Germany (Narodnoe khoziaistvo...1960, op. cit., p. 204).

When we compare these data, it must be borne in mind that in the Catholic countries of Europe and in part in the USA, the percentage of divorces is reduced artificially by church prohibition. In the USSR, however, the percentage of divorces increased primarily as a consequence of postwar difficulties, primarily material in nature, as well as due to the fact that not all marriages were sufficiently firmly based in the psychological and moral sense.

This permits us to conclude that as these temporary factors are overcome, the actual motives for marriage in the USSR will increasingly approximate the moral ideal for relationships between the sexes, and the institution of marriage itself will become stronger and more stable.

Leningrad Chair of Philosophy,
USSR Academy of Sciences

Footnotes

1) Paper presented at 8th International Seminar on the Family, Oslo.

2) Professor Nelson Foote comments on the family in the United States today: "The stablest families, as demographers have repeatedly demonstrated, are found among people in the 'professional class' or 'professional group'.... Members of this group usually favor liberal divorce laws, larger employment of women (married women included) and greater equality between man and wife in the family circle. Marriages between persons in this group usually involve young people of approximately the same age. They marry across ethnic, class, and religious lines more freely than do others." (Problemy sotsial'nykh izmenenii XX veka. Obzor dokladov Tret'ego Mezhdunarodnogo sotsiologicheskogo kongressa. Amsterdam, avgust, 1956 god, Moscow, Izd-vo Sov. Nauka, 1957 p. 52.)

3) The real incomes of workers (including elimination of unemployment and reduction in the working-day) multiplied by a factor of 5.8 from 1913 to 1962, and the real incomes of the peasants (including those used to increase the indivisible capital and reserves of the collective farms) by a factor of about seven. The housing available in towns and urban settlement rose from 180,000,000 square meters in 1913 to 1,014,000 square meters in 1961. (SSSR v tsifrakh v 1961 godu. Kratkii statisticheskii sbornik, Moscow, Gosstatizdat, 1962, pp. 348, 350, 381.)

***

Questions of Social and Nationality Policy

Istoriia SSSR, 1963, No. 1

M. S. Djunusov

SOVIET AUTONOMY AND THE VESTIGES OF NATIONALISM

The article titled "A Contribution to the Description of the Process of Coming Together of
Soviet Nations in the Course of Building Socialism and Communism" [K kharakteristike prots-
essa sblizheniia sovetskikh natsii v khode stroitel'stva sotsializma i kommunizma], published
in Istoriia SSSR, 1962, No. 3, has called forth an
objection on the part of a Comrade Sh. of the
city of Ufa. In a letter to the editor he adduces
the Bashkir ASSR as an example, in an attempt
to cast doubt upon the vitality of Soviet autonomy.

He begins his letter by referring to data from
the most recent Soviet census, indicating that
the proportion of Bashkirs using the Bashkir
language was 53.8% of the total in 1926, 58.3%
in 1939, and 61.9% of the entire Bashkir population in 1959. Commenting on these data, he ad-
vises that we "not be moved by the fact that
small nations are increasingly using their native tongues!" "In this connection," he writes,
"I should like to ask the question: why is the area
inhabited by the Bashkirs called the Bashkir
ASSR? The fact is that the Bashkirs are a minority of the population of the Bashkir ASSR
(there are only 150,000 Bashkirs out of a population of 3,300,000)." (1) "The question arises:

does the existence of a Bashkir ASSR, in which
the Bashkirs are a minority of the population,
make any sense? I think it doesn't! As soon as
the Bashkir ASSR became the Ufa Oblast' of a
unified Russian Soviet proletarian republic, all
these national state superstructures, which even
today have in reality no more than decorative
meaning, would disappear! I refer to the Council
of Ministers of the BASSR, the Supreme Soviet
of the BASSR, etc." "I think," the writer of the
letter continues, "that all our national political
structures (constituent and autonomous republics, autonomous oblasts and okrugs) should be
dealt with in the same manner. This will result
in the disappearance of one more hindrance to
our advance to a communist, proletarian tomor-
row."

In order to demonstrate how completely untenable and deeply mistaken is the view advanced
in the letter by Comrade Sh., we will have to
turn back to the historical roots of Soviet autonomy and also demonstrate its unchallengeable
vitality.

It is common knowledge that one cannot have
a deep understanding and appreciation of the present without a knowledge of the past. Let us recall

what prerevolutionary Bashkiria was like. Its native population, like all the non-Russian peoples, experienced not only acute social (class) oppression but the grossest national oppression as well.

V. I. Lenin, in his The Development of Capitalism in Russia [Razvitie kapitalizma v Rossii], employed numerous sources. Among them was the book by N. V. Remezov, Sketches from the Life of Wild Bashkiria (An Epic of Pioneering) [Ocherki iz zhizni dikoi Bashkirii (pereselencheskaia epopeia)], Moscow, 1889. (2) The author demonstrated that after the evolution of serfdom in Russia, the flow of population into Bashkiria from the central district of the country (Tambov, Viatka, Tula, Riazan', and other gubernias) increased, and Russian landlords, merchants and tsarist officials rapidly began to expand their landholdings there. The lands of the Bashkirs were acquired by them at unbelievably low prices by every conceivable kind of malfeasance, bribery and trickery. Remezov's book, Lenin observed, "is a lively description of the way in which the 'colonizers' felled the forest for making ships and transformed the fields 'freed' of 'wild' Bashkirs into 'wheat factories.' This is a tidbit of colonial policy that will stand comparison to any of the feats performed by the Germans in any old Africa." (3)

The outlying steppe districts, including Bashkiria, were, in Lenin's words, a colony of central Russia in the period after the reforms. Commercial agriculture developed. The age-old relationships of subsistence economy were destroyed. The people were deprived of political rights. The colonial policy of tsarism stood as an obstacle to the development of the national culture and language of the Bashkir people. As a consequence it was condemned to die out. The Bashkir population diminished annually by tens of thousands. In 1912 the death rate among Bashkirs and Tatars in certain uezds of Ufa Gubernia was as follows: Sterlitamak Uezd — 27.76%; Belebei — 25.91%; Menzelinsk — 32.87%; Birsk — 28.53%; while for Russia as a whole the figure for 1913 was 3%. (4)

Russian capitalism was by nature the same as English, French and American capitalism. The incorporation of Bashkiria, like that of the other non-Russian areas, into the stream of capitalist development was progressive not because Russian capitalism was in any way different from others. The reason lay in the concrete historical conditions of the development of Russia and of the peoples incorporated into the tsarist empire.

As history progressed, it developed that more than a hundred nations and peoples at various stages of social development and belonging to the most widely differing linguistic groups came to be encompassed within the boundaries of the unified Russian state. Revolutionary collaboration and cooperation in the struggle for liberation developed among these peoples. One vivid example of this is the participation of the Bashkirs, headed by Salavat Iulaev, in the anti-feudal uprising of E. Pugachev.

Since they experienced national oppression by Russian tsarism, a considerable portion of the population was naturally captured by the ideology of nationalism, and had an attitude of outrage, often of hatred, toward the Russian nation. "But the Bashkirs did not regard all Russians as plunderers and colonizers. On the contrary, refugees from Muscovy and former serfs were given shelter in safe places that the Voevodas and their agents could not reach." (5) The joint war of liberation was a great school of consolidation on the part of the working people of various nationalities. It would be a mistake to underestimate the role and significance of the traditions of friendship of the working people of the various nationalities of our country.

These traditions were raised to a new level and filled with a new content by the multinational working class of Russia. In Bashkiria, as throughout the country, the proletariat was multinational in composition. It consisted primarily of new arrivals. Thus, in 1897, there were 19,300 workers in Ufa Gubernia, including 4,600 who were born in other gubernias. (6)

The revolutionary forces of all the peoples — large and small, advanced and backward — headed by the Russian proletariat, participated in destroying the "prison of the nations." The working people of each nationality made its contribution to the struggle for liberation. Formerly backward and oppressed peoples like the Bashkirs, among whom there was no, or virtually no, industrial proletariat, participated in the revolutionary movement chiefly through the national liberation and agrarian movement.

Of all the forms of revolutionary-democratic struggle, the national liberation movement is the most complex. It may be participated in by a variety of classes united, to some degree, by a common ethnic interest, while their class interests tend to divide them. The peasants constituted the great mass of the Bashkir national liberation movement. The leadership of this movement in 1917 was at first seized by nationalist elements taking the form of the Bashkir regional "Shuro." Its leaders opposed both the Soviets and the Kerensky government because it refused autonomy to the Bashkirs. In evaluating the Bashkir movement for autonomy headed by nationalist elements, Lenin stated, according to memoirs: "We do not regard the Bashkir movement as a counterrevolutionary movement directed against us.... We believe that the national movements of the peoples of the East are entirely natural and very necessary. The peoples of the East come to the social revolution only through national revolution." (7) In a meeting with Lenin in January 1918, representatives of Bashkiria declared that "the Bashkir movement, if it is granted the autonomy it demands, will not be directed against the Soviets but will constitute a tremendous force in the struggle against Dutov." (8)

The granting of autonomy to the formerly oppressed peoples by the Soviet government promoted a clear-cut differentiation of class and political forces among the participants in the national liberation movement. This had a major influence upon the fluctuating petty bourgeoisie (consisting, in the main, of the middle peasantry). As a result of the triumph of the Red Army at the fronts and the undeviating execution of Lenin's nationality policy, this class began to take the side of the Soviets. Thus, those Bashkirs who had been tricked by their national leaders and were in the ranks of Dutov's and Kolchak's troops deserted to the Red Army in 1919. The

laboring masses of the Bashkir peoples thus accumulated their own political experience. They freed themselves of the influence of the nationalist ideology. Their road of struggle for the Soviet government was unique and tortuous. (9)

The example of the Bashkir peoples wholly and completely supports the conclusion formulated by Lenin on March 19, 1919, at the Eighth Congress of the RKP(b) in his closing remarks on the report on the Party Program. "And now," said Vladimir Il'ich, "the essence of the question of the self-determination of nations is that different nations are following an identical historical road, but by bypaths and zigzags differing to the highest degree, and that the more cultured nations are proceeding quite differently from the less cultured." (10)

In the struggle against the Soviet government, the Bashkir nationalists employed the sentiments of national insult left behind by the system of national oppression. Lenin observed: "The Bashkirs have no confidence in the Great Russians because the Russians have a higher culture and employ their culture to plunder the Bashkirs. Therefore, in these remote places the name 'Great Russian' means to the Bashkir 'oppressor,' 'swindler.' We have to consider this and we have to struggle against it. But this is a long-term proposition. This is not the kind of thing that anybody will eliminate by decree. We have to be exceedingly cautious in this matter." (11)

* * *

The conclusions and proposals offered by Comrade Sh. are not new. They coincide to a considerable degree with what was stated more than forty years ago by the great-power chauvinistic elements fighting stubbornly against execution of the Leninist line for the establishment of Soviet national autonomy.

The granting of autonomy to the Bashkir and Tatar people was opposed by leading personnel of the Ural Regional Executive Committee, Tuntul, Syromolotov and others. At the conference on calling a Constituent Assembly of the Soviet of the Tatar-Bashkir Republic, Tuntul voiced the theses of the Ural Regional Executive

Committee, which stated: "We believe that the Federated Soviet Republic can be built only on an economic basis — on the basis of powerful, economically united and closely knit regions. Organization on an ethnic basis will carry with it disorganization and the destruction of the entire economy, as well as of the proletariat, which will come under the tutelage of all kinds of chauvinists." (12) The same position was taken at the conference by K. Grasis, the representative of the Kazan' party organization. Moreover, after the conference, he published in the newspaper Znamia revoliutsii [Banner of the Revolution], organ of the Kazan' Soviet of Workers', Soldiers', and Peasants' Deputies, anti-Leninist articles against the establishment of autonomous republics in general and of the Tatar-Bashkir Republic in particular; for this he was removed from the post of chairman of the Kazan' Revolutionary Committee. At this conference Grasis, Tuntul, Shamigulov and others were decisively rebuffed by the delegates.

At the request of the people in the Urals, Lenin had a meeting with Tuntul, Syromolotov and Shamigulov. During the conference Tuntul said, on behalf of the Ural Regional Executive Committee: "We believe that the decree issued establishing the Tatar-Bashkir Republic is harmful. If it is carried out it will destroy the economic foundations of the industries of the Urals. Further, we take our stand on the internationalist position of the Soviet government. This decree will only incite national passions." (13)

According to participants in the conference, Lenin listened to Tuntul attentively and then said: "Tuntul really understands this question in an oversimplified fashion." "Very oversimplified," he repeated with emphasis. "You've got to think hard about this, Comrade Tuntul. I mean think. Of course, it is important that the ties to industry should not be broken, but won't they be stronger if we proceed on the nationality question in the fashion stated in our Program, the Program of our party....Well, Comrade Tuntul? ... Think it over. Of course, it is very important to know the actual ethnic composition by territory, with figures at hand. We must approach all nationalities with careful attention." (14)

Subsequently, Syromolotov described the position of the Ural Regional Executive Committee, and particularly of Tuntul, as follows: "The position of Comrade Tuntul and that taken by the Ural Regional Executive Committee was at loggerheads with that of the party....This was outright opposition to the decree on the Tatar-Bashkir Republic. The 'economic' deviation propounded by Comrade Tuntul with respect to territorial organization was a clear expression of profound differences of principle with Lenin's nationality policy. In actuality, the Ural Regional Executive Committee, which was strongly influenced by great-power chauvinism, was not in agreement with Lenin's line." (15)

Lenin had precisely such chauvinistically inclined persons in mind when he said: "These are objections to which I would reply: scratch some Communists and you'll find a Great Russian chauvinist." (16)

A portion of the leading personnel in Kazan', including party members, spoke out against the establishment of the Tatar-Bashkir Republic, and later of the Tatar ASSR. On this subject, I. I. Khodorovskii (who was then, in 1920, chairman of the Kazan' Gubernia Committee of the RKP(b) and later of the Gubernia Executive Committee) later wrote: "We opposed the organization of the Tatar Republic on the territory of what had been Kazan' Gubernia. We were motivated by the following: 1) the Tatars have not produced communist personnel to whom the leadership of the new republic could be turned over and, 2) the formation of the republic would result in reduction to the minimum of the possibilities of grain procurement (and the surplus appropriation system) (a), we will not be able to collect the grain, and the Tatar comrades lack the strength and courage to collect grain in their republic as we did in Kazan' Gubernia." (17)

Lenin decisively rejected this position taken by the Kazan' personnel.

Establishment of the Soviet nationality republics and regions was an act of the utmost political importance. Lenin ascribed extraordinary significance to the granting of autonomy to all the peoples of Russia, including those of the Middle Volga. He personally guided the solution of the problem of autonomy for the Bashkir and Tatar peoples. On this matter, Lenin met with a group of leading Bashkir-Tatar personnel, separately with a group of Bashkir personnel and representatives of the Ural Regional Executive Committee in May 1918, and with delegates to the Ninth Congress of the RKP(b) from the Kazan' party organization in April 1920. The Political Bureau of the RKP(b) Central Committee repeatedly discussed and adopted resolutions on problems of establishment of the Bashkir and Tatar Republics. Comrade Sh., if he came to his conclusions "as a result of long-term practical and theoretical study of this question," could not but know the history of the struggle waged by Lenin and the Party Central Committee against Great Russian chauvinist elements and for establishment of Soviet autonomy for the Bashkir people.

In March 1919 agreement was arrived at between the government of the RSFSR and the Bashkir government with respect to autonomy for Bashkiria. Some members of the former Bashkir "Shuro" subsequently served the cause of strengthening the Soviet government in all good faith. Other members of the Bashkir nationalist government — as, for example, Validov (Zaki Validi) — became enemies of Soviet rule.

The greeting by the Presidium of the USSR Supreme Soviet, the Council of Ministers of the USSR, and the Party Central Committee to the working people of the Bashkir ASSR on the 40th anniversary of the establishment of that republic states: "On March 23, 1919, the decree, signed by Lenin, on the establishment of the Bashkir Autonomous Soviet Republic was published. That date has become a national holiday for the people of Bashkiria. The triumph of the October Revolution ended forever the lack of political rights and the oppression of the Bashkir people, and brought them onto the highroad of economic and social development." (18)

As an example of the wise approach of our party to the establishment of national statehood for the peoples of the USSR, the discussion on the Tatar-Bashkir Republic should be noted. As we know, in March 1918 the People's Commissariat of Nationalities drafted a Regulation on joint autonomy

for the Tatar and Bashkir peoples. However, within one year, in March 1919, the Bashkir ASSR was established. Nevertheless, some portion of the personnel in Tataria continued to press stubbornly for establishment of a Tatar-Bashkir Republic.

This question was discussed at the Second All-Russian Congress of Communist Organizations of the Peoples of the East, held November 22-December 3, 1919. And on December 13 of the same year, the Political Bureau of the RKP(b) Central Committee adopted the following resolution: "In view of the fact that a considerable portion of the All-Russian Congress of Communist Organizations of the Peoples of the East and, in particular, all the representatives of the Communists of Bashkiria are opposed to establishment of a Tatar-Bashkir Republic, no such Republic is to be established, and the March 22, 1918, decree of the People's Commissariat of Nationalities on the Tatar-Bashkir Soviet Republic is to be repealed. We propose to the members of the party that hereafter they cease agitation for a Tatar-Bashkir Republic. We will discuss separately the question of a Tatar Republic, if Communist Tatars request this." (19) On February 2, 1920, V. I. Lenin, reporting to the First Session of the Seventh Meeting of the All-Union Central Executive Committee [VTsIK] and the Council of People's Commissars, declared: "We granted autonomy to the Bashkir Republic. We must establish an autonomous Tatar Republic and apply the same policy toward all the Eastern peoples." (20)

A few days after the meeting, Lenin received in the Kremlin the leaders of the Central Bureau of Communist Organizations of the Peoples of the East under the RKP(b) Central Committee. In his recollections of this meeting, S. G. Said-Galiev has written: "We boldly attempted to 'convince' Il'ich that there was essentially no difference between the Tatars and the Bashkirs. To this Il'ich replied by posing approximately the following series of questions to us:

" 'Is there a difference in the languages and dialects of the Tatars and Bashkirs?'

" 'Yes, but very insignificant and then only among the peasants,' was our reply. Then we pointed out that hostility for the Tatars is limited only to a narrow group of chauvinistically inclined Bashkir intellectuals. Then Il'ich put approximately the following question:

" 'Well, and who was it who recently physically attacked Tatar teachers and even mullahs as a colonizing element and drove them from the Bashkir villages — Bashkir intellectuals or the peasants themselves?'

" 'Of course,' we answered, 'the peasants did this, but this was a result of the agitation of the Bashkir intellectuals.'

" 'And who organized regiments and brigades of Bashkir peasants and succeeded in leading them in a struggle against all other groups?'

" 'Also the Bashkir intellectuals,' we mumbled in very low voices.

"The meeting was silent for a few seconds. We held our tongues, because there was no place for us to go. Il'ich forced us, so to speak, into a corner.

"With these three simple questions, Il'ich gave us a beautiful lesson on how a nationality, itself only just liberated but comparatively stronger (reference is to the Tatar nation — M. D.), must not take upon itself the role of benefactor with respect to weaker peoples, and must avoid even more strongly acting against the desires of the latter. Thereafter, the meeting centered its attention entirely on the question of the Tatars and the Tatar Republic, and it was taken for granted that it would be established without those Bashkirs about whose fate we had been so 'worried.' " (21)

* * *

The Bashkir nation, like all nations on earth, regardless of numbers, has its distinctive features, historically established. The Bashkirs have a distinctive art, literature, and mode of life. If a nation exists, that nation will have its specific needs. For nations living compactly in a given territory, nationality states have been established within the Soviet Union as a whole.

The Bashkir people has all the characteristics necessary for the establishment of national statehood. These characteristics are: the real existence of the Bashkir language, a territory in which the Bashkir people is developing in friendship with other peoples of the USSR, a relatively compact distribution of Bashkirs, the existence of an essential minimum of the native population whose name is borne by the given republic. When favorable conditions were established, the Bashkir people, like all the peoples of our country, progressed in all spheres. The numbers of the Bashkir nation are growing, as is indicated by the census figures (see Table 1). (22)

As this table indicates, the Bashkir population is increasing steadily. In a 32-year period, the number of Bashkirs in the country rose by 275,000.

Interesting phenomena have occurred in the realm of language. The development of schools

Table 1

Census	Number of Bashkirs in USSR, thousands
1926	714
1939	843
1959	989

and publishing in the native language has facilitated the widening of the sphere of application of the Bashkir language. Socialism restored the native language to the people, so to speak. Thus, in the 1926 census, out of 714,000 Bashkirs, only about half (384,600) regarded Bashkir as their native tongue. (23) In the 1939 census, 843,000 Bashkirs were found, of whom 496,900 regarded Bashkir as their native language. Thus, in a 12-year period, the percentage of people recognizing Bashkir as their native tongue increased by 26.2%, while those regarding themselves as Bashkir by nationality increased 18.2%. This means that the Bashkir people began to re-acquire its native tongue. This process continued intensively during the subsequent 20 years. In the 1959 census, 600,000 persons recognized Bashkir as their native language. From 1939 to 1959 the number

Table 2

Census	Percentage of Bashkirs regarding Bashkir as their native tongue
1926	53.8
1939	58.3
1959	61.9

of Bashkirs increased by 17%, while the number using the language rose by 23%. (24) One of the distinctive characteristics of the manifestation of an objective trend toward many-sided development of socialist nations and their languages, as seen in the case of the Bashkir people, consists of the constant increase in the percentage of persons who recognize Bashkir as their native tongue. This may be seen from Table 2. (25)

Apparently, Sh. holds that the right to establish national statehood is possessed only by those people who constitute a majority in a given territory. However, Lenin's principles of national statehood proceed from the need to guarantee that all peoples, large and small, be enabled to effectuate their right to establish national state structures. As far back as 1913 Lenin posed the question: "Why can there not be autonomous national areas with populations not only of half a million, but even of 50,000? Why cannot areas of that kind be combined in diverse ways with adjacent areas of various sizes into a single autonomous 'territory,' if this is convenient or necessary for economic circulation?" (26)

The fact that the Bashkirs did not constitute a majority in Bashkiria (25.3% in 1926) was known at the time this republic was established. However, guiding itself by Lenin's instructions, the Communist Party proceeded to establish autonomy for the Bashkir people.

The fact that the republic is called Bashkiria has profound meaning. The Bashkir people thus realizes its right to the establishment of Soviet national statehood. In this, national sovereignty manifests itself. Nowhere is the Bashkir population settled as compactly as on the territory of this republic. This circumstance was taken into consideration in determining the boundaries of the republic. In 1926, 87.76% of the entire Bashkir population lived in Bashkiria, and in 1959 — 75%. (27) In no other part of the Soviet Union are there conditions for establishing Soviet national statehood for the Bashkir people than on the territory of the Bashkir ASSR.

National state structures have been established in the USSR so that all the basic nationalities populating our country may have national statehood. Evidence of this can be seen in Table 3. (28)

Table 3

	Population, thousands, 1959	Percentage of USSR total
15 major nationalities of constituent republics	187,632	89.85
Basic nationalities of autonomous soviet republics	13,400	6.42
Basic nationalities and peoples of autonomous oblasts and national okrugs	2,788	1.33
Nationalities and peoples having no national statehood	5,006	2.40

Thus, nine-tenths of all the nationalities inhabiting the USSR have Soviet national state structures. As early as the first years of Soviet government, Lenin observed: "We have given to all the non-Russian nationalities their own republics or autonomous regions." (29)

Comrade Sh.'s proposal to liquidate the autonomy of the Bashkir people is in complete contradiction to the Leninist nationality policy. Let us cite Lenin's direct instructions on this matter. The chairman of the Central Executive Committee [TsIK] of the Tatar ASSR, S. G. Said-Galiev, wrote a letter to Lenin in 1921 in which he posed the following questions:

"1. Is the existence of small autonomous republics of the Russian Soviet Federation necessary in general and, in particular, is the existence of Tataria necessary?

"2. If the answer is yes, then for how long a period or, in other words, until what tasks have been fulfilled and what goals have been reached?" (30)

Lenin answered: "To the first question — yes. To the second question — for a long time to come." (31)

An example of the manner in which our party has invariably been guided by the Leninist postulate that autonomy is something we need for a long time to come is the restoration of the autonomy of the Balkar, Chechen, Ingush, Kalmyk and Karachaevan peoples, which was violated under conditions of the Stalin personality cult. As we know, these peoples are less numerous than the Bashkirs. Whereas there were 989,000 Bashkirs according to the 1959 census, there were 419,000 Chechen, 106,000 Ingushes, 106,000 Kalmyks, 81,000 Karachaevans and 42,000 Balkars. (32) The party is concerned with maintaining the rights and interests of all the peoples of the USSR, small and large.

As the socialist nations develop, their independence does not grow weaker but, on the contrary, is reinforced. Providing genuine equality to the peoples means, at the same time, provision of the foundations, material and cultural, for further strengthening the national sovereignty. The following provision in the CPSU Program constitutes a generalization and theoretical expression of this experience: "The nations flourish under the conditions of socialism and their sovereignty is reinforced." (33) This applies to the Bashkir socialist nation among others.

In carrying out the Leninist program of eliminating the economic and cultural backwardness of formerly oppressed peoples, our party provided for more rapid rates of industrial development in Bashkiria. Thus, from 1913 to 1960 the gross production of large-scale industry in Bashkiria increased by a factor of 186, while in the RSFSR as a whole it increased by a factor of 60. It is characteristic that as resources have accu-

mulated in the country, the rates of development of industry in Bashkiria, as in other republics, have increased. If we take the gross output of large-scale industry in Bashkiria in 1913 as unity, the index number rose to 10 in 1940, 41 in 1950, 145 in 1958, 164 in 1959, and 186 in 1960. The most rapid rates of industrial development in the Bashkir ASSR were achieved in the postwar period. As compared to 1940, the gross production of large-scale industry in the republic increased 3.6 times by 1950, 11.9 times by 1958, 13.5 times by 1959, and 15.3 times by 1960 (34)

In the 26 years since adoption of the present Constitution of the USSR, considerable changes have taken place in the geographic distribution of the nationalities of the USSR. The populations of the republics have become more multinational. This occurred primarily as the result of an influx of professional and skilled workers from the RSFSR. Some portion of the Russian workers living in the RSFSR has today entered into the population of other Soviet republics, particularly the republics of Central Asia and Kazakhstan. However, these changes, no matter how considerable they have been, do not change the picture, as we see from Table 4. (35)

Table 4

Census	Total no. of Russians (millions)	Of whom, resident in RSFSR (millions)	Percentage of entire Russian population
1926	77.8	74.0	94.2
1959	114.1	97.9	85.7

More than 80% of the Russian population lives on the territory of the RSFSR. The rest of the population is distributed as follows: 6.2% in the Ukraine, 0.6% in Belorussia, 0.9% in Uzbekistan, 3.5% in Kazakhstan, 0.4% in Georgia, 0.4% in Azerbaidjan, 0.3% in Moldavia, 0.5% in Kirgizia, and 1.5% in the other constituent republics. (36)

Thus, the changes in the distribution of nationalities provide no basis for any fundamental reconsideration of the organization of national statehood in the USSR. However, this does not rule out the possibility of individual refinements. The forms of statehood of various peoples may lag behind the real process of development of the nation that gives its name to the republic. Therefore these forms must be so improved that they do not constitute a brake upon the development of the nation and so that they will promote a fuller display of their creative forces in building communism.

At the Twenty-Second CPSU Congress, N. S. Khrushchev observed: "The development of socialist nations finds its expression in the improvement of the national statehood of the USSR. The party will, in the future, continue to meet the needs arising in this field. Fullest use must be made of all the opportunities inherent in the Soviet principles of federation and autonomy." (37) An important stage in the improvement of these forms will be marked by the new USSR Constitution now being elaborated. It will reflect the changes that have occurred in the life of Soviet society as a consequence of the complete and final triumph of socialism in the USSR and its entry into the period of the building of communism in all respects. Among these, it will reflect the changes that have occurred in the development of socialist nations and in their relationships. The party will take as its point of departure the need for a complete, comprehensive utilization of the opportunities inherent in Soviet nationality statehood for the peoples of the USSR. The national superstructures constitute an important factor in the building of communism in our multinational country. The significance of the national states is by no means just a matter of words

The road to communism lies, on the one hand, through the development of the Soviet national statehood of the peoples of the USSR and, on the other, through their being brought closer together in all respects. Neither aspect must be elevated to an absolute. When speaking of the further development of Soviet nationality statehood, one cannot leave out of consideration the ever-increasing geographic mobility of the population. Boundaries between republics are losing their former significance, and the forms and

methods of collaboration among the peoples of the USSR are being perfected. At the same time, consideration must be given to the maturing need for further development of the nations.

To liquidate the nationality statehood of the peoples of the USSR, as is proposed by Comrade Sh., would mean to deal irreparable damage to the building of communism, to undermine the established and validated forms of collaboration among more than a hundred nations and nationalities, whose friendship has been cemented by the Communist Party. The view held by certain theoreticians to the effect that the nation giving its name to a republic must constitute a majority in it has been repudiated by experience.

As long as a nation exists, the basis for the existence of national statehood is retained. Lenin observed that experience in state organization will continue "until the state in general withers away." A variety of political forms, freedom to secede from the state, and experience in state organization constitute, in Lenin's view, "conditions for accelerating the process of the voluntary coming together and merging of nations." (38)

Among the many socio-economic factors making for the withering away of all states, it is necessary to consider processes such as the erasure of class differences and the merging of nations. Class differences will be wiped out very much more rapidly than nationality distinctions. Therefore it is no accident that the socialist state of the USSR has already become a government on behalf of the entire people. It serves equally the working class, the collective farm peasantry, and the intelligentsia.

Certain changes are also occurring in the Soviet nationality statehood of the peoples of the USSR. The Party Program states: "The boundaries between the constituent republics of the USSR are increasingly losing their former significance, inasmuch as all nations enjoy equal rights, their lives are built on a uniform socialist basis, and there is equal satisfaction of the material and intellectual needs of each people. They are all unified by common vital interests into a single family and are moving jointly to a single goal — communism." (39) The erasure of national state boundaries is a process of many stages and long duration. National states will exist, in our opinion, until the process of the merging of nations has been completed. This, we repeat, does not rule out the possibility of development, change and improvement in their forms.

The merging of nations is one of the factors making for the complete disappearance of national state organizations. As far back as 1916 Lenin pointed out that "an accelerated coming together and merging of nations, which will be climaxed by the withering away of the state," will occur on the basis of socialism. (40) If we consider the fact that nationality distinctions will continue to exist for a long time, the groundlessness of proposals to liquidate the national statehood of the small peoples of the USSR becomes obvious.

* * *

Comrade Sh. attempts to support his erroneous hypothesis by the further concept that the existence of the Bashkir ASSR creates "unjustified privileges for a minority." "Inasmuch as this area, which has a population of 3,300,000," he reasons, "is called the Bashkir ASSR, it is natural that Bashkirs must be at the helm of the republic at all costs! As a consequence, the choice of leaders is based not on their political and practical qualities — which are the proletarian principles of personnel selection — but primarily on their nationality. Everything else is secondary. Inasmuch as these leaders owe their promotions to their nationality, they naturally make every possible effort to stimulate everything bearing upon that nationality." Let us also attempt to demonstrate the erroneousness of these assertions by our correspondent.

The principle of privilege certainly reflects a bourgeois-nationalist approach to nationality relations. The state organization of socialist nations is created on the foundation of internationalism. If the Bashkir ASSR is the Soviet national state of the Bashkir people, this does not mean that the Bashkir population is given any kind of privilege. All nations and peoples in our

country are equal and enjoy the same rights.

The Leninist principle of the selection of personnel on the basis of their practical and political qualities is at the same time an internationalist principle. Proletarian internationalism implies assistance to and cooperation with formerly oppressed peoples in overcoming the backwardness of the former. Lenin taught that internationalism on the part of the oppressing nation "must consist not only in observing a formal equality of nations but in the kind of inequality that would serve to make good, by the acts of the oppressing nation, the large nation, the inequality that had come into being in reality. Anyone who fails to understand this does not understand a true proletarian approach to the national question." (41)

Ethnic factors cannot but be considered in the choice of personnel. This was particualrly important in the first years of development of statehood of the formerly oppressed peoples of the USSR. It was no accident, for example, that the Central Committee of the RKP(b), in its consideration, on June 8, 1920, of the problems related to the organization of the party and the government in the Tatar Republic, proposed "that the Kazan' Gubernia committee employ its influence in such a manner that even if the Tatar deputies do not constitute a majority at the Congress of Soviets of the Tatar SSR, they should not constitute a minority in the composition of the Central Executive Committee of the Tatar Republic." (42)

The Communist Party advanced as a first-priority undertaking the training and promotion of personnel of the native nationalities. The system of measures employed for this purpose has come to be known in history as the nativization of the machinery. We cite two documents. The 4th Bashkir Regional Party Conference of February 1921 stated in its resolution: "Any federation must be headed by people of the same nationality, people of that nation whose name is borne by that portion of the federation." The 6th Plenum of the Bashkir Regional Committee (July 1932) resolved "to carry out and organize, as a first-priority undertaking, a complete census of Bashkir personnel, and systematically and undeviatingly to promote and to seek out such personnel from the lower ranks; to include Bashkir personnel in all bureaus of the Party committee." (43)

During the first years of Soviet power, it was not possible to apply the same high standards to the selection of local personnel as were established in the centers of the proletariat. Thus, in 1927 the machinery of the Bashkir Republic included only 97 persons of the native nationality, constituting 7.9% of all personnel in the given category. Of these, only two had higher education, one incomplete higher education, and 44 had elementary education or were self-educated. (44) In the letter to Lenin cited above, Said-Galiev asked the following question: "Is that opinion correct which holds that 'Communists of the formerly dominant nations, being more advanced in all respects, should play the role of teachers and nurses with respect to the Communists and all the working population of the formerly oppressed nationalities whose name is borne by a given autonomous republic (or region or commune), and yield place to the latter as the latter develops?' " (45) Lenin replied: "Not 'teachers and nurses,' but helpers." (46) Members of the Russian nationality contributed no small amount of effort to training personnel of the nationality intelligentsia.

The nativization of the machinery presumed the solution of a complex combination of problems. In the first place, it presupposed the training of intellectuals and professional personnel from among the local nationality and a general rise in the culture of the people. This was a task that could not be resolved by a "cavalry charge." Further, nativization pursued the objective of strengthening the Soviets, the alliance of the working class and the peasantry, and the friendship among the nationalities of the Soviet Union. In the execution of the Leninist nationality policy, the main danger at that time was Great Russian chauvinism. Under the conditions existing in Bashkiria it was also necessary to fight against anti-Bashkir Tatar chauvinism, which denied the distinct existence of the Bashkir nation and strove to have it regarded as a part of the Tatar nation. The Plenum of the

Bashkir Regional Committee of the CPSU, held in 1931, regarded as a major shortcoming in the activity of the Party organization "the weakness of the struggle against great-power tendencies on the part of the Tatars." (47) At the same time, attention was directed to reinforcing the struggle against Bashkir nationalism.

The task of nativization of the machinery in the Soviet nationality republics and regions was successfully fulfilled. This is confirmed by data for the Bashkir ASSR. As early as 1932, the Bashkirs, comprising 23.5% of the population of the republic, constituted the following proportions of the leading personnel of the republic: 24.7% in rural Soviets, 24.3% of the members of the raion executive committees, 32.2% of the members of the Central Executive Committee. (48) As the economic and cultural backwardness of the formerly oppressed nations was overcome, the composition of personnel of the local nationality improved. The need for special campaigns to nativize the machinery disappeared. It became possible to pose higher standards for local personnel.

The history of the building of socialism in Bashkiria and other republics shows how the problem of creating a national intelligentsia and professional category was solved step by step. It is necessary to take a historical approach to ethnic factors in the choice of personnel as to all other phenomena. Beginning with the second half of the 1930's, the problem of nativization of the machinery was no longer posed in Bashkiria. Instead, planned work was undertaken to develop personnel representing all the basic nationalities populating the republic. For example, the membership of the Supreme Soviet of the Bashkir ASSR, elected in March 1959, included 76 Bashkirs, 76 Russians, 45 Tatars, 9 Ukrainians, 6 Belorussians, 1 Latvian, 3 Maris, 1 Mordvin, and 3 Chuvashes. (49) The Bashkirs now constitute 22% of the population of the republic and 34.5% of the deputies. If one considers the need to develop Soviet national statehood for the Bashkir people and bears in mind the task of overcoming completely the vestiges of their former backwardness, this ratio is justified. This circumstance must not be interpreted as the granting

of privileges to personnel of the Bashkir nationality.

Comrade Sh. writes that "the heads of the republic demand that Bashkirs be enrolled in higher
educational institutions at all costs, and this is
achieved by reducing the qualifications required.
This does terrible damage to our proletarian
cause and incites ethnic antagonism." In order
also to understand this problem correctly, it is
necessary to apply the historical approach here
as well and to take an internationalist position.

Of 4,778 students in the secondary schools of
Ufa Gubernia in 1910, there were only 12 Bashkirs. (50) This was a historic injustice. The 9th
Bashkir Party Conference in February 1925 resolved as follows: "To enroll into the industrial
and factory schools at enterprises a student body
consisting no less than half of Tatars and Bashkirs, and if there is an inadequate number at the
enterprises, to enroll the children of the very
poorest section of the peasantry roundabout."
(51) At first, it certainly was necessary to reduce the qualifications required of students of
the formerly oppressed nationalities for entry
into the educational institutions. In 1925 there
were only three persons enrolled in study for
every hundred of the Bashkir population, while
for the USSR as a whole the figure was 7.1. As
early as the 1927-1928 school year, there were
six persons enrolled for every hundred Bashkirs,
while the average for the USSR was ten. (52) The
gap in the level of development of education was
gradually overcome. Under today's conditions,
when the economic and cultural backwardness of
formerly oppressed peoples has been essentially
overcome, measures are still required for their
more rapid cultural development.

Certain differences still exist among the nationalities of the USSR with respect to the degree
that they are involved in mental labor. They will
be overcome in the process of building communism. The differences are shown in Table 5. (53)

There are five peoples (Russians, Armenians,
Georgians, Jews and Estonians) among whom the
percentage of educated people is greater than the
percentage of these nationalities in the population
of the USSR. The opposite picture may be observed among the other nations. The Bashkirs

Table 5

Nationalities	Given na-tionality, in % of USSR total (January 15, 1959)	People with higher and specialized secondary educa-tion in % of USSR total (December 1, 1960
Russians	54.65	62.7
Ukrainians	17.84	15.2
Belorussians	3.79	2.9
Uzbeks	2.88	1.1
Tatars	2.38	1.5
Kazakhs	1.73	0.9
Azerbaidjanis	1.41	1.1
Armenians	1.34	1.5
Georgians	1.29	1.8
Lithuanians	1.11	0.8
Jews	1.08	4.9
Moldavians	1.01	0.4
Latvians	0.81	0.7
Tadjiks	0.71	0.3
Turkmenians	0.51	0.2
Bashkirs	0.47	0.2
Estonians	0.47	0.5
Kirgiz	0.41	0.2

constitute 0.47% of the population of our country,
but only 0.2% among those having higher and
specialized secondary education. They are 0.8%
of the population of the RSFSR and 0.37%
among the college students of the Federation.
(54) Thus, public attention to the training of intellectuals and professionals from among the
nationalities cannot yet be diminished. The meeting of the Supreme Soviet of the Bashkir ASSR
in July 1958, which discussed the question "Measures to Effectuate the Law on Strengthening the
Ties Between School and Life and Further De-

veloping the Public Education System in the USSR," resolved that in colleges and universities "it is necessary to open the doors wider to rural youth, to train them in ample time, and to select the most able ones so as to enable them to pass competitive entrance examinations." (55)

The people of Bashkiria have somewhat less than normal medical services. In 1959 there were 11 physicians (excluding dentists) per 10,000 population, while for the RSFSR as a whole there were 18.6, in the Tatar ASSR — 16.9, in the North Ossetian ASSR — 28.8, and in the Yakut — 20.6. (56) Our party has established the following principle in its program: "The benefits which are increasing in the process of the building of communism must be justly distributed among all nations and nationalities." (57)

* * *

In his letter, Comrade Sh. also deals with the question of the language of small nations. "The languages of all the small nations of our country," he declares, "have no prospects for the future since the development among the people of characteristics of a communist proletarian society will be expressed, in the linguistic field, in a gradual forgetting of the language of their own small nations and in the acquisition of the Russian language as their native language. What's the point of knowing, in addition, one's native tongue when it is an inhibiting factor in one's intellectual and material development?"

Here the author piles up a veritable mountain of errors. In the first place, it is erroneous to contend that the native tongue is an inhibiting factor in the cultural development of the nation. In the second place, it would be mistaken to suppose that the building of communism signifies the "abolition" of ethnic distinctions. The existing experience in the development and flourishing of the Bashkir culture during the period of socialism, as of that of all formerly oppressed peoples of the USSR, demonstrates that the native tongue is a powerful factor in their social progress. It serves as a vehicle of communication and mutual understanding among human beings. As a consequence of the utilization of the native tongue and its introduction into administration, the Soviet government has become near and dear to the working masses. Instruction in the native tongue facilitates the cultural growth of the nation. This is explained by the fact that the native tongue is mastered in the family from earliest childhood. Language is directly interwoven with the thought process. In early childhood, man acquires the habit of thinking in his native tongue. (58) He expresses his ideas and feelings through the medium of the native tongue. The school system is based upon the fact that the child has established the habit of thinking in his native tongue and it develops this thought process.

The desirability of instructing children in their native tongue has been proved by the entire experience of world civilization. With this circumstance in mind, our party recognized in its first Program "the right of the population to receive education in its native tongue, assured by the establishment of schools required for this purpose at state and local government expense," while the second Program included "complete fulfillment of the principles of the unified labor school, with instruction in the native tongue." (59)

The right to teach children in their native tongue is a great triumph of socialism. The Bashkir people, like all formerly oppressed peoples, employs its native tongue as a factor in the development of the national culture. A scientific grammar of the Bashkir language has been developed, as well as a scientific terminology. Scientific and creative literature is published in that language. In 1913 not a single book was issued in the Bashkir language, but in 1959 213 books with a total printing of 1,000,000 were issued. Six magazines with a total circulation of 559,000 and 22 newspapers with a total single-issue circulation of 102,000 are published in Bashkir. (60) During 1950 to 1959, the number of magazines in the Bashkir language doubled, their total circulation increased more than seven-fold, and that of newspapers increased 60%.

It is erroneous to hold that the national languages have already ceased to serve as a means for the development of the socialist culture of the peoples of the USSR. A tremendous upswing in the cultural level of the working population of our country will occur in the period of the building of communism — on the one hand, on the basis of the development of the cultures of the nationalities and, on the other, in terms of a close coming-together of the nations. The party sees its task in the field of the development of national languages to be "to assure, in the future as well, unhindered development of the languages of the peoples of the USSR and complete freedom for each citizen of the USSR to speak, to rear and teach his children in any language, not permitting any privileges, limitations or compulsion in the use of any language. Under conditions of brotherly friendship and mutual confidence of the peoples, the native tongues are continuing to develop on a basis of equal rights and mutual enrichment." (61)

In Bashkiria, as in all the national republics and regions, a policy of equal rights for languages is pursued. It is provided in the July 8, 1958, resolution of the Supreme Soviet of the Republic: "To establish that education in the schools of the republic shall be in the pupils' native tongue. To grant parents the right to determine what school (Russian or native) their children shall be enrolled in. In those schools in which instruction is in the Bashkir language or in the native language of a non-Russian nationality, the teaching of Russian is conducted if the pupils or their parents so desire. In schools in which instruction is in the Russian language, the pupils may, if they choose, study the Bashkir language, and children of other nationalities may study their native tongue." (62)

It was in the period of socialism that the international community of people constituted by the Soviet peoples came into being. Hitherto history has known human communities based on principles such as race, clan, tribe, nationality, and nation. The Soviet people is a social unit of a higher order than a national community. The Soviet people has a single language for international communication. This is the Russian language. The Party Program states: "The Russian language has, in point of fact, become the common language of inter-national communication and collaboration with all the peoples of the

USSR." (63) The Russian language carries on the function of inter-national communication among the Soviet peoples without any decrees or compulsion to accomplish this. The tsarist government, which pursued a chauvinist policy of forced Russification of the non-Russian peoples, prohibiting the use of "dogs' dialects," could not achieve its goal of having the peoples of Russia come to acknowledge the Russian language as their second native tongue.

In the development of relationships among nationalities, such factors as psychology and human sentiment play a role. Any use of compulsion with respect to nationalities not only does not break down their structure, their social life, but, on the contrary, promotes the strengthening of their decision to preserve their nationality and all its attributes, and to preserve their language. Lenin criticized the proposition advanced by the bourgeois-liberal newspaper Den' [The Day]: "If Russia is fated to be one and indivisible, it is necessary to defend firmly the principle that the Russian literary language be the state language." He wrote: "We know better than you that the language of Turgenev, Tolstoy, Dobroliubov, and Chernyshevskii is great and strong. We wish more strongly than you that the closest possible communion and brotherly unity be established among the oppressed classes of all nations inhabiting Russia, without distinction. Naturally, we insist that each person living in Russia have the right to study the great Russian language.

"There is just one thing we do not want: the element of compulsion. We do not want to drive people to heaven with a club....We think that the great and strong Russian language does not stand in need of anyone's being compelled to study it for fear of the stick." (64)

The policy of compelling peoples to employ particular languages, fervently pursued by the tsarist government, made it difficult to disseminate the Russian language among the peoples of our country. It would be no exaggeration to state that the 45 years of Soviet government, during which all the national languages have developed freely, has witnessed a much wider spread of the Russian language among the peoples of the USSR than did the 300 years of tsarist Russia when it was inculcated by force.

The policy of equality of languages, a policy pursued without deviation by the Soviet government, has provided broad access to the Russian language for the peoples of the USSR. As far back as 1925, the Bolsheviks of Bashkiria wrote in a resolution of a regional party conference: "We consider the Russian language to be the common language of the USSR, and hold that a knowledge of it by the entire population of the Union would greatly facilitate the coming-together of the working people of various nationalities and also promote their cultural and governmental development. We regard it as absolutely necessary to engage in systematic instruction in the Russian language as a subject in the Bashkir-Tatar schools and also in schools of other nationalities, and to give adequate time and attention to this...." (65) Similar decisions were adopted by the party organizations of other national republics and regions.

During the period of socialism, which provided free and harmonious development of all nations and nationalities, a substantial portion of the non-Russian peoples mastered the Russian language to such an extent that they regard it as their native tongue. This tendency is testified to by the following data: during the last 32 years the number of persons of non-Russian nationality, who regard their native tongue to be a language other than that of their own nationality, rose from 8 million to nearly 12 million. Of these, those who regard Russian as their native tongue increased from 6.6 million to 10 million. (66) This is an indication of the great vista opened by socialism for the spread of the Russian language among the peoples of the USSR.

The increase in the numbers of the Russian nation is occurring not only from among the Russian population, but as a consequence of voluntary entry therein of persons of non-Russion nationality. It is no accident that the Russian population increased from 77 million in 1926 to 114 million in 1959. In 1926 the Russian population outnumbered the other peoples of the USSR by only 9 million people; in 1959 — by 19 million. Moreover, it must be borne in mind that the incorporation into the USSR of the western areas

of the Ukraine, Belorussia and Moldavia, and of Lithuania, Latvia and Estonia brought an increase of about 20 million in the non-Russian population. These data indicate the intensity with which the process of entry of non-Russian peoples into the Russian nation is proceeding. There is no reason whatever to assume that this process will slow down in the future. By all indications, it will accelerate.

However, this course must not be regarded as the main trend in the coming-together of nations. What we have here is a transfer of a particular portion of the population from one national group to another. The appeal made by Comrade Sh. to the non-Russian peoples to abandon their national language contradicts the objective course of the historical process.

Comrade Sh. takes a one-sided and oversimplified view of the dialectic of the development of nations; he sees only one side of the picture. But the fact is that a coming-together of nations is a more complex and multifaceted process than the influence of the culture of the Russian people upon the cultural life of other people. The coming-together of nations is a process of mutual influence and mutual enrichment of the cultures of the socialist nations. The coming-together of nations takes place through their comprehensive development and further flourishing. The author of the letter does not differentiate between the concept of coming-together and that of the merging of nations. The complete merging of nations is a matter for the future. In that portion of the Party Program describing this communist society, we read: "Communism will witness an ever more all-embracing coming-together of the nations on the basis of a complete unity of economic, political and intellectual interests, brotherly friendship and cooperation." (67) The complete merging of nations is a question of worldwide order.

The merging of nations means the dying out of the community based on nationality. This is a natural process. It will occur just as naturally as the tribal and clan type of community was overcome during the period of initial appearance of class society, and the ethnic community was overcome in the period of formation of nations. Worldwide communism, as the highest form of organization of social life, will comprise an international community of human beings not limited either territorially or by linguistic barriers.

As long as nations exist, ethnic peculiarities will exist. Yet Comrade Sh. already proposes that, for all practical purposes, we disregard the distinctive features of nationality in governmental and cultural policies.

We know from history that chauvinism is often covered up by communist phraseology. Chauvinists employ the banner of struggle for a proletarian line to oppose consideration of factors of nationality in governmental and cultural policy.

Our public cannot take a dispassionate attitude toward manifestations of chauvinism. Prior to the 20th Party Congress, inadequate attention was often given to this sphere of ideological struggle. Here is one example of the fact that outstanding representatives of Soviet Russian culture regarded this to be an abnormal situation. A. A. Fadeev, in one of his letters to S. N. Preobrazhenskii, who was editing a collection of his articles for publication, asked that he find the original of some articles (on Soviet patriotism and national pride) and incorporate them in his compendium. He wrote to the editor: "It's important to find the original version. There I express myself better on other peoples, not only on the Russians, and, most important, on the position of the peoples in old Russia. Because the whole trouble is that in those days we were compelled to cross out everything written about great-power chauvinism and certainly that isn't Lenin's way!" (68)

Our party has restored the Leninist traditions of struggle against nationalism and chauvinism. the Party Program poses the problem of "conducting an irreconcilable struggle against manifestations and vestiges of all nationalism and chauvinism." (69) "The party," we read in it, "does not permit us either to ignore or to exaggerate nationality distinctions." (70)

At the present stage in the development of national relationships among the peoples of the USSR, the struggle against manifestations and vestiges of nationalism is of particular importance. These vestiges constitute an ideological obstacle on the path of further coming-together

of the socialist nations and the mutual enrichment of their cultures.

Today, nationalism among a number of the formerly backward peoples often manifests itself in the form of chauvinism directed at other nationalities resident in the national republics and regions. This demonstrates that there is no fundamental difference between nationalism and chauvinism. They have identical social roots. Under certain circumstances, nationalism may be converted into chauvinism. They feed each other.

In recent years, our Party Central Committee has sharply condemned certain party organizations for distorting nationality policy and, in particular, for omitting the necessary consideration in their work for training and appointing personnel of the multinational composition of the republics. Unfortunately, these lessons have not been considered in all places. Any approach to an evaluation of the merits of personnel only in terms of their ethnic affiliation results in reinforcement of national prejudices and offends the easily wounded national sentiment of people of other nationalities. The Party Program makes a special point to the effect that the party conducts a decisive struggle against such errors. "Any manifestation of national insularity in the training and employment of personnel of various nationalities in the Soviet Republics is impermissible. Elimination of manifestations of nationalism is in accord with the interests of all nations and ethnic groups of the USSR." (71)

The forms in which nationalism manifests itself are many. Nationalism is expressed in a narrow and one-sided view of the sovereignty of socialist nations. The rights of nations must not be thought of in isolation from their inter-national duties — the duties facing all the peoples of the USSR. The party press of the Baltic Soviet Republics has condemned the attempts of some leading personnel to compel all personnel of other nationalities to study the language of the local population. Nationalism is manifested in the effort to make use of the broad rights granted to each nationality in our country against the interests of some particular nation. National prejudice is also manifested in the tendency to retreat into the shell of narrowly nationalist traditions and in unwillingness to adopt the superior experiences of other peoples.

No nation can get along without employing the experience in the development of the economy and culture of other peoples, or without making use of its traditions. In full accord with this objective tendency of mutual enrichment and influence of the nations, our party is taking all the measures necessary to make the best of national traditions the property of all the peoples of the USSR.

The struggle against nationalistic and chauvinistic vestiges is a most important task in the education of the working population to communism. The study of the rich and instructive history of the struggle of the Communist Party and its local organizations with national deviationism, with great-power chauvinists and nationalists, is a powerful weapon for the ideological tempering of personnel.

Footnotes

1) The writer of the letter adduces inaccurate data on the Bashkir population of the republic. He writes that only 150,000 Bashkirs live in Bashkiria. However, according to the 1959 census, there are 983,000 Bashkirs in the USSR, of whom three-fourths live in the Bashkir ASSR. The Bashkirs constitute 22% of the population of the republic (see Ob urovne obrazovaniia, natsional'nom sostave i vozrastnoi strukture naseleniia SSSR po dannym Vsesoiuznoi perepisi naseleniia 1959 g. Soobshchenie TsSU pri Sovete Ministrov SSSR, Moscow, 1960, p. 7; P. G. Pod'iachikh, Naselenie SSSR, Moscow, 1961, p. 110).

2) N. V. Remezov served in the Ufa Gubernia Zemstvo land surveying department and worked as a surveyor. He was eyewitness to the terrible plunder of the lands of the Bashkirs.

3) V. I. Lenin, Soch., 4th ed., Vol. 3, p. 218, Footnote 3.

4) Natsional'naia politika VKP(b) v tsifrakh, Moscow, 1930, p. 31; SSSR v tsifrakh v 1961 godu, Moscow, 1962, p. 369.

5) P. F. Ishcherikov, Ocherki iz istorii kolonizatsii Bashkirii, Ufa, 1933, p. 25.

6) Chislennost' i sostav rabochikh v Rossii, Vol. 1, 1906, p. XV, Point 2.

7) Obrazovanie Bashkirskoi Avtonomnoi Sovetskoi Sotsialisticheskoi Respubliki, a collection of documents and materials, Ufa, 1959, p. 83.

8) Ibid., pp. 83-84.

9) See B. Iuldashbaev, Obrazovanie Bashkirskoi ASSR, Ufa, 1958; Kh. S. Sapranov, Druzhba rozhdalas' v bor'be, Moscow, 1959.

10) V. I. Lenin, Soch., Vol. 29, p. 173.

11) Ibid., p. 172.

12) Revoliutsiia i natsional'nosti, 1935, No. 8, p. 20.

13) Ibid., p. 22.

14) Ibid., pp. 22-23.

15) Ibid., p. 21.

16) V. I. Lenin, Soch., Vol. 29, p. 172.

17) Izvestiia TsIK SSSR, April 22, 1930.

18) Iubileinaia sessia Verkhovnogo Soveta Bashkirskoi ASSR, posviashchennaia 40-letiiu obrazovaniia BASSR, Ufa, 1959, p. 3.

19) Quoted in collection Sovetskoi Tatarii sorok let, Kazan', 1960, p. 12.

20) V. I. Lenin, Soch., Vol. 30, p. 301.

21) S. Said-Galiev, "Tatrespublika i tov. Lenin," Proletarskaia revoliutsiia, 1925, No. 9 (44), pp. 112-113.

22) Natsional'naia politika VKP(b) v tsifrakh, p. 36; BSE, Vol. 4, p. 361; Chislennost', sostav i razmeshchenie naseleniia SSSR, Moscow, 1961, p. 25.

23) Natsional'naia politika VKP(b) v tsifrakh, p. 36.

24) Iu. I. Pisarev, Narodonaselenie SSSR, Moscow, 1962, p. 91.

25) G. Maksimov and A. Isupov, "Natsional'nosti SSSR po dannym Vsesoiuznoi perepisi naseleniia," Vestnik statistiki, 1960, No. 4, p. 13.

26) V. I. Lenin, Soch., Vol. 20, pp. 32-33.

27) Natsional'naia politika VKP(b) v tsifrakh, p. 51; P. G. Pod'iachikh, op. cit., p. 110.

28) P. G. Pod'iachikh, op. cit., pp. 102-104.

29) V. I. Lenin, Soch., Vol. 33, p. 31.

30) Ibid., Vol. 36, p. 661.

31) Ibid., p. 499.

32) Chislennost', sostav i razmeshchenie naseleniia SSR, pp. 25-27.

33) Programma Kommunisticheskoi partii

Sovetskogo Soiuza, Moscow, 1962, p. 112.

34) Narodnoe khoziaistvo RSFSR v 1960 g., statistical annual, Moscow, 1961, pp. 81, 82, 86.

35) Table compiled from data in Natsional'-naia politika VKP(b) v tsifrakh, pp. 36, 44; I. Iu. Pisarev, op. cit., p. 88.

36) I. Iu. Pisarev, op. cit., p. 89.

37) Materialy XXII s'ezda KPSS, Moscow, 1961, p. 190.

38) V. I. Lenin, Soch., Vol. 22, p. 324.

39) Programma KPSS, p. 113.

40) V. I. Lenin, Soch., Vol. 22, p. 311.

41) Ibid., Vol. 36, p. 556.

42) Cited in Sovetskoi Tatarii sorok let, p. 20.

43) Rezoliutsii oblastnykh konferentsii Bashkirskoi partiinoi organizatsii i plenumov obkoma KPSS, Ufa, 1959, pp. 139, 192.

44) Natsional'naia politika VKP(b) v tsifrakh, p. 246.

45) Cited in V. I. Lenin, Soch., Vol. 36, p. 661.

46) Ibid., p. 499.

47) Sovetskoe stroitel'stvo, 1932, No. 1 (66), p. 136.

48) Vlast' Sovetov, No. 30, p. 21.

49) Materialy iubileinoi sessii Verkhovnogo Soveta Bashkirskoi ASSR, Ufa, 1959, p. 100.

50) Kul'turnoe stroitel'stvo Bashkirii za 15 let (1919-1934), Ufa, 1934, p. 5.

51) Rezoliutsii oblastnykh konferentsii Bashkirskoi partorganizatsii i plenumov obkoma KPSS, p. 235.

52) Ibid., p. 236; Natsional'naia politika VKP(b) v tsifrakh, pp. 274, 276.

53) Chislennost', sostav i razmeshchenie naseleniia SSSR, p. 25; Vysshee obrazovanie v SSSR, Moscow, 1961, p. 49.

54) Vysshee obrazovanie v SSSR, p. 128.

55) Zasedaniia Verkhovnogo Soveta Bashkirskoi ASSR piatogo sozyva (vtoraia sessia). Steno-graphic report, Ufa, 1959, p. 14.

56) Narodnoe khoziaistvo RSFSR v 1960 g.

57) Programma KPSS, p. 114.

58) It must be borne in mind that the native tongue may be that of another nationality. For example, no small number of young Ukrainians, Belorussians, Uzbeks, Kazakhs and others stated, according to the 1959 census, that they regarded Russian as their native tongue. One in eight non-Russians regarded his "first" native language to be Russian.

59) KPSS v resoliutsiiakh, 7th ed., part 1, Moscow, 1954, pp. 40, 419.

60) Narodnoe khoziaistvo RSFSR v 1959 g., Moscow, 1960, pp. 540-542.

61) Programma KPSS, p. 115.

62) Zasedaniia Verkhovnogo Soveta Bashkirskoi ASSR piatogo sozyva (vtoraia sessia), p. 117.

63) Programma KPSS, pp. 115-116.

64) V. I. Lenin, Soch., Vol. 20, pp. 55-56.

65) Resoliutsii oblastnykh konferentsii Bashkirskoi partiinoi organizatsii i plenumov obkoma KPSS, p. 242.

66) Chislennost', sostav i razmeshchenie naseleniia SSSR, pp. 25-27; Natsional'naia politika VKP(b) v tsifrakh, p. 38.

67) Programma KPSS, p. 64.

68) A. A. Fadeev, Soch., Vol. 5, Moscow, 1961, p. 550.

69) Programma KPSS, p. 116.

70) Ibid., p. 113.

71) Ibid., p. 116.

Editor's Note

a) Russian: prodrazverstka — a forced levy of goods on peasantry, practiced in the early twenties.

* * *

Voprosy filosofii, 1963, No. 4

E. V. Tadevosian

THE FURTHER CONVERGENCE OF THE SOCIALIST

NATIONS OF THE USSR

In the course of the building of communism in the USSR on all fronts, mutual contact among the socialist nations is always growing broader and deeper. The increased physical mobility of the population is playing an important role in this respect. The brotherly mutual assistance of the peoples of our country, their striving for a more and more complete international union of their labor resources and material means in the common interests of the building of communism, is one of the things that is expressed in the movement of population between republics.

In his report to the November Plenum of the CPSU Central Committee (1962), N. S. Khrushchev stated: "A constant exchange of skilled personnel among our nations is proceeding, and the greater the scale of the building of communism becomes, the greater this exchange will be. The experience acquired in the course of our multi-national state teaches us that without mutual brotherly assistance by qualified personnel it is impossible to assure rational development of the productive forces, and correctly to combine the interests of the state with those of the individual republics.

It is essential that the party committees be guided strictly in their work by these principles" (Razvitie ekonomiki SSSR i partiinoe rukovodstvo narodnym khoziaistvom, Gospolitizdat, 1962, p. 27).

The new stage in the development of relations among nationalities in the USSR, associated with the transition from socialism to communism, has been dealt with in general terms more than once in our literature. But certain of its aspects have had little study. This pertains particularly to the problem of the intensification of population migration and the role of this factor in the flourishing and convergence of the socialist nations. The publication of the findings of the Soviet Census of 1959 and the data for the nationality republics and regions opens new opportunities for scholarly treatment of this problem.

Causes of the Increasing Physical Mobility
of the Soviet Population

The further internationalization of all aspects of

the life of Soviet society is a predictable progressive process flowing primarily from the material conditions of the building of communism in a multi-national country. The splendid undertakings of creative effort for communism, the rapid growth and improvement of the productive forces, the enormous scale of certain construction projects, and the unbroken scientific and technical progress define the objective need for further deepening and expansion of collaboration and mutual assistance among the peoples of the USSR. No nation or republic is capable of successfully carrying out, by its own forces alone, the vast construction of the foundation for communism in material goods and technology. It can only be built and is being built by the combined efforts of the entire Soviet people.

As the transition from socialism to communism advances, the productive forces increasingly outgrow the bounds of the national republics taken individually. Even at present, the building of great hydraulic engineering and power systems takes on a scope that extends vastly beyond the borders of the republics. Thus, the building in Tadjikistan of the Nurek Hydroelectric Station of 2,700,000 kw capacity, or of the Toktogul Power and Irrigation Center in Kirgizia, capable of saving 7,500,000 acres in Kirgizia, Tadjikistan, and Uzbekistan from drought, is a consequence of the needs of all Central Asia and requires the further development of various ties among the republics. The establishment of unified zonal power systems in the Trans-Caucasus, the Baltic area, Central Asia and other areas and, in the immediate future, of a single power system for the European portion of the USSR and then of the entire Soviet Union, will bring the socialist nations even closer together. The significance of planned joining of their efforts to gain goals common to the entire people increases accordingly. Out of this arises the exceptional importance of the steps taken by the party to establish large international economic districts and to improve the management of the economy.

The establishment of the foundation for communism in material goods and technology is as-

sociated with accelerated opening up of new districts and the building of new industrial centers, the opening up and intensive exploitation of natural resources on the territory of all the nationality republics. This results in major population migrations and an increasingly mixed ethnic composition. In the space of only two decades (1939-1959), the population of Western Siberia alone increased by 24%, that of Eastern Siberia by 34%, that of the Far East by 70% (while the USSR as a whole showed a rise of 9.5%). During the same period the population of the Komi ASSR increased by a factor of more than 2.5; that of Krasnoiarsk Krai by 30%, including a 120% increase in the Taimyr (Dolgano-Nents) National Okrug; that of Magadan Oblast by 37%, including a 115% increase in the Chukchi National Okrug. Motivated by patriotic striving to make an even greater contribution to the building of communism, people of all the nationalities of our country, particularly the youth, are voluntarily going wherever the front line of the struggle for the future runs. At the end of 1961, more than 1,200,000 youth sent by the Komsomol of all the republics had arrived at the shock construction projects of the major branches of industry.

The more complex and grandiose the tasks undertaken by Soviet people, the greater the extent to which the broad masses of the working people of the most diverse nationalities are drawn into the common work of the international production teams. The Karaganda Steel Works was built by people of 30 nationalities, the Kremenchug Hydroelectric Station by people of 41, while Soviet people of more than 50 nationalities are erecting the Bratsk Hydroelectric Station; among these, Russians number 70%, Ukrainians over 13%, Belorussians about 7%, Chuvash – 1.4%, Tatars – 1.4%, Mordvins – 1%, etc.

The results achieved by joining the material and personnel resources of the socialist nations were particularly clearly manifested in the opening of the virgin lands. During the first two and a half years alone, Kazakhstan received from its brother republics 166,000 tractors (in 15-h. p. conversion), 60,000 harvester combines, 67,000 trucks, and a large quantity of other agricultural equipment. Over 600,000 workers and skilled experts came to the Kazakh steppes. The population of Kazakhstan rose by more than 40% from 1954 to 1961 as a consequence of the influx of personnel from the brother republics.

Thus, as the CPSU Program observes, "the appearance of new industrial centers, the opening up and exploitation of natural wealth, the mastery of the virgin lands, and the development of all forms of transport increase the mobility of the population, and promote expansion of the mutual communion among the peoples of the Soviet Union" (Materialy XXII s'ezda KPSS, p. 405).

It must be emphasized that the mobility of the population under the conditions of socialism differs fundamentally from the mobility of the population in the capitalist countries both in its socio-economic basis and in its direct causes. As we know, two historical tendencies are characteristic of capitalism with respect to the nationality question: the awakening of national life and national movements, and the development and hastening of relationships among nations, the breakdown of barriers among nationalities, and the internationalization of economic, political and cultural life. The last-named tendency is particularly characteristic of imperialism and naturally results in increasing population mobility among nationalities. However, under capitalism, the breakdown of barriers among nations takes place through the dominance of certain nations and the subordination of others, and is accompanied by relationships of ethnic inequality and discrimination. Nor can it be otherwise in societies marked by class antagonism. Therefore, population mobility, intensified by the tendency toward internationalization, does not really bring the nations closer together, but results in further ethnic introversion and national egotism. The results of international migrations prove to be contradictory. Under these conditions, voluntary mass-scale population movement is impossible, particularly among the oppressed nationalities. It is due rather to poverty, unemployment, national and racial oppression, and unevenness in the development of

different countries and peoples and to other causes.

By contrast to this, the rise in the mobility of the population under socialism reflects the harmonious unity of effect of the two major interrelated trends in the development of the socialist nations — the rapid and all-round flowering of each nation and the uninterrupted convergence of all the Soviet peoples, the strengthening of their unity, their mutual influence and mutual enrichment. The higher the level of development of nations, the deeper and more diversified does their interrelation become, and the more intensive is the exchange of personnel and the corresponding movement of the population. This, in turn, is an important prerequisite for the further flourishing of any people. It is not accidental that it is precisely in those nationality republics in which the Communist Party and the Soviet government provided higher rates of economic and cultural progress under socialism so as to overcome their backwardness most rapidly, that the increase in population has been highest. Thus, while for the USSR as a whole, the population rose by 15.9% from 1926 to 1939, the corresponding figure was 25.6% for Turkmenia, 32.2% for Georgia, 37.6% for Uzbekistan, 38.7% for Azerbaidjan, 43.9% for Tadjikistan, 45.4% for Armenia, and 45.7% for Kirgizia. In the twenty years from 1939 to 1959, although the average population growth in the USSR as a whole was 9.5%, the largest rise was in the Kazakh SSR (52.6%) and the Kirgiz SSR (41.5%).

Of course, it would be wrong not to take into consideration the role of other factors in this process and, above all, the rise in the natural growth of population in the nationality republics as a consequence of the particularly rapid rise in the material well-being of peoples oppressed before the Revolution. However, even allowing for this, the influence of migrations among nationalities is quite significant. For example, the population of the Kazakh SSR in 1953, that is, on the eve of the opening of the virgin lands, was only 3.5% of the population of the USSR, while its territory, containing enormous wealth, was about 12% of that of the Soviet Union. It is clear that the utilization of the vast opportunities for the development of industry and agriculture in that republic was and is directly dependent upon the influx of personnel from the other nationality republics. This influx will make a substantial addition to the overall growth in population in Kazakhstan.

Under conditions of complete equality among nationalities, strengthening of the friendship among the peoples and the socio-political and ideological unity of the working people, and the development of the internationalist consciousness of Soviet people, favorable political and ideological prerequisites are being established for mass-scale free movement of the population in rapidly developing parts of the country. Moreover, the tendency for the republics to become more mixed in ethnic composition will be furthered by measures such as specialization in the field of production, research and planning efforts, and in other spheres; the development of competition and dissemination of progressive experience, requiring a considerable expansion of skilled personnel among the nations; the establishment of inter-republic organizations in large economic districts, and so forth.

The Increasingly Mixed Ethnic Composition of the Soviet Republics

Every republic contains people of at least several other nationalities. Even if we consider only comparatively large ethnic groups in the population (numbering more than 1% of the population of the given republic), one finds four such nationalities in Lithuania, Armenia and Estonia, five in Belorussia, six in Kazakhstan, Azerbaidjan, Moldavia, Kirgizia and Tadjikistan, seven in Latvia and Turkmenia, nine in Georgia, and ten in Uzbekistan.

The course of the building of socialism and communism in those republics which were particularly backward prior to the Revolution and which progressed rapidly during the years of Soviet power, has clearly manifested a tendency toward reduction in the percentage of the indigenous nationalities despite the fact that they have grown in absolute numbers. At the same time, the percentage of members of other peoples in the population of the nationality republics and oblasts has constantly risen. Whereas in 1926, only 5% of the total number of Russians in the USSR lived in the other republics, by 1959 14.2% did. In 1926, Russians were 3.6% of the population of Georgia, in 1939 they were 8.7%, and in 1959 — 10.1%. The corresponding figures for Uzbekistan were 4.7%, 11.7%, and 13.5%, and in Kirgizia — 11.7%, 20.8%, and 30.2%. The number of Ukrainians in Kirgizia doubled from 1927 to 1938, while in the three Trans-Caucasian republics they increased by 140% from 1926 to 1959, and in Georgia almost three-fold.

The propagandists of anti-communism, bending every effort to weaken the enormous influence of the achievements of the Soviet republics upon the working population of the former colonial countries, have attempted to falsify the real significance of the rising mobility of population in the USSR. Grossly distorting the true state of things, they declare that the increasing ethnic mixture to be found, for example, in Central Asia, testifies to a continuation of the old, prerevolutionary policy of artificial "Russification" and forced colonization of the ethnic districts. They deliberately ignore the fact that the intensified migration of the population in the USSR has exactly the opposite socio-economic and political basis and, accordingly, yields different results than migration due to the colonialist strivings and interests of imperialism. One need only examine the remarkable triumphs of the Soviet nationality republics, which are to a substantial degree due to self-sacrificing, truly selfless aid (including the provision of highly qualified personnel) by the Russian, Ukrainian and a number of the other peoples of our country, and to compare all this with the fruits of the control of colonizers, old and new, in many lands of Africa, Asia, and Latin America, in order to understand the real worth of the mouthings of the imperialist "defenders" of the freedom of nations.

It is widely known that people sent by many nationalities of the USSR, and primarily the Russian, played an outstanding role in uplifting the economy and culture of a considerable number of republics, oblasts and national okrugs. No more than some thirty years ago, for example, the Komi ASSR (then an autonomous oblast) was one of the most backward places in the country, where virtually the entire population was concentrated in a rural locality. In the years that have passed, with the direct aid of representatives primarily of the Russian, Ukrainian, and Belorussian peoples, the productive forces in the republic have developed rapidly. There has been intensive utilization of natural riches, a number of branches of modern industry have made their appearance, the Kotlas-Vorkuta Railroad has been laid, and so forth. The urban population of the Komi ASSR now constitutes considerably more than half the total.

It must be noted that during the first years of Soviet power, many republics felt acutely the lack of economic resources and trained personnel and were naturally unable to take direct part in the development of the economy and culture of other peoples. In addition, the overwhelming majority of the population of these republics was rural. Therefore assistance to the backward nations came primarily from the Russian and certain other comparatively well-developed nations (the Ukrainian above all). Migration of members of other nationalities was comparatively slight. But even then it was considerably more rapid than in pre-Revolutionary Russia, where conditions of national oppression and inequality pushed members of the non-Russian nationalities into an isolated, xenophobic way of life. In the process of the building of socialism, in which the nationality republics scored unprecedented triumphs in all fields, including the training of personnel and their education in internationalism, there was an increase in the migration of the population of various nationalities, and it took on a more bilateral and multilateral character. Thus, whereas in 1926 there were only 28,000 Azerbaidjanis living in the RSFSR, the figure was 71,000 in 1959; the corresponding figures for Armenians were 195,000 and 256,000; of Abkhazians — 98 and 1,400, and so forth. The fact that the territory

of the Russian republic diminished by 14% during those years must also be taken into consideration.

In general, the percentage of that portion of the population of the basic nationality which lives in its native republic to the total numbers of that nationality in the USSR has diminished during the period of socialist construction, as an overall rule, by several percentage points, although it remains quite high (from 75% to 97%, except for the Armenian SSR, where only 55.7% of all Armenians in the Soviet Union live). As far as certain of the autonomous republics are concerned, such as the Mordvin, Bashkir, Tatar and Chuvash, whose development proceeded in direct association with the rapid growth of industry between the Volga and the Urals, the migration of their populations outside their own republics was comparatively high. Whereas 88% of the Bashkirs in the USSR lived in the Bashkir ASSR 35 years ago, today the figure is 75%, while the corresponding figures for the Chuvash are 60% and 52%, and for Tatars — 42% and 29%. The Mordvin ASSR today has only 28% of all the people of that nationality in the USSR, while over 7% live in Orenburg Oblast, 3.4% in Bashkiria, and 2.5% in Tataria. There are even some 11,000 of that nationality in Sakhalin Oblast.

The truly democratic foundations of the Soviet government provide exceptionally favorable conditions for mass-scale free and voluntary migration of the numerous nationalities of the USSR. The complete equality of all nations in our country (like the functioning of the socioeconomic factors noted above) cannot but promote the strengthening of the processes of migration. There is an expanding participation of people of all nationalities in the affairs not only of their own, but of other republics. There is developing among Soviet people a sense of the territorial oneness of the entire Soviet people, an understanding of the fact that the national territory is, above all, a component part of the territory of the USSR utilized in the common interests of all its nations and nationalities.

As a consequence, the boundaries separating the republics of the USSR are losing their significance. For the status and rights of Soviet people of any nationality do not essentially change at all because of the fact that some territory is transferred from one republic to another. Seeking a rapid development of the various districts, and guided by the common interest in the struggle for communism, the socialist nations are themselves acting as initiators of change in republic boundaries if this is called for by economic or other demands for progress in our country. Thus, at the end of January, 1963, there was published the Decree of the Presidium of the Supreme Soviet of the Kazakh SSR, "On the Transfer of Part of South-Kazakhstan Territory of the Kazakh SSR to the Uzbek SSR" (O peredache chasti territorii Iuzhno-Kazakhstanskogo kraia Kazakhskoi SSR v sostav Uzbekskoi SSR). In view of the fact that in Uzbekistan, cotton growing is a leading branch of agriculture, while in Kazakhstan it has not progressed very far, Kazakhstan gave to the brother republic of Uzebekistan more than 8,700,000 acres of the Hungry Steppe, which has been opened primarily to cotton farming by the joint efforts of the peoples of Central Asia.

The increasingly multinational nature of the Soviet republics is further internationalizing socialist national statehood. The organs of the Soviet republics reflect the interests of the entire population independent of national composition. This internationalization of our government structure does not at all mean "denationalization," as some comrades wrongly conclude (see, for example, P. G. Semenov's article in Sovetskoe gosudarstvo i pravo, 1961, No. 12). At the present stage the activity of the agencies of the Soviet nationality republics and oblasts is properly being effectuated in national forms. However, in content and character it is becoming increasingly international, and this is facilitated by the increasing ethnic mixture of the population. Therefore the matter at issue is not "denationalization" but the harmonious coordination of the ethnic and international factors in the statehood of the peoples of our country. Numerous facts testify to this.

Historical experience shows that the Soviet nationality republics provide broad and equal opportunities for the development of the non-native population that has arrived from other areas. Therefore one cannot agree with those who, taking note of the rapid increase in ethnic mixture of the population of a number of republics, and the formation of a more or less compact mass of people of other nationalities living in them (as in Kazakhstan, for example), propose that special autonomous areas be established as a consequence. Today there is no need for this. Proposals of this type reflect a past stage in the development of ethnic relationships in the USSR.

During the first years of Soviet authority, when Soviet autonomy had only just been established and the new socialist principles of mutual relations among nations were still developing and becoming established in a persistent and complex struggle with the heritage of the past, independent ethnic statehood and national boundaries served as an important means of assuring free and equal development of the peoples, their rights and unique ethnic cultures. Today, when the nations are increasingly converging in every way on the basis of their common interests and struggle for the triumph of communism, when the ideology of friendship among the peoples has won the minds of the overwhelming majority of Soviet people, and when equality of nationalities has firmly entered the everyday life of our society, there is no need to establish any new autonomous areas and to draw new ethnic borders as a consequence of the migration among nationalities occurring in the country. On the other hand, measures of this type can only complicate and slow down the population movement now constantly intensifying, the exchange of personnel among the republics, and other forms of international communion and interpenetration.

This, of course, does not mean that the existing forms of autonomy in the Soviet Union have already exhausted their possibilities. Even in the period of the all-round building of communism these forms play an important role in the strengthening of the friendship among the peoples and in bringing them together, and in providing a new rise in the economy and culture of all nations. However, it does not follow from this that it is necessary to supplement the existing autonomous areas by new ones, if a compact group of another nationality takes shape in some republic. Under conditions in which nations are converging at an accelerated pace, with the consequence, in a longer perspective, of complete merging, the establishment of new autonomous areas would have the effect of segregating certain national groups to some degree from the basic mass of the population of the republics. The dialectics of the development of relationships among nationalities during the transition from socialism to communism is such that the autonomous areas established earlier, reflecting definite results of the preceding long-term history of the shaping of nations, are still necessary, but the formation of new autonomous areas on this basis is no longer necessary.

Under the conditions of rapid increase in the ethnic diversity of the population of the Soviet republics, it is particularly important to carry into life rigorously and consistently the Leninist internationalist principle of selection and advancement of personnel on the basis of their practical and political qualities. The By-Laws of the CPSU regard this as one of the duties of every party member. The most determined and irreconcilable struggle is needed against manifestations, which are still encountered, of national egotism, chauvinism and nationalistic narrow-mindedness, which interfere with a proper evaluation of the progressive nature of the process of internationalization of the population of the republics and lead to statements of opposition to the growth of the population of other than the indigenous nationality, exchange of personnel, study of national languages on a voluntary basis, etc. Instances of this have been discovered in recent years in a number of republics and rigorously condemned by the party.

"The rising scale on which communism is being built," we read in the CPSU Program, "demands a continuous exchange of personnel among nations. No manifestations of xenophobia in the training and utilization of personnel of various nationalities in the Soviet republics are permissible. The elimination of manifestations of nationalism would correspond to the interests of all the nations and peoples of the USSR. Each Soviet republic will be able to flourish and grow stronger only in the great family of the brotherly socialist nations of the USSR" (Materialy XXII s'ezda KPSS, p. 408).

The Role of Population Mobility in the Convergence of the Soviet Nations

The increasing ethnic diversity of the Soviet republics, conditioned, as has already been observed, by a number of objective factors, is of vast importance to the further convergence of the socialist nations and peoples. The mutual influence and enrichment of people of various nationalities and the shaping of common traits of culture, morality and mode of life, and internationalist upbringing, are manifested most intensively and directly in the united, close-knit inter-national joint personnel of Soviet enterprises, in labor performed together.

Today not only republics but cities and districts, and thousands upon thousands of work forces at industrial enterprises, construction sites, collective farms, state farms, and even individual brigades have become truly international. This is particularly clearly visible in the example of the rapidly growing new industrial centers such as Sumgait in Azerbaidjan, Rustavi in Georgia, Angren, Begovat or Chirchik in Uzbekistan, etc. A unified, brotherly family of members of dozens of different nationalities works in each of them. In the town of Sumgait, whose population increased from 1939 to 1959 by a factor of 8.2, there are people of more than 40 nationalities, including Azerbaidjanis, Russians, Georgians, Ukrainians, Belorussians, Armenians, etc. People of about 30 different nationalities work at the Chirchik Electrochemical Works and the Begovat Cement Works. There are people of 34 nationalities at the Chilik State Tobacco Farm in Kazakhstan, and 33 in the Lenin Collective Farm of Alamedy Raion, Kirgiz SSR. Workers of nine nationalities belong to the Brigade of Communist Labor at the Turkmenian oil fields of Nebit-Dag headed by A. L. Reznikov, Hero of Socialist Labor, and there are five nationalities represented in the team of the distinguished oil well foreman of Azerbaijan, Hero of Socialist Labor Akif Djafarov.

In the new industrial and agricultural centers, whose multi-national personnel consist primarily of young people, one sees the highest percentage of mixed marriages. Throughout the USSR, the percentage of marriages to persons of other than one's own nationality is constantly increasing. This testifies once again to the overcoming of the former ethnic introversion and exclusion. In 1927, 7.5% of the marriages in the Ukraine were between persons of different nationalities, while in 1937 the figure was already 19%. In Armenia the corresponding figures are 1% and 7.4%. The inter-republic migration of population promotes further spread and deeper mastery of the Russian language by people of all the nationalities of the Soviet Union. The importance of this to the development of our economy and culture is difficult to overestimate. It is not accidental that the need for a knowledge of the Russian language is felt so acutely in personnel groups of mixed nationality, because Russian serves the purposes of mutual exchange of experience and of bringing the cultural achievements of each socialist nation and world culture to each nationality.

The national languages are progressing rapidly under the conditions of freedom and complete equality of nationalities in the USSR. During the years of Soviet power about 50 nationalities acquired written languages of their own for the first time. Every citizen of the USSR is guaranteed complete freedom to speak, educate, and teach his children in any language whatever. Among a number of nations, the number of people who regard the language of their nationality as their native tongue continues to increase. In 1926, 53.8% of the Bashkirs fell into this category, 58.3% in 1939, and 61.9% in 1959. Among the Uzbeks, 97.8% regarded Uzbek as their native tongue in 1939, and 98.4% in 1959. Under such conditions, as Lenin foresaw, there is a logical tendency among all nationalities to learn Russian voluntarily.

This last trend is entirely progressive. Today the Russian language has become, in actuality, the second native tongue of the peoples of the USSR, the common language of their inter-national communication and collaboration, playing, in point of fact, the role of the precursor of a zonal language for dozens of different nationalities. (1) This expansion of its functions and sphere of employment has a deep objective foundation. In the first place, the Russian language is the language of a people which has had, and now has, the decisive role in the development of our society, and has created glorious revolutionary traditions and a rich culture. In the second place, historically it has happened that the overwhelming majority of the people of our country do speak freely in Russian, and that it is the native tongue of nearly 60% of all Soviet people. Moreover, the languages of the two most numerous peoples of our country after the Russians, the Ukrainians and Belorussians, who number more than 45,000,000 persons, are related and similar to the Russian language. Third, and last, it is the most advanced language in our country, and has the strongest and most beneficial influence upon the progress of other national languages.

The results of the USSR Census of 1959 demonstrate that the dissemination and depth of mastery of the Russian language among peoples of the non-Russian languages are constantly rising. Whereas in 1926 the number of persons of other nationalities listing Russian as their native tongue was 6,600,000, in 1959 it had risen to about 10,200,000. In the RSFSR, of approximately 20,000,000 representatives of non-Russian nationalities, 4,700,000, or 23.5%, listed Russian as their native tongue. The following highly significant fact is evidence of the significance of ethnic mobility in that process. We find that Russian is regarded as the native tongue considerably more often by members of non-Russian nationalities living most scattered outside their republic than by those within the republic. Whereas in the Tadjik SSR, 99.3% of the Tadjiks list their native tongue as Tadjik, of those living in the RSFSR, 86% do so. The comparable figures for Lithuanians are 99.2% and 83.8%, and for Azerbaidjanis the figures are 98.1% and 89.7%, etc.

In the dissemination of the Russian language among other nationalities, a specific role is being played by migrations within the same republic, associated particularly with the increase in the urban population at the expense of the rural. Statistical data show that among the urban population, which is as a rule more inter-national in composition and more advanced socio-economically and culturally, the mastery of the Russian language is deeper and broader than among the rural population. Of 10,200,000 persons of non-Russian nationalities who regard their native language as Russian, 7,760,000 live in the cities, while among the rural population, which is greater than the total urban, only 2,430,000 take this attitude. The data for individual republics and towns are similar.

Of course, it would be a mistake to regard population mobility as the only or the principal factor in expanding and deepening knowledge of the Russian language among the socialist nations. More significant factors are operative here, to which reference was made above. Also important is the fact that Soviet people of all nationalities, recognizing the vast positive role of the Russian language in the development of the peoples of the USSR, speak out with increasing frequency, and with full freedom and voluntarily, in favor of a thorough study of that language in school. For example, in Uzbekistan in 1960, with a total of about 6,000 schools, among those with a majority of Uzbeks and others of non-Russian nationality there were 317 schools in which instruction was in the Russian language, while in nearly 1,000 schools, two or three languages of instruction were used, including Russian. But along with all this, the increasing mobility of the population in turn facilitates gradual linguistic convergence of nations and nationalities both in terms of mutual influence and enrichment of the national languages, and in the form of the transformation of one of them — Russian — into the common tongue of all these socialist nations. To a certain degree, these processes mark the beginning of the erasure of linguistic differences, which, as we know, are the most stable of all ethnic differences.

It should be observed that in our literature on the erasure of nationality differences, two one-sided points of view were current until the 22nd Congress of the CPSU. Some writers, justly emphasizing the principle that one must not identify convergence with merger, also asserted that the convergence of the nationalities now occurring among us did not yet signify any erasure of the differences among them. (2) Others, on the contrary, admitting that differences were being erased, arrived at an essentially erroneous characterization of the present stage of ethnic relationships in the USSR, supposing that not only convergence of nations, but also their merger, is now going forward. (3) But the fact is that the dialectical relationship between the two processes does not admit of their being either counterposed to each other or identified.

The erasure of ethnic differences is indubitably a considerably more long-drawn-out process than the erasure of class boundaries. Whereas the latter will be essentially overcome in our country within two decades — i.e., in the course of the movement toward communism — ethnic differences will remain for some time. Even under communism there will still be in progress a further, more profound and all-sided convergence of the nations on the basis of the complete unity, the complete identity of the economic, political, and intellectual and ethical foundations of the communist nations. This is why, in the CPSU Program, the present stage in the development of ethnic relationships in the USSR is described in its entirety as the stage specifically of further convergence, and not merging, of nationalities. It is precisely because the erasure of ethnic differences is a gradual process that it must not be confused with a disappearance of each and every point of difference among nationalities or with the complete mutual assimilation of nations, which can only be the ultimate result of this process in the comparatively remote future. This is why the party is against the artificial, administrative "acceleration" of the erasure of ethnic differences, and against everything that inhibits the objective course of events in that direction. At the 22nd CPSU Congress, N. S. Khrushchev stated: "Of course we also find people who complain about the fact that ethnic differences are disappearing. To them we reply that Communists will not put in moth-balls and preserve unto eternity the differences among nations. We will give aid to the objective process of ever more intimate convergence of nations and nationalities occurring under the conditions of the building of communism on a voluntary and democratic basis" (Materialy XXII s'ezda KPSS, p. 192).

In the course of the building of socialism in our country there has come into being a new, hitherto unknown historical community of people — the Soviet people. Being inter-national, it constitutes the most inclusive of the societal forms yet known (clan, tribe, nationality, nation). That inter-national socialist community of all Soviet people which, at the present stage, does not rule out differences among nationalities, comes increasingly to overlap the narrower national communities. The inter-national USSR-wide economic community has long since come to predominate over the community of economic life of each individual nation. In a characterization of the mental set of any nationality, what is decisive is not the distinctively national, but the traits common to all, etc. The increased geographic mobility of the population facilitates further development of those progressive processes corresponding to the objective laws of the comprehensive building of communism. In the increasingly multinational nature of the Soviet republics we find reflected the further strengthening of the unity of members of the various nationalities having the USSR as their common socialist fatherland, the socialist economy as their common economic foundation, a common social and class structure, a common Marxist-Leninist view of the world, common intellectual and moral characteristics and a common goal, the building of communism.

Footnotes

1) See M. D. Kammari, "Stroitel'stvo kommunizma i dal'neishee sblizhenie natsii v SSSR," Voprosy filosofii, 1961, No. 9, p. 42.

2) See, for example, I. P. Tsamerian, Sovetskoe mnogonatsional'noe gosudarstvo, ego osobennosti i puti razvitiia, Moscow, 1958, p. 262; same author, "Razvitie natsional'nykh otnoshenii v period razvernutogo stroitel'stva kommunizma," Voprosy filosofii, 1959, No. 7, p. 40; B. G. Gafurov, Nekotorye voprosy natsional'noi politiki KPSS, Gospolitizdat, 1959, p. 78. In his most recent writings, Tsamerian arrives at a proper solution of the question (see his article, "Zakonomernosti vozniknoveniia i razvitiia sovetskogo mnogonatsional'nogo gosudarstva," Voprosy filosofii, 1962, No. 11, pp. 46-47; Novyi etap v razvitii natsional'nykh otnoshenii v SSSR, Moscow, 1962, p. 65).

3) See, for example, M. F. Valeev, "Bratskoe sotrudnichestvo i sblizhenie narodov SSSR v bor'be za pobedu kommunizma" (in the compendium Iz opyta raboty partiinykh organizatsii po vypolneniiu reshenii XX i XXI s'ezdov KPSS, Moscow, 1961, p. 54).

* * *

Ethnic Processes and Relations

Sovetskaia etnografiia, 1961, No. 4

V. K. Gardanov, B. O. Dolgikh, and T. A. Zhdanko

MAJOR TRENDS IN ETHNIC PROCESSES AMONG THE PEOPLES OF THE USSR*

Our country's entry into the period of full-scale construction of communist society also brings on a new stage in the development of relationships among the nationalities in the USSR. The Seven-Year Plan envisages a vast growth of the economies of the constituent republics. It clearly expresses the Leninist nationality policy which makes for an even greater all-round flourishing of the economy and culture of all the peoples of the multinational Soviet state. At the same time, the socialist division of labor, the growth of new and multifarious forms of economic and cultural ties, and of comradely cooperation, mutual assistance and friendship, create a firm basis for an ever-closer coming together of the peoples of our country.

Thus, the present historical stage in the development of nationality relationships in the Soviet Union is characterized by a profound and ever-advancing process of the approximation of the socialist nations, which have flourished and achieved enormous successes along the road to the building of communism.

The theoretical foundations of the development of socialist nations and peoples as they move toward communism have been elaborated and illuminated in a number of the writings of V. I. Lenin and in the most important programmatic documents of the Communist Party. They were reflected in the decisions of the 20th and 21st Party Congresses, in the resolutions of the plenary meetings of the CPSU Central Committee and in the plans for the development of the national economy. They are already being put into practice. Therefore, study and generalization of the specific paths of development followed by various Soviet peoples from the first years of the Soviet government to the present day are most important, as is discovery of the interrelationships of nationalities that have come into being at the present stage in history.

Investigation of the complex problem of current processes in the development of nationalities and their future prospects requires data from the various humanistic disciplines: philos-

_____
*This article is based upon a paper read at the April 4, 1961, meeting of the Department of Historical Sciences, USSR Academy of Sciences.

ophy, history, ethnography, economics, law, linguistics, the study of literature and art, etc. One of the important problems, requiring research chiefly in the data of ethnography, is that of the processes of ethnic development currently in progress in our country.

Therefore the USSR Academy of Sciences' Institute of Ethnography has undertaken an investigation of current processes in the development of nationalities in various parts of the Soviet Union — Central Asia, the Caucasus, the Volga, the Far North, and so forth — using ethnographic field data and analysis of USSR census data. (1) It has undertaken to study and analyze the status of each ethnic group, including, if possible, the very smallest, and to determine the pathways along which they will develop, approach each other and, in some cases, merge. Inasmuch as this work is only getting under way, it is possible at present to make public only certain preliminary data on some of the most important aspects of the problem under consideration.

Current processes of ethnic development in the USSR are occurring essentially in two directions:

1) continuation of the consolidation and development of the socialist nations and nationalities; and

2) the general process of intensified coming together of the socialist nations and nationalities of our country, on the basis of the development of brotherly cooperation and friendly international ties in the fields of economics, culture and intellectual life — a process accompanied by the establishment of forms of culture and everyday life common to the USSR as a whole.

Naturally, the progress of these processes is not uniform.

As we shall see, they proceed unevenly in various parts of the country, but have occurred side by side from the very first years of Soviet power. The first of these two trends was of major significance in the early stages of development of Soviet society, until socialism finally triumphed in our country; and the second is now coming to the fore, acquiring broader scope and reality in the present stage of our history, the stage of the full-scale construction of a communist society.

***

As we know, the historical basis for the formation of socialist nations among the various peoples of the USSR was not uniform. It depended on the level of socioeconomic and ethnic development at which they found themselves in the period of the establishment of the Soviet government. (2) Among the most numerous and highly developed peoples — the Russians, Ukrainians, Belorussians, Georgians, Armenians, and others — the process of transformation of the old bourgeois nations into socialist nations began after the establishment of the Soviet government. The process of formation of socialist nations took a different form among peoples who had not passed through the stage of capitalism and had not become capitalist nations. This group included the majority of the peoples of the borderlands of pre-revolutionary Russia, including those of Central Asia and Kazakhstan, the North Caucasus and Dagestan, the Ural-Volga area and Siberia, the Far East and the Far North. A considerable number of them had become nationalities during the medieval period. However, under conditions of the landlord-bourgeois system of political and ethnic oppression by tsarism and the dominance in many parts of the country of pre-capitalist relationships (feudal, semi-feudal and, in places, even pre-feudal) their ethnic development was inhibited, and numerous small, isolated and insular ethnic groups persisted within them — remnants of those tribes of ancient and medieval times which had, for many centuries, participated in the ethnogenesis of the given people.

As a result, internal ethnic barriers and stable population groups of foreign origin persisted until the October Revolution among a number of large nationalities which had come into being much earlier and among some nations. The latter were frequently the result of the presence among these peoples of fragments of other nationalities cast there at some time by the waves of turbulent political events in areas distant from the places of origin of these fragmented groups. These groups subsequently adopted the language and many of the characteristics of the culture of the people whose territory they came to inhabit, and with which they are now gradually merging (for example, the Arabs, Gypsies, Iranians, and Bokhara Jews in Central Asia). However, a much more widespread and significant phenomenon has been the continued existence of local population groups of the same ethnic origins as the principal inhabitants, which have become separated from the major local people due to historical, geographic, or other circumstances, and have retained local dialects and certain distinctive ethnographic characteristics. Finally, a very large number of the ethnographic groups which have continued to exist in Soviet times originated in earlier tribes and clans which, despite many centuries of existence as neighbors of, or within, slave and feudal societies with class structures, retained their clan traditions and the characteristics of tribal life. It must be particularly emphasized that, because of general social and economic backwardness, even the bourgeois nations, formed during the capitalist epoch on the southeastern frontiers of our country, retained, at the time of the socialist revolution, remnants of ethnic subdivisions of the precapitalist epoch.

As an example, take the Georgians who, although they had become a bourgeois nation in the second half of the 19th century, retained into the first decades of the 20th century numerous internal subdivisions deriving from the prior tribal and political divisions of the Georgian people. The most important and distinctive of them were the Kartalins, the Kakhetins, the Gudamakars, the Mtiulians, the Khevsurians, the Pshavians, the Tushins, the Mokhevians, the Imeretius, the Rachins, the Guri, the Adjarians, the Meskhians, and the Djavakhians. During the early years of the construction of socialism, there were a number of peoples of the Soviet East among whom a significant and very negative role was played by remnants of the clan-tribal division of the population, the continuing influence of feudal clan chieftains, and the tradition of residence by clan, remnants of clan communal water and land utilization, etc. As we know, there were areas in which bourgeois nationalists developed a "theory" of "the transition to socialism via the clan." They involved clan elders, bais and feudal lordlings in the leadership of collective farms and local soviets during the years of collectivization.

The remnants of clan-tribal division also had a negative influence upon the national development of various peoples. Studies in historical ethnography have revealed the extraordinary complexity of the clan-tribal structures of certain peoples of the USSR in the comparatively recent past. In recent years, the most careful studies of clan-tribal organization were those pertaining to the peoples of Siberia, the Kirgiz, the Turkmens, the Karakalpaks, the Bashkirs, the Dagestani peoples, and others. (3) The resultant data demonstrate that the earlier division into tribes and clans was retained for a long time, in residual form, in the process of the formation of peoples during the feudal and capitalist periods. Thus, until the 19th and early 20th centuries, the Karakalpak were divided into 12 large tribes, 102 clans and innumerable smaller kin groups. The mountain people of the Caucasus, particularly those of Dagestan, were marked by extreme clan-tribal fragmentation.

It should be noted that study of clan-tribal composition and the territorial distribution of clan-tribal groups, and compilation of detailed historical-ethnographic maps, which have become an important part of the work of expeditions of the Institute of Ethnography of the USSR Academy of Sciences, are today being performed by ethnographers not only for the purpose of investigating problems of the historical past (ethnogenesis, history of social structure, family and customs, etc.). It is also of great significance for the study of contemporary ethnic processes, inasmuch as it provides the initial data for this purpose, i.e., a picture of the ethnic status of each people in the 1920's and 1930's, when consolidation of socialist nations began.

Study of the processes of ethnic development of the peoples of the USSR shows that the formation of the various national republics and oblasts played an enormous role in their consolidation into nations. Established and reinforced on the basis of the Soviet system, the governmental autonomy of the peoples of the USSR was a most important condition of their successful all-round progress on the path to communism. Soviet national state structure became the major weapon by means of which the Communist Party and the Soviet government directed the economic, political, and cultural development of the formerly oppressed and backward peoples of the colonial borderlands of Russia, liberated by the Great October Socialist Revolution.

Their success in the construction of socialism and their closely related success in national consolidation facilitated a transition to higher forms of national state structure — the conversion of a number of autonomous republics into constituent republics, and of a number of autonomous oblasts into autonomous republics. The triumph of socialism in the USSR and the resultant fundamental changes in the class structure of Soviet society and in the intellectual profile of the Soviet people have essentially completed the process of the formation of socialist nations and nationalities in our country, as well as the process by which their national state structure was achieved. This was recorded in the new Constitution of the USSR of 1936. However, this does not mean that no changes occurred thereafter in the national development of the peoples of the USSR, or that none are occurring today. On the contrary, the transition to the construction of communism opened a new epoch in the lives of the peoples of our country, and consequently a new epoch in their national development. The socialist nations and peoples that have come into being in the USSR are currently continuing their development on the road to communism.

The essence of present-day ethnic processes related to the consolidation and further development of socialist nations is expressed primarily in the disappearance of the insularity and isolation of small ethnic groups and their gradual assimilation into socialist nations, and in the increasingly monolithic character of these nations. Census data, when studied in combination with ethnographic materials, provide a good reflection of this progressive process of ethnic approximation and merging under socialist conditions, with complete equality of all groups in the population, naturally and freely, without any elements of pressure from outside exerted by the administrative agencies of any republic. This ethnic process, occurring under the conditions of our Soviet reality, differs fundamentally from the policy of forced assimilation practiced by tsarist

Russia, which led, not infrequently, to tragic consequences — the extinction of entire peoples.

During the first years of Soviet power, when the process of formation of socialist nations had just begun in our country and was particularly weak in the borderlands, the awareness of membership in some tribe or other ethnographic group frequently still predominated, among many peoples of the USSR, over their awareness of membership in nations. This was reflected in the data of the census at that time. Thus, the census of 1926 still listed numerous clan-tribal groups.

Consider, for example, the Uzbeks, a portion of whom (the so-called seminomadic Uzbeks) retained clan-tribal organization. In addition to the Uzbeks proper (numbering 3,905,000), (4) the census of 1917 and that of 1926 recorded separately such ethnographic clan-tribal groups of the Uzbek people as the "Turks," whose total number exceeded 60,000 (5) (there were about 24,000 in the Fergana valley), (6) the Kipchaks (33,500), (7) the Kurama (50,000). (8) All of these, although they spoke the Uzbek language, considered themselves distinct from the Uzbeks. In particular, the Fergana "Turks" usually even listed their tribal designation in the "nationality" column of their internal passports.

The 1959 census no longer revealed any Kurama. They had finally merged with the Uzbeks. Only 100 persons in Fergana called themselves Kipchak. However, a little over 4,000 persons listed themselves as "Turks" (chiefly in Fergana and Samarkand oblasts). Ethnographic studies in the field, carried out by parties of the USSR Academy of Sciences' Institute of Ethnography and the Uzbek Academy of Sciences in the Fergana Valley in 1951-1954, (9) also confirmed that the former separate existence of the Uzbek-speaking clan-tribal groups had essentially ended, and that there is no longer any doubt that their awareness of membership in the Uzbek nationality will win out in the near future.

The process of approximation to and merger with the Uzbeks of the Karakalpaks interspersed among them in the Fergana Valley and particularly in Samarkland oblast, which had begun before the Revolution, has also advanced a long way, as is demonstrated by the latest investigations by parties of the Karakalpak Branch of the Academy of Sciences of the Uzbek SSR. (10)

A process of merger of ethnographic groups with the main body of the nation is also occurring among the Tadjiks, who do not have clan-tribal division, but among whom small peoples retaining their ancient tongues, fundamentally different from the Tadjik, had for a long time lived isolated lives in the mountain districts. The majority of these people have long known not only their own language but Tadjik. We speak here of the Yagnobians and the so-called Cis-Pamir peoples. Census data describe the gradual approximation of these groups to the Tadjiks. Thus, the Yagnobians, living along the headwaters of the Zeravshan, were found by the 1926 census to number 1,800 (11) while the 1959 census showed about 600 persons calling themselves by this name, although approximately the same number as in 1926 identified Yagnobian as their native tongue. The same situation is true of the Cis-Pamir peoples inhabiting the Gorno-Badkhshan Autonomous Oblast. They are now called the Cis-Pamir Tadjiks. These eight small groups were not taken cognizance of by the 1926 census. In 1939 they totalled 38,000 persons, all told. In the 1959 census they no longer appear as distinct ethnographic groups, inasmuch as all called themselves Tadjiks by nationality. However, many Shugnans, Rushans, Vakhans, Bartans, Iazguls, and Badzhui gave these languages, and not Tadjik, as their native tongues. The total number of Cis-Pamir peoples proved to be somewhat larger than in 1939 in terms of native language. Aside from the growth in population, this was doubtless due to the greater care with which the latest census was taken in the remote mountain areas.

However, stable retention of local languages and certain ethnographic differences in culture do not in any way negate the real progressive process of merger with the Tadjiks of these small groups lost in the high valleys and at one time wholly out of touch with the rest of the world. The merger is occurring on the basis of the Tadjik language, which is widely known both among the Cis-Pamir Tadjiks and the Yagnobians. The building of roads, air and automotive transport,

large-scale industrial construction, the rise in culture, and the resettlement of a portion of the high mountain peoples into the valley have broken down the age-old isolation of these areas.

The process of ethnic development of large socialist nations in the republics of the Transcaucasus is occurring in another form.

In the Armenian SSR, a closer unity and merger of various ethnic groups of the Armenian people has occurred in accordance with the socialist transformation of the bourgeois nation. Approximately the same thing happened in Georgia, where socialist transformations led to the erasure of numerous ethnic lines of demarcation that had existed deep in the Georgian nation in the capitalist stage. Today, the internal subdivisions among the Georgians have lost their former significance, and have disappeared almost entirely in the formation of the Georgian socialist nation. This nation now includes the Kartvelian peoples with their distinctive languages, related to Georgian; the Svans, Mingrelians and Laz. In the past these had considered themselves distinct. Although these groups of Georgians do, in part, continue to use their former language in everyday life (particularly within the family), their societal and political life and culture are developing with the use of the Georgian language, which is now their chief means of communication. The 1959 census showed that 720 persons considered Mingrelian, Svan, or Laz to be their native tongues. As far as national consciousness is concerned, only a few more than 10 individuals termed themselves Mingrelians, and less than 10 called themselves Svans, while only 232 of the 318 persons terming themselves Laz designated that as their native tongue. The Tsova-Tushins (Batsbians) living in Georgia have also been completely assimilated. Although current linguistic classification places the Batsbian language in the Nakh family of North Caucasian languages, which includes Chechen and Ingush, it has been very strongly influenced by the Georgian, as P. K. Uslar noted as long ago as the middle of the 19th century. A recent study of the Batsbian language demonstrated that the influence of the Georgian has been most strongly felt in the vocabulary. (12) This has greatly facilitated the Georgian acculturation of the Tsova-Tushins (Batsbians). The long historical contact and intimate interrelationships of the Tsova-Tushins and the Georgians were consummated, in the Soviet epoch, by assimilation into the Georgian socialist nation.

Considerable success has been achieved in the development of the Azerbaidjani socialist nation, which has been gathering into itself the various ethnic groups living in the Azerbaidjani SSR. The process of assimilation of the Tats and Talysh, speaking Iranian languages, had begun in Azerbaidjan long before the Revolution. Today these peoples have substantially merged with the Azerbaidjanis, and have thus come to be part of the Azerbaidjani socialist nation. However the Azerbaidjani Talysh still retain certain distinctive ethnic aspects in culture and everyday life. (13) The situation is somewhat different with respect to the Azerbaidjani Tats. The 1926 census showed 28,000 Tats (some of those listed in that census dwelt in Dagestan). The 1959 census listed 11,-000 Tats, the bulk of whom live in small isolated groups in Dagestan and the mountainous parts of Azerbaidjan, while the bulk of the Azerbaidjani Tats, including those of the area of Baku (Apsheron), have now merged completely with the Azerbaidjani socialist nation and regard themselves as Azerbaidjanis. A similar situation is observed among the Udin, the aboriginal inhabitants of Azerbaidjan, who played an important role in the ethnogenesis of the Azerbaidjanis. Today the Azerbaidjan Udins have almost completely merged with the Azerbaidjanis, and only small isolated groups regard themselves as Udins.

The process of national development of the peoples of the Northern Caucasus is taking a distinctive path. Until the October Revolution they retained many characteristics of the clan-tribal way of life and had not, by that date, attained the point of final ethnic consolidation. After the establishment of Soviet power they achieved such unity in the economic, political, and cultural sense, in the process of the construction of socialism, as to develop into socialist nations and nationalities. Thus, peoples of the Northern Caucasus which had not, before the October Revolution, passed through the capitalist stage, made a gigantic step in their national development under the conditions of the Soviet system, bypassing the phase of the bourgeois nation.

As a consequence of national consolidation, the former divisions into "community" tribes within the socialist nations and nationalities of the Northern Caucasus, constituting remnants of patriarchal-feudal relationships, disappeared. Thus, for instance, until the Revolution, the Adygeis were divided into the Abadzekhs, Beslenis, Bzhedukhs, Temirgois, Shapsugs, and other tribes; the Abazins into two main branches (Tapantas and Shkaraus), each of which retained a division into six tribes. The Balkarians were divided into the Baksan (Urusbi), Chegem, Khulam, Bezengi, and Madkar "communities." The Ossetes, Ingushas, Chechens, and other North Caucasian mountaineers were also divided into tribes and "communities." Today the traces of these former internal divisions among the peoples of the Northern Caucasus are barely discernible, although prior to the October Revolution they were still quite clearly reflected in the level of socioeconomic development, in certain elements of material culture and peculiarities of dialect among the ethnic subdivisions of the Adygeis, Abazins, Balkarians, Ossetes, and Chechens.

An important part in the consolidation of the peoples of the Northern Caucasus into nationalities was played not only by the profound socioeconomic transformations carried out during the Soviet epoch, but by the cultural revolution and, specifically, by the development of writing in their native tongues. The establishment of uniform literary tongues among the peoples of the Northern Caucasus, who have recently acquired writing, greatly assisted in the successful development of their national culture, in the gradual elimination of dialect peculiarities in language. It helped strengthen the concept of membership in a single nationality on the part of the previously insular ethnic groups of a given people which had, until recently, retained in residual form the memory of their clan-tribal membership as a counterbalance to national consciousness.

In discussing current processes of ethnic development among the peoples of the North Caucasus, Dagestan must be treated separately. Even in the Caucasus, which is so rich in nationalities,

Dagestan is distinguished by an extreme multiplicity of languages and ethnic fragmentation. It is natural that under these conditions the processes of ethnic development and national consolidation should take on extremely complex forms.

About 30 peoples and ethnic groups having distinct languages, and more than 70 registered dialects, exist at present in the Dagestani ASSR. The native population of the Dagestani ASSR includes a large group of peoples of the Caucasian language family, as well as the Turkic-speaking Kumyks and Nogais, and the Iranian-speaking Tats and Mountain Jews. Among the peoples speaking the Caucasian languages one find the larger Dagestani peoples such as the Avars, Lezgins, Dargins, Laks, and Tabasarans. Written scripts were developed for these tongues after the October Revolution. Their literature has developed in these languages, and education in the elementary grades is conducted in them. This fact, as well as the ancient historical connections and close geographic ties, and the economic ties which have been greatly strengthened during the Soviet period, have resulted in some of these major peoples of Dagestan becoming the nuclei for consolidation around them of smaller ethnic groups similar to them in language, way of life and culture.

An important place in this process is occupied by the Avars, with the thirteen neighboring nationalities of the so-called Ando-Tsezian (Ando-Didoi) group and the Archins, who have long been in their orbit. The ethnic groupings undergoing consolidation around the Avars inhabit chiefly the western raions of the Dagestani ASSR. They include the Archins, whose language is midway between the Avar and the Lezgin branch of the Dagestan tongues, and the following peoples in the same linguistic group as the Avars themselves: Andi, Akhvakhs, Bagulals (Kvanaduns), Botlikhs, Godoberins, Karatins, Tindals, Chamalais (within the Andi sub-group), Bezhtins (Kapuchins), Gunzebs, Ginukhs, Khvarshins, and Tsezes (within the Tsez or Didoi sub-group). (14) The ethnic group consolidating around the Avars is coming to be the largest people in Dagestan. According to the 1959 census they number 239,-000, which constitutes more than 22% of the en-

tire population of the Dagestani ASSR. The major language among this group of peoples has become Avar, although the Ando-Tsezes and Archin continue to use their native tongues in their everyday life. (15)

The next largest group undergoing consolidation in Dagestan is the Dargin group found in the central raions. This group includes, in addition to the Dargins, such closely related groups as the Kaitags and Kubachins, whose languages were formerly usually regarded as independent, but are now considered dialects of Dargin. The linguistic closeness of the Kaitag and Kubachin to the Dargin has facilitated the process of consolidation into a single nationality, which may be considered to be essentially completed. According to the 1959 census, the Dargins number 148,-000 persons, constituting 14% of the population of the Dagestani ASSR.

The group of Dagestan peoples speaking the languages of the Lezgin branch is complex. It includes the Lezgins, Tabasarans, Aguls, Rutulians, and Tsakhurs, living in the southeastern raions. The 1959 census showed the number of Lezgins in the USSR to be 223,000, of whom 98,000 live in Azerbaidjan; 109,000 Lezgins live in Dagestan, and constitute more than 10% of the population there. The Tabasarans now number 35,000 persons. Inasmuch as they, like the Lezgins, have their own written language, (16) their national culture is developing independently, although the Lezgin language is rather widely used among the Tabasarans.

It was held at one time that the small peoples of Dagestan, lacking written languages and speaking tongues of the Lezgin branch, were merging with the Lezgins and losing their distinctive ethnographic features. This view, later found to be erroneous, specifically led to the situation in which the Ethnographic Map of the peoples of the USSR, published with the participation of the Institute of Ethnography, did not show the Rutulians and Tsakhurs, their territory being indicated by the same color as that of the Lezgin. In Dagestan, too, local agencies ceased, in estimating the population, to distinguish the Rutulians and Tsakhurs as distinct groups, but included them in the Lezgins. A more careful study of the processes of consolidation of the peoples of Dagestan, performed by the Dagestan Expedition of the Institute of Ethnography in 1950-1954, permitted a more exact treatment of the problem of the small peoples of the Dagestan-speaking languages of the Lezgin group. It was found that despite certain evidence of growing closeness between these peoples and the Lezgins, it is premature at present to speak of their merger with the latter. Here we must take into consideration, first, their linguistic disunity. Membership in a single language group does not mean that the Aguls, Rutulians, and Tsakhurs can communicate with the Lezgins in their own tongues. Knowledge of Lezgin is required for this. At the same time, the degree of dissemination of Lezgin among the small peoples of the Lezgin group is comparatively minor and far from uniform. The Lezgin language has gained widest dissemination among the Agula, many of whom know this language and employ the Lezgin script. On the other hand, the majority of the Rutulians and Tsakhurs do not know Lezgin.

The needs of economic and cultural development of the peoples of Dagestan require that their ethnic fragmentation, a consequence of the former age-old xenophobia and the isolation of small groups of people, living in the high and until recently inaccessible raions of this "land of mountains," be ended as rapidly as possible.

The socialist transformations, and the processes of national consolidation occurring on their basis, have fundamentally changed the lives of the Dagestani mountain people, unified them, and opened wide the doors to the surrounding world. Whereas formerly it was only a small portion of the population, chiefly adult males, who left their rural communities and entered into contact with the outside world, today the entire population, regardless of sex, beginning with children of school age, is in constant communication with the surrounding world through the factory, collective farm and school, and with the help of the press and radio. For the ordinary inhabitant of Dagestan, the dimensions of the world have grown immeasurably. Formerly the Dagestani mountaineer frequently had to know a foreign language in order to go to the bazaar in the next village, but this language would take him no further, since the knowledge of this second language was limited to a comparatively small territory. Today, thanks to the appearance of the literary languages of Dagestan and their dissemination among a whole group of related peoples, it is possible for a member of even the smallest people in Dagestan, with the aid of one of these languages, not only to communicate with a considerable number of his fellow tribesmen, but to take active part in the development of the national culture, literature, and art.

This clearly shows the historically progressive nature of the national consolidation of the small peoples of Dagestan around a related people having its own script and literary language.

However, along with this, a second tendency, expressed in the process of creation of a Dagestan-wide national community, is now manifesting itself to an ever-increasing degree.

The individual peoples of Dagestan, who have become unified by a community of economic and cultural life within the framework of a single autonomous republic, increasingly regard themselves not only as Avars, Dargin, Kumyk, Lezgin, Lak, etc., but also as Dagestani. Due to the diversity of languages in Dagestan, Russian has naturally come to be the principal language of inter-nation communication there.

It has, in the true sense of the word, become the second native tongue of all the peoples of Dagestan. Today when an Avar meets a Lezgin, a Kumyk meets a Lak, and a Dargin meets a Tabasaran, they will usually communicate in Russian. In Dagestan, where endogamy was widespread until recently and helped maintain the insularity of the societies and tribes, mixed marriages have now become commonplace. (17) The husband and wife and, in cities, their children will frequently converse with each other only in Russian.

The dissemination of the Russian language in Dagestan is also attested to by the fact that certain of the small peoples there (the Tsakhurs, and Rutulians) prefer not to adopt the language of a neighboring, larger Dagestani people with a written language, but to have their children taught in the Russian language from the very first grade.

Thus, a further unification of the peoples of Dagestan is proceeding on the basis of the Russian language.

A characteristic picture of ethnic development is also observed among the peoples of Siberia and the Far North. Prior to the October Socialist Revolution, of all the Siberian peoples, only the Yakuts and Buryats had jelled into nationalities. The so-called small peoples of the North — Chukchi, Koriaks, Evens, Evenks, Khanty, Mansi, and others — were peculiar early ethnic formations. Some of them had retained tribal and clan divisions almost in their primitive forms. The peoples of Siberia and the North were the most backward ethnic groups in our territory. A series of special political, economic, and cultural measures on the part of the Soviet government were required to raise their living standard and culture. The largest Siberian peoples — the Buryats and Yakuts — were given the status of autonomous republics. The consequence of socialist transformations was that the Buryats and Yakuts took shape as socialist nations. The Altai, Khakass, and Tuvans were organized territorially into autonomous oblasts.

The consolidation of the Altai and Khakass as nations is particularly significant. Prior to the Revolution, both of these were merely groups of fragmented tribes. It was only during the Soviet period that they consolidated into socialist peoples. The formation of autonomous political units for them played a tremendous part in this. The small peoples of the North, scattered over immense territories, were in part unified into national okrugs and raions. This also facilitated the approximation of portions of these ethnic groupings. Scripts were developed in the native tongues of a number of the small peoples of the North (the Chukchi, Koriaks, Evens, Evenks, Khanty, Mansi, Sel'kups, Nanai, etc.). All the foregoing developments facilitated the rise of the culture of the peoples of Siberia and the North, and the overcoming of their backwardness. However, the native population does not constitute a majority in any of the autonomous republics, oblasts, and okrugs of Siberia, inasmuch as many Russians, Ukrainians, Belorussians, and the like, live there. Some of them have been

there for long periods, while others came during the Soviet years in connection with the development of socialist industry and agriculture in Siberia.

The reorganization of the economy and daily life promoted the approximation and merger of certain of the small peoples of the North with the Yakuts, Komi, or Russians, although this process is still far from complete. Analogous processes are observed in other parts of the Soviet Union, as for example along the Volga, where some groups of Mordvins, Chuvashes, Mari and other peoples, located among the mass of the Russian population, are gradually assimilating with the latter.

* * *

It must be noted that phenomena inhibiting the progressive process of overcoming the isolation and insularity of the small ethnographic groups, the process of ethnic development of nations, still exist. In certain republics, attempts have been made to force the assimilation of small peoples into the major nation artificially. Such acts are fundamentally opposed to the nationality policy of the Communist Party and the Soviet government. They have brought harm, beyond any question, to the successful progress, under our Soviet conditions, of the merger of small ethnic groups in the population with the large socialist nation in question in each case, and will interfere with the healthy incorporation of these groups into such a nation in the future.

Cases are still encountered of insensitive attitudes toward the national self-consciousness of members of the small peoples. The psychological aspect of this matter is of enormous significance for a proper solution of the problem of interrelations among nationalities, as Lenin emphasized. (18)

Religious differences and prejudices frequently interfere with the approximation of a small people to a large one. Finally, the retention of archaic customs and rites, which in the past had given expression to the unity of the clan and the strength of clan relationships in the community, plays a major negative role.

Thus, in Central Asia and the Caucasus, the traditional succession of funeral feasts, participated in by an enormous number of fellow clansmen of the deceased, is still widespread. As in ancient times, clansmen participate in collecting money for funeral expenses, weddings, and bride-price. Although Soviet legislation prohibits payment of bride-price, it continues to be practiced in some places. There are cases of mutual cover-up by all members of a clan, resulting in crimes by persons in public service, concealment of thefts of public property, etc. Among some peoples the laws of clan exogamy, under which weddings even between distant relatives are taboo, still have not lost their force. We have long known that the folk tradition of "respect for elders," which is considered positive, is frequently a survival of the harmful patriarchal custom of blind obedience to the aged — the <u>aksakals</u>, whose conservative views in the past determined "public opinion" in the village or mountain settlement. Unfortunately, in the solution of problems of the family and everyday life, people sometimes continue to give inordinate regard to the backward opinions, permeated with customary and religious prejudices, of the older generation. This inhibits the uprooting of old customs and ceremonies.

Not long ago an article by Comrade A. Kazakbaev, Secretary of the Central Committee of the Communist Party of Kirgizia, was published in which he observed that it is not uncommon there to encounter such remnants of patriarchal life as clan vendettas, bride-purchase, polygamy, and so forth. "One hears, now and then, in the collective and state farms," he writes, "questions such as why the person chosen as chairman of the collective or chief of a farm was from such-and-such a clan, and not from another. It is certainly true that irreconcilable proponents of such vestiges of the past are encountered with increasing rarity, but they continue to harm our common cause." (<u>19</u>)

It is particularly important to note that patriarchal customs are sometimes defended by the intelligentsia of the given nationality, which does not hesitate to participate actively in their observance. In so doing, they disseminate the false formula that a given custom is "a law of our nation." In other words, archaic customs contradictory to the Soviet way of life are regarded as part of the national culture. The author of the article cited above notes that civic organizations and their active members frequently prefer not to interfere in such matters, and do not try to build a negative public opinion with respect to them, out of fear "of violating national traditions." The writer reminds us that the resolution of the Central Committee of the Communist Party of the Soviet Union on the responsibilities of party propaganda demands an uncompromising struggle against these survivals of bourgeois nationalism, and against the revival and artificial inculcation of reactionary customs and habits under the guise of "national traditions."

* * *

Side by side with the continuing development of socialist nations, the general process of approximation of the nations and peoples of the USSR is taking place. This is proceeding simultaneously in two directions: a) an ever closer approximation of socialist nations and peoples within the limits of large historical-ethnographic regions; and b) the approximation of peoples on an all-union scale, which is accompanied by the formation of all-union traditions and cultural features, higher communist forms of collaboration, and an increase in the friendly fraternal ties among the peoples of our country, who have common basic interests.

A process of regional approximation of the population is observed in such large areas of our country as Central Asia, the Caucasus, and so forth. The peoples living in these areas have been in the most intimate economic and cultural contact from ancient times. They are united by common history and are sometimes of similar origin. The similarity of conditions of physical geography and the cultural interchange over many centuries have resulted in the establishment of numerous similar modes of economic activity and common cultural traits. Economically speaking, these are major economic-geographic regions, while from the ethnographic point of view they are major historical ethnographic regions. Valuable habits of labor have been developed in these regions. They are still valid. They are being studied with a view to preserving and improving them in the general perspective of development of our country's economy.

Thus, in Central Asia the most valuable of the economic traditions of the native inhabitants of the agricultural oases — the Tadjiks, Uzbeks, Turkmens, and Karakalpaks — is irrigation agriculture, which has existed in some of these places since the Third or Fourth Millennia B.C.E. The peoples of Central Asia have developed distinctive and unique methods of irrigation suited to various natural conditions — oases, mountains, foothills, and delta areas. The traditions of mountain pastoralism among the Kirgiz and some of the Tadjiks, of steppe pastoralism by the Kazakhs and Kirgiz, and of desert pastoralism by the Turkmens, are combined with their own adaptation, handed down from their ancestors, to life and work under the severe natural conditions of those areas.

Southern Siberia and, even more so, the Far North constitute special historical-ethnographic and economic areas. Over a period of many centuries, the peoples of Siberia and the Far North have established the specific habits of labor necessary in local geographic conditions. We know that centers of industry in the North occupy very limited territory. Large expanses of taiga and tundra, occupying about a third of the entire territory of the USSR, are utilized only by the small peoples of the North, numbering 130,000 persons in all. Reindeer-breeding, hunting for land and sea mammals, and fishing continue to be economically profitable occupations in these enormous areas. The peoples of the North have acquired the practical habits required for these branches of the economy. One need only point out that virtually the entire stock of reindeer of the Soviet Union, totalling 2,000,000 head, are herded by members of the small Northern peoples. The types of Arctic clothing and footwear developed by the peoples of the North have gained wide acceptance among the entire population of that area.

The work experience of the peoples of the Caucasus, in particular their customs of mountain agriculture and pastoralism, is also of major economic significance. The population of the mountain areas of the Caucasus has, over a period of many centuries, developed various methods of working the land suited to local conditions. For example, in Dagestan they have long practiced terraced grain and fruit-tree cultivation with irrigation. This system makes rational use of even the smallest piece of land.

Aside from the specific, unique, traditional economic customs rooted in local conditions (natural-historical) and shared by people inhabiting large regions of common ethnographic history, traditional joint characteristics of material and intellectual culture also have a long history. Some of these (common religious faiths, rites, and customs) have been or are being outlived under the conditions of contemporary socialism, while others not only retain their value under today's circumstances, but may do so even in the communist future, when the process which will occur will not be that of approximation, but of merging of nations. In some creatively reworked form, these features will be characteristic of the population of specific regions and areas, constituting a peculiarity of the local culture and way of life. Here we have in mind a skillful and functional creative utilization of the many valuable elements of folk experience in the area of rational planning and orientation of homes, their maximal adaptation to the climate of the given area; practical forms of clothing, diet, the daily schedule of working time under the given natural conditions and, finally, of artistic traditions in the field of native decorative work, etc.

The historically conditioned regional ties among people inhabiting the historical-ethnographic regions of our country were not affected even in the past by the differences in language and political boundaries. Under the conditions of the socialist system, these ties are being successfully strengthened and developed, this time on a new, high, socialist foundation of economic collaboration and brotherly friendship.

As an example of this type of cooperation among the peoples of Central Asia we may cite their irrigation projects produced in the prewar and war years by the joint efforts of collective farmers of the various republics, the construction of the Chardzhou-Kungrad railway line in the Kara-Kum desert, etc. Numerous power plants — the Kairak-Kum and Uch-Kurgan hydroelectric plants, and the Chardarin Reservoir on the Syr-Dar'ia — have been built by the joint efforts of various republics. Three republics — Uzbekistan, Tadjikistan, and Kazakhstan — are combining their efforts in opening the Hungry Steppe to agriculture. One could multiply the examples of inter-republic economic ties at the governmental level. These will be increased in the years immediately ahead in connection with the realization of the great undertakings planned by the January Plenum of the Central Committee of the Communist Party of the Soviet Union for the irrigation and opening of the desert and delta regions of Central Asia and Kazakhstan.

As another example we may cite the Transcaucasus, where economic community came into being before the Revolution, during the capitalist era. However, under the conditions of Soviet power, in which the economy of the republics of the Transcaucasus has been developed in accordance with a unified plan, the economic ties among these peoples have grown immeasurably. This has substantially reinforced the economic foundations of the friendship among the peoples of Georgia, Azerbaidjan, and Armenia. The economic collaboration and mutual aid of the Transcaucasian republics have found clear expression in such actions as the creation of a unified power system in the Transcaucasus, the building of the Stalin Iron and Steel Mill of the Transcaucasus in Georgia, which uses iron ore from Azerbaidjan, and the construction of the Transcaucasus Gas Pipeline through which gas from the Karadag deposit in Azerbaidjan will be transmitted through Baku to the Georgian and Armenian capital cities, Tbilisi and Erevan.

The ties among the socialist nations of the major historical-ethnographic regions in the fields of science, culture, art, and so forth, are growing and becoming stronger with each passing day.

The fact that people from neighboring republics work and live side by side at industrial en-

terprises and in cities, and that there are collective and state farms of mixed nationality, is of very great importance to the process of gradual approximation by the peoples of our country. There are cases on such collective farms, of which there are very many particularly in Central Asia and Kazakhstan, in which a special kind of division of labor is established with the most functional use of the work skills of each nationality. Thus, cotton-growing is done by teams of Tadjiks, Uzbeks, or Turkmens; cattle-raising by Kirgiz or Kazakhs, who are experienced in this; Koreans do the rice planting, and so forth.

The resettlement of collective farmers and state farm workers from isolated farmsteads and small settlements scattered over their former holdings into large socialist settlements with modern conveniences, as well as the new forms of social and cultural life and family structure (in particular, the increase in mixed marriages which in the past were in many cases taboo under religious law or the prejudices of custom) — all these phenomena of present-day life are active factors in the progressive process of approximation of various nations and small nationalities both in rural localities and particularly in the cities.

The process whereby peoples have been drawing closer in the country as a whole began before the Revolution. However, under the conditions of the tsarist autocracy this process was complicated, on the one hand, by the policy of Russification of the tsarist government, and on the other by the increase in local nationalism as a reaction to this policy. As a consequence of the application of the Leninist nationality policy and the achievement of practical equality among all the peoples of the USSR, the process of drawing closer lost its antagonistic characteristics. It was expressed most clearly in the selfless help given by more developed nations (the Russian, Ukrainian, and so forth) to peoples who were backward in economic and cultural development as a consequence of the colonial oppression of the tsarist autocracy. It was only as a consequence of this all-round assistance in the field of economics, culture and the rest that a real non-capitalist development of these peoples and their involvement in socialism became possible.

The friendship and unity of all the peoples of the Soviet land were manifested with tremendous force during World War II. In the postwar period, the construction projects of communism and the opening of the virgin territories played an enormous role in this respect. These undertakings gave rise to a national movement for the accelerated development of the economy and culture of the Soviet land.

Reinforcement of the ties among the peoples of the Soviet Union is greatly furthered by the proper distribution of productive capacities over the territory of the country, the USSR-wide division of labor, the development of the national economy in accordance with the Seven-Year Plan and the specialization and many-sided development of the economies of the individual republics and the large economic-geographic regions. All this constitutes the foundation for establishment of higher forms of economic collaboration and, at the same time, of a firm basis for the growth of a more intimate collaboration, communion, and cultural relationships among the republics.

Industrialization and the growth of the urban population are also important factors facilitating contact between members of various nationalities. The census data of 1959 are very suggestive in this respect. They show that virtually all the cities of Central Asia, the Caucasus, and the Baltic have an extremely mixed population in terms of nationality. This makes these cities important centers of the international unification of the working population. Here representatives both of the native population and of other Soviet peoples work side by side at industrial enterprises, in government offices, and in schools and higher educational institutions. It is increasingly common to find as many as ten nationalities and even more on a single collective or state farm. These include not only people native to the area, but those of the most varied origins.

Here it is appropriate to recall Khrushchev's recent speech at the conference of leading agriculturalists in Kazakhstan. "You should pride yourselves on the fact that in your republic, members of 100 nationalities and peoples of the So-

viet Union live and labor in friendly fashion, as a single family, and in political and moral unity." [20]

The Russian language is playing an extremely important part in the process of the approximation of the socialist nations and the small peoples of the USSR. It is gradually becoming their second native tongue. According to the data of the 1959 census, 124,100,000 persons of the total of 208,800,000 inhabitants of the USSR, or 59%, regarded Russian as their native tongue. [21] A great proportion of these (113,900,000) are Russians, but 10,200,000 persons of other nationalities, or 10.8% of them, [22] have adopted Russian as their native tongue. Unfortunately, the census does not provide information on the Russian language as a second language, and therefore we cannot present precise data on this generally observable phenomenon.

In the constituent republics, despite the fact that the Russian language has become the customary second language, the position of the native language is observed to be stable or, perhaps, to show some increase as the language of choice of the given republic (to a considerable degree as a consequence of the successful process of national consolidation).

At present, we learn from the 1959 census, the bulk of the population in the majority of the 15 constituent republics consists of the native nation of that republic. In three republics, the indigenous nationality represents more than 80% of the total population (88% in Armenia, 83.3% in the Russian SFSR, 81.1% in Belorussia); in three from 70 to 80% (79.3% in Lithuania, 76.8% in the Ukraine, and 74.6% in Estonia); in six from 60 to 70% (67.5% in Azerbaidjan, 65.4% in Moldavia, 64.3% in Georgia, 62.2% in Uzbekistan, 62% in Latvia, and 60.9% in Turkmenia); in one it is over 50% (Tadjik — 53.1%), and finally there are but two in which it is less than half (40.5% in Kirgizia, and 30.0% in Kazakhstan). [23]

These data also present convincing information on the dominance of the national official languages. The flourishing of the languages of the socialist nations, the press and the enormous literature published in these languages, their significance in the development of education and in the cultural life of the republic, all demonstrate that the broad dissemination of the Russian language occurs here not on the basis of the ouster or even reduction in the role of the nationality languages, but parallel with the growth and flourishing of the latter — i.e., as a second language. This is an important fact refuting the slanderous concoctions of foreign writers to the effect that a policy of Russification is allegedly being pursued in the Soviet Union.

The role of the Russian language in the contemporary life of the socialist nations of the USSR was well expressed by the Secretary of the Central Committee of the Communist Party of Uzbekistan, Sharif Rashidov, in his speech at the Second Congress of the Intelligentsia of Uzbekistan: "A thorough study of the Russian language and the treasures of Russian literature, science, and engineering is of vast importance to the strengthening and development of the ties among the working people of the various nationalities of our country. It is thanks to the Russian language that the achievements of each republic in the field of science, engineering, and culture become the property of all the peoples." (24)

The Russian language plays a special role in those autonomous republics and oblasts inhabited by a number of nationalities. The multi-national Dagestani ASSR, the Kabardino-Balkarian ASSR, and the Karachaevo-Circassian Autonomous Oblast are instances of this. In these autonomous units, the Russian language is the primary means of communication among the resident native peoples speaking different languages.

A similar situation is observed in the Far North, where intensive linguistic and cultural coming together of ethnographic groups is in process. In the Yakut and Komi ASSRs the small peoples frequently convert to the use of the Yakut and Komi languages. On the other hand, the process of mastery of the Russian language by the native peoples is quite perceptible in the North as a whole. Writing and education in the languages of the peoples of the Far North, as a transition stage in acclimatizing these peoples to a higher culture, played a very positive role in its time. Even today a considerable amount of textbook publishing is done in the languages of the Far

North. However, these books are not always used. It is significant that the Chukchi of the Nizhne-Kolyma raion of the Yakut ASSR themselves proposed conversion of their schools to the Russian language in 1950, and won their point, as did the Koriaks of the Koriak National Okrug of Kamchatka Oblast in 1955-1956.

At the same time we know that neither the Russian language nor the dozens of other official languages in use in the multi-national Soviet state are forced upon anyone. Every Soviet citizen has the right to choose as he wishes from among these languages the one which he deems most desirable for himself and his children in terms of education and use as a means of communication with other persons. This freedom of choice of language is one of the distinctive characteristics of Soviet democracy. It is emphasized in the Law on Strengthening the Ties Between Education and Practical Life and on the Further Progress of the System of Public Education in the USSR. This law states that steps must be taken to guarantee to parents in the constituent and autonomous republics the possibility of resolving as they wish the matter of the school to which they send their children, in terms of language of instruction. If the child is sent to a school where instruction is in the language of one of the constituent republics, the child may also study Russian, if he so desires. If education is in the Russian language, he may study the language of the given republic.

There is yet another most important aspect of the development of the nationalities of our country that must be considered here. This is the matter of the new, Soviet-wide forms of culture and life, whose formation is intimately related to the ethnic processes in progress.

Prior to the October Revolution, certain of the ethnographic features of culture and family structure of each people were determined by the backward level of socioeconomic development, the poor standard of living, the insularity of the people and their isolation from more cultured areas. Therefore many elements of culture and life were, from the very onset of the construction of socialism, doomed to disappearance or fundamental transformation, inasmuch as they were incompatible with the new life. Their destruction and displacement occurred throughout the Soviet period and continues to this day. The formation of a culture of the peoples of the USSR that was socialist in content and national in form took place simultaneously with the process of the construction of socialism.

The socialist content includes elements of culture held in common by all the socialist nations, such as Marxist-Leninist philosophy, a high level of political ideology, a conscious communist attitude toward labor. It is also manifested in socialist realism in the field of literature and art, etc., i.e., in the traits that characterize the cultural and moral nature of Soviet people regardless of nationality.

The vivid and unique national features of the culture and life of each socialist nation incorporate all the progressive traditions and forms inherited from their ancestors which have prospects of further development in the future.

The socialist content gives rise to and unifies the forms of national culture, so different in language, everyday customs, and art forms, which, in our country, develop not in isolation but in intimate contact and interrelation with each other.

The treatment of the problem of an all-union culture is of fundamental significance, particularly if we bear in mind that bourgeois theoreticians, who advocate a non-national, cosmopolitan culture, try to assert that socialist culture is incompatible with national culture, allegedly depriving it of its distinctiveness and destroying it.

Unfortunately, there are some practical workers and researchers who picture the all-union culture as something featureless and gray, lacking vivid artistic aspect. They are inclined to substitute for it the concept of "European" culture which often, however, can hardly be regarded or recommended as a model to be followed by all peoples of the world. For example, the so-called European types of clothing, mechanically introduced into the Eastern republics from the cold and temperate zones (suits with ties, felt hats, etc.), could not be regarded as convenient or adapted to hot climates. More serious thought than is now given to this subject must be given

to creative modification of certain local forms of native costume and to the development, on the basis thereof, of new, beautiful, hygienic and convenient types of clothing. European features of material culture do not by any means represent a civilized way of life at all times or as a matter of course.

The Union-wide culture is international. A unique and intensive process of continuous coming together and interpenetration of the national cultures of large and small peoples is occurring before our very eyes. This historically unprecedented phenomenon deserves special research into all its aspects. It is manifested in science, literature, the plastic arts, theater, the motion picture, music. Cooperation in cultural life is acquiring constantly broader dimensions. The best books of the writers of the various republics are being translated into the Russian and other languages. It is ever more common to see writers and poets turning to themes from the lives of peoples of some nationality other than their own. The artistic intelligentsia of one nation familiarizes the population of the other republics with its art. The tradition of ten-day festivals of literature and the arts which had arisen in Moscow has now been replaced by the new custom of joint meetings of writers of the different republics, mutual exchanges of road tours by the national theaters, choral and dance companies. The socialist art of one people finds its way to the heart of the other and becomes familiar to it. All this enriches the life of the mind, assists in the development of high esthetic tastes, and accelerates the cultural progress of the entire Soviet people.

Talented works of literature and art and the distinguished works of the plastic artists of the various nations are becoming the property of the Soviet land as a whole, serve to represent the culture of the Soviet Union in foreign lands, and inspire people of all continents.

The same thing occurs in everyday life. Ethnographic observations permit numerous examples to be cited of the all-union dissemination of elements of the material culture of various peoples: articles of clothing, dishes, etc. The embroidered Ukrainian blouse has become a favorite item of clothing in Central Asia. In remote Turkmen mountain villages women and girls make themselves Hutsul jackets, decorating them with Ukrainian or their own national embroidery motifs. The convenient, loose Uzbek woman's dress of attractive hand-woven shoi silk has spread throughout Central Asia. The smart Central Asian skullcap is worn during the summer all over our country. This is also true of rugs and wall hangings of various types. Applied and decorative art works of the various peoples are the most favored gifts, and may be found in the home of any worker or collective farmer, alongside his favorite books translated from other languages into his own.

Union-wide literature is a most important factor in the growth of internationalism and the coming together of the peoples of the Soviet Union.

Evaluations of the cultural heritage and household traditions of the peoples of the USSR are frequently erroneous, and this brings very negative consequences in its train. On the one hand there are efforts, clearly nationalistic in tendency, to make a fetish of the entire ancient culture and numerous residual aspects of the old way of life. In this connection we cannot pass over in silence the efforts of certain architects to artificially create an allegedly "national" style for public buildings and dwelling houses, with an uncritical use of elements of religious architecture: mosques, mausoleums, etc. Dissemination of these forms of culture and art inhibits the processes of transformation of the way of life, and creates conditions for the retention of ideological stagnation, including a particularly religious world outlook. The Alisher Navoi Theater of Opera and Ballet in Tashkent, of which A. V. Shchusev was the architect, may be regarded as a genuine example of a creative approach to the national architecture and decorative arts of the Uzbek people, and of the reworking of its cultural traditions in the spirit of socialist realism. The finest Uzbek craftsmen in the folk arts — wood and alabaster carvers and the like — took part in the decoration of the theater.

At the same time, unfortunately, the importance of a careful attitude toward the cultural heritage,

the preservation and further creative development of valuable rational elements in this heritage, are frequently ignored on the plea that these are merely "survivals of the old way of life," which allegedly have no place in Soviet reality. "Leftist" attempts to emasculate national forms in the culture of the peoples, a contemptuous attitude toward the folk experience of many centuries, toward work skills, artistic tastes and craftsmanship, have negative results. It is no secret to anyone that entire branches of beautiful applied art are being irretrievably lost in many republics due to the inattentive, negligent attitude of local agencies to folk art cooperatives and craftsmen.

Local climatic conditions are by no means always taken into consideration in standard plans for towns, rural settlements, and houses. There are many cases in which current architectural work designed for application in the Central Asian districts of the country or the Transcaucasus ignores the customs of the local population, such as the habit induced by the hot climate of spending a considerable portion of non-working time in the open air, on cool roofed verandas and in gardens. Both in the rural localities and towns of these districts, life in the intense heat of summer is very difficult unless dwelling houses are surrounded by massed greenery — shady gardens, pools, and irrigation ditches — and equipped with large, shaded terraces.

The experience and useful skills of the peoples of the North are also still inadequately used. Local agencies frequently attempt to involve the limited labor supply available among the peoples of the North in branches of the economy in which their experience cannot be utilized — coal and ore mines, and lumbering. At the same time, the traditional pursuits of the North face a shortage of experienced reindeer-herders, hunters, and fishermen. Houses made of prefabricated panels, not suited to the severe climatic conditions of the tundra, are shipped to the North, as are clothing and footwear made to suit the needs of the central districts of the country, while local types of clothing are pronounced "survivals of the old way of life," etc.

It is necessary to design and introduce the

industrial manufacture of items of material culture which suit the conditions of the various geographic zones. Here, on the one hand, due consideration must be given to the work experience of the native peoples, while on the other full use must be made of scientific and engineering progress. Together they can result in the most appropriate types of houses, clothing, furniture, utensils, etc.

Very instructive in this respect are Khrushchev's recent statements in the Virgin Soil Territory and at Alma-Ata, specifically with respect to the broad utilization of reeds, a native material of construction, in the steppe areas, and on the usefulness of the yurt, under present conditions, as housing for shepherds on range pastures. (25) There are some "leftist" officials who have frequently spoken of the yurt as the very embodiment of the "old way of life." The fact is that this form of lightweight portable dwelling, developed by the pastoral peoples of the plains over many centuries, and which has long ceased to be the primary form of dwelling among the Kazakhs, Kirgiz, and other Central Asian peoples who have abandoned the nomadic way of life, would even today be desirable in the range pasturelands. Khrushchev was also right in pointing to the need for the manufacture of high-quality felts or equivalent synthetic substitutes as covering for the yurt which would be capable, under continental climatic conditions, of providing good protection against the cold of night, the morning damp, rain, and the merciless rays of the sun. The efforts of local agencies to substitute canvas for felt proved very unsuccessful, because canvas admits cold and moisture, while canvas-covered yurts are hot and stuffy during the day. Yurts covered with foam plastic are now being experimented with. (26) It would also be desirable, in terms of the need to improve the yurt, to consider the experience of the Mongolian People's Republic, where the design and internal arrangement of the yurt are well adapted to the cultural and daily living requirements of the livestock farmer of today. No less important is the problem of mobile housing for the reindeer-breeders and hunters of the North. The status of the Caucasian ankle-length sheep-

skin cloak with very broad padded shoulders [burka], a garment exceedingly well suited to the needs of the mountain shepherd, is about the same. Today, unfortunately, the manufacture of these cloaks has been reduced to a minimum.

Many very pressing practical problems of economic progress are indissolubly connected with the national progress and national cultures of the peoples of the USSR, and demand ethnographic data for their proper solution. Thus, for example, evaluation of ethnic aspects of the life of the population and the work skills of the various peoples is important for the solution of problems of redistribution and strengthening of labor resources in the newly pioneered districts of the country. National differences in clothing, housing, and food must be considered in compiling plans for providing the population of various zones with the commodities they need to improve their living standards. Further reorganization of the daily lives of the rural population of the various national districts and the development of their culture constitute a special branch of government planning — one for which ethnographic data are necessary.

The questions raised in the present article do not by any means exhaust the problems involved in investigating the processes of national development of the peoples of the USSR during the transition to communism. Thus, for example, the problem of the change now occurring in the psychological makeup of the socialist nations is exceedingly interesting and complex. It requires the joint efforts of researchers in various specialties, as do a number of other theoretical questions. It seems to us that the study of such a form of socialist internationalism as the improvement in the friendly relations between the socialist nations of the USSR and those of foreign lands, facilitating the struggle of the progressive forces of the world against reaction, colonialism, and racist barbarity, would be of particular importance.

Footnotes

1) V. K. Gardanov, "The Work of the Dagestan Expedition in 1950," Kratkie soobshcheniya In-ta

Etnografii AN SSSR, No. XIV, Moscow, 1952, pp. 34-38; L. I. Lavrov, "Some Results of the Dagestan Expedition of 1950-1952," ibid., No. XIX, Moscow, 1953, pp. 3-7; Narody Dagestana, M. O. Kosven and Kh. O. Khashaev, eds., Moscow, 1955; T. A. Zhdanko, "A New Historical Phase in the Leninist Nationality Policy (A Contribution to the Problem of the Development of the Socialist Nations of Central Asia on the Road to Communism)," SE, 1960, No. 2; Ia. R. Vinnikov, "The Present Distribution of Peoples and Ethnic Groups in the Fergana Valley," Sredneaziatskii etnograficheskii sbornik, II, TIE, nov. ser., Vol. XLVII, Moscow, 1959; L. S. Tolstova, Karakalpaki Ferganskogo oazisa, Nukus, 1959; I. S. Gurvich, "Ethnic Processes Presently Occurring In Northern Yakutia," SE, 1960, No. 5, etc.

2) See Resolution of the 10th Congress, RKP(b), "Current Tasks of the Party with Respect to the Nationality Question," KPSS v rezolyutsiyakh i resheniyakh s'ezdov, konferentsii i plenumov TsK, Part I, 7th ed., 1954, pp. 558-563.

3) Ia. R. Vinnikov, "The Clan-Tribal Makeup and Distribution of the Kirgiz in Southern Kirgizia," Trudy kirgizkoi arkheologo-etnograficheskoi ekspeditsii, Vol. I, Moscow, 1956; S. M. Abramzon, "The Ethnic Composition of the Kirgiz Population of Northern Kirgizia," ibid., Vol. IV, Moscow, 1960; T. A. Zhdanko, "Outlines of the Historical Ethnography of the Karakalpaks," TIE, nov. seriia, Vol. IX, Moscow, 1950; R. Kuzeev, Ocherki istoricheskoi etnografii bashkir, Part I, Ufa, 1957.

4) Vsesoyuznaia perepis' naseleniia 1926 goda, Vol. XVII, Moscow, 1928, p. 12.

5) B. Kh. Karmysheva, "The 'Tiruk' Ethnographic Group Among the Uzbeks," SE, 1960, No. 1, p. 6.

6) Op. cit., supra 4, Vol. XV, Uzbekskaia SSR, pp. 144-149; Vol. VIII, Kirgizskaia SSR, pp. 216-219.

7) Ibid., Vol. XVII, p. 12.

8) Ibid.

9) Sh. I. Inogamov, Etnicheskii sostav naseleniia i etnograficheskaia karta Ferganskoi doliny v granitsakh Uzbekskoi SSR, author's abstract of candidate's degree dissertation, Tashkent, 1955; Ia. R. Vinnikov, Sovremennoe rasselenie narodov i etnograficheskikh grupp v Ferganskoi doline.

10) L. S. Tolstova, "The Karakalpaks of the Fergana Valley"; same author, "The Karakalpak Ethnographic Group Among the Uzbeks of Samarkand Oblast," Vestnik Karakalpakskogo filiala Akademii Nauk Uzbekskoi SSR, Nukus, 1960, No. 2.

11) Op. cit., supra 4, Vol. XVII, p. 12.

12) Iu. D. Deshiriev, Batsbiiskii iazyk, Moscow, 1953.

13) Ocherki obshchei etnografii, S. P. Tolstov, M. G. Levin, and N. N. Cheboksarov, eds., Aziatskaia chast' SSSR, Moscow, 1960, pp. 90-92.

14) Even P. K. Uslar noted the presence of a common language ("Bolmats" — the soldier's tongue) among the Avars and Ando-Tsezians proper. See P. K. Uslar, Etnografiia Kavkaza. Iazykoznanie, Vol. II, Tiflis, 1899, p. 5. The Soviet linguists M. S. Saidov and Sh. I. Mikailov observed that "Bolmats," which was initially a means of oral communication among the peoples of the Avar group, had acquired written form as of the 19th century and formed the foundation of a literary language of the Avars. See M. S. Saidov, "The Unvoiced Lateral LI and the Unvoiced Velar Kh' in the Avar Literary Language," in Iazyki Severnogo Kavkaza i Dagestana, Moscow, 1948; same author, "The Origin of Written Language Among the Avars," Iazyki Dagestana, No. I, Makhachkala, 1948; Sh. I. Mikailov, "The Paths of Formation of the Avar Literary Language," Iazyki Dagestana, No. II, Makhachkala, 1954.

15) Certain researchers classify the Archin language in the Lezgin group, noting, however, the pronounced influence of the Avar and Lak languages. See E. A. Bokarev, "Dagestanskie iazyki," in Mladopis'mennye iazyki narodov SSSR, Moscow-Leningrad, 1959, pp. 248, 260.

16) The written language of the Tabasaran dates only from 1932.

17) The system of marriage among close relatives, characteristic of Dagestan, was, as accurately stated by L. I. Lavrov, one of the specific reasons for the retention of the diversity of languages there. See L. I. Lavrov, "The Reasons for the Multiplicity of Languages in Dagestan," SE, 1951, No. 2, pp. 202-203.

18) V. I. Lenin, Soch., Vol. 19, p. 452.

19) A. Kazakbaev, "Traditions or Survivals?",

88

Izvestia, June 8, 1960.

20) Izvestia, March 25, 1961.

21) Central Statistical Bureau of the USSR Council of Ministers, Uroven' obrazovaniia, natsional'nyi sostav, vozrastnaia struktura i razmeshchenie naseleniia SSSR po respublikam, kraiam i oblastiam po dannym Vsesoyuznoi perepisi naseleniia 1959, Gosstatizdat, Moscow, 1960, p. 12.

22) Ibid., p. 12.

23) Ibid., pp. 13-16. For the reasons for some reduction in the percentage of the native nationalities in Kazakhstan and a number of other republics from 1939 to 1959, see ibid., p. 16.

24) Pravda Vostoka, December 12, 1959.

25) N. S. Khrushchev, "New Stage in the Conquest of the Virgin Soil and the Tasks of Agriculture in Kazakhstan," speech at conference of agriculturalists at Alma-Ata, March 21, 1961, Izvestia, March 25, 1961.

26) Ch. Aitmanov and S. Il'in, "A New Yurt for the Shepherd," Pravda, June 12, 1961.

Sovetskaia etnografiia, 1962, No. 2

L. P. Potapov

ETHNOGRAPHIC STUDY OF THE SOCIALIST CULTURE AND MODE OF LIFE

OF THE PEOPLES OF THE USSR

The present stage of development of Soviet society, which has adopted a firm program for the construction of communism, poses new problems for Soviet science, in particular for ethnography. The decisions of the 22nd Congress of the CPSU and the new Program of the Communist Party of the Soviet Union have provided a clear definition of the role of the social sciences in the next two decades.

Ethnographers, whose field places them in intimate association with the rank-and-file of the people, facilitate the successful progress of Soviet society toward communism by their researches. Ethnographic studies of the contemporary culture and mode of life of the numerous nations and nationalities of our country have frequently provided the key to solution of various practical problems in the building of communism. Because of their direct observations of the life of the peoples, ethnographers are in a position to offer specific proposals with respect to numerous complex problems.

The present article contains a brief survey of studies conducted by Soviet ethnographers in in-

vestigating the contemporary culture and mode of life of the peoples of the USSR and of certain related proposals bearing on the further development of ethnographic research.

* * *

Ethnographic study of the culture and mode of life of the peoples of the USSR began in the first years of the Great October Socialist Revolution, in conjunction with the practical needs of the Soviet state. The awe-inspiring objectives involved in construction of a socialist society were resolved by the Communist Party and the Soviet government under the conditions of a multi-national state. The 10th Congress of the VKP(b), led by V. I. Lenin, elaborated a practical program for building socialism among the Soviet peoples in the very first stage of the history of the young state, which had abolished colonial oppression within our country and had successfully defended itself in the struggle with international imperialism. It was necessary to eliminate the economic, political and cultural backwardness of many formerly oppressed peoples and nations, which differed as to language and origin, historical antecedents, economic status, level of cultural advancement, and distinctive characteristics of their mode of life. In order to assist these nationalities to advance along the path of social, economic and cultural progress, we had to know not only their status at that time but their historical past, ethnographic features of their culture, etc.

Ethnographers proved to be among the first in the Soviet historical sciences to place their work at the service of the construction of socialism. The Soviet government supported the establishment of centers of scientific ethnography in the country. One such center was founded in 1917 under the Academy of Sciences (the Commission for Study of the Tribal Composition of the Population of the USSR and Its Adjacent Countries [KIPS]. In 1919 ethnographic scholarship and personnel training were organized on a large scale in Leningrad, first at the Geographical Institute, then at Leningrad University, and also in Moscow University. Ethnographic centers soon appeared in Kiev, Minsk, Tbilisi, Baku, Tashkent, Irkutsk and other cities. The ethnographic researches of those years were devoted to study of the current state of the economy, culture and mode of life of the peoples and were given practical application in the delimitation of national boundaries, in which ethnic composition and ethnographic characteristics were given major consideration in establishing various agencies and offices of Soviet government among peoples in remote borderlands. The researches were also used in arranging for marketing their products and provision of supplies to them; in organization of the development of education, medical affairs, cultural and enlightenment activities, and so forth. Many ethnographers went out to do field work for government agencies and institutions and took a practical part in the development of the culture of the nationalities. At the same time, ethnographers were trained from personnel of local government institutions and party organizations. They were, of course, also intimately involved with the practical reorganization of the lives of the peoples under study.

The Committee for Assistance to the Peoples of the Northern Borderlands under the Presidium of the VTsIK [the Committee of the North], which played a major, positive role in organizing and developing economic and cultural progress among the backward peoples of the USSR and which is widely known for its work, included in its membership not only prominent figures in government but leading ethnographers. The role of ethnographers in preparing censuses, in developing scripts for numerous formerly backward peoples, particularly those of the Far North and Siberia, etc., was considerable.

Thus, a characteristic feature of the ethnographic studies of the initial period in the history of the Soviet state was their intimate relationship to the practical undertakings and needs of Soviet construction. However, as research and description, these studies naturally reflected forms of culture and daily life of the peoples which, although chronologically current, were essentially old and outdated and carried over from the prerevolutionary past.

The publication of these ethnographic works began as far back as the first half of the 1920's. The first ethnographic study devoted to the present day (1) was more of historical than scientific interest. It contained ethnographic observations and semi-literary essays. The compendium is characterized by an effort to differentiate the old from the new mode of life, given birth to by Soviet reality. In the mid-1920's the ethnographers published a symposium, The Komsomol in the Countryside [Komsomol v derevne], which undertook to demonstrate the role of Komsomol youth in building the new life. (2) This marked the beginning of discussions in Leningrad and Moscow on the urgency and need for ethnographic study of the new Soviet culture and mode of life in the villages.

The second half of the 1920's saw the expansion of publication of ethnographic materials, mainly by various museums (chiefly the central ones), which at that time conducted large-scale research and, as a rule, were centers of the movement for regional study that was developing on a mass scale. The Museum of Anthropology and Ethnography of the USSR Academy of Sciences issued a number of symposia in which theoretical studies and ethnographic field research were published. However they reflected only old characteristics of the mode of life of the peoples of the USSR, which were going out of existence. (3) The Ethnographic Division of the Russian Museum in Leningrad published three volumes of its Materials on Ethnography [Materialy po etnografii], but here too the data were predominantly descriptive of the old mode of life and peasant culture, (4) although an effort was made to present ethnographic observations on the mode of life of the countryside in Soviet times (1919-1925) as well. The Museum of Ethnology in Moscow and the Moscow Regional Museum began to publish ethnographic monographs and symposia. (5) Ethnographic study of the peoples of the USSR was participated in by scientific societies as well — the Geographic Society, the Society of Friends of Natural Science, Anthropology and Ethnography — which all published the results of their researches. (6) Monographic descriptions of the village began to appear. (7) The Commission for Study of Tribal Composition engaged in particularly large-scale publishing activity. It issued a number of valuable ethnographic maps and monographs. (8)

At the end of the 1920's and in the early 1930's, when our peasantry took the path of mass collectivization, upon which the policy of abolition of the kulaks as a class was based, ethnographic study of the peoples of the USSR again made a useful contribution to the building of socialism. During those years studies of the social structure of many peoples of the USSR, as it existed at the time of the October Revolution, were conducted. Both ethnographers and historians were able, in specific researches, to expose the notorious "theory of clan structure" which was allegedly characteristic of various peoples. Basing themselves on this "theory," local right-wing elements, particularly bourgeois nationalists, denied the existence of exploiting classes among the many millions of peasantry of a number of peoples, among them the Kazakhs, Kirgiz, Turkmens, Yakuts, Altais, Khakass, etc. Taking this "theory" as their point of departure, right-wing elements in general, and bourgeois nationalists

in particular, took a stand against collectivization, against the elimination of exploiting classes, and so forth. The special researches of ethnographers and historians fully confirmed the correctness of the course taken by our party toward eliminating exploiting elements even among peoples where class society was in fact present, although the bourgeois nationalists denied this. (9)

The ethnographers correctly posed the question of the reactionary role of vestiges of clan society among many Soviet peoples in the period of the building of socialism. At the same time, the first studies devoted to the collective farm peasantry of various Soviet peoples — the Russian, Ukrainian, Belorussian, Uzbek, Turkmen, Tadjik, Armenian, Altai and others — began to make their appearance. (10)

However, in those years ethnographic study of the collective farm peasantry was not properly developed. The result was that the first origins of new forms of culture and mode of life among various Soviet peoples under the influence of the practical activity of the Communist Party and the Soviet government were inadequately studied and recorded by ethnographers; this applied particularly to Siberia and the Caucasus. One of the most fundamental turning points in the history of our state, which brought about a basic change in the culture and mode of life of all the peoples of the USSR without exception, proved to be quite inadequately researched in the ethnographic sense. As a consequence, theoretical works generalizing this most important problem of the day did not appear. Of course, the guiding center for ethnography was responsible for this state of affairs. At that time the ethnographic center was part of the structure of the Academy of Sciences in Leningrad where, during those years and in the subsequent 1930's, the dominant tendency was to concentrate ethnographic work on the study of prerevolutionary culture and life and on description of various vestiges of primitive communal society. There were also efforts to treat ethnography as a science concerned solely with primitive society and its vestiges in present-day life. Soviet ethnographers had to put forth no little effort and time to overcome that mistaken tendency.

Ethnographic study of the culture and mode of life of the peoples of the USSR developed on a broader and deeper basis only after the Second World War — i.e., in the past 15 or 16 years. A most important feature here is the fact that it is not only the collective farm peasantry but the working class of a given nationality that is now under study. As we know, a working class made its appearance in a number of socialist nations and peoples only after the October Revolution in conjunction with the rapid development of various forms of industry among them. Ethnographic study of the culture and mode of life of the workers under these conditions is of major theoretical and practical interest, and reveals important aspects of this process. This was demonstrated, for example, in a monograph by the young Turkmen ethnographer, Sh. Annaklychev, The Mode of Life of the Oil Workers of Nebit-Dag and Kum-Dag [Byt rabochikh-neftianikov Nebit-Daga i Kum-Daga], which he presented as his dissertation in the Institute of Ethnography of the USSR Academy of Sciences. (11) Ethnographic study of the contemporary culture and mode of life of the workers fills a major gap, the existence of which usually made it impossible to provide a complete and scientific description of the culture and mode of life of a people having its own working class. Study of the mode of life of the workers was undertaken by the Institute of Ethnography. Its example was followed by a number of scientific institutions in our country, as well as by various research institutes in the lands of the socialist community (particularly Czechoslovakia). One of these first efforts was publication of an article by N. N. Cheboksarov on the mode of life of the workers of Moscow. (12) Ethnographic studies of the Russian workers of the Central Urals (the Nizhnii Tagil Expedition under V. Iu. Krupianskaia) have been and are being conducted. A large monograph by Krupianskaia is in preparation. She and others have published a number of articles. (13) The distinctive features of the mode of life of the Ural workers of Sverdlovsk, Perm and Kirov oblasts have been studied by G. S. Maslova (these data have been published in the synposium Materials and Researches on the Ethnography of the Russian Population of the Euro-

pean Portion of the USSR [Materialy i issledovaniia po etnografii russkogo naseleniia Evropeiskoi chasti SSSR]. (14) In the Southern Urals the same work was done by V. E. Gusev, who published an article titled "Experiences in Ethnographic Study of the Workers of the Old Factories in the Southern Urals" [Iz opyta etnograficheskogo izucheniia rabochikh starykh zavodov Iuzhnogo Urala]. (15) Considerable work was done in study of the way of life of the workers of the Sormovo Machinery Works, Red Sormovo, and of the textile city of Ivanovo, by personnel of the State Museum of Ethnography of the Peoples of the USSR (these data, unfortunately, were not published and were employed only in displays of the museum). Expeditions of the State Historical Museum engaged rather widely in collection of ethnographic materials. In the two volumes of the Transactions [Trudy] of that museum, edited by A.M. Pankratova, valuable materials were published on the position and mode of life of the workers of the Three-Mountain Mills in Moscow, the metallurgical industry of the Urals, and the workers of the Donbass, of Sormovo and others. (16)

Ethnographic studies of the culture and mode of life of the workers were conducted on a larger scale in the Ukraine. This made it possible to incorporate their results in the large work of theoretical generalization, The Ukrainians [Ukraintsy]. The data and researches on this problem were also reflected in a number of studies by Ukrainian scholars. (17)

Studies of the mode of life of the workers were initiated in Belorussia by ethnographers of the Institute of Art Study, Ethnography, and Folklore of the Academy of Sciences, Belorussian SSR, working at enterprises in the city of Minsk. The first results of this work are already being published. (18)

However, the volume of ethnographic research into the workers' mode of life is clearly inadequate. Research of this nature is being conducted on a larger scale in Georgia. Here a study is being made of the culture and mode of life of the workers of the Chiatura manganese industry and the Tkvibuli anthracite basin, of industrial enterprises built in the years of the socialist Five-Year Plans (the Kasin Cement Works, the

Zestafoni Ferroalloys Mill) and in the postwar period (the Kutaissi Auto Works, the Rustavi Integrated Iron and Steel Mill). Questions about the appearance of new groups of workers, their settlements and types of housing are being elaborated. Their families and family lives are being studied. Of the writings published in Russian, note must be taken of the interesting work of A. I. Robakidze and the writings of certain others. (19) A study of the workers in Armenia and Azerbaidjan has been begun. A number of studies in the Armenian language have been made (E. G. Karapetian, "The Culture and Mode of Life of the Workers of the Dzerzhinskii Machine-Tool Works" [Kul'tura i byt rabochikh stankostroitel'-nogo zavoda im. Dzerzhinskogo]; T. S. Temurchian's "Mode of Life and Culture of the Workers of the Armenian Textile Industry" [Byt i kul'tura rabochikh tekstil'noi promyshlennosti Armenii]). A. G. Trofimova has written a monograph titled The Culture and Mode of Life of the Baku Oil Workers (An Experiment in Ethnographic Research) [Kul'tura i byt bakinskikh neftianikov (Opyt etnograficheskogo izucheniia)] and "The Family and Family Life of the Azerbaidjani Oil Workers of Baku" [Sem'ia i semeinyi byt bakinskikh neftianikov-azerbaidzhantsev]. Unfortunately, not all of these works have yet seen publication.

The ethnographic study of the mode of life of the workers of the Central Asian republics and Kazakhstan is under way on a partial scale. In Uzbekistan this research is being conducted among workers of the agricultural machinery works of Tashkent. Its results are reflected in the writings of F. A. Aripov and G. Dmitrieva. (20) Already published is "Ethnographic Data on the Mode of Life of the Uzbek Workers of Tashkent and Andizhan" [Etnograficheskie materialy o byte rabochikh-uzbekov Tashkenta i Andizhana] by K. L. Zadykhina. (21) On Turkmenia there are the writings already referred to by Sh. Annaklychev, and on the culture and mode of life of the workers of Kirgizia there is an article by S. M. Abramzon, "The Past and Present of the Kirgiz Miners of Kyzyl-kiia" [Proshloe i nastoiaschee kirgizskikh shakhterov Kyzyl-Kiia]. (22) In Kazakhstan an ethnographic study of the

Kazakh workers of the Karaganda anthracite basin is under way.

The workers in the Baltic states and in the autonomous republics along the Volga and in Siberia have as yet not been touched by ethnographic study. This lag in ethnographic study of one of the most important problems of the present day is clearly impermissible.

Available data indicate that ethnographic study of the workers, which Soviet ethnographers have undertaken for the first time, is clearly neglected in many centers of scholarship in the constituent and autonomous republics. Therefore steps must be taken to eliminate this serious shortcoming.

The situation is considerably better with respect to ethnographic study of the culture and mode of life of the collective farm peasantry. In this regard it is already possible to speak of a history of the elaboration of a new problem in research, and of a considerable amount of experience accumulated by Soviet ethnographers. Note should be taken of the organizational work of the Institute of Ethnography of the USSR Academy of Sciences in the development of this activity. It convened two union-wide conferences of ethnographers (1951 and 1956) and has not only established contacts with various research institutions but has organized coordination of their work in ethnographic study of the culture and mode of life of the collective farm peasantry and workers of the peoples of the USSR. These measures, along with the publicizing of this new subject matter through the journal Sovetskaia etnografiia, have yielded positive results in attracting the attention and interest of Soviet ethnographers to this most important current problem.

The decisions of the 20th Congress of the CPSU and certain resolutions of the Presidium of the USSR Academy of Sciences taken for the purpose of effectuating the decisions of that congress (23) have played an important role in developing research into the most pressing problems of the day. However, a decisive turn in the direction of ethnographic study of problems of the building of socialism and gradual transition to the all-out building of communism occurred only after the historic 21st Extraordinary Party

Congress, which clearly defined the tasks of the social sciences. In the Seven-Year Plan of the Institute of Ethnography of the USSR Academy of Sciences, study of the socialist culture and mode of life of the collective farm peasantry and workers among various peoples of the USSR and the publication of collective works of theoretical generalization became the center of emphasis. A major special expedition has been organized on this problem. Its work embraces many areas of our country.

* * *

In order to provide some understanding of the scale and the most significant results of ethnographic study of the culture and mode of life of the collective farm peasantry of the USSR, it is necessary to make a brief survey of these investigations in the postwar period. Although, as yet, we lack works of generalization on the mode of life of collective farm peasantry for the Soviet Union as a whole, virtually all the constituent and autonomous republics and oblasts have been covered, and dozens of different nationalities have been embraced by these studies. However, these researches were conducted unevenly, as a consequence of which some nations and nationalities, including some of the largest, have been covered only to a small degree, and in some cases have not been studied at all. On the other hand, greater attention and better coverage have sometimes been given to individual small nationalities.

Ethnographic study of the socialist culture and mode of life of the Russian collective farm peasantry has clearly had inadequate ethnographic study. One can list no more than a few dozen published articles and pamphlets on this theme. (24) True, the Russian collective farm peasantry is the subject of two substantial monographs. We have in mind the books on the villages of Viriatino and Korablino written by teams. (25) Both books, particularly the former, result from long-term study of the culture and mode of life of the collective farm peasantry and yield valuable scientific materials and conclusions. The authors of the monograph on Viriatino village

introduced a new technique for field work. They initiated the surveying of each individual collective farm family and obtained very valuable material reflecting a picture of family structure, the cultural level of the collective farmers, and so forth. They made the first attempt to study the family budgets of collective farmers and to define the share of women's incomes in them. This made possible a more profound description of the pronounced improvement in the position of women in the modern Russian peasant home, and revelation of new forms of family relationships.

It is impossible in a brief survey article to offer evaluations of individual works, even major monographs. But one thing is clear: although these books and certain of the pamphlets and articles are doubtless of merit, they are quantitatively too few to permit truly deep and broad generalizations from the experience of the socialist reorganization of the culture and mode of life of the Russian collective farm peasantry. In this regard one can name only one special monograph and 20 or 30 published articles, pamphlets and authors' abstracts of dissertations. (27) However, Ukrainian ethnographers have reflected the study of the culture and mode of life of the collective farm peasantry in the above-cited work of theoretical generalization, The Ukrainians [Ukraintsy], which provides a general description of the socialist culture and mode of life of the collective farmers of the Ukraine. A positive role in the elaboration of this problem is played by the journal of ethnographers of the Ukraine, Narodna tvorchist' ta etnografiia, which systematically publishes articles and materials on these questions.

In recent years ethnographic study of the collective farm peasantry has also gotten under way in the Moldavian SSR, where a number of writings have been published and preparations for the publication of others are under way. (28)

With respect to Belorussia we refer the reader to a work by M. Ia. Grinblat and L. A. Molchanova, New Phenomena in the Mode of Life of the Collective Farm Village. An Attempt at an Ethnographic Study of the Bol'shevik Collective Farm, Khoinitskii Raion, Gomel' Oblast [Novye iavleniia v bytu kolkhoznoi derevni. Opyt etnograficheskogo izucheniia kolkhoza 'Bol'shevik' Khoinitskogo raiona Gomel'skoi oblasti], Minsk, 1958. Unfortunately, the authors published this valuable monograph in abbreviated form. Writings by A. I. Zalesskii and others, (29) as well as a number of dissertation abstracts, (30) are devoted to individual questions in the area of the mode of life of Belorussian collective farmers.

Some time later, a beginning was made toward ethnographic study of the present mode of life and culture of the collective farm peasantry in the constituent republics of the Baltic area, particularly Estonia. Until recently publications on these themes were limited solely to small articles in the periodical press. (31) The symposium Family and Family Life of the Collective Farmers of the Baltic Area [Sem'ia i semeinyi byt kolkhoznikov Pribaltiki], now in preparation, is a more substantial work on the same subject. (32) In recent years the plans of the institutes of history of the academies of sciences of the Lithuanian, Latvian and Estonian SSRs (1958-1965) have seen a considerable expansion of the attention devoted to current problems. Teams at these institutes have already prepared essays, "The Latvians," "The Lithuanians," "The Estonians," for the volume Peoples of the European Portion of the USSR [Narody Evropeiskoi chasti SSSR] in Peoples of the World [Narody mira], in which materials on the present mode of life and culture of the peoples of the Baltic states get considerable attention. Work has begun on large monographs on the socialist transformation of the economy, mode of life and culture of the collective farm population. Some dissertations by young scholars and graduate students at these institutes are devoted to contemporary problems. Research into the contemporary culture and mode of life of the collective farm peasantry of the Baltic states is being engaged in systematically by the Institute of Ethnography of the USSR Academy of Sciences. A monograph by L. N. Terent'eva devoted to the culture and mode of life of the Latvian peasantry, published in the Transactions of the Institute of Ethnography, USSR Academy of Sciences [Trudy Instituta etnografii AN SSSR], is of considerable significance. The writer studied the collective

farms of certain raions of the Latvian SSR over a considerable term of years. The book makes a detailed and rounded examination of all aspects of the contemporary lives of collective farmers. L. N. Terent'eva has also published a number of articles on this subject matter. (33) In 1959 the Institute of Ethnography of the USSR Academy of Sciences undertook a study of the contemporary culture and mode of life of Estonian collective farmers in Roplas raion.

Ethnographic study of the contemporary culture and mode of life of the collective farm peasantry of the Volga republics has now gotten under way. Publications on this subject are in preparation in the Mari, the Bashkir, the Chuvash and the Komi ASSRs. Large-scale work is under way in the Tatar ASSR, where a study is in progress of the contemporary culture and mode of life not only of the Tatar collective farm peasantry (work of N. I. Vorob'ev), but of Russian peasants living in Tataria (a study by E. P. Busygin of the clothing, settlement pattern and dwellings of the Russian rural population). Unfortunately, a number of interesting and valuable dissertations on the peoples of the Volga have not been published and are known only from authors' summaries. (34)

A more gratifying picture is seen if we review the work on ethnographic study of the mode of life and culture of collective farm peasantry of the Central Asia republics. A considerable service in this respect has been performed by the Division of Central Asia and Kazakhstan of the Institute of Ethnography of the USSR Academy of Sciences, which published as early as 1954 (jointly with the Institute of History of the Tadjik SSR Academy of Sciences) the first monograph devoted to a study of the Tadjik collective farm peasantry. The Division has established firm contacts with corresponding research institutions of Central Asia and Kazakhstan and has assisted them in organizing and developing ethnographic study of contemporary life. Inasmuch as there is a considerable literature on this subject with respect to the peoples of Central Asia, it would be desirable to offer a general description of it here. To begin with, we note a number of major monographs devoted to the culture and mode of life of the Tadjik, Uzbek, and Kirgiz collective farm peasantry. (35) These books which, on the basis of colorful concrete material, shed light upon various aspects of culture and mode of life of the collective farm peasantry among the peoples of Central Asia, provide material for some important generalizations and conclusions. Moreover, there are some brief monographs and articles containing valuable material and observations on the culture and mode of life of collective farm peasantry of the Central Asia peoples. (36) A considerable number of such articles have been published by the journal Sovetskaia etnografiia. (37) Perhaps a dozen monographs — dissertations for the candidate's degree defended at the Institute of Ethnography of the USSR Academy of Sciences alone — may be added to these. (38)

With respect to the peoples of the Caucasus, it may be said that virtually all the scholarly institutions of the Caucasian republics that could be expected to be involved are in fact engaged in ethnographic study of contemporary life. However, the number of writings published on culture and mode of life of the collective farm peasantry is as yet small. (39) Even smaller is the number of ethnographic writings on the collective farm peasantry of Azerbaidjan. (40) On the peoples of Armenia there are in print only a work by D. Vardumian in the Armenian language (41) and the book by A. Avdal. (42) With respect to the North Caucasus we must note I. Kh. Kalmykov's monograph, The Culture and Way of Life of the Circassian Collective Farm Aul [Caucasian or Central Asian mountain village] [Kul'tura i byt cherkesskogo kolkhoznogo aula]. (43)

Valuable materials and general evaluation of the culture and mode of life of collective farmers of the various peoples of Dagestan are contained in a collection of articles published by the Institute of Ethnography of the USSR Academy of Sciences. (44) For certain of the nationalities of the Caucasus (the Abkhazians, Adygeis and Azerbaidjanis) the results of studies of these questions have been set forth in dissertations for the candidate's degree, most of which, unfortunately, have not yet been published. (45)

Quantitatively, the greatest amount of ethnographic literature of the socialist culture and

way of life is that on peoples of Siberia, the Far North and the Far East. Most backward and oppressed in the past — politically, economically and culturally — these peoples have been the object of particular attention and concern on the part of the Communist Party and the Soviet government, as well as of the entire Soviet people. Here ethnographic study is of primary significance and is utterly essential to socialist construction, inasmuch as the steady advance of these nationalities to communism is occurring under highly unique circumstances and requires unremitting attention and aid to these peoples on the part of the Soviet state in all its branches. The triumphs and difficulties in socialist reorganization of the lives of the so-called small peoples of Siberia have had rather extensive reflection in the literature of Soviet ethnography. A major work of generalization by M. A. Sergeev has been published, which presents a history of the building of socialism among these peoples. (46) A book by V. N. Uvachan, an Evenk scholar, is on the subject of the transition to socialism of the small peoples of the North as illustrated by the materials for the Evenk and Taimyr National Okrugs. (47) A book by N. M. Koviazin has been published on collectivization in the National Okrugs of the Far North of the USSR. (48) In connection with the 30th anniversary of the Nen National Okrug, an article has been published by L. V. Khomich on the socialist culture and way of life of the Nentsy. (49) A work by E. V. Iakovleva has been published in Khabarovsk under the title The Small Nationalities Along the Amur After the Socialist Revolution [Malye narodnosti Priamur'ia posle sotsialisticheskoi revoliutsii], 1957. There is, it would appear, no Siberian nationality which has not had some light shed on it in our literature with respect to its mode of life and culture under socialism. (50) However, with few exceptions, these data are scattered among various articles and essays and, as a rule, have not been generalized. It is pleasant to observe that scholars, who themselves come from these nationalities, are participating in study of the socialist culture and modes of life of the Siberian peoples.

Siberia has acquired centers of research —

branches of the Academy of Sciences of the USSR (the Iakut and the Far Eastern branches), as well as local research institutions that do not fall into the system governed by the Academy (the Tuvan, Khakass, and Mountain-Altai Institutes of History, Language and Literature). All these scholarly institutions have begun fruitful research. Together with the scholars of Moscow, Leningrad and other cities, they are engaged in publication of ethnographic studies devoted to the socialist culture and mode of life of the nationalities of Siberia. It is the progress of these researches that has made possible the appearance of a work of generalization such as The Peoples of Siberia [Narody Sibiri], in which particular attention is given to description of the socialist culture and modes of life of the Siberian nationalities. (51) This same circumstance favored the appearance of various monographs on the histories of particular Siberian peoples (the Iakuts, Buriats, Altai, Khakass, Tuvans and others), in which light is shed upon the Soviet period and the culture of these peoples, socialist in content and national in form.

* * *

This brief historiographical survey of the study of the socialist culture and mode of life of the peoples of the USSR makes it possible to provide a general evaluation of the degree to which this subject matter has been covered in Soviet ethnography, and to touch upon the question of its theoretical and practical significance. Despite inadequate study of many large districts and a considerable number of the peoples of our country, we do nonetheless possess a number of significant published, and some dozens as yet unpublished, monographs, many of which have been defended as dissertations in the Institute of Ethnography of the USSR Academy of Sciences and other scholarly institutions. Some hundreds of articles and pamphlets have been published, both in the major cities and locally. Therefore, considerable material has by now been accumulated, and no few conclusions and generalizations have been arrived at. This makes it possible, even at this stage of research, to draw some

preliminary conclusions. A distinguishing characteristic of all these researches and publications is their great variety in scope and degree of illumination of the data. Some of them are devoted solely to investigation of particular aspects of the contemporary culture and mode of life of a people, while others yield a broader picture. There are studies descriptive of the culture and mode of life of the peasantry in terms of data on some single typical collective farm. But there are also investigations and descriptions that rest upon data of collective farms of one or several districts of a republic or oblast, krai, or okrug. Some of these works constitute general essays on the culture and life of a nationality as a whole.

One must emphasize the fact that all these studies contain extensive concrete material. Unfortunately, they are frequently submitted on the descriptive level alone. It goes without saying that descriptive data are very much needed, particularly in the first stage of research, but the fact that they are inadequately generalized and not always employed to arrive at conclusions, however modest in nature, must be considered a shortcoming of many ethnographic studies devoted to contemporary life. However, even considering this significant shortcoming, the published works are in their overwhelming majority of great scholarly value. Some writers or groups of writers adduce rich and variegated data from the widest range of aspects of the people's lives. This material is testimony to the abrupt improvement — simply incomparable with prerevolutionary times — in the material circumstances, the rise in the level of culture, and the fundamental improvement in the mode of life of the collective farm peasantry in all, even the most inaccessible and remote, scantily inhabited areas of our country. These vast data are the best proof of the fact that the organization and leadership of the Communist Party, in mobilizing the people to build socialism and to develop theoretical and practical methods of socialist reorganization of the lives of the Soviet peoples, followed by the building of a communist society, have yielded and are yielding fruitful results.

The next important conclusion deriving from

these studies is that the culture of the Soviet nationalities has, during the period of the building
of socialism, developed as a culture socialist in
content and national in form. Demonstration of
the validity of this law must be regarded as one
of the major achievements of Soviet ethnography.
The articles and books of ethnographers demonstrate in specific terms just how new national
forms of culture and mode of life come into being, and how old national forms yield to new, due
to their incompatibility with the new conditions
of life, because they inhibit further development.
True, some rational forms of the old culture and
mode of life continue to live and develop (sometimes after undergoing transformations). Numerous published and unpublished ethnographic
studies clearly refute the lying propaganda of
the imperialists, American in particular, who
spread inventions to the effect that national cultures in the USSR have been suppressed. (52)

The studies in ethnography provide a foundation for the assertion that development of the
socialist culture and mode of life of each separate nation or nationality in the USSR occurs not
in isolation, but in interaction with the culture
and mode of life of the other nations and nationalities of our country. This interaction leads to
an inevitable merging of the socialist nations
and nationalities on the basis of the common socialist content of their culture. At the same time,
ethnographic materials show that the level of development of culture and mode of life, as well as
the level of economic prosperity, are not identical among the different nationalities of the USSR.
As a result of a number of specific circumstances
chiefly rooted in the historical past, the various
nationalities of the USSR entered the period of
gradual transition to communist society at different levels of development of socialist culture
and mode of life. And although some numerically
large nationalities or nations which were greatly
retarded in the past have today completely over-
taken in economy and culture certain more advanced nations and nationalities with rich cultural traditions and cultural heritage, there are,
nonetheless, socialist nationalities, particularly
among those small in numbers, who for a number of reasons have not succeeded in advancing

as far along the path of historical development.

Much material for important theoretical generalizations is provided by ethnographic studies
of the processes of national consolidation among
Soviet peoples, and the paths they have taken in
national development. These studies are of great
importance. Unfortunately, the scope of this
article does not permit us to pause to consider
this problem, which was recently treated at
length in the pages of the journal Sovetskaia etnografiia (1961, No. 4). I wish merely to emphasize that ethnographic researches indicate that
along with progress of socialist culture and mode
of life in its national forms and alongside processes of consolidation of various nationalities,
there has been an increase in the process of
merging and, in part, even combination of the
cultures of various socialist nations and nationalities.

The practical significance of certain ethnographic investigations of current themes, in connection with the problems of building socialism
and communism among the peoples of the USSR,
is readily seen in the experiences of the Institute
of Ethnography of the USSR Academy of Sciences.
The Institute has established and is strengthening ties with the State Planning Commission of
the USSR, the Economic Commission on Nationality Affairs of the Supreme Soviet of the USSR,
and with a number of ministries (Public Health,
Agriculture, and others). The ethnographers
submit data to the State Planning Commission to
assist them in planning the supply of industrial
commodities to various areas of the USSR with
due consideration for distinctions of nationality
and the needs of the population (for example, with
respect to grades, types and color patterns of
fabrics, ready-to-wear clothing, certain foodstuffs, household furnishings, and so forth). Ethnographers are participating in designing types
of modern housing according to national traditions of the population and local climatic conditions of various zones of our country. The practical effect of this work is improvement in the
living standard and satisfaction of the needs of
the population. Ethnographic research data are
needed in examining questions pertaining to settlement of newly opened or sparsely populated

portions of our country in conjunction with its industrial or agricultural development; in resolving problems with respect to directions and methods of more rapid economic and cultural development of the small peoples of Siberia and the Far North; in discovering possibilities for employment of youth and graduates of the national schools of certain areas in local industry and farming, in work in other areas, and so forth. It is hardly necessary to prove how important the researches of ethnographers are in the struggle with various religious vestiges of the past in the mode of life, and in determining the reasons for their vitality and methods of overcoming them. Ethnographic data and evaluations of socialist cultures and modes of life are highly necessary for major works both on the history of individual Soviet peoples and those of a more general nature.

In the light of the problems placed before Soviet science by the 22nd Congress of the CPSU, study of the contemporary culture and mode of life of the Soviet nationalities has to be greatly expanded and deepened. It is necessary that broad strata of rural people be embraced in the research — not only the collective farm peasantry but persons working in state farms and members of the rural intelligentsia.

Since 1959 there has been in the Institute of Ethnography, USSR Academy of Sciences, a combined expedition on the study of processes of building communism in the culture and mode of life of the working class and collective farm peasantry of the peoples of our country. The expedition includes 18 field parties, of which eight are studying the contemporary culture and mode of life of the Russian population, including that of the inhabitants of Siberia (the Angara-Enisei party) and Kazakhstan (study of the population that has opened the lands of Virgin Soil Krai). Local scientific personnel are taking an active part in the work of the expedition. The Institute of Ethnography has the job of providing a high level of coordination and administration in planning and executing ethnographic investigations into the current mode of life and culture of the Soviet peoples. A major aspect of the research has to be the process of gradual merging of the various nationalities and mutual enrichment of the socialist cultures. In studying the process of merger and combination of the socialist nations and nationalities of the USSR, ethnographers face the problem of discovering those specific conditions that help this process to advance, as well as factors inhibiting it. The CPSU poses as one of the objectives of its new Program active assistance to the mutual enrichment of national cultures and drawing together of the socialist nations. Ethnographic researches must assist our party in solution of this problem.

"The historical experience of the development of socialist nations," we read in the new CPSU Program, "demonstrates that national forms are not being frozen but are changing, advancing and coming closer to each other, and are being freed of all that is outdated and in contradiction to the new conditions of life." (53) Ethnographic studies must answer the practical question as to which of the national features, particularly which customs and habits, are of assistance to a people in building a communist society and which, contrariwise, inhibit this process. The CPSU calls upon the Soviet people to struggle against those customs and habits that interfere with the building of communism. Ethnographers can and must assist in this.

Treatment of the current level of culture and state of the mode of life of each nationality must be considered an important task in ethnographic research. This is of major significance in assisting in the most rapid and successful advance of all the peoples of our country along the road to communism. But it is not only the level of culture and the status of the mode of life of a nationality that have to be investigated. It is most important to study new phenomena that can be considered to be elements of the culture and mode of life of the future communist society — sprouts of communism. Ethnographers, who are normally in direct contact with the rank-and-file of the people, should record everything that helps these embryonic aspects of communism to develop and grow strong, as well as that which interferes with them. Particular attention must be given to study of religious survivals in the everyday life of the collective farm peasantry and workers of the various peoples of the USSR, to investigation of the reasons for retention of these survivals, and to outlining specific measures to enable them to be overcome as rapidly and completely as possible. The practice, pursued by expeditions of the Institute of Ethnography, of compiling reports of their observations of the state of culture and mode of life in the districts under study, which serve to reveal shortcomings and difficulties in this respect, should be followed by other scientific institutions conducting ethnographic field studies. The intimate relationship between research activity and the practical work of building communism among the nationalities under study must be the guiding rule for scientific ethnography. Ethnographers basing themselves upon the method of direct observation of reality, a method founded on intimate contact with the masses of the people, must reinforce their role in educating the working people for communism. It is necessary to publish major studies generalizing the experience of the building of socialism and the laws of development of the culture and mode of life of the peoples of the USSR. It is particularly necessary that researches be published which generalize this experience among the formerly most backward peoples who bypassed the capitalist path of development thanks to the October Revolution. It is necessary to publish studies exposing the bourgeois ideology and reactionary theories of bourgeois scholars. Special studies recording the first steps in building the new, communist mode of life would be extremely desirable. This subject matter is just beginning to be treated in our scholarly literature. It must be further developed in the years immediately ahead. (54)

The success of future ethnographic studies will depend to a significant degree upon the extent to which creative contact is established between ethnographers on the one hand, and historians, philosophers, economists and representatives of the other social sciences on the other. The major theoretical generalizations which ethnographers will have to make with respect to a number of the problems under study will be impossible without the participation and assistance of philosophers. Without pausing here for consideration of this problem, I note, for example, the

problem of formation of socialist nations and the processes of consolidation into nations. The very concept of a socialist nation demands refinement at the present stage of scientific knowledge. This is equally true of the concept of nation as such, particularly as compared with categories such as nationality, people, and so forth.

If we consider the problem of religious survivals in the modes of life of the peoples of the USSR, of study of the reasons for their vitality and adaptability to the socio-economic conditions of the present day, the participation of philosophers is needed here as well. It is most desirable that we investigate not only the forms of social consciousness and their relationship to the material conditions of contemporary Soviet life, but, it seems to me, we must also study the individual consciousness, if one may so express oneself, the individual psychology of collective farmers and workers who have not yet broken with religion. For vestiges of religion today are retained not in the social consciousness of collective farmers and workers, but in their individual consciousness, their personal psychology, which is shaped to a considerable degree under the influence of the family. Social consciousness, on the other hand, is irreconcilable with all vestiges of the past in the mode of life and is a force of great power in the struggle for a new way of life and for elimination of religious and other vestiges of the past. In this respect it would appear that activation of social consciousness provides the most viable and serious mode of struggle against these vestiges, which are rooted in the family. Study of a number of questions pertaining to the forms taken by the contemporary Soviet family, to the processes of its development, and to the reflection in it of the general processes of development of Soviet society, are also unthinkable without active participation of Soviet philosophers. Soviet ethnographers are very much in need of the creative assistance of philosophers in developing theoretical studies of the most important problems of ethnography devoted to the study of present-day life. In turn, special ethnographic studies devoted to Soviet nations and nationalities must also be useful for specialists in philosophy. Creative contact among the various social sciences can only assist in successful fulfillment of the tasks defined by the 22nd Congress of the CPSU.

Footnotes

1) Staryi i novyi byt, a symposium edited by Prof. V. G. Tan-Bogoraz, Leningrad, 1924.

2) Komsomol v derevne, essays edited by Prof. V. G. Tan-Borgoraz, Moscow-Leningrad, 1926.

3) See, for example, Sbornik Muzeia antropologii i etnografii, Vol. VI, Leningrad, 1927; Vol. VII, Leningrad, 1929; Vol. VIII, Leningrad, 1929.

4) Materialy po etnografii, published by the Ethnographic Division, State Russian Museum, Vol. III, No. 1, Leningrad, 1926; No. 2, Leningrad, 1927; Vol. IV, No. 1, Leningrad, 1927; No. 2, Leningrad, 1929.

5) N. I. Lebedeva, "Zhilishche i khoziaistvennye postroiki Belorusskoi SSR...," Trudy Gos. tsentr. muzeia narodovedeniia, No. 1, Moscow, 1929; B. A. Kuftin, "Material'naia kul'tura russkoi Meshchery," Part 1, Trudy Gos. muzeia Tsentral'noi Promyshlennoi oblasti (cited below as TsPO), No. 3, Moscow, 1926; "Voprosy etnologii TsPO (1-e soveshchanie etnologov TsPO)," V. V. Bogdanov and S. P. Tolstov, eds., Moscow, 1927; "Kul'tura i byt naseleniia TsPO (2-e soveshchanie etnologov TsPO)," same editors, Moscow, 1929.

6) S. I. Rudenko, Bashkiry, Part II, Byt Bashkir, Leningrad, 1925; N. I. Lebedeva, "Narodnyi byt v verkhov'iakh Desny i v verkhov'iakh Oki," Memuary Etnogr. otd. O-va liubitelei estesvoznaniia, antropologii i etnografii, No. 2, Moscow, 1927.

7) E. S. Radchenko, "Selo Buzharovo Voskresenskogo raiona Moskovskogo okruga," Trudy O-va izucheniia Moskovskoi oblasti, No. 3, Moscow, 1929.

8) Kazakhi, Leningrad, 1927; "Ukraintsy-pereselentsy Semipalatinskoi gubernii," Materialy Komissii ekspeditsionnykh issledovanii AN SSSR, No. 16, Leningrad, 1930; "Bukhtarminskie staroobriadtsy," ibid., No. 17, Leningrad, 1930, etc.

9) P. Pogorel'skii and V. Batrakov, Ekonomika kochevogo aula Kirgizstana, Moscow, 1930; L. P. Potapov, Ocherk istorii Oirotii, Novosibirsk, 1933; S. P. Tolstov, "Genezis feodalizma v kochevykh skotovodcheskikh obshchestvakh," Izv. GAIMK, No. 103; A. N. Bernshtam, "Problema raspadeniia rodovykh otnoshenii u kochevnikov Azii," Sov. etnografiia, 1934, No. 6, etc.

10) Trudy In-ta po izucheniiu narodov SSSR (IPIN): Vol. I, Trud i byt v kolkhozakh. Iz opyta izucheniia kolkhozov Leningradskoi oblasti, Belorussii i Ukrainy, Leningrad, 1931; II, Kolkhozy sovetskogo Vostoka (Uzbekistan, Turkmeniia, Tadjikistan, Armeniia), Leningrad, 1931; L. P. Potapov, "Poezdka v kolkhozy Chemal'skogo aimaka Oirotskoi avtonomnoi oblast...," Trudy IPIN, No. 1, Leningrad, 1932.

11) Sh. Annaklychev, Byt rabochikh neftianikov Nebit-Daga i Kum-Daga. Istoriko-etnograficheskii ocherk, Ashkhabad, 1961. See same author's article, "Nekotorye storony byta rabochikh neftianikov Nebit-Daga," SE, 1959, No. 1.

12) N. N. Cheboksarov, "Etnograficheskoe izuchenie kul'tury i byta moskovskikh rabochikh — Ocherk pervyi. Proizvodstvennaia zhizn'," SE, 1950, No. 3.

13) See, for example, V. Iu. Krupianskaia, "Opyt etnograficheskogo izucheniia ural'skikh rabochikh vtoroi poloviny XIX v...," SE, 1953, No. 1; same author, "Nekotorye aspekty etnograficheskogo izucheniia rabochikh," KSIE, AN SSSR, XXIX, 1958; T. K. Gus'kova, "Nekotorye etnograficheskie osobennosti naseleniia b. Nizhne-Tagil'skogo gornozavodskogo okruga v kontse XIX-nachala XX veka," SE, 1958, No. 2.

14) TIE, new series, Vol. LVII, Moscow, 1960.

15) Uch. zap. Cheliabinskogo ped. in-ta, Vol. I, No. 1, 1956.

16) "Istoriko-bytovye ekspeditsii 1949-1950 gg.," Trudy GIM, No. XXIII, Moscow, 1953; Istoriko-bytovye ekspeditsii 1951-1953 gg. Materialy po istorii proletariata i krest'ianstva Rossii kontsa XIX-nachala XX v., Moscow, 1955.

17) M. P. Prikhod'ko, "K voprosu o razvitii zhilishcha rabochikh Donbassa," Narodna tvorchist' ta etnografiia, 1957, No. 2; same author, "Kharakternye cherty sovremennogo narodnogo zhilishcha rabochikh," ibid., 1958, No. 2, and others; A. S. Kunitskii, Sotsialisticheskii byt rabochikh Voroshilovgradskogo zavoda im. Oktiabr'skoi revoliutsii, author's summary of dissertation, Kiev, 1953; same author, "K voprosu o metodike etno-

graficheskogo izucheniia rabochikh Ukrainy,"
KSIE, XXIX, 1958; same author, "Samostoiatel'noe
rabochee zhilishchnoe stroitel'stvo na Lugansh-
chine," Narodna tvorchist' ta etnografiia, 1960,
No. 2; same author, "Ob izuchenii rabochego
byta na Ukraine," ibid., 1957, No. 1; V. T. Zinich,
Sotsialisticheskii byt i kul'tura rabochikh Kieva,
author's summary of dissertation, Kiev, 1960;
same author, "Sovremennyi brak i svad'ba u
rabochikh," Narodna tvorchist' ta etnografiia,
1957, No. 2; same author, "Novye cherty v semeinom bytu rabochikh," ibid., 1957, No. 3; same
author, "O nekotorykh novykh obshchestvennykh
prazdnikakh i kollektivnom dosuge rabochikh,"
ibid., 1958, No. 3, and others; M. T. Lomova,
Kul'tura i byt rabochikh-neftianikov goroda
Borislavlia; V. Iu. Pastushchin, Byt rabochikh
Borislavskogo neftianogo raiona, author's summary of dissertation, Kiev, 1954; L. P. Shevchenko,
"Sotsialisticheskie preobrazovaniia v kul'ture i
byte rabochikh Krolevetskoi tkatskoi arteli im.
20-letiia Oktiabr'skoi revoliutsii," SE, 1954, No.
4; V. T. Zinich and M. P. Prikhod'ko, "Cherty
kommunisticheskogo v byte i kul'ture rabochikh
Ukrainskoi SSR," Narodna tvorchist' ta etnografiia,
1960, No. 4; D. I. Figol', "Kommunisticheskie
cherty v proizvodstvennom i obshchestvennom
bytu rabochikh g. L'vova," Narodna tvorchist' ta
etnografiia, 1961, No. 1; V. I. Naudko,
"Dobrovol'nye narodnye druzhiny i voprosy
obshchestvennogo byta rabochikh," ibid.

18) Among published works, see: V. M. Ivanov,
"Cherty novogo v byte rabochikh sovetskoi Belo-
russi," Narodna tvorchist' ta etnografiia, 1959,
No. 1; same author, "Obshchestvennyi i semeinyi
byt brigad kommunisticheskogo truda Belorusskoi
SSR," Narodna tvorchist' ta etnografiia, 1960,
No. 3; A. I. Zalesskii, "Ob izuchenii byta rabochego
klassa v SSSR," Voprosy istorii, 1955, No. 5, and
others.

19) A. I. Robakidze, Nekotorye storony byta
rabochikh chiaturskoi margantsevoi promyshlennosti, Tbilisi, 1953; see as well articles by the same
author, "K nekotorym spornym voprosam etnograficheskogo izucheniia novogo byta," SE, 1952,
No. 2; "Nekotorye storony semeinogo byta
chiaturskikh gorniakov," ibid., 1953, No. 4; L. Kh.
Akaba, "Materialy o byte rabochikh abkhazov

Tkvarcheli," Trudy Abkhazskogo In'ta iazyka,
literatury i istorii, Vol. 31, 1960, and others.

20) F. A. Aripov, Iz istorii formirovaniia
uzbekskikh rabochikh kadrov (po istoriko-etno-
graficheskim materialam zavodov sel'skokhozi-
aistvennogo mashinostroeniia UzSSR), author's
synopsis of dissertation, Tashkent, 1961; same
author, "Nekotorye dannye ob izuchenii sovremennogo byta rabochikh Uzbekskoi SSR," Narodna tvorchist' ta etnografiia, 1961, No. 2; G.
Dmitrieva, "K izucheniiu material'noi kul'tury
uzbekskikh rabochikh," Nauchnye raboty i so-
obshcheniia otdel. obshch. nauk AN UzSSR, Vol.
2, 1961.

21) Sredneaziatskii etnograficheskii Sbornik,
II, TIE, new series, Vol. XLVIII, Moscow, 1959.

22) SE, 1954, No. 4.

23) Specifically, the resolution of the Presidium
of the USSR Academy of Sciences, July 4, 1958,
in conjunction with the discussion of the results
of the Joint Session of the Division of Social
Sciences, USSR Academy of Sciences (June 1958),
devoted to theoretical problems of the building
of communism in our country.

24) It is of course impossible to list them all,
but some should be mentioned, such as G. S. Maslova, "Kul'tura i byt odnogo kolkhoza Podmoskov'-
ia," SE, 1951, No. 1; same author, "Seleniia i
postroiki kolkhozov Moskovskoi oblasti," ibid.,
1951, No. 2; L. A. Pushkareva and M. N. Shmeleva,
"Predvaritel'nye itogi izucheniia kul'tury i byta
kolkhoznogo krest'ianstva v Kalininskoi oblasti,"
SE, 1958, No. 4; L. N. Chizhikova and M. N.
Shmeleva, "Sovremennoe russkoe krest'ianskoe
zhilische," SE, 1955, No. 1; M. Simonov, Kolkhoz
imeni Lenina Taganrogskogo raiona Rostovskoi
oblasti, Rostov-na-Donu, 1953; Ot oskudeniia k
portsvetaniiu. Proshloe i nastoiashchee sel
Novo-Zhivotinskogo i Mokhovatki Berezovskogo
raiona Voronezhskoi oblasti, edited by P. N.
Prudkovskii and R. V. Vorotnikov, Voronezh,
1958; "Po kolkhozam Gor'kovskoi oblasti," an es-
say in economic ethnography by N. V. Tazikhina,
Izv. VGO, 1949, No. 3; L. Pushkareva, G. Snesarev,
and M. Shmeleva, "Religiozno-bytovye perezhitki
i puti ikh preodoleniia," Kommunist, 1960, No. 8,
and others.

25) Selo Viriatino v proshlom i nastoiashchem.

Opyt etnograficheskogo izucheniia russkoi kolkhoznoi derevni, 1958, TIE, new series, Vol. XLI, Moscow, 1958; "Riazanskoe selo Korablino," Uch. zap. Riazanskogo gos. ped. in-ta., Vol. XVIII, Riazan, 1957.

26) I. F. Simonenko, Sotsialisticheskie preobrazovaniia v bytu trudiashchikhsia sela Neresnitsy Zakarpatskoi oblasti (in Ukrainian), Kiev, 1957. [This footnote is not keyed in text.]

27) For example: A. A. Lebedeva, Sotsialisticheskoe pereustroistvo khoziaistva i byta Zakarpatskoi oblasti Ukrainskoi SSR, author's synopsis of dissertation, Moscow, 1952. See essays on individual collective farms of Chernovtsy oblast: M. Burbank and N. Gol'nev, "V kolkhoze im. B. Khmel'nitskogo," Slaviane, 1954, No. l; for Vinnits oblast: Nikolai Dalekii, Kolkhoz im. Kirova, s. Miziakovskie khutora (in Ukrainian), L'vov, 1947; on Kiev oblast: V. F. Kolesnik, "Novoe v bytu kolkhoznogo krest'ianstva," Narodna tvorchist' ta etnografiia, 1960, No. 2; M. O. Kuz'menko, "Novuiu sotsialisticheskuiu zhizn' vospevaiut trudiaschiesia Rovenshchiny," ibid., 1960, No. 3; F. I. Samoilovich, "Novyi byt i kul'tura sela 'Pervoe maia,'" ibid., 1960, No. 1; P. S. Repchenko, "Ob istoricheskikh peremenakh v sele Bugaevke Gradizhskogo raiona Poltavskoi oblasti," Nauchnye trudy Poltavskogo s-kh. in-ta, Vol. 6, 1959; O. M. Kravets and O. F. Kuveneva, "Novoe v obshchestvennom i semeinom bytu kolkhoznikov Sovetskoi Ukrainy," Narodna tvorchist' ta etnografiia, 1961, No. 1; K. N. Cherkashin, "Novoe v kul'ture i byte trudiashchikhsia Novograd-Volynskogo raiona," ibid., 1961, No. 3.

28) There are few publications on this. See N. F. Nikolaev, "Rost sotsialisticheskoi kul'tury moldavan s. Zhury," SE, 1951, No. 2; K. V. Stratievskii, "Rost material'nogo sostoianiia i kul'turnogo urovnia kolkhoznogo krest'ianstva Moldavskoi SSR za gody vtoroi piatiletki," Uch. zap. Kishinevskogo ped. in-ta, Vol. 6, 1957; P. Usik, "Sela meniaiut oblik," Kommunist Moldavii, 1960, No. 2.

29) Belaruski etnagrafichny zbornik, Academy of Sciences of the BSSR, Trudy In-ta isskustvovedeniia, etnografii i fol'klora, Vol. I, Seriia etnografii i fol'klora, No. 1, Minsk, 1958. The symposium contains the following articles: M. Ia. Grinblat and L. A. Molchanova, "Monograficheskaia rabota o kul'ture i byte kolkhoznikov v kolkhoze 'Bol'shevik' Khoinitskogo raiona Gomel'skoi oblasti"; A. Zalesskii, "O nekotorykh chertakh v poslevoennom semeinom bytu belorussikikh kolkhoznikov"; N. I. Kasiuk, "Tekhnika sovremennogo domashnego tkachestva na Sluchine"; K. P. Kabashnikov, "Belorusskoe ustnoe poeticheskoe narodnoe tvorchestvo sovetskoi epokhi." See also: L. A. Molchanova, "Osnovnye itogi etnograficheskoi ekspeditsii 1959 goda po severnym raionam Belorussii," Vestsi AN BSSR. Seriia gramadzkikh navuk, Minsk, 1960, No. 1; A. I. Zalesskii, Byt belorusskikh krest'ian v partizanskom krae, Minsk, 1960 (in Belorussian).

30) O. A. Gantskaia, Material'naia kul'tura kolkhoznikov Bobruiskoi oblasti BSSR (1952); I. L. Poroshkova, Pobeda kolkhoznogo stroia i ee otrazhenie v belorusskom narodno-poeticheskom tvorchestve (1953); I. V. Mironov, Pod'em material'nogo blagosostoianiia i kul'turnogo urovnia trudiashchikhsia Belorussii v poslevoennyi period (1945-1953) (1959).

31) See A. Luts, "Novoe v bytu estonskikh rybakov i zadachi ego izucheniia," SE, 1960, No. 3; A. K. Krastynia, "O stroitel'stve zhilykh domov kolkhoznikov v Latviiskoi SSR (Planirovka i zastroika kolkhoznykh poselkov)," ibid.; L. Efremova, "Nekotorye itogi etnograficheskogo izucheniia kolkhoznikov-rybakov Vidzeme," ibid; V. Ia. Kalits, "Novye cherty v bytu ostrova Kikhnu," SE, 1961, No. 3. Also see author's synopses of dissertations: I. P. Butkiavichius, Sovremennoe litovskoe krest'ianskoe zhilishche, 1956; A. I. Vishniauskaite, Semeinyi byt litovskikh kolkhoznikov, 1955, and others.

32) This symposium is published in TIE, new series, Vol. LXXVII, Moscow, 1962.

33) L. N. Terent'eva, Kolkhoznoe krest'ianstvo Latvii (Istoriko-etnograficheskaia monografiia po materialam kolkhozov Ekabpilsskogo raiona Latviiskoi SSR), TIE, new series, Vol. LIX, Moscow, 1960; same author, "K voprosu o perekhode ot khutorskogo rasseleniia k kolkhoznym poselkam v Latviiskoi SSR," SE, 1954, No. 1; same author, "Formirovanie novykh obychaev i obriadov v bytu kolkhoznikov Latvii," SE, 1961,

104

No. 2, and others.

34) V. P. Ezhova, Sovremennaia kul'tura i byt mordovskogo naseleniia Ten'gushevskogo raiona, 1954.

35) N. N. Ershov, N. A. Kisliakov, E. M. Peshchereva, S. P. Rusiaikina, Kul'tura i byt tadzhikskogo kolkhoznogo krest'ianstva, TIE, new series, Vol. XXIV, Moscow-Leningrad, 1954; O. A. Sukhareva and M. A. Bikzhanova, Proshloe i nastoiashchee seleniia Aikyran, Tashkent, 1955; S. M. Abramzon, K. I. Antipina, G. P. Vasil'eva, E. I. Makhova, D. Suleimenov, Byt kolkhoznikov kirgizskikh selenii Darkhan i Chichkan, TIE, new series, Vol. XXXVII, Moscow, 1958.

36) For example: T. A. Zhdanko, "Byt kolkhoznikov-pereselentsev na vnov' osvoennykh zemliakh drevnego orosheniia Kara-Kalpakii," Trudy Khorezmskoi ekspeditsii, Vol. II, Moscow, 1958; M. A. Bikzhanova, Sem'ia v kolkhozakh Uzbekistana (Po materialam kolkhozov Namanganskoi obl.), Tashkent, 1959; I. V. Zakharova, "Material'naia kul'tura kazakhov-kolkhoznikov iugo-vostochnogo Kazakhstana (Po materialam Alma-Atinskoi i Dzhambulskoi oblastei)", Trudy In-ta istorii, arkheologii i etnografii AN Kazakhskoi SSR, 1956, No. 3; V. V. Vostrov, "Kazakhi Dzhanybekskogo raiona Zapadno-Kazakhstanskoi oblasti," ibid.; N. S. Sabitov, "Obshchestvennyi i semeinyi byt kolkhoznikov Alma-Atinskoi i Dzhambulskoi oblastei," ibid; U. Shalekenov, "Byt karakalpakskogo krest'ianstva Chimbaiskogo raiona v proshlom i nastoiashchem," Trudy Khorezmskoi ekspeditsii, Vol. III, Moscow, 1958; K. L. Sadykhina, "Uzbeki del'ty Amu-Dar'i," Trudy Khorezmskoi ekspeditsii, Vol. I, Moscow, 1952; I. V. Zakharova, "Material'naia kul'tura uigurov Sovetskogo Soiuza," Sredneaziatskii etnograficheskii sbornik, II, TIE, Vol. XLVII, Moscow, 1959; N. V. Kuzembaev, O kul'ture v bytu naseleniia aula i sela, Alma-Ata, 1957; M. R. Ryskulbekov, "Perekhod kirgizov ot kochevogo k sovremennomu sotsialisticheskomu khoziaistvu" [Doklady Kongressa vostokovedov], Moscow, 1960; I. Moshiiakhov, "O zhiznennom urovne tadzhikskogo naroda," Uch. zap. Tadzh. s-kh. in-ta, Vol. 4, Seriia obshchestv nauk, 1960, No. 1; B. N. Abisheva, "Ot velikogo pochina do brigad i kollektivo kommunisticheskogo truda (Na materialakh Kazakhstana)," Izv, AN KazSSR, seriia istorii, arkheologii i etnografii, No. 2, Alma-Ata, 1960; A. V. Karelin, "Uluchshaetsia byt tselinnikov (Sovkhoz 'Razdol'nyi', Kokchetavksoi oblasti)," Sovkhoznoe proizvodstvo, 1960, No. 5; A. Dzhumagulov, Sem'ia i brak u kirgizov Chuiskoi doliny, Frunze, 1960; S. M. Abramzon, "Preobrazovaniia v khoziaistve i kul'ture kazakhov za gody sotsialisticheskogo stroitel'stva," SE, 1961, No. 1.

37) See articles: S. M. Abramzon, "Ob etnograficheskom izuchenii kolkhoznogo krest'ianstva," SE, 1952, No. 3; same author, "Kirgizskaia sem'ia v epokhu sotsializma," ibid., 1957, No. 5; same author, "V kirgizskikh kolkhozakh Tian'-Shania," ibid., 1959, No. 4; T. A. Zhdanko, "Byt karakalpakskogo aula," ibid., 1949, No. 2; same author, "Byt kolkhoznikov rybolovetskikh artelei na ostrovakh iuzhnogo Arala," ibid., 1961, No. 5; N. A. Kisliakov, "K voprosu ob etnograficheskom izuchenii kolkhozov," ibid., 1952, No. 1; O. A. Korbe, "Kul'tura i byt kazakhskogo kolkhoznogo aula (K 30-letiiu Kazakhskoi SSR)," ibid., 1950, No. 4; G. P. Snesarev, "O nekotorykh prichinakh sokhraneniia religiozno-bytovykh perezhitkov u uzbekov Khorezma," ibid., 1957, No. 2; Ia. R. Vinnikov, "Novyi byt turkmenskikh kolkhozov Maryiskoi oblasti," ibid., 1950, No. 1; L. S. Tolstova, "Materialy etnograficheskogo obsledovaniia gruppy 'karakalpak' Samarkandskoi oblasti Uzbekskoi SSR," ibid., 1961, No. 3; same author, "Karakalpaki Bukharskoi oblasti Uzbekskoi SSR," ibid., 1961, No. 5, etc.

38) G. N. Valikhanov, Sovremennyi byt kazakhskogo aula; V. V. Vostrov, Kul'tura i byt kazakhskogo kolkhoznogo aula; L. Shinlo, Sotsialisticheskii byt kolkhoza imeni Frunze Kantskogo raiona Kirgizskoi SSR, and others.

39) I. V. Chkoniia, "Novye byt v kolkhozakh Makharadzevskogo raiona," Materialy po etnografii Gruzii. Trudy In-ta istorii AN GruzSSR, Vol. 6, Tbilisi, 1953 (in Georgian); M. A. Ochkauri, "Sovremennaia khevsurskaia zhenskaia odezhda," ibid.; Sh. Inal-Ipa, "Duripsh (Opyt istoriko-etnograficheskogo izucheniia kolkhoznogo byta abkhazskoi derevni)," Trudy Abkhazskogo In-ta iazyka, literatury i istorii, Vol. 29, 1958; G. A. Chachashvili, "Nekotorye voprosy kul'tury i byta sovremennogo naseleniia Samgori," KSIE,

XXIX, 1958; I. V. Chkoniia, "Sem'ia i semeinyi byt kolkhoznikov Gruzinskoi SSR," Materialy po etnografii Gruzii, Trudy In-ta istorii AN GruzSSR, Tbilisi, Vol. 9, 1960; Sh. Inal-Ipa, Abkhazy (in Georgian), Sukhumi, 1960; A. I. Robakidze, "Novye cherty sovremennogo gruzinskogo krest'-ianskogo zhilishcha," SE, 1961, No. 1; see also: L. Kh. Akaba, "Etnograficheskoe izuchenie abkhazov za gody Sovetskoi vlasti," Trudy Abkhaz-skogo In-ta iazyka, literatury i istorii, Vol. 32, 1961.

40) M. N. Nasirli, Sel'skie poseleniia i krest'-ianskie zhilishcha Nakhichevanskoi ASSR, Baku, 1959; M. N. Bigirov, Blagoustroistvo kolkhoznykh sel i byt krest'ian Azerbaidzhana, Baku, 1957; G. R. Imanov, Korennoe izmenenie dukhovnogo oblika azerbaidzhanskogo krest'ianstva za gody Sovetskoi vlasti, Baku, 1960.

41) D. Vardumian, Novyi byt loriitsev, Erevan, 1956.

42) A. Avdal, Byt kurdov Zakavkaz'ia, Erevan, 1957. See also: T. F. Aristova, "Materialy po etnografii kurdov Armenii (Sovremennaia kul'-tura i byt kurdskikh kolkhoznikov Armenii), Izv. AN Armianskoi SSR. Obshchestvennye nauki, 1961, No. 1.

43) Press of the Karachaevo-Circassian Institute of History, Language and Literature.

44) Narody Dagestana, Moscow, 1955.

45) See L. A. Vitukhnovskaia, Opyt monografi-cheskogo issledovaniia sotsialisticheskoi kul'-tury abkhazskoi kolkhoznoi derevni, author's condensation of dissertation, Moscow, 1950; G. A. Guliev, Sotsialisticheskaia kul'tura i byt kolhoz-nogo krest'ianstva Azerbaidzhana, author's condensation of dissertation, Moscow, 1953; E. L. Kodzhesau, Semeinye otnosheniia shapsu-gov v proshlom i nastoiashchem, Moscow, 1954, and others. Among published works we choose: A. Kh. Akaba, "Abkhazy Ochamchirskogo raiona (Opyt etnograficheskogo issledovaniia kul'tury i byta kolkhoznikov)," Kavkazskii etnograficheskii sbornik, I, TIE, new series, Vol. XXVI, Moscow, 1955.

46) M. A. Sergeev, Nekapitalisticheskii put' razvitiia malykh narodov Severa, TIE, new series, Vol. XXVII, Moscow-Leningrad, 1955.

47) Perekhod k sotsializmu malykh narodov Severa, Moscow, Gospolitizdat, 1958.

48) See Izv. Vsesoiuzn. geograf. o-va, No. 1, 1955.

49) "K tridtsatiletiiu Nenetskogo national'-nogo okruga," SE, 1959, No. 5.

50) See, for example, V. F. Vorob'ev, "O pre-obrazovanii khoziaistva i byta naseleniia severo-zapadnoi Iakutii," Uch. zap. Leningr. ped in-ta, Vol. 136, 1957; L. A. Fainberg, "Khoziaistvo i kul'tura taimyrskikh nganasan," SE, 1959, No. 2; A. V. Smoliak, "Materialy k kharakteristike sotsialisticheskoi kul'tury i byta korennogo naseleniia Chukotskogo raiona," Sibirskii etno-graficheskii sbornik, II, TIE, new series, Vol. XXXV, Moscow-Leningrad, 1957; L. P. Potapov, "Opyt izucheniia sotsialisticheskoi kul'tury i byta altaitsev," SE, 1948, No. 1; same author, "Shortsy na puti sotsialisticheskogo razvitiia," ibid., 1950, No. 3; same author, "Sotsialistich-eskoe pereustroistvo kul'tury i byta tuvintsev, ibid., 1953, No. 2; L. V. Grebnev, Perekhod tu-vintsev aratov-kochevnikov na osedlost', Kyzyl, 1955; V. I. Vasil'ev and V. A. Tugolukov, "Etno-graficheskie issledovaniia na Taimyre v 1959 godu," SE, 1960, No. 5; Sovremennoe khoziaistvo, kul'tura i byt malykh narodov Severa, a collection of articles, ed. B. O. Dolgikh, TIE, new series, Vol. LVI, Moscow, 1960; Ch. Taksami, Vozro-zhdenie nivkhskoi narodnosti, Iuzhno-Sakhalinsk, 1959; M. D. Kaplan, "Izmenenie kul'tury i byta nanaitsev v rezul'tate sotsialisticheskikh pre-obrazovanii," Izv. Vsesoiuzh. geograf. o-va, Vol. 93, 1961, No. 2; Z. P. Sokolova, "O neko-torykh etnicheskikh protsessakh, protekaiush-chikh u sel'kupov, khantov i evenkov Tomskoi oblast," SE, 1961, No. 3, etc.

51) Narody Sibiri, eds. M. G. Levin and L. P. Potapov, Moscow and Leningrad, 1956 (series Narody mira. Etnograficheskie ocherki; gen. editor S. P. Tolstov, Corr. Member, USSR Acad. Sci.).

52) See, for example: R. Pipes, "Muslims of Soviet Central Asia: Trends and Prospects," The Middle East Journal, Washington, Part 1, Vol. 9, No. 2, 1955 (see review by T. A. Zhdanko in SE, 1958, No. 4.).

53) Materialy XXII s'ezda KPSS, Moscow, 1961, p. 407.

106

54) The first effort at a work of generalization in the field of contemporary way of life is the interesting book by V. Sinitsyn, Byt epokhi stroi- tel'stva kommunisticheskogo obshchestva, Chelia- binsk, 1960. See review by M. Kammari, "Stroi- tel'stvo kommunizma i voprosy byta," Kommu- nist, 1961, No. 5; see also A. M. Apartsyn, "O razvitii kul'tury i byta kolkhoznoi derevni v period razvernutogo stroitel'stva kommunizma," Zap. Leningr. s-kh. in-ta, Vol. 78, 1960; I. Kry- velev, "Vazhnaia storona byta (O sozdanii sovre- mennykh prazdnichnyka obriadov)," Kommunist, 1961, No. 8.

* * *

Questions of General Sociological Method

Vestnik drevnei istorii, 1967, No. 2, pp. 7-30

K. K. Zel'in

PRINCIPLES OF MORPHOLOGICAL CLASSIFICATION OF FORMS

OF DEPENDENCE

Glossary of Marxist and Other Special
Terms Used in This Article

1. Social system — the combination of a particular system for the production of material goods (the base) with the social and political structure (the superstructure) corresponding to it. This must not be confused with the concept called by the same name in American sociology. — Ed.

2. Production relations — relations among human beings for purposes of production: master-slave, lord-serf, capitalist-worker, members of a cooperative, members of a socialist society.

3. Economic compulsion — the need, on the part of a free man lacking means of production (land, tools, materials), to seek employment with someone who possesses these.

4. Surplus value — the value produced by a hired worker over and above the equivalent of his wages.

5. Use values — objects useful as such, regardless of market value.

6. Commodity — goods offered for sale on the market.

7. Labor power — that which the worker sells an employer; the worker's ability to put out more labor than the value of his labor power (his wages, roughly speaking) is the inducement to the employer to employ him.

8. Ancient form of property — Greco-Roman forms specifically, not antiquity in general.

9. Caste — as used here, and generally in standard English translations of the Marxist classics: a ranked juridical category of people. This concept does not involve either religious sanction or the idea of ritual pollution, as in India. — Ed.

10. Social relationships — societal, i.e., characteristic of or found everywhere in a given form of society, not unique small-group or individual relationships.

11. Superstructure — all human organization (political, military, religious, legal, etc.) and

thought derived from and resting upon the economy, which is the base.

12. Classical slavery — Greco-Roman forms, specifically, that of classical antiquity.

13. Simple reproduction — a non-expanding, non-contracting economic level of output.

14. Reproduction of the base — the inherent economic practices (laws) causing a given economic system (slavery, feudalism, capitalism, socialism, etc.) to persist.

15. Liturgy — as used here: any of several public offices which wealthy citizens in ancient Greece and the Hellenistic successor-states were required to hold in rotation. — Ed.

Note. All definitions except those marked "Ed." were supplied by the translator.

* * *

Whereas, in biology, recent decades have witnessed a tremendous interest in problems of systematization, and it is acutely felt that treatment of these problems is a task whose solution is necessary to biology as a whole, (1) no significant advance is to be seen in this regard in historiography. Not only have no attempts been made to deal with methodological problems in taxonomic research (2) and its connection with general problems of historical research, but even in writings devoted to specific analysis of particular sources, higher taxonomic categories continue to be employed, sometimes uncritically and often without the necessary attention to those narrower concepts that enter into them, without analysis in depth of the criteria distinguishing one set of definitions from others, and without an attempt to establish any more or less rigorous taxonomic entity.

The concept of social system has come to be of overriding significance in Marxist literature. "Marx," wrote Lenin, "was the first to place sociology on a scientific basis by formulating the concept of the socio-economic system as the totality of given production relations, and by demonstrating that the development of these systems is a natural historical process." (3) According to Lenin, it was precisely the concept of social system that made it possible to approach the process of historical development as a natural historical process and to escape the confines of subjective sociology.

But while recognizing the full scientific value of this concept, we cannot, for all that, fail to see that researchers working with the concept of social system in treating concrete historical material often, and over a long period, saw their task as primarily that of assembling certain facts that would, in their opinion, prove that a given society was classifiable under a given system (for classical antiquity, the slaveholding system), without giving sufficient consideration to the numerous different forms of relationships that entered as elements into this general concept. At times they would rather unconvincingly stuff into a general category, descriptive of the given system (i.e., "slavery"), relationships which were at least deserving of special scholarly study and definition. (4)

For it would be incorrect, after taking some higher taxonomic category as point of departure, to give special value to, or even select, facts that would seem to substantiate it. For example, we must not employ the concept "the slavery of classical antiquity" in this fashion and, having decided that slaveholding was dominant in antiquity, proceed to "discover" slaves (or people who seem to us to have been slaves) — and the more of them the merrier — without particularly considering what was specific in the socio-economic relationships placed under the category "slavery," and without establishing with sufficient persuasiveness whether those relationships played a determining role in production. We know, too, how difficult it is, in the light of the condition of the sources, to answer the latter question. When considered in the fashion described, the category "slaveholding system" encompassed all of antiquity from the appearance of states in Egypt and Mesopotamia at the end of the Fourth Millennium B.C.E., to the fall of the Western Roman Empire, i.e., it was applied, so to speak, without consideration of space and time. Marx's words in another connection (on the political economy of John Stuart Mill) are applicable to that sort of approach: "A wondrous optical illusion — to see everywhere relationships that have hitherto prevailed on earth only in exceptional cases." (5)

In this connection, it seems to us instructive to compare the situation in historiography with what is currently happening in the field of biology. There people are insisting that one must abandon the typological concept of the species as something fixed and homogeneous, that it must be replaced by a dynamic conception, and that a species must be studied from the standpoint of its variability, taking into consideration the diverse conditions making for the formation of species and populations. (6) These factors must also be taken into consideration in the analysis and classification of a category such as that of socio-economic relations. The incompleteness, low level, and, to some degree, primitivism of systematics should, in our opinion, be recognized as one of the factors inhibiting progress in historical scholarship.

In the realm of the science of society, we remain now, in some respects, at the same level in the development of systematics that zoology was at over 2,000 years ago, when scientists were operating with broad morphological concepts — birds, fishes, quadrupeds, etc. — and did not base themselves upon the totality of significant criteria identified as the result of comparison of experimental data, not to speak of the examination of species of animals with consideration of their phylogenesis, ecology, geographic conditions, and other factors on which the "new," contemporary systematics bases itself. In making use of such broad concepts, associated with only a few criteria and, often, by no means the most significant but those accessible to superficial observation, certain species of animals appeared to fit into categories that would today seem, at the very least, to be inappropriate to them. (7)

When we familiarize ourselves today with the status of taxonomic problems in biology, we see that that science takes a different approach to the solution of these questions, and we not only cannot fail to associate ourselves with the demand for a critical approach to the theory and methods of systematics propounded by biologists, but we cannot remain indifferent to the lack of

any such critical approach, often encountered in the realm of historiography. The words of the authors of one of the manuals on methods of zoological systematics — "An acute need is felt for analysis and firm formulation of the principles on which the taxonomic method rests" (8) — are wholly applicable in the study of historical phenomena as well.

In biology, the species was, for a long time, the principal fundamental unit of a taxonomic system. Today more than 300,000 species of plants and more than a million of animals are known. Those species comprise the factual material, which had to be named, described, and arranged in an ordered system. Is there anything, even if in only a few respects, corresponding to this in the history of human societies?

It is absolutely clear that it would make no sense, for purposes of historical study, to classify the people in a given society by particular physical or psychological criteria. What is important is not the isolated individual, but man as a member of society — the relationships among individuals. These relationships — and, above all, relationships in the sphere of material production — come into being, in considerable measure, independent of men's conscious activity. Thus the lowest taxonomic unit in the study of various social structures is a relationship between human beings. And if we wish to understand the basic criteria of that structure, we must study the totality of socio-economic relationships.

Proceeding from the foregoing in our further analysis, it is necessary at this early stage to express two considerations of a general character that are, in our view, significant. One of them corresponds to what is seen in modern systematics in the field of natural science, while the other is associated primarily with the special features of the history of human societies. The first is that we must abandon the examination of relationships as in some way invariable and homogeneous. Relationships, like species, display variability and a whole series of variants and transitional forms. In studying them, one cannot limit oneself merely to purely morphological criteria, but must give consideration to the factors cited above — the ecological, geographical, historical, and, what is particularly significant, genetic and transformational connections of the given relationship, as well as its reproduction.

The second consideration, which is, incidentally, related to the first, resolves to the fact that, in history, we never encounter a relationship in isolation. This relationship is always an element of a particular system and a more extensive whole (a tribe, a commune, a state, a temple estate, etc.).

Let us first pause to consider a single relationship in isolation. It also comprises a kind of small system whose elements are associated with each other. In every dependence relationship in class society, it is thus possible to identify three component elements: a) the nature of the connection between the one who occupies the dominant position and the dependent individual; b) the degree and nature of the dependence of an exploited individual; and c) the social position, scope, and nature of the power of the one who subjects the other and makes use of his labor. In other words, "who" exploits "whom," and "how"? What are the principal features of these three elements in precapitalist societies?

In Capital, Marx more than once contrasted capitalist and precapitalist society in the following respect. In capitalist society, it is economic compulsion that rules as the decisive factor, while in precapitalist societies, economic life is based upon extra-economic compulsion. The former is characterized by a striving for surplus value, the latter by a striving to accumulate use values. Under capitalism, the commodity economy attains its highest development, whereas in precapitalist societies, this supreme level of development of commodity production, in which the wealth of society takes on the commodity form, is not seen. Thus, we are faced with a logical dichotomy: two broad categories embracing all social structures organized into classes: 1) precapitalist and 2) capitalist societies.

Wherein lies the difference between them, if we compare the basic socio-economic relationship under the capitalist system with that which

all socio-economic relationships in precapitalist societies have in common without, for the present, going into detail on these differences and discriminating among them? Who exploits whom, and how, in the one case and in the other?

Under the capitalist system, the means of production are in the hands of the capitalist, while the worker is deprived of these means. The workers are compelled to sell their labor power so as not to die of hunger. This is economic compulsion: "Poverty drives them to the market," wrote Lenge, "where they await a master who will deign to buy them." (9)

In precapitalist societies, for all the diversity of the forms of dependence existing in them, there is one thing always found in relationships between exploiters and exploited. This is the fact that, in these relationships, it is most often possible to observe the existence of direct compulsion (in its most diverse variants). The slave or serf works not because he is driven by poverty or fears that he will die of hunger, but because he is compelled to work in the interests of another. It is only capitalism that "separates property in the land from relationships of dominance and slavery." (10)

When we examine this fundamental difference between the capitalist system and all the social structures of the precapitalist period, which differ from each other in many respects, we are faced with two questions: 1) what gave rise to this distinction? and 2) what differentiates the forms of dependence in precapitalist societies from each other; wherein lie the causes of these differences?

The economic structure of precapitalist societies was, in substantial measure, based upon direct dominance. The condition for the existence of such a structure was the comparatively low level of development of the productive forces. (11) Only large-scale industrial production makes it possible to replace direct compulsion, no matter what form it takes, by economic compulsion, under which a free worker, deprived of means of production, is compelled, under the pressure of need, to sell his labor power to the capitalist. In all precapitalist societies, it was relationships on the land that were of decisive significance — whom the land belonged to, who worked on it and how, what the relationships were between the owner of the land and those who worked it.

We may hope to obtain the answer to the second question only after careful study of the concrete historical material on precapitalist societies, data which show the unusual abundance and diversity of forms of socio-economic relationships. This diversity of relationships was completely clear to the author of Capital. Speaking of corvée rent, he wrote: "Further, it is clear that in all forms under which the immediate worker remains the 'master' of the means of production and the conditions of labor needed to produce the means of his own existence, property relationships must take the form, under these circumstances, of a direct relationship of dominance and enslavement, and the direct producer emerges as unfree; this is an unfreedom that may be mitigated from serfdom, with corvée labor, to simple quitrent dues." (12)

Thus, although in all relationships of dependence in the sphere of material production one observes the uniform principle of direct dominance and subordination, this principle has manifested itself in the most diverse forms.

As stated above, each individual relationship always constitutes some component of the structure of the "economic system (Gemeinwesen)," as Marx expressed it, (13) and therefore the meaning and form of the dependence can be understood only against the background of, and in conjunction with, the entire system. It is precisely in this connection that it is necessary to emphasize the difference between biology and history.

Synecology, or the science of plant and animal communities, would seem to have certain points in common with what is to be seen upon investigation of social structures. The members of a given botanical (or zoological) species in a community live in a given environment, by which they are influenced (favorably or unfavorably), and themselves, in turn, exercise an influence upon the lives of other organisms in such a community and, in general, upon the surrounding environment. Both abroad and in our country, some ecologists believe it possible to speak of the "sociology" of plants, (14) and others go even further and recognize associations of plants (phytocoenoses) as organisms of a, so to speak, third order. (15) On this matter, we cannot but accept the view of the Soviet editor of MacDougall's work, V. V. Alekhin, that such a comparison is a mechanical analogy, "inasmuch as the phenomena of these orders are qualitatively different, and phytocoenoses do not and cannot, of course, contain sociological regularities of any kind." (16)

Analogies with biological concepts are quite familiar in the science of society. We refer, above all, to the 19th century organic theory of society (Herbert Spencer, Scheffler), under which society is regarded as an organism, and organs and functions are discovered in its structure similar to the organs and functions of a living organism (brain, stomach, kidneys, their functions, etc.). The organic theory has long since been recognized as untenable. But the standpoint of MacDougall and others who regard a forest or a marsh as an organism of a special sort is also not convincing. Nevertheless, one cannot but observe that the idea of an analogy between an organism and a complex system (an association of organisms, or even human society) arose among both sociologists and biologists. We are trying to say that it would be erroneous to transfer the phenomena or laws observed with respect to plant or animal communities to human society, but one cannot fail to recognize that certain similar relationships do exist. This similarity lies not in the presence of identical regularities but in the fact that, in both cases, we find an intimate connection between the individual components of the given system and the whole. (17) One can hardly deny that, in society, each socio-economic relationship is dependent upon the whole, and that it must be examined against the background of the entire economic structure of the extensive whole of which it is a part. Lenin did not avoid the use of the term "organism" with respect to society, although there are no grounds whatever for thinking that he was a partisan of the organic theory. We find him employing this term in connection with the notion that society is an entity of sorts, all the elements of which are interrelated. (18)

Of what does this "entity," this structural unity, consist?

Usually it is held that the structure of society is in a unique relationship with the form of property. Let us turn to a work in which this notion is put forth with extreme precision and is the guiding idea in solving the fundamental problem of interest to the author and in the treatment of the vast amount of concrete historical data assembled in that work — E. M. Shtaerman's The Crisis of the Slaveholding System in the Western Provinces of the Roman Empire [Krizis rabovladel'cheskogo stroia v zapadnykh prov- intsiiakh Rimskoi imperii], Moscow, 1957.

"As we know, the nature of production rela- tions is determined by the forms of property in the means of production. The forms of property determine the situation and mutual relationships among various social groups." (19) This is the author's point of departure. Each of the forms of property corresponds to a particular and dominant socio-economic relationship expressing a mode of exploitation. (20) Then four forms of property in the Roman Empire are listed — slaveholding, communal, the property of private persons in what were termed "salti exempti," (a) and governmental (imperial). The diverse information in the sources is examined in the further presentation on the premise that the four forms of property are the key to an explanation of both the socio-economic development of the empire and its political destiny and even of the ideological struggle. The conceptual rigor, originality of thought, and exceptional erudition displayed make this work an outstanding phe- nomenon in our historical literature.

However, from the standpoint of method, it is difficult to agree with certain of the author's statements.

What is the slaveholding form of property? We read that it was characterized by classical slavery, in which the owner had unlimited power over the slave, who was deprived of means of production and was the property of the owner and, at the same time, it was also marked by lim- itations upon the ownership of the principal means of production, the land, by the owner. (21) The first part of this definition indicates an in-

dividual (albeit, in the opinion of the author, dominant) socio-economic relationship. The second portion pertains not to this relationship between exploiter and exploited, but to a charac- terization of the social structure as a whole. Let us examine that second portion.

"Of course," the author comments, "private property of land did exist and the owner was, in practice, able to dispose of the property belong- ing to him at his discretion" (ibid). Thus, the holder of an estate in classical antiquity was a private property-owner, and the characteristic criterion of private property — the ability to dispose of it at will — was present. Nonetheless, in the author's opinion, this was a limited form of ownership. The limitations were these: a parcel which had not been worked for two years could be occupied by anyone who so wished; town lands existed and an effort was made to keep them intact; dues and expenses were paid by landholders to the towns; prices of foodstuffs were regulated; the emperor, in some cases, confiscated lands in the provinces in order to establish colonies there, etc.

Naturally, it may be said that the presence of urban lands and the tendency to maintain such lands intact do not in themselves signify a lim- itation upon the property of citizens in the land, any more than do price controls placed upon foodstuffs by the towns. It may also be said that the emperor's confiscation of land in the prov- inces is a phenomenon of a different order from the limitation of the property rights of land- owners and slaveholders by the town as an entity. But, nonetheless, in our view the essence of the problem under examination does not lie in this. It would be of greater importance to shed light upon two other questions: 1) is the concept of limited property compatible with the concept of tenure, and, if these concepts coincide, what was the significance not only of the form of property, but of the form of land tenure upon the birth and development of given socio-economic relation- ships; 2) is the form of property (in the given instance, that which is termed the ancient) unambiguously determined by the dominant socio- economic relationship — i.e., the mode by which, to use the words of Marx, "unpaid surplus labor

113

is pumped out of the direct producers" (22) — and, if that is the case, how is this connection between form of property and form of exploitation to be understood?

Both these questions, it would appear, will have to be resolved on the basis of data from the sources. Here, however, we shall adduce only a few thoughts of a general character.

Inasmuch as Marx expressed the concept of unfreedom already cited — "which may be mitigated from serfdom, with corvée labor, to simple quitrent dues," it may be assumed that the form of property will either remain the same or change. If it remains the same (i.e., feudal), then, consequently, the forms of "unfreedom" depend not upon that (i.e., the form of property) or, more accurately, not only upon that, but upon something else in addition. If it (the form of property) changes, then what form will come to take its place? Usually the former assumption is accepted — i.e., that in all these cases the prior form of property remains in effect, to be replaced later by the capitalist form.

From the foregoing we must also draw the conclusion that it was not the form of property alone which determines the forms and character of exploitation, but also the form of tenure and a number of other factors. Only thus is it possible to explain "the infinite variations and gradations" of the economic forms of appropriation of surplus labor.

Marx's definition of property is, in our view, sometimes understood somewhat narrowly. After all, Marx wrote in his well-known letter to Annenkov (23) that social relationships "as a whole (my emphasis — K.Z.) form what is today known as property." [This letter is published in English in The Correspondence of Karl Marx and Friedrich Engels, International Publishers, N.Y., p. 11.] But if we regard each of the forms of property as characterized by one particular socio-economic relationship expressing the mode of exploitation, we will naturally begin to see that relationship everywhere, or to search for it and no other (as often happened in our historiography during the 1930's), although the diversity of the factual data does not bend itself to such interpretation.

It seems to us that the reason for this lack of correspondence between theory and reality is the failure to take into account the degree (24) and the particular regard in which precapitalist societies differ from capitalist. Their class structures are marked by greater complexity: they contained a veritable ladder of social statuses. (25) And whereas, even then, "the oppressor and the oppressed were in eternal antagonism to each other," this antagonism was different in nature and considerably more difficult to understand because of the complexity of the social structure.

It is this which explains the numerous and, in our view, not entirely successful attempts to explain the class struggle of classical antiquity. In these explanations, society is sometimes presented as having been split into two basic classes — slaves and slaveowners — and among the latter are listed classes or strata that characterized capitalist society in the 18th and 19th centuries — a reactionary landholding aristocracy, a moderate and unstable class of traders, etc. Yet the source data do not yield to efforts to fit them into this customary framework and explain them by means of the categories we commonly employ. It goes without saying that the unpersuasiveness of particular efforts does not at all prove that the postulate of the significance of class struggle in the process of historical development is invalid, but testifies only to the difficulties of comprehending that struggle as it occurred in ancient times.

Precapitalist societies contained not only classes, as is the case in capitalist society, which lacks castes, but also contained castes, and the classes and castes usually failed, in very substantial measure, to coincide. The classes of contemporary capitalist society are based on an assumption of equality before the law, which did not exist prior to capitalism. (26) The presence of castes and of corresponding forms of property prevented social elements similar in their place and role in production from merging into a unified class. The process of historical development led rather early to the appearance, within the confines of particular castes, of acute contradictions. Division into classes as such was observable, but membership in a caste (for example, citizenship in a polis — i.e., the opportunity to make use of rights not available to non-citizens and unfree persons, and also to exploit the latter in one way or another) was more important than the specific forms of dependence within the caste (such as a landlord-tenant relationship, or that between the owner of a workshop and a craftsman, etc.). (27) But when the development of society led to a situation in which some possessed means of production (often on a large scale) while others lacked even the means of existence, this contradiction inspired struggle within the caste for a citizen's right to enjoy support by the state, to receive a lot, etc. It was for this reason that, for example, in Greece during the 4th century B.C.E. and later, one could observe actions by the demos against the δυνατοί — i.e., rich citizens — but not actions by peasants, craftsmen, etc.

All the foregoing permits the conclusion, in our opinion, that unless juridical categories are considered, it is impossible to understand, and to explain in historical terms, the very forms of dependence and class struggle in precapitalist societies. The forms of property placed definite limits upon distribution of means of production among the castes, but did not in themselves unambiguously determine the functioning of the social system, which in fact depended upon a number of internal and external conditions.

One of the principal tasks of historical research lies in identifying the connection that existed between the entire system of any one of the precapitalist societies and the complex of diverse, developing socio-economic relationships between castes and classes (and not merely a relationship, but the dominant one). Property in the means of production is the foundation of production relationships. But the complexity of this task lies in the fact that the totality of production relations is determined both by the system as a whole (its morphology) and by the morphological and functional features of the individual socio-economic relationships that go into the make-up of the system. This complexity is also related to the fact that in precapitalist societies we always encounter various forms of per-

sonal dependence and many variants of the application of extra-economic compulsion. This finds expression both in the structure of the system as a whole and in particular socio-economic relationships.

The existence of castes makes it inevitable that they will not coincide with the classes. People's juridical status may be identical while their actual statuses (i.e., forms of dependence) differ. (28) The caste of people who held land from the pharaoh in Hellenistic Egypt embraced very different social elements (29) — from the peasant who was sent under compulsion to do some job on orders of the administration, up to the person who was also "a landholder from the pharaoh" but who had a large estate and considerable financial means, and who himself held numerous people in dependence. In ancient times a slave could, under certain circumstances, find himself in conditions identical with or even superior to those of a freeman. (30) On the contrary, an individual could be juridically free and yet be under conditions of severe dependence and be subjected to compulsion and oppression. In the history of the ancient world, it is possible to observe the rise of classes within the castes and constant change therein depending upon general historical conditions, while the castes were distinguished by a high level of stability (compare, for example, the common social and juridical position of the slaves in Greece and their actual status in various branches of production at various times in its history).

When we speak of the legal status of particular persons and their economic status, we would like our thought to be properly understood. At early stages in social development, the use of force in economic relationships by individuals or the state (and other juridical entities) was unavoidable. Compulsion was a necessary component of the economic system. Public law in general is no mere element of the superstructure, and in precapitalist societies it is indissolubly associated with the economy and serves as an expression of that economy, (31) inasmuch as the latter is based upon extra-economic compulsion. The law states, in general form, to whom compulsion may be applied and, in part, what kind of compulsion is applicable. This law comes into being on the basis of the system of social relationships and, at the outset, juridical status coincides to a certain degree with the factual situation — dominant or dependent — of particular sections of the population. Their political position defines their role in the country's economy, and they constitute caste-classes. But the application of law is determined not only by this general structure of society, but also by a number of other factors which we have already discussed. Therefore one soon observes a lack of correspondence between the juridical and actual situations, although, in the process of further development, they may again approach each other more nearly.

The difference between capitalist and precapitalist societies does not lie in the fact that, in the former, everything is determined by economics and, in the latter, by politics or religion, as was asserted even in Marx's day, (32) but in the fact that, under the capitalist system, this influence of the economy upon other aspects of the life of society is, so to speak, stripped naked, revealed directly, while prior to the era of capitalism it was mediated by the establishment of certain juridical categories in prevailing law. One might say that the form of property determines the possibility for a given social element to function in a certain way in production, places specific limits on its productive activity, and clears the way for the transformation of persons belonging to class-castes deprived of certain rights and privileges into unfree persons oppressed or deprived of means of production, but does not unambiguously predetermine how this social element will function and what place it occupies (or will come to occupy with the passage of time) in the system of production. This latter problem is not subject to solution modo geometrico, by the deductive method, on the basis of analysis of the form of property, but only as the result of a historical study, which must demonstrate the direction in which the process of social development has proceeded.

The Delphic manumissions, with the condition of the paramon, make clear the full meaning of "unfreedom" as a general legal institution. Un-

der this condition — i.e., the obligation to work for the manumitter, usually until the death of the latter or for a stated number of years — the socio-economic relationship continued to exist in approximately the same form as before: the paramonarius was required to perform all his "slavish tasks" (δουλιχὰς χρείας)   and the manumitter had the right to punish him "as he desired" in case of offense. Slaves undertook this nonetheless because, despite these conditions, they did cease to be slaves and their social status changed, although personal dependence upon the former slaveowner continued, sometimes for many years.

The existence of this kind of dual relationship of a dependent person — i.e., a connection directly with the individual upon whom he was dependent, and a connection defining his position in the system as a whole — enables us to understand why a terminology corresponding to relations in a society of that structure must not be mechanically transferred to relations in societies of a different morphological character: the socio-economic relations could be similar (and this similarity was no accident), but social systems could be entirely dissimilar in structure. (33)

The form of property does not in itself define, for example, the actual existence of "the classical type of slavery." The existence and development of this slavery depend upon a set of historical conditions promoting or interfering with its development.

Slavery is a widespread institution at a certain stage of social development, but this does not mean that virtually all peoples have passed through a slaveholding system. It seems to us that the determining factor in this regard is not the presence of slavery, but the change in its role (at the given time in history) in the entire socio-economic structure. For clarification of the concepts of "slave" and "classical slavery," it is not inappropriate to employ certain propositions from the theory of classes of things (logical classes) in mathematical logic.

A class is usually understood to be a set. The relations that may exist between two classes may differ. Certain operations with certain

116

classes give rise to new classes. As we know, the operation called multiplication (or intersection) of classes consists of the formation of a new class. The components of that class consist of those and only those things which belong to both classes. (34) This new class is termed the product or intersection of the original classes. This is the kind of operation we are dealing with when we examine slaves in the juridical sense (as objects of property) and slaves "in the economic sense" as they are frequently understood, reference being to the factual position of various elements in society (lack of means of production, cruel compulsion, etc.). To clarify this we believe it appropriate to have recourse to an example adduced by Tarskii.

If we take circles of any diameter (i.e., things in a particular class) and angles of any size (i.e., things in another class), multiplication of these two classes yields a new class, as, for example, if the vertex of one angle is placed in the center of one of the circles. This new class of things will be the figure termed a sector of a circle (C).

If a similar operation is performed with two classes — "slaves" in the sense of a caste (A) and "slaves" in the sense of persons deprived of means of production and subjected to extra-economic compulsion (B), this leads to the formation of a new class comprising those and only those slaves in the juridical sense of the term who also satisfy the second condition (i.e., do not possess means of production and are subject to compulsion).

Or, if we employ Euler circles:

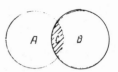

Their position (C) will characterize the relationships usually understood as "classical slavery." Such a sector of classical slavery may come into being very early and exist for a long time, but that will not suffice to justify our speaking of a slaveholding mode of production. This will be possible and will seem persuasive when and only when we are able to determine that this sector is expanding, that a caste is increasingly taking on the character of a class, while the relationship of slavery is becoming dominant in the totality of socio-economic relationships comprising the given system.

We noted above that coincidence between juridical status and actual situation is seen at the outset of the process of socio-political development. This does not contradict what has been discussed here, inasmuch as, while juridical status remains about the same even at a later date, the socio-economic relationship will have changed. At the outset that was a relationship of a different type from that which obtained several centuries later (the slave could possess means of production, and his factual position was different), while here we are dealing with people deprived of means of production and subject to extra-economic compulsion. In the former case, the intersection leads to patriarchal slavery; in the latter — to classical slavery. Therefore one may agree with the assertion that "in Rome there was doubtless a moment in the development of slaveholding for which our concept 'class of slaves' and 'caste of slaves' coincide" and that "this coincidence occurred in an early period of Roman history, the period of relative weakness and underdevelopment of the relationships of slaveholding." (35) We can only guess at the situation in this regard in the early period of Roman history. The caste of slaves and the class of slaves came to approximate each other more closely rather than diverging, on a different basis than in the early period and at a considerably later date, in the 2nd and 1st centuries B.C.E.

These considerations also render comprehensible the fact that the slaveholding system held on and even continued to develop during the first two centuries of the Roman Empire, as Shtaerman demonstrated convincingly in her writings, despite the fact that wars of conquest ceased for a long time. This is all the more important because war was not necessarily the source of supply of slaves.

Of course, the concept "slaveholding system" is broader than that of "classical slavery." The latter may not exist while a slaveholding system does. Slaves may not necessarily be subjected to cruel compulsion, may not be "working animals," may possess property and even the right to take legal actions, but if they are, in general, occupied in production and play a more important role in that realm than free persons, to the point of being the decisive elements there, they have to be regarded as the fundamental class and the system as one of slaveholding. Thus, what is decisive is, of course, the role of slaves in production. (36) But in order for a system to be identified as slaveholding, it will not suffice that slavery, or even "classical slavery," be present if it exists only as a small sector and if it is impossible to discover a tendency toward further development. This, moreover, does not prevent this sector, under changed historical conditions, from coming into motion and increasing sharply in significance.

We are therefore in a position to shed light upon the logical error committed by those historians who listed as slaves persons deprived of means of production and subject to extra-economic compulsion. The operation they performed was not one of multiplication (intersection) but one of combination (addition) of two (logical) classes, which results in a set consisting of those, and only those, elements which belong to one class or the other (or both). (37) If we again have recourse to Euler circles, we obtain:

A is Class 1, B is Class 2, and C is the intersection. The entire shaded surface (A, B, C) is the

combination. It suffices to look at the diagram in order to see how great is the difference between intersection and combination. The effort to discover a large number of slaves sometimes leads to confusion of these two operations and to the mechanical lumping together of slaves in the juridical sense with people who are free but deprived of means of production and subject to compulsion, although the content of these two concepts differs.

Some may object that slaves, in the eyes of ancient law, were not in any sense a caste, but a thing. This view is set forth quite clearly in G. F. Il'in's article "Šūdras and Slaves in the Law Codes of Ancient India" [Shudry i raby v drevneindiiskikh sbornikakh zakonov], (38) in which the author, who rightly contends that no distinct varna of slaves existed, adds that "no such varna could exist, for the very same reason that slaves could not comprise a caste anywhere; for even in ancient India, with its primitive and undeveloped slaveholding, slaves were excluded in principle from the category of persons existing in law and were subject to the laws that regulated property in things." That argument is about as convincing as it would be to say, on the same grounds, that slaves were not a class in India either (or anywhere else), inasmuch as a class is a group of people occupying a particular position in production, while a slave was a thing, not a person!

Slaves did not have the rights of the free and were constantly contrasted to the latter (compare δοῦλοι – ἐλεύθεροι). They comprised a portion of the population of the state differing sharply in legal respects from other portions and, consequently, from our standpoint they comprised a caste, despite the fact that the ancients regarded them as things (although not always, by any means). In general, the ancients had no concept of caste in the modern sense, or of class-caste, even for other sections of the population. These are our concepts, concepts which we use when we wish to shed light not upon the distinct usages of terms designating slaves, among the Greeks for instance, but upon the real circumstances in which a given portion of the population found itself.

In our further presentation we will employ the term "slaves" to denote people belonging to the caste of slaves — i.e., recognized as such by prevailing law and constituting the property of other people, or of groups, or even of a "divinity," but not necessarily a commodity, not necessarily deprived of means of production or even of juridical rights, and not necessarily subject to the cruelest forms of oppression. By "classical slavery" we understand the intersection (39) of the logical class of slaves in this sense with the class of persons deprived of means of production and forced into involuntary labor. Only this usage will enable us to avoid a paradoxical conclusion with respect, for example, to day laborers in Hellenistic Egypt, who were freemen and at the same time allegedly slaves. (40)

The ideas we have expressed are applicable in equal measure to the problem of feudalism. The feudal system of society is sometimes so defined that the definition could be applied to certain societies recognized as slaveholding. If, in fact, it is stated (41) that, with respect to the level of productive forces, the feudal epoch is characterized by a predominance of economically self-contained estates and simple reproduction, with elements of commodity and money relationships, this is just what we observe in most of the societies classed as belonging to the slaveholding system. A second criterion, pertaining to the mode of production, certainly applies to some of these societies although, of course, not to all — a combination of large-scale landed property and the existence of a number of petty farms. Finally, if we take class antagonism as a basis, an antagonism between large landholders and the dependent peasantry they exploit may also be seen, at the very least, in the ancient East and in the Hellenistic countries.

The concept of the "feudal system" defined by these criteria proves to be excessively broad if we direct attention to the fact that these criteria lack any reference to the political structure of feudal society, which was an expression of its socio-economic structure, fundamentally related to extra-economic compulsion.

We see the same phenomenon in the definition of feudalism in the "Introduction" to Volume III of World History [Vsemirnaia istoriia]. Here we read that the land was the property of the feudal lord, that landed property was the basis of medieval feudal society, and that personal dependence of the peasants on the feudal lords, and the extra-economic compulsion deriving therefrom, comprised the typical characteristics of the feudal system. (42) Extra-economic compulsion, however, is a typical characteristic of all precapitalist societies. Furthermore, the formulation "the feudal lords' ownership of the land was the basis of medieval feudal society" suffers from a defect of logic, inasmuch as the concept "feudal lords" enters into the definition but is not itself defined. What is more, one cannot define as feudal lords all large landholders on whose lands the direct producers (peasants) worked, inasmuch as one could then find feudalism in ancient Egypt and in Mesopotamia, which the authors of the Introduction justly criticize scholars abroad for doing, (43) basing themselves exclusively (or primarily) upon a picture of the political system. The logical structure of the conclusion is similar in the two cases. Just as a political system considered separately from its socio-economic base takes on an extra-historical character, so the socio-economic relationships of precapitalist society, when taken in isolation from the political structure, prove to be lacking in the differentia specifica that comprise this structure — the form of property and the system of caste-classes.

We do not regard as acceptable the definition of feudalism as a type of society given in historiography abroad, for example, by Ganshof, (44) inasmuch as the economy, the social structure, and the principal forms of dependence are inadequately described in that definition. Nevertheless this author points to certain significant criteria of the feudal system which are lacking in the definitions of a feudal social system cited above: the development of forms of dependence embracing society as a whole; the extreme fragmentation of property rights; the fragmentation of public authority; the employment of rights belonging to the state in the personal interests of individuals, etc.

In characterizing a system of society in the precapitalist era, it is not permissible, or so it seems to us, to disregard its political system, inasmuch as the latter comprises an expression of the fundamental principle of the economies of those times, which were built upon the employment of extra-economic compulsion.

If, in a caste system, a portion of the rights vested in the central authority, relative to the population of a given district or region, is held by a given social stratum (to be precise, the military, as for example the knights in Eastern Germany in the 12th through the 16th centuries), this population, even while most of it remains free, eventually falls into dependence upon the neighbor who holds the rights in question. This is not yet either feudalism or serfdom. But if the feudal-lord-to-be employs his power in such a fashion as to place the population subordinated to him in a position of economic dependence and burdens it with levies (or appropriates levies intended for the central authority), and constricts the personal freedom of his neighbor peasants or craftsmen (for example, their freedom of movement), then he becomes a genuine feudal lord.

We have already pointed out that the existence of a particular individual socio-economic relationship is in itself not enough to determine whether we are dealing with a slaveholding system or with feudalism, because both in antiquity and in the Middle Ages one encounters the most diverse forms of dependence, some of them very similar to one other. Also inadequate is the criterion that has usually been adduced to prove that we are dealing with slaves — the fact that the people so designated in the sources are the property of others and may be bought and sold. To confine oneself to this is merely to record the existence of slavery, but that does not settle the question of the role of slaves in production.

It seems to us that the principal difference rests not in these individual characteristics of slavery or feudalism, but in the nature of the social system out of which a slaveholding or feudal system may later develop. When extra-economic compulsion was dominant, the organi-

zation of the state — i.e., of the apparatus of compulsion — had to be of vast significance to socio-economic relationships, or, to be more accurate, that political organization, that system of juridical categories which embraced a given portion of the population, was an expression of the economy. The direction of social development was determined in some measure by the locus and extent of power.

If that power belonged to the civil community (here we are not thinking of political arrangements, which might take various forms — oligarchical or democratic, for example), then it is natural that that kind of community would counterpose itself both to foreigners and to unfree elements falling under the authority of its citizens. This still did not mean that its further development would necessarily follow the path of an increase in slaveholding, let alone that it would result in "classical slavery," although it contained the possibility of developing in such a direction.

It is another matter if some portion of political authority was in the hands of individual persons who had the opportunity, by using that authority, to subordinate their fellow-citizens — or (in case of conquest) people of other tribes — to themselves economically. Once again, we have here not a complete, fully formed system of feudalism, but only certain possibilities of movement in that direction.

Finally, if what confronts the dependent and underprivileged mass of the population is neither the privileged and ruling community of citizens nor individual persons endowed with stated political rights, but rather the state in the person of the holder of political power (with unlimited or even with limited authority) who is sometimes also the ultimate owner of the land — in this case, all strata of the population depend upon him, directly or in mediated form. In such a state, it is not the totality of citizens or persons belonging to a given caste and possessing political rights who stand opposed to the rest of the population, which lacks political rights or is in a state of dependence. The line of demarcation runs, rather, between those strata from which the ruling caste was formed and in whose interests the machinery of government operated (which could include diverse socio-economic elements — officials, landholders, aristocrats, and, later, major figures in trade — but always people intimately associated with the machinery of government), and all the rest of the population, free and dependent. (45)

In offering this thought, we do not at all wish to picture the state as some sort of independent force standing above society. No. In this case as well, a political organization is an expression of the socio-economic system, an instrument for the suppression of a given portion of society in the interests of another, dominant portion. But the exploitation of the immediate producers may be organized in diverse fashion, and the role of the state in this organization of exploitation may differ. The state was not only an instrument for the suppression of the exploited, but was capable of exploiting them itself; or, to be more precise, by making direct use of its institutions, its machinery, its vast power, the ruling strata of the population, comprising the ruling caste, could exploit the bulk of the people. In antiquity we see this in Eastern countries (Egypt, for example), and later in the Hellenistic states and in the Roman Empire. It would be wrong to equate such a system of organization of production relations with slaveholding or feudal society. The difference is conditioned both by the nature of the entire social system and by the special features of the forms of dependence. These forms may be very diverse, (46) but a characteristic feature of them has been wide application of governmental compulsion.

* * *

In order to overcome the difficulties that arise in application of the concept "slavery" to concrete historical material, there is need, it seems to us, for greater clarity and completeness of content in the concepts with which we have to operate, with the object of attaining a certain systematization of the factual data in all their variety. Toward that end, it is obviously necessary to enter into a more detailed examination of the criteria that describe the forms of dependence and

that we employ in defining them, inasmuch as the combination or, on the contrary, the absence of various of these criteria determines this diversity. On the other hand, it is important to take note of the principal differences which have existed in social systems where we encounter forms of dependence. On the basis of the foregoing, it may be asserted that if we confine ourselves to overly general definitions without more detailed analyses of these systems (such as, for example: "what we see here is a slaveholding society," "an underdeveloped slaveholding society," or "a slaveholding society with survivals of the preclass system"), we will not be able to attain satisfactory results in the understanding and explanation of historical phenomena.

As we have seen, most of the forms of dependence in precapitalist societies are characterized by the existence of direct compulsion. But whereas we do find this in a majority of cases, the degree and form of this compulsion are very diverse. Control may be found to exist both over the person of the exploited individual and over the means of production and means of consumption. In precapitalist societies we can see, in most cases, control either over the worker's person or over both his person and the means of production, or control over a portion of the means of production (the land, for example). On the other hand, both kinds of enslavement may be complete or partial. Thus, we emerge with the following forms of dependence:

A. The individual is free and:

a) the means of production are in the hands of the exploiter. This form of dependence may also be encountered in precapitalist societies, but control of the means of production alone is, as a general rule, characteristic only of the capitalist system;

b) the basic portion of the means of production (the land, for example) is at the disposal of the ruling caste or class-caste alone, but there are free people who are deprived of the right to own this land (for example, the metics in Athens).

B. The individual is enslaved

1. entirely:

a) the means of production belong wholly to the ruling caste or class-caste;

b) the means of production are partly in the hands of the exploited;

2. partially:

a) the means of production belong to members of the ruling caste;

b) the means of production are partly in the hands of the exploited.

The authority of the master over the person of a dependent individual is always, to some degree, combined with control of the means of production, although the forms of this control may differ.

The four forms of dependency relationships in precapitalist societies given here (B, 1a and b; 2a and b) are derived by pure logic via the concepts of complete or partial appropriation of persons or means of production. But it is clear from this classification of concepts how different the character of forms of dependence may be. A dependent individual may be in complete bondage to his master (individual or collective), and all means of physical compulsion may be applied to him, and yet he may not be a slave (see the description of work in the ore mines of Ethiopia, borrowed by Diodorus III, 12-14 from Agatarchides), or modes of compulsion may be limited in one degree or another (compare the limited power of the Spartiate over the helots on his lot or the proviso in some Delphic manumissions concerning the right to punish a paramonarius, but not so as to cripple him, e.g., SGDI, 2261: πλαγαῖς ἀσινέοις).

The "bondage" of the dependent individual is conditioned by various forms of compulsion. He may be bound to the person of his master or to the latter's property (primarily land) and be a sort of appendage to that property. On the other hand, the dependence may be permanent and transmitted from generation to generation: it may be traditional or temporary.

Marx ascribed much significance to tradition in socio-economic relationships. He wrote on this in connection with the question of whether serfs had the right to accumulate property, (47) and he asserted that "in the primitive and undeveloped state attained by this relationship in social production and the mode of production corresponding thereto, tradition has to play a decisive role." By tradition we are to understand

here the regular reproduction of the base and the corresponding relationship, giving stability to the given mode of production.

"Traditional" social acts also occupy a place of prominence in the sociology of Max Weber. In particular, he also points to the fact that simple repetition of events gives them the significance of a kind of norm. (48) With respect to classical antiquity, it was Shtaerman who first directed attention to the role of tradition in one of the most interesting chapters of her monograph on slavery in the Roman Empire during the 1st and 2nd centuries C.E. (49) She examines the significance of tradition in connection with the question of the condition of the given form of socio-economic relations (their stability or observable decline) and of phenomena in these cases in the realm of ideology.

We should like to approach the problem of tradition from a somewhat different viewpoint. Is it possible to discriminate between traditional and nontraditional forms of dependence? This question was dealt with by Oertel in his speculations about liturgies, (50) which he regards as nontraditional, by contrast to "traditional dependence." On this matter it may be said that there is a difference here, but it is relative in nature. The liturgies which all wealthy citizens of Athens were required to bear were, of course, something other than the traditional burden that fell upon many slaves, but these liturgies, too, became traditional in considerable measure. Likewise, the μερισμός in Ptolemaic Egypt of the 2nd and 1st centuries B.C.E. — i.e., compulsory short-term rental of land — was a short-term liturgy (51) which was repeated but did not at all become a universal law and is in no sense evidence that holders of land from the crown were "serfs." However, the very repetition of a measure helps it to begin to take on the nature of a tradition. Thus, it becomes necessary, in each specific instance, to consider this criterion in relationships of dependence.

The factor of compulsion may find expression in the confiscation of products of the labor of a dependent individual (all or only a portion of those products), in the imposition of penalties for misdeeds (from the standpoint of the possessor of authority), in limitations on freedom of movement (again, the degree may vary: total attachment to the given place or prohibition against moving to a given place; prohibition of following one's master's move or, on the contrary, the obligation to do so, etc.; assignment to work in a rigidly defined craft, etc.). Thus, even a single aspect of dependence — the presence of extra-economic compulsion — may determine numerous variants of relationships.

It is also impossible to content ourselves with a general assertion as to the presence or absence of means of production in the hands of a dependent individual. Means of production may be lacking in whole or in part. A dependent individual may, for example, possess implements but no land, or he may have land but be limited in his right to dispose of it. Or, again, he may have a certain amount of property, even of a variety of types — real estate (a house, for example), or movable property, or money, or both, and sometimes even persons dependent upon himself. On the other hand, he may lack not only means of production but means of subsistence, which he obtains from his master in the form of a monthly allotment, etc.

Also of significance are the mode and scale of appropriation of the products of dependent persons. These products may be taken from them in whole or in part, in kind or in the form of money. The dependent individual has to work for his master, and here again he may have to give the latter his labor time in full or only in part (corvée in the Middle Ages, the operae of the coloni as indicated by the inscription from Saltus Burunitanus, and so forth). In this regard, it is also important where he works — on the land or in the mines, in the home of his owner or in his workshop.

This is important because these conditions of work influence the form of dependence (see, for example, the conditions of labor and the status of workers in the weaving shops of Hellenistic Egypt), and particularly because they are related in different ways to the general environment of developing commodity exchange. Also of significance is the question of whether the labor of the dependent person is supervised and, if so,

how, or whether he is granted the right to work more or less independently, and merely required to provide a specified level of earnings (in kind or in money; compare, for example, the condition of slaves under the conditions of ἀποφορά in Athens during the 4th century B.C.E.

The scale of extra-economic compulsion — its level and intensity — is by no means necessarily proportional to the level of authority over the means of production. One can imagine, for example, a situation in which the exploited possess a portion of the means of production (implements, for example), work on their own and have the use of part of the harvest received, and even have the right to accumulate certain financial surpluses, and yet at the same time are subjected to the cruelest compulsion. The helots of Sparta, for example, were in approximately these circumstances.

We have already noted that the study of a single socio-economic relationship in isolation cannot be fruitful. The dependence upon the whole is dual: this whole, one element of which is the given relationship, determines the significance and place of the given relationship in the entire structure of society, while this whole may itself be exploiter or exploited. (52) As we have seen, this dependence of the part upon the whole acquires particular significance in precapitalist societies in conjunction with the existence of castes in these societies, and with the process of appearance and initial development of class contradictions in the true sense, and of classes in the sense of social groups whose members occupy a similar place in production.

On the whole, taking into consideration the complexity of social ties and the diversity of relations, and attempting to systematize, in some measure, the forms of dependence, we are faced with the need to solve a dual problem: a) to establish the taxonomic units for these forms, and b) to carry out similar work for the systems into which particular socio-economic relationships enter.

Both individual relationships and entire systems thereof appear and develop within particular natural and historical conditions. Therefore it is impossible not to observe that, from the time of archaic Greece to the end of classical antiquity, all forms of direct compulsion existed and changed under conditions of the growth (or, correspondingly, decline) of commodity production, which could not but be a shaping and modifying factor in the development of diverse forms of dependence. The operation of this factor could manifest itself in different ways. In many cases, the development of commodity exchange facilitated an increase in extra-economic compulsion, inasmuch as the exploited and dependent person became a kind of commodity and was converted into a thing purchased and sold, while the possibility that his value could be realized in the market satisfied the drive for profit (χέρδος) that manifested itself so vividly, for example, in Greek society as early as the first half of the 4th century B.C.E. (Xenophon), and promoted its further development.

On the other hand, the increase in commodity exchange could sometimes lead to a certain weakening in the direct power of the master over the dependent person, and to the latter's beginning to enjoy greater independence; although his legal position had not changed, his present factual situation differed from what it had been when he was working on someone else's farm under the direct supervision of his owner. Now he was required to bring to his master something of the order of quitrent after selling the products of his specialized labor outside their relationship.

The position of a dependent individual, whatever it was, was influenced by the transformation of the dominant individual into a trader with an interest in selling on the market the products of the labor of the persons dependent upon him. It could happen that the dependent individual himself became a trader. The effort on the part of the state to make use of the benefits of commodity exchange also led to the development of distinctive forms of compulsion, in combination with the principles of commodity production — from complete enslavement, with employment of the cruelest forms of compulsion, to comparatively mild forms of dependence, resolving to the payment of a portion of one's income to the state.

Finally, inasmuch as commodity production did not by any means embrace all forms of labor, the products of the labor of dependent persons did not necessarily have to go beyond the confines of the given economic unit (individual or collective), in which case relationships of dependence were characterized by their relative independence from the development of commodity exchange.

The diversity of forms of dependence is facilitated by the diverse concrete historical conditions of their genesis and subsequent development. One can only welcome the fact that Soviet scholarship has begun to express awareness of the erroneousness of underestimating the role of the geographical environment in the development of societies. (53) Gurevich is inclined to ascribe very high significance to the combination of natural conditions "in the appearance and intensive development of the system of classical slavery in the lands of the Mediterranean or, for example, in the retardation of the evolution of many peoples of the equatorial belt."

Although we do not consider it possible to come to so firm a conclusion on the problem before us without careful preliminary analysis of the very essence of forms of dependence and of "empirical circumstances," we must recognize, nonetheless, that without a study of the interaction of a given system of socio-economic relationships and the natural environment in which it appeared and developed, as well as of the historical circumstances — interrelationships with other social systems, the rate and nature of political development, and so forth — it is also impossible to understand the development of the forms of dependence of interest to us.

It has already been remarked above that, in analyzing and classifying forms of dependence, it is necessary to take into consideration their genesis and the distinctive features of this particular genesis. In general, two modes of such genesis may be observed: dependence may develop either in the form of individual socio-economic relationship, of the nature of private law, or as the result of political influence, within the purview of public law. The first type of genesis includes, for example, such instances of the establishment of dependence as the dependence of a debtor upon a creditor resulting from

124

the indebtedness of the former when he is unable
to pay off his debt; dependence following upon a
court decision or as the result of sale of oneself;
the appearance of dependence as the result of a
contract concluded with a person or a divinity
(such as, for example, the private rental of land,
the dependence of χάτοχοι in Hellenistic Egypt)
or, finally, bondage as the result of outright compulsion (by brigands, pirates, a magnate in the
Late Roman Empire, etc.).

But dependence is often in the realm of public
law and appears as the result of an action by the
state. For example, we may note conquest as a
factor in the establishment of dependence, a consequence of which may be enslavement or the
more or less onerous dependence of the population of entire regions. Further, one must point
to the policy of the state with respect to particular strata of a country's people (compare, for
example, the edict of Ptolemy II Philadelphus on
σώματα λαιχά in Syria). The demands of the
state treasury (in China under the Han dynasty,
in Hellenistic Egypt, in the Late Roman Empire)
were of great significance in classical antiquity.

The socio-political structure, containing the
prerequisites for development of particular relationships, played the most significant role of all
in the genesis of forms of dependence.

Another historically important factor in the
genesis of relationships of dependence was their
nature as regards their reproduction. In this
connection, relationships of dependence also
have to be divided into two types, which we may
term the monogenetic and polygenetic forms.
The former includes those which, once having
arisen, are handed down from generation to generation without the need for repeating the process
whereby the relationship initially came into being:
reproduction is determined by the initial act of
establishing dependence (helotism, slavery by
descent from a male or female slave —
οἰχογενεῖς , slaves; serfdom). In the polygenetic forms, the process of appearance of the dependence continues to be repeated and, moreover,
this dependence arises in various ways (the development of the colonate, and slavery due to
various causes — taking of prisoners, sale of
oneself, indebtedness, etc.). Upon examination

of both the monogenetic and the polygenetic
forms, we are always able to identify the influence of two general factors — direct compulsion
or commodity production — but in different com-
binations and degrees.

It is necessary to take note of the fact that the
genesis of relationships may be similar, while
the relationships themselves, appearing as the
result of a given mode of appearance, may differ.
In comparatively late classical antiquity, in cases
of mass-scale seizure of prisoners of war, even
that portion of the population which did not participate in military operations was often enslaved
in the sense of classical slavery, whereas, for
example, mass-scale seizure of the population
of an enemy country by the Hittites did not by
any means lead to the development of classical
slavery: the captives were taken to internal regions of the country and settled on the land.
Compulsion was expressed in the fact that these
people (NAM·RA) were forbidden to leave the
locality where they had been settled, but there
is a very great difference between that and classical slavery. Thus, whereas the nature of genesis is of significance in the appearance of a
given form of dependence, what was primary
was not who these people had been, but who they
became — i.e., the place of the newly arising relationship in the system and its morphological
and functional nature.

The genesis of a single relationship cannot
play the role in history that phylogenesis plays
in biology. The whale today, despite its mode of
life and certain morphological characteristics,
is not regarded as a fish by anyone, nor is a bat
classified as a bird. What is decisive here is
not only and not even primarily morphological
analysis, but phylogenesis. In history, another
situation obtains. The identical genesis of a relationship (for example, as the result of conquest) may lead to the most diverse results.
Compare the fate of the population of Sparta
after the Doric conquest or that of the 150,000
Epirots made into slaves by the Roman consul
in 167 B.C.E. or the status of the Egyptian population in Hellenistic Egypt after the Macedonian
conquest, or, finally, the destiny of the Copts
after the Arabs became established in Egypt in

640 C.E. It is entirely possible for cases to occur in which differing conditions give rise to similar or even identical relationships which may be arranged, by their principal criteria, in groups of more universal nature, and thus comprise a particular system.

Moreover, it cannot be said that the appearance of forms of dependence is always accompanied by the employment of compulsion. Their appearance may involve "free" agreement of the parties concerned in the sense that a given individual has it in his power to make or not make the corresponding agreement. The decision is determined by conditions of advantage, economic need, and so forth. The $\theta\epsilon\rho\acute{a}\pi o\nu\tau\epsilon\varsigma$, in the Homeric period, were persons of this type, as were the $\varphi\iota\lambda o\iota$ warriors serving under a mercenary commander in Xenophon's Anabasis and Cyropaedia, hired laborers in Greece and the Hellenistic states, the clients of patrons toward the end of the Roman Empire when not only individuals but towns accepted the patronage of some powerful figure. So were the dependents of the patricians in the Late Roman Empire and the vassals of the Middle Ages. This "freedom" was for the most part illusory. But it is important to note that, in these cases, compulsion was not direct and extra-economic, but was marked by quite another character: it bore a certain similarity to economic compulsion in the capitalist era. This is understandable, for in all societies the means of production are, as a rule, in the hands of members of the ruling caste or class-caste, and therefore a situation can always arise in which a man who is not in bondage but who lacks means of production entirely, or even in part, is compelled to enter "voluntarily" into dependence upon a person possessing these means. The basic difference from the capitalist system, however, lay in the fact that the dependence arising in this manner was primarily personal in nature and tied the dependent individual to a specific patron, and that this dependence was not at all a consequence of high development of commodity production, but was usually a way out of an even more onerous dependence upon the state, or even, in the case of people who had lost their connection with that state, a means of finding some other source of support.

All of the foregoing was intended to promote the clarification of the fundamental problem of interest to us — the question of the techniques for systematizing socio-economic relationships. We wished to demonstrate that, in attempts to develop such a taxonomy, a correct method would be to proceed from the data in the sources and, first, to identify the lowest taxonomic units, and then, proceeding upward step by step — i.e., to units incorporating those below — to go on to more universal and abstract concepts. Toward that end, it seems to us that it is necessary to avoid a decision beforehand on the social system with which we are dealing, and to clarify in sequence and, as fully as the sources will permit, the criteria for the various forms of dependence, and then to take a careful look at the picture showing the totality of the relationships we have determined. This study of various forms of dependence should be associated with investigation of the structure of the system of which these forms are components.

Naturally, different criteria differ in meaning in systematics. Just as the present-day taxonomy of flowering plants is not built on some single characteristic, as was the case in Linnaeus' system, but, as we have already stated, takes into consideration a diversity of factors, phylogenesis above all, so would a system of forms of dependence, if it proves possible to create it, have to be built on more than one criterion, however significant. We cannot confine ourselves either to only that contradiction that was so vital in and characteristic of the mind of man in classical antiquity $\delta o\tilde{\upsilon}\lambda o\varsigma$ — $\dot{\epsilon}\lambda\epsilon\upsilon\theta\epsilon\rho o\varsigma$, or to the most modern formula — that a slave is a being in bondage and lacking means of production. We must, as far as possible, seek to take the most important criteria into consideration in two aspects — the criteria characterizing the relationship between the dependent individual and the one upon whom he is dependent and, on the other hand, the criteria which determine the place and significance of this relationship in the social system as a whole.

The determination of what is the significant criterion flows from the basic methodological considerations set forth above. These criteria resolve, all in all, to the following: a) control over the person of the dependent individual and/or over the means of production — i.e., the degree and forms of extra-economic compulsion; b) the place and significance of a given form of dependence in the entire structure of society (in the system of classes, castes, and class-castes); criteria indicating c) the connection between the form of dependence and the development of commodity production; and also, d) the manner in which it is conditioned by the historical environment, and its connections of genesis and transformation.

One of the problems in studying forms of dependence in the various societies of the ancient world also must be the creation of a more or less rigorous taxonomic system of forms of dependence in their necessary and intimate connection with social systems. Only on the basis of such study is it possible, it seems to us, to approach the problem of the social system more deeply and in accordance with historical reality. Lotze has observed that "gradual transitions exist between various forms and it is necessary to bear in mind at all times that all systematization is merely a means auxiliary to thought." We cannot accept this formulation without qualification. Of course, it is impossible to conceive of or describe an entity in the total diversity of its properties and functions. Every discipline must have recourse to idealized models, abstractions. But, nevertheless, scientific systematization should rest upon actual and significant traits of the entities to be investigated, and in this sense systematization cannot be regarded as a mere convenience for thought. The type of systematization of which we speak can be arrived at by careful study not only of the principal types of relationships, or of those which appear to us to be such, but also of the numerous forms which blend into each other, of which Lotze reminds us.

"Bondage," both in various epochs and within the bounds of a single period, has in reality (and not only in the minds of contemporaries) taken on a great diversity of forms, and it is only study of these forms that can yield a completely valid conclusion with respect to what the totality comprised.

If, as a result of study, we were to arrive at the same general conclusion that has been reached without the analysis that seems to me to be necessary, this conclusion would gain a firmer foundation than it now has.

Editor's Note

a) In the Roman Empire, fields which were taken from publicly held land, turned over to especially deserving citizens, and thereafter considered their property.

Footnotes

1) E. Mayr, E. Linsley, and R. Usinger, Metody i printsipy zoologicheskoi sistematiki, Moscow, 1956, p. 25; G. G. Simpson, "The Principles of Classification and a Classification of Mammals," Bull. of American Museum of Natural History, Vol. 85, New York, 1945, p. 1 ff.; J. Huxley, The New Systematics, Oxford, p. 2.

2) "Taxonomy," in accordance with common usage, is employed as a synonym of systematics.

3) V. I. Lenin, Poln. sobr. soch., Vol. 1, p. 139; compare p. 165 ff.

4) We refer primarily to the approach typical of our historiography of the ancient world during the 1930's and 1940's. The past decade has seen much change in this regard. Today many historians are no longer seeking "to reduce" "intermediate social states, as well" — i.e., forms of dependence which are not slavery — to slavery "in the broad sense of that concept" (as did L. A. El'nitskii in his Vozniknovenie i razvitie rabstva v Rime v VIII-III vv. do n.e., Moscow, 1964, p. 15).

5) Marx and Engels, Soch., Vol. 23, p. 526.

6) Mayr et al., op. cit., p. 23 ff.

7) Historians of zoology have observed that the weak side of Aristotelian zoology is classification, of which we find no systematic treatment in Aristotle (Histoire des animaux d'Aristote, translated by J. Barthélemy — Saint Hilaire, I, Paris, 1883, Preface, p. CXVII). Nonetheless, Aristotle found it necessary, at the very beginning of his Historia Animalium, to speak of the

nature of the differences among living beings, which he regarded as being in their mode of life, activities, habits, and the parts of their organisms (Aristotle, De Anim. Hist., A 487^a, p. 11 ff.:

Αι δε διαφοραι των ζωων εισι χατα τε τους βιους χαι τας πραξεις χαι τα τηφη χαι τα μορια ...), and he deals repeatedly with questions of systematics in the presentation that followed (for example, G 490^b, p. 8 ff., and elsewhere).

8) Mayr et al., op. cit., p. 10.

9) Quoted by Marx: Marx and Engels, Soch., Vol. 26, Part I, p. 349.

10) Marx and Engels, Soch., Vol. 25, Part II, pp. 166-167.

11) See Marx and Engels, Soch., Vol. 23, p. 89.

12) Marx and Engels, Soch., Vol. 25, Part II, p. 353.

13) Ibid., p. 354.

14) J. Braun-Blanquet, Pflanzensoziologie. Grundzüge der Vegetationskunde, Vienna and New York, 1964.

15) W. B. MacDougall, Ekologiia rastenii, Moscow, 1935.

16) Ibid., p. 4 (Preface by V. V. Alekhin).

17) Compare L. Bertalanffy, Das biologische Weltbild, I, Bern, 1949, p. 11: "At present, however, problems expressed in the concepts 'entity,' 'organization,' and 'form,' the taproot of which is to be found in the field of biology, are being posed in all sciences." However, Bertalanffy is inclined to place excessive emphasis on the exceptional place of biology in the system of the sciences. To be specific, the concepts of "entities" and "systems" are being advanced today for reasons other than the fact that the root of these concepts lies in biology.

18) See V. I. Lenin, Poln. sobr. soch., Vol. 1, pp. 165, 167.

19) E. M. Shtaerman, Krizis rabovladel'-cheskogo stroia v zapadnykh provintsiiakh Rimskoi imperii, Moscow, 1957, p. 25.

20) Compare, ibid., pp. 26, 30, 41, 44, 47 ff.

21) Ibid., p. 26.

22) Marx and Engels, Soch., Vol. 25, Part II, p. 354.

23) Marx and Engels, Soch., Vol. 27, p. 406.

24) See V. I. Lenin, Poln. sobr. soch., Vol. 1, p. 167.

25) Marx and Engels, Soch., Vol. 4, p. 424 ff.

26) See V. I. Lenin, Poln. sobr. soch., Vol. 2, p. 475 ff.

27) K. K. Zel'in, Bor'ba politicheskikh gruppirovok v Attike v VI v. do n. e., Moscow, 1964, p. 173.

28) Compare, for example, the marked change in the status of the slaves in Arabia after the granting of oil concessions in 1947 (R. Maugham, The Slaves of Timbuktu, New York, 1961, p. 2 ff.).

29) K. K. Zel'in, Issledovaniia po istorii zemel'nykh otnoshenii v Egipte II-I vekov do nashei ery, Moscow, 1960, p. 193; V. V. Struve, "Obshchestvennyi stroi ellinisticheskogo Egipta," VI, 1962, No. 2, p. 75.

30) Compare, for example, the positions and activity of certain slaves as depicted in documents of the New Babylonian and Persian periods, when these slaves were independent for all practical purposes, had rights before the law, disposed of both real and movable property, concluded transactions of various types, etc. (M. San Nicolò and H. Petschow, Babylonische Rechtsurkunden aus dem 6. Jh. v. Chr., Munich, 1960, No. 7; O. Krückmann, Babylonische Rechts- und Verwaltungsurkunden aus der Zeit Alexanders und der Diadochen, Weimar, 1931, p. 16; G. Cardascia, Les Archives des Murašu, une famille d'hommes d'affaires babyloniens à l'époque perse (455-403 av. J. Chr.), Paris, 1951, p. 12 ff.

31) ". . .the property relationship must at the same time present itself as a direct relationship of mastery and enslavement. . ." (Marx and Engels, Soch., Vol. 25, Part II, p. 353).

32) Marx and Engels, Soch., Vol. 23, p. 91, fn. 33.

33) Compare, for example, the essentially uncritical employment of feudal terminology by Cardascia (op. cit., p. 5 ff.) to describe the socio-economic relationships of the Persian period. We permit ourselves the term "uncritical" because such phenomena as the fief, feudataire, seigneur, vassal, beneficiaires (des groupes de fiefs), etc., are treated in this work as though they were self-evident without either definition of the terms or validation of this

usage. The fact that the king gave land away is held to be in itself evidence of the existence of feudalism (p. 8). The author, in criticizing the interpretation of one of the documents provided by an American scholar, Lutz, agrees with the latter completely in his general attitude toward the Murašu archive, in which, they both believe, one may find a large number of parallels between Babylonian feudalism and European feudalism of the Middle Ages (Cardascia, op. cit., p. 182).

34) A. Tarskii, Vvedenie v logiku i metodologiiu deduktivnykh nauk, Moscow, 1948, p. 118.

35) S. L. Utchenko, Krizis i padenie Rimskoi respubliki, Moscow, 1935, p. 141 ff.

36) The conclusion drawn by Ruben (W. Ruben, Die Lage der Sklaven in der altindischen Gesellschaft, Berlin, 1957, p. 101 ff.) is typical in this regard. He recognizes that slaves did not play the decisive role in production in ancient India, that in this agrarian country, with its small-scale production by peasants and craftsmen, employment of slave labor was unprofitable and that slaves merely helped the woman and the head of the family around the house. It can be said with truth, however, the author notes, that late Indian society takes on feudal characteristics. Nonetheless, the social system of ancient India, Ruben concludes, was slaveholding, although undeveloped as compared with that of Greece and Rome.

37) J. Kemeni, J. Snell, and J. Thompson, Vvedenie v konechnuiu matematiku, Moscow, 1965, p. 78 ff.; Tarskii, op. cit., p. 117 ff.

38) VDI, 1950, No. 2, p. 106 ff.

39) In the sense indicated above (page 13).

40) Struve, op. cit., p. 79 ff.

41) A. I. Neusykhin, Sud'by svobodnogo krest'-ianstva v Germanii v VIII-XII vv., Moscow, 1964, p. 17.

42) Vsemirnaia istoriia, III, Moscow, 1957, p. 10 ff.

43) Ibid., p. 19.

44) F. L. Ganshof, Qu'est-ce que la feódalité?, Brussels, 1957, p. 11.

45) We do not deal here with the question of what has been termed the "Asian mode of production," because that question requires separate consideration. In any case, what we are discussing here is broader and more diverse than the rule of a supreme property owner, the king, over an assemblage of small communes.

46) Marx and Engels, Soch., Vol. 25, Part II, p. 354.

47) Ibid., p. 356.

48) Max Weber, Wirtschaft und Gesellschaft, Tübingen, 1925, p. 378 ff.

49) E. M. Shtaerman, Rabstvo v Rimskoi imperii. Italiia (in press).

50) F. Oertel, Die Liturgie. Studien zur ptolemäischen und kaiserlichen Verwaltung Ägyptens, Leipzig, 1917, p. 3.

51) Zel'in, Issledovaniia po istorii zemel'-nykh otnoshenii v Egypte II-I vekov do nashei ery, p. 335.

52) That is, if one conceives of an individual relationship A → B, where A is the party holding power over the person of B and the means of production, and B is the dependent person, it may be that A or B is not a separate individual, but a group entity of some kind.

53) A. Ia. Gurevich, "Obshchii zakon i konkretnaia zakonomernost' v istorii," VI, 1965, No. 8, p. 19 [see Soviet Review, 1966, Vol. VII, No. 3].

54) D. Lotze, Μεταξὺ ἐλευθέρων χαι' δουλων Studien zur Rechtsstellung unfreier Landbevölkerungen in Griechenland bis zum 4. Jh. v. Chr., Berlin, 1959, p. 60.

Empirical Methodology and Technique

Sovetskaia etnografiia, 1964, No. 3

S. B. Rozhdestvenskaia

AN EXPERIMENT IN COMPUTER PROCESSING OF ETHNOGRAPHIC DATA

(From Materials of the Gorky Detachment of the Combined Expedition
of the Institute of Ethnography, Academy of Sciences, USSR)

The study of modern forms of culture and daily life requires the use of a broad range of sources, including survey data. Inclusive and sample surveys of factory, collective-farm, and state-farm work forces, of individual settlements, and of districts have become part of the normal practice of ethnographers. The study of individual targets by the ethnographer's traditional technique of observation, description, inquiry, and use of documentary data is combined with questionnaire data presenting information on some aspect of each object of investigation.

Inclusive surveys are of particular importance in studies of urban populations, complex in their composition and history of formation.

The criterion for choosing targets for particularly thoroughgoing ethnographic study, the proportion to be maintained among the various groups of subjects (by nationality, age, occupation, etc.), the real number of persons in each group within a factory or collective farm, or among the population of a city, a Cossack village — i.e., questions of representativeness of selec-

tion and the degree to which a sampling is in accord with the entire mass of available information — are matters that can be resolved only with the assistance of questionnaire surveys providing complete coverage of the population to be considered.

However, the processing of mass-scale survey data by manual means is extraordinarily laborious and limits the possibilities for utilization of such material. On the other hand, computer processing permits rapid calculations with data describing the frequency of various phenomena, and equally rapid establishment of interconnections among them. In this connection, the special and, it would appear, purely technical question of the time required to process the material acquires particular significance, inasmuch as when one undertakes ethnographic observations, particularly in a complex and numerically large urban population, availability of the finished results of processing of questionnaire data is particularly important in the selection of objects for study. Moreover, when survey data can be processed rapidly, our information on rapidly changing forms of culture and daily life does not lose significance, while the slow manual processing of survey data causes such information to lose its sharpness.

Simple operations of calculation — the mere totalling of questionnaire data on certain problems — make it possible, when computers are employed, to make more observations and draw more conclusions than when a questionnaire is processed by hand. For example, when manual methods are employed, the population dynamics of a new town or factory is usually calculated by periods of several years grouped together, but not individually for each year, in such categories as the date of arrival of town dwellers at their permanent address or the hiring of a worker at a factory. Likewise, the identification of the age composition of the work force of an enterprise, when done manually, yields distribution by the generally accepted age groups, but not for each year. Computer processing makes it possible to obtain, simultaneously, the population dynamics of a town, or of the personnel of an enterprise, both for each year and for several years, just as it yields simultaneously the age composition by year of birth and by age groups. This can provide significant correctives to the conclusions as well. Tables containing such data may demonstrate, for example, that two adjacent years which often fall into different reporting groups under manual processing are of the highest significance in terms of the number of persons arriving in a city or taken on at a plant, or in terms of the number of persons of a particular age. When singled out individually, they may aid in pinpointing the process whereby the population of a city or factory personnel took shape, or show the predominance of persons of a given age, while under manual processing, when summed with other data for their group, these indices may not stand out distinctly. As a consequence, the factors causing a sharp rise in the growth of a city's population (or that of a factory's personnel) may escape the eyes of an investigator, as may circumstances giving rise to the presence of an age group large in numbers but small in terms of the number of years

spanned.

The principal advantage of computer processing of survey data lies in this opportunity to discover the interrelations among individual phenomena, the degree of dependence of one characteristic of an object upon others, and the possibility of considering data on all other indices in arriving at a picture of one alone. For example, machine processing of data may simultaneously yield material not only on quantitative but on qualitative indices of the dynamics of the growth of a town or factory personnel — i.e., it may demonstrate when (by year or group of years), at what age, bearing what nationality, with what education and training in skills, from where, and for what reasons the individuals studied came to the town or were taken on at the plant. At the same time, the computer is capable of providing information on where and at what jobs individuals are working at a given moment, what their wages are, what housing they occupy, whether they are pursuing their education further, and what their family status is. All these data may be combined into a single table for each year, thus giving a complete picture both of growth dynamics (quantitative and qualitative) and of the present composition of the population of the town or factory force. To process survey data manually in this fashion is a very difficult matter, practically speaking.

We became persuaded of the advantage of computer processing of survey data from our own experience.

The data of our inclusive survey of the work force of the Vyksun Iron and Steel Mill and the sample survey of families of workers at the Krasnoe Sormovo Works, taken in 1960, were processed manually over a period of many months. But the data of the inclusive survey of the work force of the Novo-Gorky Petroleum Refinery in 1963 were processed on the spot by the computer station of the refinery immediately after collection, and yielded an analysis of the survey data incomparably more extensive than that which could be obtained with manual processing in the earlier years. (1) Two surveys, incorporating various types of information, were conducted in 1963 at the Novo-Gorky Works in the town of Kstovo, Gorky Raion. One was inclusive, dealing with the composition of the refinery's personnel and the history of its formation, including certain data on the family of each worker and his living conditions. The other was selective, concerned with family data, and conducted by members of the team in the workers' homes. It included extensive information on every member of the worker's family, the forms of family and marriage, conditions of daily life and economic circumstances, level of culture, housing and, in particular, conditions and arrangements inside the house, etc.

The data of the inclusive survey, constituting a homogeneous mass of information, were processed at the computer station. The information unit was the survey sheet, filled out for each person at the enterprise and containing, in addition to given name, patronymic, surname, and address, the following 26 points: 1. year of birth; 2. birthplace; 3. nationality; 4. native language; 5. sex; 6. job; 7. other skills; 8. working conditions; 9. how skill was acquired: on the job; at training courses; in an FZO or RU school; or in a regular educational institution; 10. education (grades completed; technical secondary school; higher education; if not graduated indicate "not graduated"); 11. whether presently taking correspondence education (at a higher educational institution, a technical secondary school, at special courses, in evening school); 12. time of arrival in Kstovo; 13. reasons for coming to Kstovo; 14. number of members of family, including the subject (living together as one household); 15. working members of this family unit; 16. children in family unit; 17. children living separately (indicate: at school, in military service, living with own family in Kstovo or other towns; workers or white-collar); 18. parents living in family of subject (father, mother, spouse's parents); 19. social status of parents: worker, peasant, or white-collar; 20. how many times married, including unofficially; 21. housing (separate or shared apartment, dormitory, privately owned or rented home); 22. square meters of housing per member of family; 23. wage of subject; 24. wages of other members of family; 25.

holding of a plot of land (size, in hundredths of hectare); 26. use of plot (orchard, truck garden, or both).

Computation of the indices under all these categories revealed the current make-up of the personnel of the factory and provided information on how it was formed. In addition to general data descriptive of the refinery personnel, the survey was processed for certain questions revealing the relationship of certain items of information to others. Thus, in revealing the history of the formation of the plant personnel, we obtained data correlating the year of arrival at the plant with other data: year and place of birth, nationality and social origin, level of training at job skill, and family status.

Questions of cultural and occupational development, depending upon economic conditions, the traditions of particular workers' families, and other circumstances, were elaborated in five tables, answering the following questions: how does family status affect the studies of younger members of the family; is continued education correlated with age and the education in the school years, and if so to what degree; is the desire to study influenced by the level of wages, housing and working conditions, and social origin; do men or women predominate among those studying in addition to working at a job, and where precisely do members of the factory personnel study?

In regard to the family, the information on marriages subsequent to the first was analyzed. We were interested in learning among whom this was most widespread — among men or women, in what age groups, under what economic conditions (earnings, availability of housing), among what national groups, among local people or in-migrants.

For purposes of processing the survey data at the computer station, we first established the form of the questionnaire sheet, so as not to have to copy each one during coding. Above all else, the phrasing of each question was thought out in such fashion that the reply to it would have to be clear, uniform with others in form, and not descriptive. Therefore complex questions, capable of providing descriptive answers of various degrees of completeness and of being broken down into a number of sub-questions, were found best. For example, the question "composition of your family" was not posed, but rather several questions – "number of members of family including yourself," "number of children," "how many children live with you," "which relatives live with you" (with remark: "father, mother, spouse's parents"), etc.

In arranging the sheet into columns, we left one for the code number.

The first stage in processing the data was coding, which was anything but mechanical work. Despite the preciseness of the questions, the answers to them, reflecting many traits characteristic of the individuals concerned, were exceedingly diverse, and the first task in coding was grouping different answers to each question (under each criterion). Thus while, as was established above, it proved more convenient to cover years of birth individually in the processing and to total them up by age groups, it made no sense to code the birthplace of each individual surveyed by a separate identification. We grouped this data in three categories: 1) natives of Kstovo Raion, 2) other raions of Gorky Oblast, and 3) other oblasts. Of course, it would also have been possible to code in detail the birthplace of each individual surveyed (by republic, oblast, raion, and even town or village), but the degree of detail of the coding was determined by the concrete tasks of the investigation. For our subsequent work, such detailed coding was not necessary. However, in other investigations, coding in extreme detail or the singling out of particular economic or geographic districts may be necessary. For example, if the construction of a railroad or power plant is being studied, it may prove desirable to identify the raions in which railroads or power plants had been completed during the same or the preceding year. Thus, it becomes possible to trace the origins of construction enthusiasts moving to the new project.

In this it must be borne in mind that information, once coded and transferred to punch cards or perforated tape, will, upon processing, no longer reveal the initial detailed content of the data, except for the categories into which it has been coded. Nor must one fail to consider the fact that the more detailed the coding, the more cumbersome it is, except for numerical material (year of birth, earnings, number of square meters of dwelling space or of plot of land). Certain questions require preliminary processing before coding. Thus, in seeking to determine the occupational composition of the work force of an enterprise, we based ourselves on a list of all skills represented there, and for coding purposes developed a grouping reflecting the actual, and not accidental, association among the skills within each group.

Thus, the elaboration of the principles of coding is a serious undertaking, the successful performance of which determines what can be done subsequently with mass-scale data.

When all the questionnaires had been encoded – i.e., when an arbitrary numerical equivalent had been assigned to each answer given in verbal form – we considered, in conjunction with the personnel of the computer station, the best arrangement of the data on punch cards: in what columns and with what necessary number of symbols each index would be entered upon the card by perforation. The computer station personnel developed procedural instructions and a model, from which the perforator experts punched the cards. The material was thus prepared for feeding into the computer. What remained was only development of the problems – i.e., formulation of the number of questions to which we wished to obtain answers. The following questions were framed: a) who is studying, relative to age and prior education (correlation of the 11th, 1st, and 10th indices); b) who is studying in the presence of aged parents and children (correlation of the 11th, 18th, and 16th indices) – the influence of family status; c) who studies when living in a shared or separate apartment, in one rented from a private individual, in a dormitory, in his own home, or with his parents, and at various levels of earnings (correlation of the 11th, 21st, and 23rd indices) – the influence of economic conditions; d) do men or women predominate among those studying and what is the environment under which those studying work (correlation of the 11th, 5th, and 8th indices) — predominance of men or women workers, and the influence of working conditions; e) who is studying from among those born in Kstovo and Kstovo Raion, from among those born in other raions of Gorky Oblast, and from among those born in other oblasts, and who are the parents of the students: 1) peasants, 2) workers, 3) white-collar personnel (correlation of the 11th, 2nd, and 19th indices).

This completed our work prior to feeding the information into the computer.

Upon receipt of the computer-processed data, numerically expressed, we had to convert the numerical material of the summary data into verbal form by decoding. The computer processing of the survey questionnaires yielded tables by which it became possible to describe the results of the survey done as follows.

The Kstovo Petroleum Refinery has an extremely small number of local people in its work force. (2) This is explained by the fact that the personnel of this new plant, which went into operation in 1958, was made up of newcomers who arrived starting in 1952, when the building of the refinery and the new town of Kstovo began. This new town rose alongside the plant, six kilometers from the small town of Kstovo, now called Staroe Kstovo. Although the people of neighboring villages (Bol'shie and Malye Vishenki, Novo-Likeevo, Velikii Vrag, and others) took part in building the refinery and the town, most of the builders and members of the plant personnel, as it had taken shape by 1958, were incoming collective farmers and workers from various raions of Gorky Oblast (42.2%) and people from other oblasts and republics (33.6%), while natives of Kstovo Raion, including the town of Kstovo and the surrounding villages, comprised 24.2%, and natives of Kstovo itself numbered only 7.6%.

The present work force includes 22.7% who came to Kstovo between 1951 and 1956 — in the period between the preparations for building the refinery and its completion. The largest single group of arrivals (30.3%), who came in a brief period, 1957 and 1958, comprises members of

the personnel taken on when the refinery began operating (12.3% in 1957, 18% in 1958). Those who came in later years (1959-1963) comprise 33.7%, while persons coming to Kstovo during the 50 years preceding the building of the plant (1901-1951) comprise only 5.7% of its personnel.

The reasons that workers came to Kstovo varied. A very small proportion were assigned to it (8.2%) or transferred from one job to another (5.2%); some came to stay with relatives who had settled in Kstovo after the construction of the refinery began (9%), and yet others came here upon discharge from the army (3.8%). For the majority (53.8%), the major attraction was the prospect of finding interesting work at a new automated enterprise in a new, growing town, situated moreover near Gorky, one of the country's major cultural centers. To this it must be added that they were attracted by the town's good location near the picturesque banks of the Volga, and by its healthful climate.

The children of workers constitute 42.2% of the staff, people of peasant origin — 47.6%; those whose parents were white-collar people number 7.7%. The small numbers of persons employed in industry among the population at the site of the building of the Novo-Gorky Refinery is naturally the reason for the presence, among the workers, of a substantial group whose parents had been peasants, that is, a group of first-generation workers.

By national composition, Russians were an absolute majority — 95.5%. Of the remainder, 44% were Ukrainians, 24% Lithuanians, 8.9% each Belorussians, Mordvins, and Jews, 8% Chuvashi, 4% Tatars, 1% each Azerbaidjanis, Uzbeks, Moldavians, Letts, Armenians, Bashkirs, Maris, Tuvans, and Iakuts. The rest combined were 4%.

As we know, the retention of the native tongue by small groups not native to an area, living among a given large national group, is important to a characterization of the ethnic processes occurring among a multi-national working class. Among the workers of non-Russian nationality (4.5% of the total staff of the Novo-Gorky Refinery), 2.3% were bilingual, while

2.2% regarded Russian as their native tongue.

Comparison of the numbers who had lost their native tongue among the various national groups shows that about half of the local Ukrainians regard Ukrainian as their native tongue. Most of the Belorussians regard Russian as their mother tongue. The Tatars, Bashkirs, and Maris showed the highest percentage of retention of native tongue, while the nationalities grouped under "other nationalities" retained it least.

Clearly, the similarity among the Russian, Ukrainian, and Belorussian languages, which facilitates transfer from one to another, plays a role in the abandonment of one's own national language for another, while those languages most remote from the Russian, such as Tatar, are retained for the longest period. At the same time, an important condition for retention or loss of the language of one's nationality is the compactness and numbers of groups of other nationalities living in the midst of one major national group. Thus, we see that the Tatars, Bashkirs and Maris, who had lived in their own autonomous republics or in compact groups in other regions before coming to Kstovo, retained their native tongue. In this new town they usually maintained a lively communication with people of the same nationality, and this facilitated retention of the native tongue. At the same time, individuals constituting the representation of other nationalities had least opportunity for such communication. Moreover, even before coming to Kstovo they had also lived outside their native ethnic environment, and this led to abandonment of their native language for Russian.

The refinery personnel is 66% male, 34% female. The age range is from 17 to 63. Seventeen-year-old apprentices constitute 0.2% of the total work force. Youths between 18 and 22 number 5.3%. Young workers from 23 to 27 constitute 34.2%, while those from 28 to 32 number 27.4%. Of those working at the plant 17.4% are between 33 and 37 years of age, and 10% fall into the 38-to-42 age group. The next two age groups are considerably smaller: 3.8% are from 43 to 47, and 2.9% are from 48 to 52. Elderly workers are few: 1.3% are from 53 to

57, and 0.5% between 58 to 63. Thus, the refinery is staffed chiefly by young people between 23 and 27 (34.2%) and 28 to 32 (27.4%). The other age groups are considerably smaller, while the groups at the two extremes – old men over 60 and youth under 18 – are negligible in numbers. This is because all the old workers are pensioned, while young people are studying in primary and technical secondary schools, whose courses of study are designed to occupy them until the age of 18. The age composition of the work force was also influenced by the fact that the building of this refinery was proclaimed a USSR-wide Komsomol Construction Project, and large numbers of young building workers had come on Komsomol passes. Many of them left when construction was complete, but a portion remained to live in Kstovo and merged into the personnel of the Novo-Gorky Refinery.

Of the trades to which the work force of the factory belong, the largest (22.8%) consists of operators and their assistants, controls workers. The second largest category (21.8%) consists of machine-tool operators, tool-and-die makers, and repairmen. Considerably smaller are the categories of laboratory personnel (6.2%), electricians (5.7%), machine-operators (3.8%), blacksmiths, carpenters, painters, furnacemen (1.4%), gas rescue crews (0.9%), process-control directors (0.1%), and so forth.

Half the workers possess one skill, 37.6% two, 9.6% three, 1.9% four, 0.4% five; 0.4% have six or more skills.

A considerable portion of the workers (29.4%) acquired their skills in educational institutions, including RU, FZO and FZU; 10% at upgrading courses, and 56% on the job, generally through the instrumentality of the work-and-instruction department of the Kstovo or some other industrial enterprise. The others acquired their skills through on-the-job training in secondary school, in the army, and so forth.

By educational level, the largest group (38.5%) are workers with incomplete secondary schooling (having graduated from seven- or eight-year schools); the second largest are those with complete secondary education (having graduated from ten- or eleven-year schools) –

29.6%.

Among those who had obtained complete and incomplete secondary education, 5.2% had graduated from higher educational institutions (in addition to which 0.6% had incomplete higher education); 11.6% had graduated from technical secondary schools (1.8% attended but did not graduate).

At present, 20.5% of the personnel are continuing their studies. Of these, 11% are going to secondary technical schools, 5.1% to evening school, 2% to higher educational institutions, 1.2% to upgrading courses, and 1.2% are preparing to take examinations in educational institutions.

By family status, the largest group (31.7%) consists of people in families of three, and the second (28.9%) takes in those in families of four. The numbers of two-member families (11.5%) and five-member families (11.1%) are equal. Families numbering six persons are 7.1%, and families of seven, eight, and nine are less than 1%; 10% are single, including unmarried young people; 30.9% of the people working at the plant live with parents.

Of the plant personnel, 40% have one child each, 25% have two, 5% – three, 2% – four, and 0.5% – five; 27%, including the single people, have no children. Of the married people, including newlyweds, only 17% have no children; 16.6% of the personnel, including the youth, are unmarried; 76% have been married once, and 6.9% twice.

Nearly half (44.6%) of the personnel live in their own apartments, 18.7% have one or more rooms in shared apartments, 14.2% live in factory dormitories of the hotel type, with all modern conveniences, and 14.2% rent from private persons; 7.4% have private homes, and 0.9% (young people) live in their parents' housing space in private or shared apartments.

Of the persons surveyed, 40% have plots of land. Of these, 15.8% use them for orchards, 4% for gardens, and 19.8% for both purposes combined.

Determination of the relationship between family status and study on the job, at evening school, upgrading courses, by correspondence at technical secondary schools or higher educational institutions showed that the presence of children in workers' families usually does not prevent young parents from studying. This is particularly due to the fact that preschool children's institutions have taken upon themselves a large part of the responsibility for care of children and for their upbringing. Most of the people studying live in separate apartments in large urban-type apartment houses with all conveniences. Dormitory life seems to create less favorable conditions for study. The least opportunities for study are enjoyed by workers who live in their own homes and have private orchards and gardens.

The processing of the survey questionnaires also is of practical value, since detailed data on the make-up of urban or rural groups may be employed in improving the organization of ideological and political work, as is discussed in the resolution of the June Plenum of the CC CPSU, "Current Tasks in the Ideological Work of the Party" [Ob ocherednykh zadachikh ideologicheskoi raboty Partii]: "The level of preparation, the ethnic and age composition of the population are not always taken into consideration in ideological and political work." (3)

Multiphasic analysis of the staffs of large industrial enterprises (such as that which we undertook) makes possible better understanding of the needs of the working people in respect of culture and ordinary services, and prior detailed planning to satisfy these. Particularly, it would be possible to plan mass cultural work more successfully, organizing automotive or amateur movie and photography clubs for some, fishing and hunting or Michurinist orchard growing clubs for others, while in work forces in which girls predominate there would be instruction in the decorative arts and Swedish gymnastics clubs (in addition to the various sports clubs, sewing and embroidery circles, vocal, dance, and drama groups that one finds everywhere). The comparative data of these surveys may be employed in resolving problems of another type – the desirability of opening technical secondary schools or branches of higher educational institutions at factories staffed by young people at a particular level of general education — as well as in answering questions pertaining to the greater or lesser need to open new kindergartens and nurseries on the basis of families consisting of two generations, including children of preschool age.

Thus, the fifteen-man Gorky Detachment of the Combined Expedition (4) was able, in the course of 18 days spent at the Novo-Gorky Refinery, to carry out a sampling survey covering 740 workers' families and at the same time to code a complete person-by-person survey of questionnaire data gathered by civically active plant personnel. As the coded material came in, it was entered upon punch cards, whereupon the computer station proceeded to process the forms. Two surveys were set up and carried out, and the mass-scale data yielded by the person-by-person survey were processed in the course of 18 days. The punch cards, which remain in our possession, make it possible to do further work with this information. Our experience has persuaded us of the desirability of using computer stations to process the data of the questionnaire surveys.

It seems to us that it would also be convenient to use computers to process other ethnographic materials, such as, for example, the data assembled for ethnographic atlases. Perhaps all that is required to make all the data both of questionnaire surveys and of information collected for the atlas comparable is to develop a more refined and unified technique for collecting data, based on the assumption that it will subsequently be coded for computer processing.

Footnotes

1) The success of this work was facilitated by the concerned attention given it by V. S. Edrenkin, manager of the refinery, and the energetic participation of M. M. Kurmanov and A. G. Parotinova, of its computer station.

2) At the same time, the data of our survey of 1960 among workers of the Vyksun Works showed that 27.5% had been born in Vyks, a small but ancient industrial center of Gorky Oblast, and 41% in Vyksun Raion.

3) Postanovleniia Plenuma TsK KPSS, June 1963, Moscow, 1963, p. 7.

4) The work of the team was participated in by schoolchildren belonging to the Ethnographic Section of the Young Voyagers' and Researchers' Club of Moscow, headed by G. A. Mamleeva, teacher, and the present author.

Filosofskie nauki, 1965, No. 4

A. L. Sventsitskii

THE INTERVIEW AS A TECHNIQUE IN CONCRETE SOCIOLOGICAL RESEARCH (1)

The interest in concrete sociological research that has appeared in our country in recent years is quite natural. It is a consequence of the tremendous changes that have occurred in Soviet society since the 20th Congress of the CPSU. Life is constantly advancing urgent problems, the proper solution of which is possible only on a foundation of concrete sociological research. Certain successes have already been achieved in such research, as evidenced by the studies of philosophers, sociologists and representatives of other social sciences at the Universities of Leningrad, Moscow, the Urals, Novosibirsk, and Voronezh, the Institute of Philosophy of the USSR Academy of Sciences, and other institutions.

At the same time, it is a generally recognized fact that questions pertaining to the methods and technique of concrete sociological research have thus far not been gone into deeply enough. Only a rigorously scientific approach to the devices and techniques of research employed can guarantee that the information obtained about any aspect of the life of society will be accurate. The success of any concrete sociological study depends entirely upon whether the techniques employed in gathering information correspond to the methodological principles of Marxism. To disregard these principles or use them improperly will inevitably lead to empiricism and the mere recording of particular phenomena.

Concrete sociological research, as practiced in our country, envisages both analysis of objective conditions and factors in the life of society, and study of the manner in which they are refracted subjectively in the human mind. One of the techniques employed in sociological investigations is that of the interview. The interview, like the questionnaire, is a form of interrogation. Before speaking of methods and techniques of interviewing, it is necessary, in our opinion, to pause to consider those common features of interrogation found both in the interview and the questionnaire. Interrogation techniques have been and are presently being

---

*The Soviet concept of methodology is different from, and rather broader than, the one commonly used in the United States: it includes certain elements of broad philosophical approach and theoretical assumptions. This is the sense in which the term "methodology" is used in this journal — Editor, Soviet Sociology.

subjected to criticism not only by Marxist sociologists but by representatives of capitalist-oriented empirical sociology. The chief shortcoming of any interrogation technique (interview or questionnaire) lies in the fact that the data obtained often testify not so much to the actual opinions, convictions, and moods of the subject as to what he imagines them to be. Yet there are numerous aspects of social life, the investigation and study of which are impossible without interrogation.

Our experience in concrete sociological research shows that interrogation techniques can play a positive role if the information obtained is compared with the results of analysis of statistical data, official and personal documents, and various other forms of information gathering. In conducting sociological research, one must avoid elevating interrogation techniques to an absolute, and using them where other methods of sociological research are necessary. This is characteristic of the empirical sociology of capitalism, which examines all societal phenomena through the prism of extreme psychologism, without consideration of objective factors. However, it must be stated that for all the methodological untenability of contemporary capitalist-oriented sociology, certain of the interrogation techniques and methods used in capitalist countries are entirely applicable to concrete research by our sociologists. Naturally, the utilization of the techniques developed by capitalist-oriented sociologists must be creatively rethought on the basis of the theory and methodology of Marxism-Leninism.

In the Soviet literature devoted to concrete sociological research, the interview technique is often termed the conversational. In our view, this identification is not entirely valid, inasmuch as there is a significant difference between the very concepts "interview" and "conversation." As a rule, any conversation presumes exchange of opinions among the participants. An interview, however, is not an exchange of opinions but the eliciting of information from one person, the subject. Naturally, this does not signify transformation of the interview into an examination or interrogatory. A well-conducted interview should have all the external characteristics of a conversation between people having respect for and confidence in each other.

In this article, the interview method will be examined only as it applies to concrete investigations in sociology and social psychology. Judging by the writings published in our country, the interview technique is not yet used widely enough among us. Most often, when an interrogation technique is necessary, the questionnaire is given preference. In our opinion, there are a great many cases in which this is not at all appropriate, and in some instances the interview is the sole basis on which the necessary information can be obtained.

The fact that our researchers lack confidence to some degree in the interview method is explained by the fact that this method has been compromised by Freudians, who employ what is termed the psychoanalytical interview to discover the "subconscious" in the mind. The teachings of Freud have been employed in capitalist-oriented sociology to develop other types of interviews. These include, for example, the clinical interview, the nondirective interview, etc., in which great attention is given to the free associations of the respondent, his qualifications, and slips of the tongue. Conclusions are often drawn solely on the basis of some arbitrary interpretation of "recall symbols." The "projective" tests, (2) such as the Rorschach, T.A.T. (Thematic Apperception Test), etc., widely employed by capitalist-oriented scholars in certain forms of interviews, also bear the imprint of Freudian concepts.

Naturally, the unscientific use of the interview technique by bourgeois philosophers does not at all signify that the very method of investigating man's mental activity through interviews is itself erroneous. The use of the interview in concrete sociological research is equally valid where it is necessary to study some aspect of the consciousness of particular groups of people and they have to be studied more deeply than is possible by the questionnaire technique. For the fact is that, because questions are necessarily standardized, any questionnaire gives the investigator information that is more superficial than does the "free" interview, not held within rigid confines.

The interview technique may be successfully employed at various stages in a concrete sociological investigation. Thus, in the process of setting up an investigation, one may conduct a small number of interviews in order to check the working hypotheses. Interviews are often employed for preliminary testing of a questionnaire. The interview may also appear as the principal technique for gathering data — for example, in the study of public opinion, the tastes of viewers, readers, buyers, etc. Finally, interviewing is very often employed with the object of supplementing and checking data acquired by other methods. The interview is used least often as the basic means for gaining knowledge of social phenomena. In our opinion, this is due to underestimation of that technique.

Let us consider, for example, research on the esthetic tastes of movie audiences. The techniques usually employed toward this end are analysis of statistical data, the study of letters, discussion-meetings (a) of viewers, discussion of films and, finally, questionnaire surveys. However, each of these methods suffers from certain shortcomings as compared with the interview. The statistics of attendance at movie theaters cannot fully explain why particular films are appreciated by viewers. Study of letters and the statements of viewers at discussion-meetings may provide rich and profound data, but the opinions of those viewers who display initiative do not, as a rule, fully represent the opinions of the entire mass of the movie audience.

In our opinion, the best method for studying the tastes of movie audiences is the survey, as it makes possible the attainment of a more representative sample. Moreover, the interview survey has, in our opinion, a number of serious advantages over the questionnaire type: it is easier for anyone to tell about something orally than to write it. For example, it is very difficult to provide, in the limited space available on a questionnaire, a detailed answer to questions such as: "Did you respond to the feelings and thoughts of the characters in the movie?" or

"What films didn't you like? Why?" We believe that in studying the tastes of movie-goers (as in quite a number of other studies), the interview technique may be successfully employed as the chief method of collecting factual material. Of course, this does not rule out utilization of other methods to supplement and control this.

Naturally, study of various aspects of the problem under investigation demands the use of concrete forms and techniques of interview. In the Soviet literature devoted to the methods of concrete social research, virtually no attention is given to classification of the various types of interviews, although there is an obvious need for this. Most sociologists in the capitalist countries distinguish two principal types of interviews: the standardized and the unstandardized (see, for example, Maccoby and Maccoby, "The Interview: A Tool of Social Science," in G. Lindzey, Handbook of Social Psychology, Reading [Mass.], 1959; C. Jonsson, Questionnaires and Interviews, Stockholm, 1957). In the former case, questions determined beforehand are presented in identical formulation and order to all subjects. Moreover, the interviewer must not reformulate any of the questions, introduce new ones, or change their order. In employing an unstandardized interview, the interviewer may himself formulate or reformulate the questions, change the order of those to which an answer must be obtained, etc. There is also the semi-standardized (or "focused") interview, which employs an interview guide with a list of the essential and the possible questions, thus offering the investigator a choice within the limits of the guide (see Merton and Kendall, "The Focused Interview," The American Journal of Sociology, 1946, Vol. 51, No. 6).

All three listed forms of collection of information by means of the interview contain nothing inherently faulty and have been employed in practice in the researches of Soviet sociologists who base themselves on Marxist methodology. The choice of any particular form of interview depends basically upon the already attained level of knowledge of the question under study. Thus, for example, it is hardly rational to employ the standardized or even semi-standardized type of interview in the initial stage of an investigation, inasmuch as it is only after many interviews have been conducted that one may proceed to determine the most desirable form for the questions and their sequence. It is useful to employ the standardized interview in surveys of large numbers of people, in order to make possible statistical processing of the data obtained. The unstandardized form of interview is very often employed as a method of supplementing and checking data obtained by other means of research. This unstandardized form of interview is particularly widespread in social research in our country today. Therefore we shall undertake below a detailed examination of the technique employed in such interviewing on the basis of a concrete investigation of job attitudes by a team of the Social Research Laboratory of Leningrad University under Iadov and Zdravomyslov.

The purpose of the study (3) was to investigate the motivations (stimuli) for job activity and their influence upon the objective results of work relative to changes in its nature due to comprehensive mechanization and automation. At the outset, 2,665 workers under 30 years of age were queried by questionnaire. The sample was chosen by randomly districted selection, based on nature of work, at 25 industrial enterprises in the city of Leningrad. The questionnaire, filled out either by the workers themselves or by a staff member of the laboratory on the basis of the words of the subject, made it possible to shed light on the degree of satisfaction with job and skill, understanding of the social significance of the work, as well as the motivations for choice of the given skill. At the same time, an individual card was filled out for each worker queried, in which the researchers recorded his performance on the job in terms of conscientiousness, discipline, and initiative.

In order to make a deeper study of the problem under consideration, interviews were conducted subsequent to the questionnaire survey. So as to make it possible to compare the results of the interviews and of the questionnaires, we interviewed 5% of the 2,665 persons already questioned. The sampling of persons interviewed was within groups whose jobs were most typical

of Leningrad industry; (4) 134 persons (88 males and 46 females) were interviewed. The present author did the interviewing. The interview followed the questionnaire in general outline and included questions touching upon the following:

1. Attitude toward the job. (Positive and negative aspects of the work. Was there a desire to change jobs? What might increase interest in the work? Degree of satisfaction with the work.)

2. Attitude toward skill. (Motivations for choice of skill. Attractive and unattractive aspects of present skill. Was there a desire to change skills? Degree of satisfaction with skill.)

3. Participation in efficiency suggestion and invention activities, in civic activities, in the movement for communist labor; furthering of education or job skills; determination of lifetime perspectives of the young worker, and his plans for the future.

In the interviews we guided ourselves solely by this general plan, while the form and sequence of questions were varied in accordance with the particular situation. About two years passed between the time of the questionnaire survey and the interviews. Because of this, we also found it necessary to determine whether the differences in answers to identical questions in the questionnaire and the interview were a function merely of time and not of the fundamental differences in the techniques of research. In order to answer this question, we conducted a control survey after the interview, employing the initial questionnaire. Thirty workers among those who had filled out the given questionnaire two years earlier were re-surveyed in this fashion. They were representatives of the category of skilled manual workers (mechanics, electricians, etc.) chosen at random at five industrial enterprises in Leningrad.

Now let us examine the techniques and procedures employed in interviewing and certain data obtained by this method in our research. A very acute problem which always arises, in one or another form in the use of surveys, is that of the sincerity of the subjects. Clearly, in order for truthful answers to be obtained, mutual confidence on the part of both participants in the interview is essential. How did the interviewer attain positive contact with the subjects?

The opening of the conversation, the first words which the investigator addresses to the subject, play an important role. In the given instance, the interviewer, introducing himself as a university researcher and having checked the identity of the subject, expressed himself approximately as follows: "We are studying the conditions of work at various enterprises, and people's opinions of their jobs and skills. Can you find the time to talk about this with me now?" Often a worker would ask why he in particular had been chosen. The interviewer replied that a computer had been used to make a random selection from among those who had previously filled out the questionnaire so as to determine what changes had occurred in the intervening period in the workers' responses to the questions asked. Our description of the principle of sampling substantially persuaded the workers that the interviewer had no preconceptions in regard to him. At any rate, we encountered no absolute refusals to be interviewed.

In making the survey it is also very important to approach correctly the framing of the initial questions. They may produce in the subject either interest and a desire to engage in conversation or, on the other hand, an effort to get out of it. These questions must be "neutral" — i.e., directed more toward eliciting factual information than toward determining personal attitudes. Thus, it would have been a gross error for us to begin the interview with questions such as: "How do you feel about your job?" Usually we began by asking the worker to tell us why he chose a given skill. The question was put in this form: "Tell me, please, how you became a mechanic (machinist, etc.)?" Following this, the interviewer's questions about the attractive and unattractive sides of this work were entirely natural.

An obligatory condition for satisfactory contact between the parties to the interview is manifestation of interest by the interviewer in the words of the subject. Of course, the interviewer must not show open approval or disapproval of the subject's opinions, but indifference and an apathetic attitude on the part of the interviewer are also impermissible. The interviewer's interest may be shown by displaying an expression of attention and by encouraging remarks. The device of challenging the subject's opinions, for the purpose of stimulating him to defend his viewpoint and thereby make clear his degree of conviction, is deserving of attention. However, this device may have a negative effect upon the relationship between the participants in the interview. Inasmuch as the subject himself may often not be clearly aware of the relationships among people in the instance under discussion, we sometimes asked him to describe the external appearance, manner, and characteristics of an individual associated with the relationships being studied. The nature of the information and its very verbal fabric permit us to form an indirect judgment about the relationships of interest to us.

Contradictions in answers are quite important. If the subject contradicts something he has previously said, there are two courses open to the interviewer. The first is to call the subject's attention to the contradiction and to ask him to explain it. The second is to seek to determine the truth by means of indirect questions. In our survey the second course was followed, chiefly because if one points to a contradiction in an individual's statement, one may provoke unwillingness to respond to subsequent questions. The chief contradictions were those in response to questions with respect to the degree of satisfaction with job and skill. To a considerable degree, these contradictions were provoked by inadequate contact between the researcher and the subject in the first minutes of the interview. Inasmuch as contact improves, generally speaking, as the interview continues, the responses become less stereotyped and more sincere.

In the course of our interviews we made use of indirect questions which, in many cases, yielded valuable information controlling and supplementing answers to direct questions. Thus, satisfaction or dissatisfaction with the job was elicited both by direct questions: "Are you satisfied with your job? To what degree?" and also by a series of indirect questions, the nature and

Table 1

Differences in Answers to Direct and Indirect Questions in Evaluating Job Satisfaction

Answers	No. of workers giving this answer to direct questions	No. of workers giving this answer to indirect questions
Completely satisfied	52	39
Satisfied	51	47
Indifferent to job	9	17
Dissatisfied	9	16
Utterly dissatisfied	13	15

Table 2

Job Satisfaction Indices in Occupational Control Groups from Questionnaires and Interviews

Occupational control groups	Index	
	Questionnaire data	Interview data
II. Skilled manual labor (mechanics)	6.15	8
III. Mechanized jobs (machinists)	5.46	5
V. Semi-automated work (metalworking automatic machine-tool operators)	4.62	3.5
VI. Automated work (operators; console operators)	4.5	4
IV. Assembly-line jobs	2.95	0.66
I. Unskilled manual labor (loading, chipping)	0.41	0.2

number of which depended upon the concrete situation, for example: "Don't you want to change to some other work?" The role of indirect questions is particularly clearly evidenced from Table 1.

As we see, the greatest difference in distribution of answers is seen in the first line. The interviews also yielded a considerably more exact determination of the number of people dissatisfied with their jobs, as well as those expressing an indifferent attitude toward them.

In determining the degree of satisfaction with the job, consideration was also given to answers to other direct questions that served as indirect questions with respect to this. Questions on motivations for study or plans for the future, for example, fell into this category. Then it was important to determine the degree to which the data on job satisfaction obtained by interview coincided with those found by questionnaire. In analysis of the questionnaire material, generalized indicators (indices) were employed. The job satisfaction index was the ratio of the number fully satisfied to those utterly dissatisfied, in the given group. In analyzing the interview data, we applied this procedure for the purpose

Table 3

Mechanics' Motivations for Choice of That Trade, According to Questionnaire Replies

Motivation	Results of initial survey (No. of workers giving this motive)	Results of re-survey (No. of workers giving this motive)
Interest in trade	19	17
Desire for good pay	8	7
"Things turned out so"	9	7
Other motivations	3	3
Unable to answer	-	4

of comparing indices of job satisfaction derived from the questionnaires and the interviews (see Table 2).

The table shows that the declining order of job satisfaction indices in the various occupational groupings resulting from the questionnaires coincides with the distribution based on interview data. A divergence is to be seen only in the sequence of groups V and VI, but here it must be taken into consideration that the difference between those indices, both in terms of questionnaire data and interviews, is very slight. Thus, the interview results in this instance provide good support for the reliability of the questionnaire data.

Furthermore, interviewing made it possible to obtain answers to questions that it was not possible to clarify fully by means of questionnaires, such as, for example, the question as to the motivations for choice of a skill. The questionnaires provided the following multiple-choice reply: 1. The skill seemed interesting; 2. The pay was attractive; 3. Things turned out so I had no other choice; 4. Other considerations (family tradition, advice of friends, etc. Specify in writing); 5. Can't answer. In filling out the questionnaires, about half the subjects underlined the third choice. On analysis of these data, the question immediately arose as to what sort of circumstances these were. The results of the interviews clarified the matter. Of 134 workers surveyed twice (by questionnaire and interview), 51 indicated in their question-

naires that "things turned out that way." But the interviews showed that only 18 of the 51 were fully justified in speaking of circumstances which "turned out so that I had no other choice." Among the other 33, it turned out that motivations included interest in the skill, the pay, advice offered by relatives and friends, etc. — i.e., motivations that fell entirely within the confines of the questions in the questionnaire specified above.

Our explanation for differences of this order between questionnaire data and interviews is the following. In the first place, the individuals questioned often underline those choices that demand no great thought. In the second place, the question: "How did you choose your present trade?" is in itself not a very simple one. In answering it, one must analyze the motivations for one's choice, and many found this difficult. We see the advantage of the interview method over the questionnaire technique, inasmuch as, when interviews were employed, all 134 persons were able to reply in adequate detail about how they chose their trades and what considerations guided them in doing so.

In conducting the study, an important question arose to which we have already made reference: to wit, is not the chief reason for the divergence between questionnaire and interview findings merely the time factor — the fact that two years had passed? Comparison of the results of the initial and control questionnaire surveys of 30 workers (mechanics) shows that the time factor

had absolutely no influence upon the deliberate-
ness of the replies (see Table 3).

Over and above what the questionnaire provides, the interview findings permit discovery
of those factors in choice of an occupation which
actually turned out so that the subjects could
choose no other skill. In most of these cases,
this was determined by place of residence: for
various reasons these individuals had to work
close to home, regardless of the nature of the
job. Other circumstances that, upon occasion,
played the chief role in choice of skill were:
parents' choice of an occupation for their children (with respect to juveniles aged 15 or 16)
without regard for their desires, and transfer
to work at another skill due to illness.

* * *

In this article we have adduced certain of the results obtained, our purpose being to examine the
unstandardized interview technique in concrete
sociological investigation. These results provide
the grounds for concluding that the interview
may be employed successfully as a technique not
only prior to questionnaire surveys but to supplement and check questionnaire survey data at
one of the final stages in social research.

Department of Psychology,
University of Leningrad

Editor's Note

a) Such gatherings, at which authors, artists
and scholars meet the public, are frequently
held under the auspices of periodicals and other
cultural institutions. They have been called
"mass interviews" by Western writers.

Footnotes

1) In preparation for a scientific conference
on problems and techniques in sociological research.

2) For further detail on "projective" tests,
see Selltitz, Jahoda, Deutsch, and Cook,
Research Methods in Social Relations, New
York, 1962, pp. 280-299.

3) For further detail on the goals and methods of this study, and for the sampling procedure, see Zdravomyslov and Iadov, "Opyt
konkretnogo issledovaniia otnosheniia k trudu,"
Voprosy filosofii, 1964, No. 4. [Translation
published as "An Attempt at a Concrete Study
of Attitude Toward Work," Soviet Sociology,
Vol. III, No. 4.]

4) For further detail on these groups see
cited article by Zdravomyslov and Iadov.

* * *

Demography, Ethnogeography, and Social Statistics

Sovetskaia etnografiia, 1963, No. 1

S. I. Bruk, V. I. Kozlov, and M. G. Levin

THE SUBJECT MATTER AND PURPOSES OF ETHNOGEOGRAPHY (1)

I

Close relationships exist between cultural and social anthropology on the one hand, and geography on the other. They date from classical antiquity, when the beginnings of ethnographic and geographic knowledge merged into a single field that might have been called the study of countries and peoples.

For a long period of time, the description of the features of life of various peoples was never conceived of without a description of the natural environment in which they lived, and vice versa: description of the elements of the natural environment was not regarded as an end in itself and was of interest only to the degree to which these elements were related to descriptions of features of the people's lives.

Herodotus, who was regarded as "the father of history," might to an equal degree be called the father of ethnography and geography. His work contains the most various information both of a historical and a geographical and ethnographic nature, with respect to the lands and peoples then known. The earliest maps to survive in our day (those of Hecataeus of Miletus [5th century B.C.E.] and of Eratosthenes [3rd century B.C.E.]) were simultaneously geographical and ethnographic maps in that, along with their geographic content, they contained ethnographic information as well: peoples were shown by legends in the areas they inhabited. The combined description of the lands and peoples, characteristic of the works of the classical scholars, was later retained in the writing of many scholars of the medieval and modern periods.

However, it must be noted that this unity of ethnography and geography was, to a considerable degree, more apparent than real, and was explained by the insufficiently clear conception then held of the distinctive features of these two sciences. Efforts to make a direct comparison of ethnographic and geographic data — without an adequate concept of the laws of socio-economic and historical development of society — had the result that the differences in culture and mode of life, social structure, and psychological sets of peoples were explained by the direct influence of differences in the natural conditions under which those people lived (differences in climate, soil fertility, etc.). (2) At first, these views were progressive and carried elements of a materialist approach to nature and society. Nevertheless, all this created the prerequisites for the appearance of theories known under the name of geographical determinism or geographical materialism, and formulated most clearly in the 17th century in the writings of Charles Montesquieu, and later in the works of H. T. Buckle and other scholars. (3)

Even in the 19th century — "the century of differentiation of the sciences" — the ties between ethnography and geography were not ended. Many researchers continued to work both as geographers and as ethnographers. The description of lands and peoples continued to be combined. Suffice it to recall the work of E. Reclus (his series La Terre et les Hommes, l'Homme et la Terre, and other writings). However, in the second half of the 19th century, ethnography and geography began to emerge as independent sciences, each having its own subject matter and investigative techniques. At that stage, the desire to continue to treat social and cultural anthropology — the study of laws characteristic of society — and geography — the study primarily of natural conditions — as one discipline, began to hinder the development of both sciences and to interfere with deeper research and correct establishment of causal relationships in each of these fields. Whereas formerly the effort to establish causal relationships between natural and social phenomena was to some degree progressive in nature, now the attempts to establish a so-called "anthropogeographical school" (the writings of F. Ratzel and others) and the school of "human geography" proved to be not only unproductive, but harmful. We shall pause below to consider certain anthropogeographical views in greater detail.

Russian science displayed particularly very close ties between ethnography and geography. This was due to a considerable degree to the multinational character of Russia. The academic expeditions of the second half of the 18th century included in their stated purposes both geographic and ethnographic investigations. The close ties between ethnography and geography were retained into the 19th century. This was facilitated by the circumstance that Russia, unlike countries of Western Europe, preserved the traditional view of social and cultural anthropology as a science concerned with the contemporary life, culture and daily habits of all peoples. Let us recall that the Russian Geographical Society, established in 1845, included a division of ethnography.

In the Society of Friends of Natural Science, Anthropology and Ethnography, which appeared somewhat later, geography occupied a prominent place. Many outstanding figures in Russian science were simultaneously geographers and ethnographers. Among them were such major scholars as N. N. Miklukho-Maklai, D. N. Anuchin, L. S. Berg, etc.

Beginning approximately in the 1920s, the ties between socio-cultural anthropology and geography began to weaken in the USSR, and they virtually ceased to exist early in the 1930s. This was due to some degree to the struggle against the anthropogeographical theories (reflected in the writings of A. A. Kruber, (4) L. D. Sinitskii, (5) etc.) which were widespread in our country, but primarily to the fact that at that time many ethnographers ceased to engage in the study of the contemporary lives of the people. The tasks of cultural anthropology were reduced to a study of the vestiges of the clan-tribal order, and it came to be understood as only an auxiliary discipline to history. Many cultural anthropologists, fearing the accusation of geographical determinism, completely abandoned consideration of geographical problems related to ethnography. This dichotomy was facilitated by the situation in the field of geography. Geographers began to direct their attention primarily either to the study of various components of the natural environment (physical geography), or to study of the distribution of branches of production (economic geography), ignoring man himself. In the apt expression of the distinguished Soviet geographer N. N. Baranskii, geography became "inhuman."

From the middle of the 1940s, a new stage began in the development of cultural and social anthropology. It posed, among its major tasks, description of contemporary peoples, their lives, culture, and daily habits under concrete socio-historical conditions and in the specific natural environments in which they lived. For their part, geographers began more and more frequently to give attention to the study of human society. A special branch developed in the field of economic geography — demographic geography. All this placed on the order of the day the need to renew the ties between socio-cultural anthropology and geography on a new basis, and resulted in the development of one of the more important facets of the former — ethnic geography.

It should be observed that in the 1920s, V. G. Bogoraz-Tan made an attempt to establish ethnogeography as a distinct discipline. However, because of the author's mistaken methodological approach, this effort had no significant success. Bogoraz-Tan believed that "...cultural anthropology studies the culture of primitive peoples ....It gives particular attention to the tribes today scattered through Australia, Africa and Northern Siberia....In more culturally advanced countries, it studies with particular attention vestiges of early society that have been retained primarily among the broad masses of the people, particularly in the countryside." (6) In his opinion, the function of ethnogeography was to be "...to devote a considerable portion of its attention...to numerous and culturally advanced peoples. Ethnogeography starts in primitive times, but in general is concerned primarily with extensive mutual relationships among the most important groups of mankind." Speaking of the objectives of ethnogeography, Bogoraz-Tan writes: "Ethnogeography classifies man into races, peoples and tribes, and includes the entire totality of culture created by man on earth, in all its historical and geographical variety." (7) As is evident from these quotations, Bogoraz-Tan understands ethnogeography very broadly, including within its scope virtually all of ethnic anthropology, the ethnogeography of modern peoples, and their history. Nor can we accept his erroneous understanding of cultural anthropology as the science only of primitive societies and vestigial phenomena.

At the present time, the need to separate out ethnic geography as a distinctive discipline within cultural anthropology is gaining broader recognition (8) although its outlines have not yet been completely defined. Below we make an attempt to define the scope of the questions falling within the purview of ethnogeography.

II

S. P. Tolstov regards cultural anthropology as a border field between, on the one hand, various branches of historical knowledge and, on the other hand, between the latter and a number of other humanities and natural sciences, primarily the entire complex of geographical disciplines. (9) Ethnogeography (or ethnic statistics and cartography) is one of the branches of cultural anthropology most closely associated with geography. Its basic task is the study of the composition and distribution of the population of the entire world and of its various regions in their ethnic aspects. This includes: study of the ethnic composition of the population of countries and regions and the territorial interrelationships of peoples (pure and mixed populations); analysis of the features of distribution of ethnic communities in the past and the present (settled and nomadic distribution, urban and rural settlement, forms and types of settlements, the degree to which territories are occupied and their population density, etc.); establishment, on the basis of these researches, of ethnic boundaries, as well as determination of the numbers of various peoples and study of the changes in these numbers.

Let us pause to give somewhat more detailed consideration to the ties between ethnogeography and population geography, a comparatively new branch of geography that began to take shape chiefly in the postwar period. In the first attempts to define the range of problems entering into the geography of populations, one finds a certain confusion of geographic and anthropological subject matter. Thus, for example, R. M. Kabo, in his article "Priroda i chelovek v ikh vzaimnykh otnosheniiakh kak predmet sotsial'no-kul'turnoi geografii" [Nature and Man in Their Interrelationships as the Subject Matter of Socio-Cultural Geography], defines the goals of demographic geography as follows: "It studies the differentiated forms of work of various types of human population distribution, their mode of life and socio-cultural features in terms of spatial differences, as well as the complex correlation of all these elements that characterize each individual socio-territorial group of human beings." (10) It is not hard to see that this definition includes among the tasks of geographics a study of purely anthropological problems. To say nothing of the fact that such a definition is not theoretically justified, it also fails to correspond to practical reality. Demographic geographers do not usually study "the mode of life and socio-cultural features of people."

V. V. Pokshishevskii has defined the objectives of demographic geography more correctly. In his opinion; it is "...a branch of economic geography studying (in their dynamics and development) the structure, distribution and territorial organization of populations, considered in the process of social reproduction; determining the laws, particularly spatial, that govern changes in all these population characteristics." (11) If we accept this definition, the boundary between ethnic geography and population geography becomes sufficiently clear. In population geography as a part of economic geography, man is regarded in the abstract, primarily as a producer and consumer of material goods. In ethnic geography, he is regarded primarily as the bearer of the "ethnos," that is, as a member of a particular ethnic community. However, it must be emphasized that in studying various aspects of a given object of study, these two fields of knowledge are in constant contact.

Ethnography is related to geography in the broad meaning of this concept by investigation of the influence of human activity (that of peoples and ethnic groups) on the establishment of cultural landscapes. Ethnobotany and ethnozoology are related, in similar degree, to geography and to cultural and social anthropology.

It must be emphasized immediately that ethnography has nothing in common with the anthropogeography that used to be popular. Anthropogeography claimed that it established universal laws of distribution and migration of populations in accordance with features of the geographic environment, and also undertook to prove that geographic factors allegedly played a determining

role in the progress of society. Anthropogeographers gave fundamental attention to problems of man's adaptation to his natural environment, and contended that he was dependent upon that environment. They held that the laws of nature determined the conditions of population distribution and man's way of life. The development of society and changes in its life were explained by the increase in population density. In attempting to demonstrate that the natural environment had a governing influence upon social development, they gave little attention to the determining role of production and therefore engaged primarily in study of primitive forms of economy and culture, where the influences of natural forces were more pronounced. Anthropogeography served as the foundation for the reactionary doctrine of geopolitics that justified the imperialistic wars of the capitalist states by referring to the failure of state boundaries to correspond to what was called the Lebensraum of nations, etc.

Marxism-Leninism has established that natural conditions do not govern the course of social development, although they influence it, and place their imprint upon the culture (particularly the material culture) and the mode of life of people, and upon the nature of their geographical distribution. Man transforms nature, and utilizes it for his purposes, but geographic conditions influence the human choice of tools and means of labor, and the distinct forms taken by work skills. Ethnogeography should study all these problems.

Thus, as distinct from anthropogeography, ethnic geography considers the interrelationships among ethnic groups and the geographic environments on the historical level, emphasizing the mediating influence of geographic factors and the dominant role of socio-economic conditions.

III

In practice, geographical description plays a significant role in any anthropological study. It is understood that it is impossible to provide any more or less complete characterization of the life of a people, its material and intellectual culture, without analysis of the geographic medium in which this people lives. In the multi-volume series <u>Narody mira</u> [Peoples of the World], work on which is now coming to completion at the Institute of Ethnography, geographic description occupies an important place.

The objectives of Soviet ethnography include analysis, on the basis of Marxist-Leninist methodology, of the modes of life of all peoples — large and small, highly developed and backward in their development. This objective can be met only with examination of all factors influencing the mode of life of a population, both historical and socio-economic factors and natural ones.

It is most important to give attention to the nature of the geographic medium when working on atlases of historical anthropology. Scientific mapping of various elements in economic life, housing, clothing, and the rest, can be carried out only if all factors in the natural environment, economic life, etc., are taken into consideration.

The concept of "ethnic geography" embraces in full two important branches of cultural anthropology: ethnic cartography and ethnic demography. Let us consider these in greater detail.

Ethnic maps (maps of national composition or maps of peoples) help us to gain an understanding of the most important events of political life and to reveal the essence of national movements developing in various countries of the world. They serve as an important source for the solution of problems having to do with changes in national territory. Characteristic of each people is a given territorial distribution. The geographical position of this territory and the natural conditions related thereto have a significant influence upon the distinctive features of development of various aspects of the material and intellectual culture of peoples, while its territorial relationships to other peoples define many features of its ethnic history. Thus, ethnic maps, which make possible detailed and visual expression of the spatial relationships and connections among the data and phenomena of cultural and social anthropology, are transformed from an illustration to the text into a new source of cognition of anthropological laws.

The development of ethnic cartography abroad has been governed chiefly by particular practical needs. Thus, ethnic mapping of the countries of Europe was related primarily to various plans for reshaping boundaries between states and first embraced so-called "disputed" territories (Macedonia, Istria, etc.), which have complex ethnic compositions and have been the causes of international conflicts and military clashes. At the same time, large regions and even entire states remained outside the purview of ethnic geography. Recent decades have seen a number of rather detailed ethnic maps of various colonial and dependent lands of Asia and Africa (former French Indo-China, the Western Sudan, etc.). The compilation of these maps was often associated not with scientific goals, but with the search for new means of penetration by the capitalist monopolies into the economic systems of the native population.

In our country, because of its multinational character, ethnic mapping has attained a high level. The ethnic maps that P. I. Keppen and A. F. Rittikh compiled in the second half of the 19th century and the postrevolutionary maps of L. S. Berg, I. I. Zarubin, P. E. Terletskii and others have become widely known.

In 1917 a Commission for the Study of the Tribal Composition of Russia and Adjacent Lands (KIPS) was established under the Academy of Sciences. It carried out major work in compiling anthropological maps of many regions of the country.

The cartographic labors of KIPS and other institutions were of significant assistance to the directing agencies in nationality policy. Lenin thought highly of the significance of ethnic maps. Having examined the project of the Turkestan Commission on Elimination of Nationality Friction, Lenin wrote of the need "to compile a map (ethnographic, etc.) of Turkestan, with subdivisions for Uzbekia, Kirgizia, and Turkmenia," and "to clarify in detail the conditions for merger or separation of these three parts." (<u>12</u>)

Investigations in the field of ethnic cartography gained considerable scope after the close of World War II, when the rapid rise of the national liberation struggle of the peoples of the colonial and dependent countries attracted the attention of the broadest strata of the Soviet public. At that time, planned work to compile ethnic maps of the various regions of the earth began in the Institute of Ethnography of the USSR Academy of Sciences, where a laboratory of ethnic statistics and cartography was founded. In 1951 a school map of the peoples of the USSR was published. Then, starting in 1956, anthropological maps of Indostan, the peoples of China, the Mongolian People's Republic, Korea, the peoples of Indo-China, the peoples of the Near East, the peoples of Indonesia, Malaya and the Philippines, the peoples of Africa, as well as a general map, "Narody mira" [Peoples of the World], appeared in succession. Early in 1962 a map of the peoples of the USSR, compiled on the basis of the 1959 census, was published by the Institute of Ethnography in cooperation with the Main Administration of Geodesy and Cartography. A large Atlas narodov mira [Atlas of the Peoples of the World], to consist of 70 maps, including 15 large-scale maps of the USSR as a whole, tables and texts, is in preparation. Moreover, in recent years, a large number of ethnic maps were published in various editions by the Institute of Ethnography of the USSR Academy of Sciences (chiefly in the multi-volume series Narody mira [Peoples of the World]), geography textbooks, various encyclopedias, etc.

Studies of ethnic demography, which are important both for science and practical affairs, have not been developed as fully. Nevertheless, material on ethnic demography occupies a significant place in the textual matter appended to these demographic maps for regions of the earth and for the earth as a whole. They are grouped together in the large publication of the Institute of Ethnography, Chislennost' i rasselenie narodov mira [Numbers and Distribution of the Peoples of the World], published at the end of 1962 in the series Narody mira [Peoples of the World]. This publication provides a detailed description of the nationality composition of all countries of the world and continents, the numbers of the various peoples, and a description of their distribution. It also deals with theoretical problems having to do with the fundamental principles of identification, classification and determination of the numerical size of various peoples.

IV

A number of methodological problems have arisen in the work on ethnic cartography and ethnic demography, some of which have already been solved and some of which are awaiting solution. In the first place, principles must be developed for identification and classification of ethnic communities, principles for delimitation of ethnic territories and establishment of ethnic boundaries, as well as techniques for compilation of ethnic maps; the nature of the utilization of various indirect indices must be established so as to determine the boundaries of population distribution, etc.

Description of ethnic communities is one of the most important objects of ethnography. However, each individual investigator usually deals with limited areas and a small number of peoples. When ethnographic maps are to be compiled, the need arises for identification of peoples on a single scale over the surface of the earth as a whole, and for the choice of some particular and definite system of classification.

The major subjects of investigation in ethnic cartography are peoples — i.e., all forms of ethnic communities: nations, nationalities and tribes. Therefore, the first objective of ethnic cartography is the selection of criteria making it possible to identify peoples as such, and not parts of peoples (ethnographic groups) or other types of human communities (political, religious, racial, etc.).

The most reliable criteria for identification of peoples are the indices for nationality or native tongue employed in the censuses of certain countries. However, in the majority of multinational countries, there are no such questions in the census sheets. Moreover, there are many countries of the world containing considerable population groups that are in the process of consolidation or assimilation with other groups, as well as groups of people among whom consciousness of national affiliation is being pushed out by, for example, a consciousness of political or religious affiliation.

In order to establish laws of distribution of given phenomena over the earth's surface, it is necessary to classify them and to base this classification upon objective and significant characteristics. What are the characteristics that may be employed in classifying peoples? The mixed anthropo-linguistic and religio-linguistic system of classification commonly used abroad has no basis in science, inasmuch as ethnic boundaries usually do not coincide either with racial or religious boundaries.

Currently, the system of linguistic classification is the one in widest use for grouping various peoples. Similarity of languages permits a conclusion that there is a certain cultural affinity among the peoples concerned. The process of formation of language families was closely related to the diffusion of mankind over the earth's surface. Languages most closely related to each other are frequently encountered among neighboring peoples connected by common origin, long periods of life side by side under a single government, and having close economic and cultural ties.

Note must be taken of a number of difficulties and shortcomings involved in the employment of linguistic classifications and deriving from the fact that the classification is based upon only one of the characteristics of a people — its language. This classification makes it impossible to take into consideration important ethnic processes, one of the indicators of which is bilingualism. This often creates the impression that sharp ethnic or cultural contrasts exist where actually nothing of the sort is true (for example, among various groups of Swiss). In a number of cases (at the points of juncture between language families), this system of classification complicates the demonstration of the significant similarity among neighboring peoples (for example, in India between the Dravidic-speaking peoples and those of the Indic linguistic group).

The problem is to develop a system of classification of peoples which, along with consideration of language, would take other characteristics into account.

Let us pause to consider certain specific problems of ethnic cartography.

Many different methods are employed in the compilation of ethnic maps. Some of them (the method of legends, the area method, the method of qualitative or color background, etc.) are widely employed for other special types of maps, while some (the ethnic-territorial technique, the technique for showing ethnic composition and population density together) are employed only in ethnic cartography. Demonstration of the ethnic boundaries of various peoples and of certain most important features of population distribution is achieved best of all by the latter two methods. The method of ethnic territories reflects the geographical distribution of populations not only in districts where peoples are distributed in compact masses, but in mixed areas populated by representatives of various nationalities. The method, developed in the Institute of Ethnography of the USSR Academy of Sciences, of combining on a single map illustration of the ethnic composition and of population density makes it possible to give an idea of the distribution of peoples and of their numbers. However, the combination of two indices, to an equal degree of detail, on a single map, presents great difficulties, and in certain cases yields negative results (for example, the readability of maps is impaired, and ethnic boundaries are shown in less detail). It would seem that the best prospects are offered by further development of the technique of ethnic territories, in which a map shows both ethnic boundaries and, in less detail, a number of other indices of importance to anthropology (the indication of unpopulated or thinly populated districts, of nomadic and semi-nomadic populations, the use of special symbols to indicate the ethnic composition of cities, etc.).

In compiling ethnic maps, the investigator finds, no matter what portion of the world he is dealing with, a lack of sources. The uneven degree of study that various peoples of the earth have had, and in some cases the virtually complete absence of direct data on population distribution, long hindered the compilation of detailed ethnic maps for many parts of the world. (13) Our experience in drafting the "Narody mira" map, as well as the regional and ethnic maps, demonstrates that the employment of a large number of sources from a very wide variety of fields of knowledge (handbooks on particular countries, travelers' descriptions, monographs on individual peoples or districts, works in linguistics, data on economics and geography, various large-scale maps, etc.) also permits satisfactory determination of population boundaries by indirect means. Thus, for example, in many countries peoples may be distinguished by their economic specialization. Data to the effect that irrigated territories exist in southwestern Afghanistan permit identification of settlements of Tadjik farmers among the Afghan tribes engaged in pastoralism. Chinese and Indians in Malaya are localized in regions of plantation economy. The tea plantations of Ceylon employ chiefly Tamils emigrated from Southern India. The tin mines of Malaya are worked by Chinese. The oil fields of Iran employ chiefly Arabs, Indians and Bakhtiars, and so forth.

Analysis of the specific circumstances of territorial interrelations among peoples has made it possible to derive certain general laws of their population distribution. The peoples inhabiting the earth, in their overwhelming majority, live in compact groups. Areas having mixed ethnic composition are found most frequently at the junctures between peoples: mixing is usually greater among those neighboring peoples who speak similar languages. Ethnic composition becomes more complex as one proceeds from rural to urban localities, from backward districts to districts of highly developed economy. In large cities, one may encounter representatives of many nationalities. This is particularly characteristic of lands into which immigration has been considerable, where the bulk of the newly arrived population settled specifically in the cities. Dominant among urban populations are representatives of peoples at a higher level of socio-economic development. Sometimes cities constitute bodies of foreign nationalities in the native environment. In a number of cases, these laws were employed in the work of ethnic cartography for more precise definition of ethnic boundaries, when specific data on a given area were sparse.

In describing the status of the work and the major problems of ethnic cartography, it is necessary to note that historical ethnic cartography has had little development. Here we may cite only the works of B. O. Dolgikh on the distribution of the native peoples of Siberia prior to the advent of the Russians, and the maps of clan and tribal composition of Kirgiz and Turkmenians, compiled by Ia. R. Vinnikov and S. M. Abramzon. (14) However, undertaking such studies might assist in the solution of a number of problems of ethnogenesis, and would also make it possible to add greater precision in other historical problems.

V

Ethnic demography (one of the most important branches of ethnic geography) is at the juncture between ethnography and another discipline — demography. The basic object of ethnic demography is establishment of the ethnic composition of the population of some region of the earth's surface, determination of the numbers of various peoples and of ethnographic (including religious, racial, caste, etc.) groups. It is also the study of the dynamics of the ethnic composition of populations and the numbers of various peoples in the course of the general process of the socio-historical and economic development of societies. Another important objective of ethnic demography is analysis of the basic indices (birth rate, death rate, marriage rate, composition by sex, age and class, level of education, etc.) in their ethnic aspect, and identification of the relationship between these indicators and the features of life, culture, and daily habits of a particular people.

The role of ethnic demography is determined by the significance which the Marxist dialectical method ascribes to the need for an organic combination of quantitative and qualitative analysis of social phenomena and processes. However, as already observed above, ethnic demography has not yet been developed to any great extent, and a number of its important methodological problems await solution.

The major raw data for ethnodemographic researches are provided by census materials. This applies above all to censuses whose questions include that of ethnic (nationality) affiliation. At the present time, a comparatively small number of countries ask these questions (included among them is the majority of the socialist countries), while in certain countries, which do employ the question of ethnic affiliation (the old censuses of Indonesia and a number of the countries of the Western Sudan), the results obtained require further processing. (15) In making use of population censuses containing data on the language of the people (native tongue, colloquial language, knowledge of a particular language, etc.), the researcher faces the fairly complex problem of correcting these data. This requires detailed analysis of the relationship between linguistic and ethnic affiliation. An even more complex problem arises in cases where the researcher has at his disposal only data providing indirect information on ethnic affiliation. This would apply where the data deal with religious or racial composition, country of birth or citizenship, etc. Sometimes the investigator is just not able to determine the precise numbers of a people and is compelled to confine himself to approximate estimates.

Let us consider in somewhat greater detail the questions related to the study of the dynamics of the numbers of various peoples, inasmuch as these are the questions that have hitherto remained untouched by wide-scale scientific researches. It used to be held that study of population dynamics should be reserved to demography as such, but demographers have not given and have been unable to give attention to these problems because of the specific nature of the subject at hand, due to the fact that study of the dynamics of the numbers of various peoples and of the factors determining these things is impossible without knowledge of the specific features of the lives of these people, the peculiarities of their culture and way of life. (16)

Population dynamics are determined by such factors as the natural movement of the population, and migrational and ethnic processes. The first of these factors — natural population dynamics and the totality of the indices related to it (marriage rates, birth and fertility rates, death rate, etc.) — is central to the attention of demographers, but even here demographers are not in a position to take proper account of the ethnic aspect of these problems. The second factor — migration

— is, as a rule, treated by demography in a considerably more superficial manner. The third factor — ethnic processes (consolidation, assimilation, etc.) — is outside the sphere of demography.

The principal role in population dynamics is played by natural dynamics, which are characterized primarily by birth and death rates, the difference between which yields the natural rate of population increase. The indices of natural population dynamics vary, in different countries of the world and among various peoples, within rather broad limits (the birth rate ranges from 15% to 50% and more, the death rate from 7% to 30%).

Death rates are rather closely related to the general level of socio-economic and cultural development of particular peoples, although in the past decade, as a consequence of the spread into the underdeveloped countries of comparatively inexpensive means of combating epidemic disease (particularly antibiotics, DDT and sulfamides), this relationship is not as clear-cut as in the past. Suffice it to note that the death rate in Ceylon, in Malaya, and in a number of other economically backward countries of Asia and Latin America has today been reduced nearly to the level at which it stands in advanced industrial countries. If he analyzes the specific death rates of particular population groups, especially among the peoples of underdeveloped countries, the anthropologist is in a position to determine the relationships between these indicators and distinctive features of life among the population, specific aspects of its daily mode of life, diet (in particular, the use of intoxicants and narcotics), clothing, and the like, and in some cases he finds a relation to various traditional rituals and customs affecting health. In this work, the anthropologist is required constantly to make use of the data of medical geography, which studies the geographical distribution of diseases.

The general demographic situation in the world in the last few decades is characterized by a rise in the average natural increase as a result of rapid reduction in the death rate in many economically backward countries, accompanied by a high birth rate. Study of the reasons for this high birth rate is complicated by the fact that, unlike the death rate data, birth rate figures do not display such a close relationship to development of public health measures, and even less to the level of prosperity of the population. An increase in this level by no means always results in an increase in birth rate. The birth rate in the economically backward countries is considerably higher than in the advanced industrial countries. It is generally higher among the laboring classes of the capitalist countries than among the so-called "prosperous classes," and often higher among oppressed national minorities than among the dominant peoples. Peoples living under identical socio-economic conditions also often differ sharply in birth rate. Thus, in the USSR, the birth rate among Armenians and Azerbaidjanis has been more than twice as high as among Latvians and Estonians.

In studying the differences in birth rate among the peoples of the earth, the anthropologist has to analyze a complicated concatenation of varied factors. An important place among these is occupied by the group of anthropological factors related to distinctive features of life, culture and household practices. These factors include the traditional attitude toward age at marriage, as well as forms of family organization and social tradition encouraging large families or, on the other hand, tending to reduce the birth rate.

The tradition of a high birth rate appears in the very earliest stages of human history. It apparently dates from primitive society, in connection with the need to maintain the very existence of the clan or tribe under difficult conditions of life, when the death rate was very high. Subsequently, views with respect to large families became traditional and were reinforced by the standards of custom, reflected in religious dogmas, etc. This latter circumstance must be emphasized inasmuch as in many countries of the world religion has a significant influence in preserving the tradition of bearing many children: Hinduism and Islam provide specific conditions for these high birth rates. The influence of Catholicism in this direction is also considerable in the Americas. Analysis of such situations is of considerable scholarly interest.

Processes of migration have played and continue to play an important role in the history of lands and peoples: the establishment of the ethnic composition of many regions has been governed primarily by the influence of migrational processes. Of particular interest to anthropologists, as previously observed, are migrations of a distinctly national character — i.e., those in which a single nationality (or several nationalities) participates, and in which other nationalities in the same country do not participate. The origin of such migrations is usually related to particular socio-economic features in the lives of these peoples. When such migrations occur, the national composition of a country and the nature of population distribution change most sharply.

The migration of some portion of a people outside the limits of the principal country or district of its habitation, or reduction of its numbers in that district, does not exercise a direct influence upon the total number. Nevertheless, such migrations have rather significant indirect influence upon population dynamics. A portion of a people migrating to another country, particularly if that country is rather remote from the former place of habitation, usually finds itself in different natural and socio-economic circumstances, and since the migrants themselves usually have a very distinctive sex-and-age distribution (with predominance of the young age groups and of males), the indices of their natural movement change sharply. Thus, for example, the French who migrated to Canada were distinguished by a higher birth rate and higher rates of natural increase than those in France itself. Moreover, migrations have a strong influence upon the development of ethnic processes. There have been numerous cases in which a portion of a people that has moved to another country and mixed with the indigenous population has wholly broken its former ethnic ties and been transformed into an independent people (the establishment of nations in the lands of the Americas, etc.).

Finally, when we turn to the general question of the influence of ethnic processes upon population dynamics, the ethnographer most frequently encounters two types of such processes: ethnic consolidation and assimilation. The processes of ethnic consolidation, which in the past underlay the formation of most of the great nations existing today, are presently characteristic of various countries in Asia and Africa, where related tribes are merging into peoples and nations. Processes of assimilation are currently found everywhere, but are most characteristic of the advanced countries of the world, where large peoples, usually the basic nationalities of the country, absorb foreign minorities coming into their midst. Ethnic assimilation is particularly intensive among groups of immigrants that are wholly separated from their ethnic base, learn a new language, enter into mixed marriages, and often merge with the basic nationality of the country by the second or third generation. The similarities that may exist in culture and language between the immigrants and the basic nationality of their new homeland also affect ethnic assimilation and the intensity with which it proceeds.

VI

As already stated above, a study of the role of geographical factors in development of the traditional forms of economy and culture of the peoples of the world at various stages in their history is part of social and cultural anthropology. Soviet ethnography has developed the concept of economic-cultural types. We are unable here to give any detailed consideration at all to this question, which has been treated in a number of published writings. (17) Therefore let us confine ourselves to a summary.

Economic-cultural types are historically developed complexes of features of the economy and culture characteristic of peoples at approximately the identical level of socio-economic development and living under similar natural geographic conditions. We speak here of historically established characteristics of economy and culture because only those peoples whose development of productive forces is at approximately the same level may be characterized as falling into an economic-cultural type. As history progresses, both this level, as well as the nature of the influence exercised upon the economy and culture of peoples by the natural-geographical environment, changes. These changes may be so profound that in place of one economic-cultural type there may arise and develop, among these same peoples and in the same geographical environment, an entirely different type.

The economic-cultural types which have been identified among modern peoples in various parts of the globe differ in terms of historic antiquity. Some of them appeared at the time of the ancient migrations of mankind during the late Paleolithic, Mesolithic and Neolithic, while others date from considerably later times — the periods of breakup of primitive-communal, slaveholding or feudal class societies. Under capitalism, the economic-cultural types of preceding epochs undergo a gradual breakdown, and in their place new zonal complexes of economic, cultural and daily habit characteristics come into being. Unfortunately they have thus far had little study by anthropologists. Similar complexes exist in the socialist epoch, but on a fundamentally new socio-economic basis. Similar types may usually be found in areas of the globe remote from each other.

The study of economic-cultural types, their historical and chronological relationships, and the changes they undergo in the course of their historical development is of major significance to the solution of many problems of ethnogenesis and the ethnic history of peoples. At the same time, the study of economic-cultural types has to be of interest for the consideration of both the general and specific manifestations of the role of the geographical environment in the shaping of the economic and cultural features of peoples of different climatic and natural zones.

Here we do not touch upon the range of questions arising not in the field of socio-cultural but in that of physical anthropology and which are closely related to ethnic geography. We have in mind, in the first instance, that branch of physical anthropology which is devoted to study of the human race. The study of problems bearing on factors of race formation in man, the classification of racial types, and the physical-anthropological composition of the peoples of the earth — this entire range of subject matter is

156

inseparable from problems of ethnic geography. Study of the role of the geographic environment at various stages in race formation, consideration of the data of paleogeography in investigating the paths and rates of distribution of ancient groups of mankind, and the elaboration of data on historical demography, which are highly important for an understanding of the processes of establishment of the physical-anthropological composition of various peoples — this is merely a brief list of those basic questions in which the collaboration of physical anthropologists with persons in the field of physical and ethnic geography is most promising.

There can be no doubt that problems of ethnic geography are related to problems of political geography, linguistic geography, medical geography, as well as certain problems that are the province of sciences abutting on the field of social and cultural anthropology, archeology in particular. The discovery of these relationships might well be the subject matter of further investigation.

Footnotes

1) Paper read at meeting of the Department of Historical Sciences, USSR Academy of Sciences, April 28, 1962, expanded and revised.

2) For example, Thucydides, in his History of the Peloponnesian War, repeatedly underscored the important influence of climate upon distinctions in the daily lives and historical development of peoples.

3) Montesquieu, in his writings (particularly in L'Esprit des Lois, published in 1748), attempted to prove the decisive significance of climate, which, in his belief, affects the psychology and, in turn, the daily life, customs, social system and laws of peoples. Montesquieu ascribed to climatic influences the custom of polygamy, all types of slavery and forms of government, etc. Another defender of the concept of the deciding influence of the geographic environment, Buckle, in his History of Civilization in England (1852), held that the organization of society depended upon climate, soil and foodstuffs. Ideas of the

direct influence of the geographic medium upon human history are encountered among virtually all major geographers of the past century: C. Ritter, E. Reclus, L. Mechnikov, etc. The latter, for example, associated the development of civilization and culture with the geographic position of various countries on the greatest rivers, seas, and the shores of open oceans.

4) A. A. Kruber, Obshchee zemlevedenie, Part III (Biogeografiia i antropogeografiia), Moscow, 1922.

5) A. D. Sinitskii, Lektsii po zemlevedeniiu (Antropogeografiia), Moscow, 1929.

6) V. G. Borgoraz-Tan, Rasprostranenie kul'tury na zemle. Osnovy etnogeografii, Moscow, 1928, p. 58.

7) Ibid., pp. 58, 42.

8) Thus, in his paper at the First Interdepartmental Conference on Population Geography, Iu. G. Saushkin wrote: "A new branch of sociocultural anthropology, ethnogeography, must be singled out for attention. It has not yet fully taken shape, and its major function is often still regarded as merely the compilation and analysis of ethnographic maps. However, this branch has a much more profound significance, as disclosed in the book by P. I. Kushner (reference is to Etnicheskie territorii i etnicheskie granitsy, Moscow, 1951 — Authors); its function is to analyze the complex, historically mediated interrelationships between a given ethnic population group and the territory it inhabits. This problem, which is at the juncture of ethnography and geography, is truly complex and is of major significance to broad scholarly investigation of the population of the USSR" (Iu. G. Saushkin, "Geografiia naseleniia i smezhnye nauki," Materialy I Mezhduvedomstvennogo soveshchaniia po geografii naseleniia, No. 1, Moscow and Leningrad, 1961, pp. 83-84). Elsewhere he writes that ethnogeography "...is of major interest to economic geography and to geography in its entirety, inasmuch as the territory, the geographical environment, places a strong imprint upon a nation (nationality) and, on the other hand, a nation greatly changes the territory it inhabits, in accordance with its established traditions of production and material mode of life" (Vvedenie v ekonomicheskuiu

geografiiu, Moscow, 1958, p. 30).

9) S. P. Tolstov, "Osnovnye teoreticheskie problemy sovremennoi sovetskoi etnografii," Sov. etnografiia, 1960, No. 6, p. 12.

10) Voprosy geografii, 1947, No. 5, p. 32.

11) V. V. Pokshishevskii, "Predmet, sostoianie i zadachi geografii naseleniia," Materialy I Mezhduvedomstvennogo soveshchaniia po geografii naseleniia, No. 1, Moscow-Leningrad, 1961, pp. 3, 4.

12) Leninskii sbornik, XXXIV, p. 326.

13) Thus, P. I. Kushner has written (Etnicheskie territorii i etnicheskie granitsy, Moscow, 1951, p. 83): "For the compiler working on a map of the ethnic composition of countries in which ethnic statistics are lacking, it is utterly useless to employ a large-scale blank for his geographic foundation, as he will not be able to fill this blank with the appropriate ethnographic detail." On this same basis, Kushner came to the conclusion that it was impossible to compile a scientifically valid ethnic map for many countries of Asia, Africa and Latin America (ibid.).

14) B. O. Dolgikh, Rodo-plemennoi sostav Sibiri v XVII v., Moscow, 1959; Ia. R. Vinnikov, "Rodo-plemennoi sostav i rasselenie kirgizov na territorii Iuzhnoi Kirgizii," Trudy Kirgizskoi arkheologo-etnograficheskoi ekspeditsii, Vol. 1, Moscow, 1956; S. M. Abramzon, "Etnicheskii sostav kirgizskogo naseleniia Severnoi Kirgizii," Trudy Kirgizskoi arkheologo-etnograficheskoi ekspeditsii, Vol. IV, Moscow, 1960.

15) Many censuses of population do not take into consideration the powerful processes of consolidation and identify the most petty tribal groups, which actually are parts of large peoples and nations in the process of formation.

16) On this matter see the following article: V. I. Kozlov, "Kul'turno-istoricheskii protsess i dina mika chislennosti narodov," Vestnik istorii mirovoi kul'tury, 1959, No. 1.

17) S. P. Tolstov, "Ocherki pervonachal'nogo islama," Sov. etnografiia, 1932, No. 2; M. G. Levin and N. N. Cheboksarov, "Khoziaistvenno-kul'turnye tipy i istoriko-etnograficheskie oblasti," Sov. etnografiia, 1955, No. 4.

* * *

Narody Azii i Afriki, 1965, No. 6

A. Ia. Kvasha

SOME PROBLEMS OF THE DEMOGRAPHY OF THE DEVELOPING

COUNTRIES OF ASIA AND AFRICA

One of the important problems of development of the young states of Asia and Africa is the fact that the population is increasing out of proportion to economic development. Since World War II, and particularly in the past decade, the average annual rates of population increase have risen considerably, most markedly in the countries of Asia and Africa (see Table 1).

The substantial increase in growth rates of population in the countries of Asia and Africa is explained fundamentally by a rise in natural increase, as in most of them the external migration balance is negative. It is this "demographic explosion," taken in conjunction with the tragic heritage of colonialism in the economies of the young independent countries, that has created

Table 1

Average Annual Growth of World Population in 1900-1964* (%)

Year	World	Europe**	Africa	Asia**
1900-1920	0.55	0.50	0.80	0.30
1920-1940	1.15	1.00	1.10	1.15
1950-1960	1.85	0.95	1.90	1.95
1960-1964	1.86	1.15	1.95	2.15

*Source: SSSR v tsifrakh, 1963, Moscow; Statistika, 1964, p. 203.

**Without USSR.

certain difficulties in economic development and in raising the living standard of the peoples. Thus, if we take as 100 the average per capita food production in 1952/53-1956/57, we find that for Africa the figure stood at 94 in 1960/61, and for the Near and Middle East it stood at 103. For Pakistan, the corresponding indices for 1952/53-1956/57 and for 1962/63 were 102 and 94, for the Philippines — 100 and 99, and for Tunisia — 99 and 88. (1)

Public figures in the African and Asian countries ascribe much significance to demographic problems. Thus, President Nasser of the UAR has stated: "I should like to say that while there will never be an end to the problems facing us (the peoples of the UAR — A.K.), the most serious of them is the growth in population by 700,000-800,000 per year." (2)

Neo-Malthusianism is one of the most important means used in the ideological attack waged by imperialism upon the peoples of the young states of Asia and Africa.

Soon after the close of World War II, writings appeared in the West that propagated, in one version or another, the idea that the chief threat to the world is the excessive rise in population in the developing countries. Among such books there are, for example, W. Thompson's Population and Peace in the Pacific, (3) World's Hunger, by Pearson and Harper, (4) and many others. They allege a direct relationship between rise in numbers and density of population on the one hand, and the aggressiveness of a country on the other. "A struggle between peoples with low and high birth-rates is inevitable, and the peoples with high birth-rates will emerge the victors. While the European peoples are still strong, they must limit the rapid growth of population in these countries," writes Thompson. (5)

Pearson and Harper assert that the earth could feed only 900,000,000 persons. The rest of mankind is "excess" and will have to be exterminated in the course of wars, constant epidemics, and starvation. Otherwise, according to these neo-Malthusians, the peoples of the industrially developed countries will be threatened by a "wave of hungry Asiatics."

1948 saw the appearance of Vogt's The Road to Survival, which became a sort of manifesto of neo-Malthusianism. (6) Comparing the rates of population growth and food production in the countries of Asia and Africa, the author comes to the conclusion that mankind can be saved from famine only by forced reduction in the rate of population growth. Vogt recommends that the United States refuse economic aid to all countries that do not pursue a policy of reducing the birth-rate and taking steps toward artificially slowing the progress of medicine.

The years that followed saw the publication in the West of a considerable number of books developing neo-Malthusian ideas. Thus, in J. Hertzler's book The Crisis in World Population, published in the United States in 1956, one reads that "in the light of our experience that doctrine (Malthus' — A. K.) has the universality of a postulate." (7) The French Malthusian Bouthoul, who in 1961 published a book with the eloquent title Save War, (8) holds similar ideas.

1964 saw the publication in the United States of The Population Dilemma, (9) written by a group of distinguished American demographers and sociologists (F. Hauser, I. Tauber, D. Boige, and others). It deals with a broad range of demographic problems, including those of the population and economic development of the countries of Asia and Africa. The authors hold that these problems may be resolved primarily by reducing the birth-rate in these countries, and not by accelerating the rates of economic development.

The "danger" of overpopulation of the earth is exaggerated beyond all bounds. Certain demographers in the West have even "discovered" the existence of a "population bomb," a weapon even more dangerous, in their opinion, than the nuclear one. For example, the situation taking shape in the young states of Asia and Africa is seen in this way by the American demographer F. Notestein. And Vogt, whom we cited above, writes: "The tempestuous growth of population is more dangerous and presents a more immediate threat than does the hydrogen bomb." (10)

The sole alternative to the "population bomb,"

in the opinion of today's Malthusians, consists of measures to reduce the size of the population. "The sole certain means of reducing population pressure, and the tensions and disturbances to which it gives rise, is population control," writes Thompson. "The alternative to such control may prove to be a return to high death-rates from starvation, poverty, and disease, and possibly a hot war in the not-too-distant future." (11)

"The world is already approaching a situation in which growth of production and other benefits will no longer be able to match the explosive force of population growth," writes the American magazine U. S. News and World Report. "In such a situation, as in times past, overpopulated nations will be compelled to choose between famine or war to win the necessary resources." (12)

Present-day supporters of Malthus include capitalist-oriented demographers who not only do not support the appeals of the "hawks" (a) to "solve the overpopulation problem" by starting a "hot war," but criticize them, sometimes very sharply, and take a stand for peace and universal disarmament. Among these scholars there is, for example, the prominent French demographer and sociologist A. Sauvy, who for many years headed the Paris Institute for Demographic Research and the UN Population Commission. Like many Western scholars who oppose nuclear war, Sauvy, in his most recent writings (with highly biased titles), From Malthus to Mao Tse-tung (1958), and particularly in his Malthus and the Two Marxes (1963), which in many respects pursues further the ideas in the former book, supports negotiations between the USSR and the USA on the most important international problems, and warns of the danger of nuclear conflict to mankind and its future. At the same time, Sauvy holds that the threat of nuclear war is accompanied by another no less dangerous threat, that of the tempestuous population growth of the underdeveloped countries. Comparing the danger of a nuclear war to a powder keg, and the second "threat" to that of nibbling rodents, Sauvy writes: "We (mankind — A. K.) find ourselves in the position

of people living on a powder keg and daily awaiting an explosion. At the same time, the foundation of the building in which they live is being gradually undermined by rodents." (13)

In Sauvy's opinion, reduction in the death-rate is merely further intensifying the food difficulties of the young states. He sees the way out of this crisis primarily in conscious limitation of the birth-rate, and not at all in radical reorganization of the economies of these countries. Thus, it is demographic and not socio-economic factors that he advances to the foreground.

The attempts of the ideologists of imperialism today to resurrect the reactionary Malthusian theory, under new conditions, are determined by the same goals as 150 years ago. They seek, by utilizing the invented threat of the "demographic crisis," to distract the attention of the working people from the struggle for their class interests, the struggle against colonialism.

What are the factors which have conditioned the so-called demographic explosion in the lands of Asia and Africa? We know that natural population growth is determined by birth- and death-rates. It is the death-rate of the peoples of Asia and Africa that has undergone the most marked changes in the postwar years. In most of these countries, the death-rate today, although it has diminished since World War II, remains higher than in the industrially developed countries. Thus, whereas in 1955-59 the average death-rate was 23/1,000 in Asia and 27/1,000 in Africa, the figures for 1958-1962 were, respectively, 20/1,000 and 23/1,000. For Europe, the corresponding figure for 1958-62 was 10/1,000. (14) The reduction in death-rate, particularly infant mortality, is even more pronounced in a number of countries of Asia and Africa, if the present situation is compared to prewar.

It must be borne in mind, however, that it is precisely in those countries where sanitary conditions are worst and the death-rate highest that statistics on the number and causes of deaths are particularly inexact and often provide a distorted picture of these processes. In Turkey and Burma, for example, mortality is measured solely in terms of the urban death-rate. However, it is in rural areas that mortality, particularly of children, is highest. (15)

Therefore the officially computed death-rates in a number of countries are, if anything, understated. However, in these cases as well, there is no doubt that mortality has diminished considerably since before the war. Thus, whereas there were 24.5 deaths per thousand annually as an average for 1935-39 in Ceylon, and 20.7 in Malaysia, these figures averaged 10.1 and 11.7 in 1955-1958, and 8.5 and 9.2 in 1961. Infant mortality has declined even further. In Ceylon, the figure dropped from 182.8 per 1,000 in the first year of life as the annual average for 1935-1939 to 52 in 1961. Despite this, mortality in these countries is still several times as high as in the advanced capitalist countries, not to speak of the socialist states. In 1961 the death rate in Indonesia was 21.4 per 1,000, in India — 22 on the average for 1951-61, and in Mali — 29 in 1960. At this time (1960), the figure stood at 12 in Britain, 10 in Sweden, 9.5 in the USA, and 7.1 in the USSR.

When comparing death-rates of the developing to those of the industrially advanced countries, it must be borne in mind that the figure for mortality, like other "crude" demographic indices, does not consider differences in the age composition of the population. However, the Asian and African countries with high mortality rates are characterized by lower percentages of older people than is the case in the "old" countries. As computed by UN experts, (16) 11.5% of the Swedish population was over 65 in 1959, while in Japan the figure was 5.9% and in Singapore (1957) — 2.1%, while the crude mortality indices were 9.5, 7.4, and 7.4, respectively. If the percentage of the elderly were the same in the latter countries as in Sweden, the crude death-rate would be 13.1 in Japan and 16.8 in Singapore. (17)

Therefore the most precise and inclusive index of mortality is average life expectancy at birth. However, determination of this figure requires complicated prior demographic calculations on the basis of a comparatively large volume of statistical data. According to estimates by UN experts, this figure (men and women together) for countries on which there is the necessary statistical information (in most cases it is available for countries where the sanitary situation is comparatively good) was 55 to 59 for Ceylon and 50 to 54 for Malaysia in the years 1955-1958. In 1960-61, the average length of life in the Republic of Gabon was 37, in Morocco — 49.6 in 1960. In India it was 45.2 for men and 46.6 for women (urban population alone) in 1957-1958, and in the UAR, 51.6 and 53.8, respectively, in 1960. For 1941-1950, average length of life in India had been 32.4 years, and in the UAR — 35.6 years in 1936-1938. Let us recall that in France an average life-span of 38 to 40 years obtained in 1817-1831, 48 to 52 years in 1908-1913, and in 1962 it was 67.3 for men and 74.1 for women.

The rising life-span and the consequent diminution in mortality in the countries of Africa and Asia are associated primarily with the institution of a number of sanitation measures against infectious diseases. The cost of medicaments and supplies for these measures is comparatively low. Moreover, many of them have been provided without charge by the socialist countries or by various international organizations. Thus, dusting marshy areas with DDT solution has reduced malaria morbidity (and consequently mortality) to a fraction of the former level. Whereas 611,000 cases of malaria were recorded in Ceylon in 1950, the figure had dropped to only 110 in 1961. For Madagascar the corresponding figures were 418,000 and 50,000, and in the Philippines 63,000 and 30,000 (18) Inoculation and quarantine measures have made possible a substantial reduction in morbidity and mortality from other infectious diseases. The employment of these measures in combination with a set of steps in sanitation and hygiene (quarantine during epidemics, inspection of water supplies) would make it possible to reduce many-fold, without significant expenditure, the morbidity and mortality from a number of infections that previously took millions of lives. These measures require a comparatively small number of skilled experts to carry them out.

Whereas for countries like Gabon and certain other young African states, the carrying out of

Table 2

Death-Rate from Infectious Diseases in Asia and Africa, 1960-1961* (per 100,000 persons)

	UAR	Ceylon	India	Burma	USA	France
All infectious diseases	66.3	65.2	163.6	228.3	10.5	26.4
Including tuberculosis	18.7	12.5	61.1	74.5	4.7	17.4

*Source: Annuaire démographique, 1963.

simple and comparatively inexpensive health and sanitation measures could raise the median life-span to approximately 43-45 years, the situation is more complicated in countries like the UAR, India, and other comparatively "older" independent states, where median life expectancy at birth ranges between 45 and 55.

To determine the sources from which reduction in mortality is possible, let us examine the structure of the death-rate as it has now taken shape in these countries, by causes (see Table 2).

In comparing the data in Table 2 it must be borne in mind that, because of incompleteness of information, they often yield a distorted picture of mortality due to particular causes. In India less than 1% of the total population is reported on. As a consequence of these circumstances, as well as the shortage of medical personnel, the cause of death is often inaccurately determined. Therefore it may be assumed that the data on deaths due to infectious diseases in Asia and Africa probably understate the real situation. In countries such as India and the UAR, efforts to combat infectious diseases and their consequences can still bring an important reduction in mortality. However, at the present stage, this requires more extensive preventive and sanitary measures (for example, vaccination, improvement in housing and diet, medical help) — i.e., measures of a socio-economic order, requiring large appropriations. Further reduction in infant mortality also requires the establishment of a broad system of medical services and improvement in the living and cultural standards of the population, i.e., measures of a socio-economic order. In countries where national public health services are making their

first steps, even simple hygienic and medical-and-quarantine measures can yield a perceptible effect rather quickly.

Turning now to idiopathic diseases (malignant tumors and cardio-vascular conditions, for the most part), the lower mortality from them in the developing countries as compared with the "old" states (22.7 deaths per 100,000 from all malignant neoplasms in Ceylon in 1960, as against 191.7 in the U.S. in 1961) is due both to inadequate diagnosis and to differences in the age structure of the population. Mortality from idiopathic diseases rises particularly sharply with age. Therefore, in countries with higher life expectancy (in the U.S., 9.2% of the population was 65 and older in 1960, while in India the figure was 2.8% in 1961, and in Ceylon only 0.2% in 1955), the death-rate due to these diseases is considerably higher. Real successes in the treatment of these diseases (malignancies above all) are presently made possible by mass-scale prophylactic measures permitting prevention, prompt identification, and cure. However, it is hardly possible to take such steps on a large scale when medicine is practiced privately, and the numbers of qualified personnel and quantity of complicated equipment available are inadequate.

In the Soviet Union, 36,000,000 persons have been covered by preventive examinations for malignancies alone. Most infectious diseases have been entirely eliminated in the USSR. The general availability of medical assistance and the rising living standard of the population have had the consequence that mortality (not only for the country as a whole but for such formerly backward areas as Central Asia, where the population was dying off in some regions before the Revolution) has declined to the lowest level on earth. (b) Within the brief period since the October Revolution, despite the immense damage done to the health of the population by world war and foreign intervention, the average lifespan of Soviet people increased from 44 in 1926-27 to 70 in 1960-61. (19)

The principal reason for these successes lies in the fundamental social transformations that improved the health of the population of our country and diminished its mortality, subsequent to the October Revolution. The choice of the correct course of social development will permit the peoples of the developing countries to create conditions promoting the elimination of that burdensome heritage of colonialism, high mortality.

The birth-rate in the countries of Asia and Africa is approximately three times as high as in Europe. Thus, whereas in Europe (except the USSR) the average birth-rate in 1955-1959 was 19 per 1,000, in Asia (except the USSR) it was 42 and in Africa 46, while the corresponding average figures for 1958-1962 were 19, 43, and 46. In 1962, the index for Tunisia was 44.4, for the UAR 41.2, for India 32.8, for Indonesia 43, for Pakistan 43-46, and in Lagos, the capital of Nigeria, it was actually 80.4.

The overall indices for the birth-rate, like those for mortality, are to a certain degree dependent upon the age structure of the population. The larger the number of young people it contains, the higher the birth-rate, all other conditions being equal. Therefore the birth-rate is measured more exactly by applying age coefficients and, in the overall, by the use of what is termed the fertility coefficient. (20) In determining the limits of the child-bearing age it is necessary to consider the ethnic features of a given country and, in particular, the average age at marriage. In such young African states as Gabon and the Central African Republic, and in certain Asian countries, a certain percentage of the births (perhaps very considerable) occurs among females under 15 years of age. However, it is precisely for those countries that the statistical data, particularly with respect to fertility by age, are either lacking or very incomplete. In the UN report cited previously we read: "The new data obtained as the result of censuses and sample surveys, and which have become available only in recent years, permit only an approximate calculation of the birth-rate figures for most African countries. Although these calculations are not entirely exact, they give us reason to assume that for northern, southern, and eastern Africa the average birth index is approximately 45-46, while in West Africa it would seem to be somewhat over 50. By these same estimates, the birth-rate in Asia (except for Japan) exceeds 35." (21)

What are the causes (other than age composition) of so high a birth-rate? A number of Western demographers associate this with the fact that the people of Asia and Africa engage in virtually no conscious birth-control, so that the birth-rate approximates the physiological maximum, and differences in the index depend solely on the health of the population. These factors certainly play a role, but this would not seem to be the primary consideration. If the differences in birth-rate were associated solely with these factors, this would be manifested statistically in the existence of a close inverse correlation between birth- and death-rates. However, analysis of the available statistical data does not permit us to draw this conclusion. Moreover, in certain Asian and African countries, where the birth-rate is virtually stable or is even showing a slight increase, a definite reduction in the death-rate is observable. Thus, on Reunion Island (a so-called overseas departement of France), where the maintenance of statistics is at a relatively high level, the fertility coefficient dropped from 203.4 in 1954 to 190.1 in 1959, while the crude death-rate also diminished from 14.8 to 13.6.

Apparently, the chief factor determining the dynamics of birth-rate processes in Asia and Africa (and not there alone) is a complex of social, economic, and cultural features of the development of the given country.

The fact that a group of factors influences the birth-rate in the developing countries is evidenced by the data in Table 3.

Table 3

Birth-Rate Indicators and Level of Economic and Cultural Development of Asian and African Countries in 1960-1961*

Country	Fertility coefficient per thous.	National income per head of population, U.S. dollars, 1960	Urban population, as % of total	Illiterate females, 15 and older, as % of total	Non-agricultural gainfully employed, as % of total
Tunisia	191.9	130	15.2	15-19	30-39
Thailand	195.0	76	11.8	43.9	10-19
Philippines	226.0	155	10.2	30.5	30-39
Pakistan	145.0	38	13.6	92.6	20-29
USA	118.0	1,541	63.0	2.3	93

*Calculated from data in Annuaire démographique, 1963, UN Report on the World Social Situation, and Statistical Abstract, USA, 1962.

The data in Table 3 show that a high level of fertility generally corresponds to a high percentage of rural people both in the population as a whole and in its gainfully employed portion.

It is necessary to give consideration; albeit in the most general form, to the exceptionally complex mechanism whereby these factors operate. For example, one cannot hold that the considerable increase in the percentage of urban population immediately results in a noticeable decline in birth-rate in the country. Thus, whereas from 1957 to 1960 the percentage of urban population in Pakistan as a whole rose from 35.8 to 38.1%, the birth-rate in the country at large remained virtually unchanged, at 41-44 per thousand.

It should not be thought that change in a population's level of culture is reflected immediately in the processes whereby it reproduces itself. This is a very complicated process, and its influence upon birth-rate processes is by no means manifested at once. The genuine cultural revolution that occurred in the Soviet years in the Central Asian republics is a matter of common knowledge. However, the birth-rate in these areas continues to be at a very high level. Thus, for example, the birth-rate in 1961 in Azerbaidjan was 42.1 per 1,000, and 41 in Turkmenia — i.e., at the same level as in a

number of Asian and African countries. We wish to emphasize that reflection of a change in the level of culture may be very long delayed in birth-rate processes, and may occur only after these fundamental changes in the culture and daily life of the population form a new set of traditions, habits, and features of the life of the population which largely determine the dynamics of the birth-rate.

However, if the process of "restructuring" the birth-rate is a comparatively slow one, where then is the way out of the "vicious circle of poverty," as the gap that has come into being between rates of population growth and the production of food in the developing countries is termed by capitalist-oriented demographers? The way out obviously lies, above all, in rates of development of the economy of those countries that will be several times as great as the high natural population growth resulting from retention of a high birth-rate and declining death-rate. Moreover, these high rates of population increase may also diminish in the future if the young states put great efforts into developing their economies.

As industry develops in the formerly backward countries, a considerable proportion of the young people, primarily men, will move from villages to the cities, with the result that the birth-rate both in the villages and in the country at large will diminish. Involvement of women in production and, as their level of education rises, in more and more skilled work will lead in turn to intensification of the processes of conscious family planning. Urbanization and a number of other factors will influence the processes of population reproduction. However, these processes may perhaps proceed more rapidly than they did in Europe, if we consider that, once having taken the path of non-capitalist development, the young states of Asia and Africa will be able to create modern industry and highly skilled personnel for it within shorter periods of time, and this in turn will promote the shaping of a pattern of population reproduction corresponding to a lower birth-rate.

It is desirable, albeit in the most general form, to present the attitude of Marxists to the problem of conscious limitation of the birth-rate. This question is discussed in many writings by Western demographers and sociologists.

In his books cited above, Sauvy seeks to prove that there exist "European" and "Asian" concepts of Marx's teachings with respect to problems of the birth-rate. Whereas "the European understanding" of Marxism (reference is to the USSR) does not admit of complete childlessness, the "Asian" takes as point of departure the need to limit the birth-rate by every possible means.

Sauvy seeks in every possible manner to rehabilitate Malthus, and sees his principal error in the fact that he propounded his theory "too early," while the considerable reduction in mortality due to the discoveries of modern medicine have now made Malthus' theory timely. Without the least hesitation, the French demographer ascribes to Marxism ideas foreign to it, affirming, for example, that Marx wrote that the development of technology leads to an absolute reduction in the labor force, and that Marxists oppose birth control. We know, however, that Marx, in formulating his law of population under capitalism, was thinking of relative and by no means absolute reduction in employment.

The position taken by Marxists with respect to the problem of reducing the birth-rate is quite definite. While giving priority in solving the problem of "demographic pressure" to fundamental socio-economic changes, which alone are capable in the final analysis of assuring the rising generation of an adequate supply of material goods, Marxist-Leninists do not in principle oppose humane measures for conscious limitation of births. As early as 1913, in his article "The Working Class and Neo-Malthusianism" [Rabochii klass i neo-mal'tuzianstvo], Lenin wrote that most certainly, while opposing Malthus' views as a social theory, Marxists stood for unconditional repeal of all laws punishing abortion or the dissemination of information about contraceptive devices. "Freedom of medical publicity and protection of the elementary democratic rights of the citizens, male and female, is one thing," wrote Lenin. "The social theory of neo-Malthusianism is quite another." (22)

Criticizing the neo-Malthusian prophecy that the capacities of modern science would lag behind the needs of modern society, Engels wrote: "Production is too low, and that's the entire problem. But why is production too low? By no means because production has attained its limits: even for today and with today's facilities. Not at all: but because this limit upon production is determined not by the number of hungry bellies but by the number of buying, solvent purses. Capitalist society does not wish and cannot wish to produce more than that." (23)

The experience of the USSR and the socialist countries of Asia testifies irrefutably that "the demographic crisis" is capable of being resolved solely by a course of fundamental socio-economic changes — the course of socialism. More and more of the countries of Asia and Africa are taking that course.

Editor's Notes

a) Russian beshenye: literally "mad dog."
b) This represents the crude rate only. Due to wars, famines, disease and lower living standards, the percentage of population over 65 was, until recently, much lower than in the USA, Sweden or some other countries. However, life expectancy at present is equal to that in the USA.

166

Footnotes

1) Production Yearbook, Vol. 17, 1963, p. 31.

2) Izvestia, Jan. 4, 1965.

3) W. Thompson, Population and Peace in the Pacific, Chicago, 1946.

4) P. Pearson and F. Harper, World's Hunger, New York, 1946.

5) W. Thompson, op. cit., p. 218.

6) W. Vogt, The Road to Survival, New York, 1948.

7) J. O. Hertzler, The Crisis in World Population, Lincoln, Nebraska, 1956, p. 103.

8) G. Bouthoul, Sauver la guerre, Paris, 1961.

9) The Population Dilemma, New York, 1964.

10) W. Vogt, People! Challenge to Survival, New York, 1960, p. 224.

11) W. Thompson, Population and Progress in the Far East, Chicago, 1959, p. 339.

12) U. S. News and World Report, Sept. 16, 1963, p. 61.

13) A. Sauvy, Malthus et deux Marx, Paris, 1963, pp. 8-9.

14) Annuaire démographique, 1960, p. 118; ibid., 1963, p. 142.

15) Ibid., 1963, pp. 538-549.

16) See Doklad o mirovom sotsial'nom polozhenii za 1963 g., UN, 1964, p. 25.

17) This device in demographic statistics is termed standardization of the age structure of the population.

18) A. Sauvy, op. cit., p. 92.

19) B. Ts. Urlanis, Rozhdaemost' i prodolzhitel'nost' zhizni v SSSR, Moscow, Gosstatizdat, 1963, p. 104.

20) The ratio of the number of children born to women aged 15 to 49, to the total size of that age group. In Soviet demography this indicator is still called the special birth-rate coefficient.

21) Doklad o mirovom sotsial'-nom polozhenii za 1963.

22) V. I. Lenin, Poln. sobr. soch., Vol. 23, p. 257.

23) Marx and Engels, Soch., 2nd ed., Vol. 31, Moscow, 1963, p. 394.

* * *

Sovetskaia etnografiia, 1965, No. 2

N. G. Volkova

CHANGES IN THE ETHNIC COMPOSITION OF THE URBAN POPULATION

OF THE NORTH CAUCASUS DURING THE SOVIET PERIOD

Research on problems of the ethnic formation of the urban population during various periods of history is one of the important aspects of the study of the history of the peoples of the Soviet Union. These matters are particularly pertinent in relation to the North Caucasus because of certain specific features of the development of urban life in that area: the recent origin of most towns, the insignificant numbers of members of the North Caucasian nationalities in them until the October Revolution, and the dominance in the urban population of Russians, Ukrainians, Armenians, and other peoples.

The Soviet period has seen a rapid rise in urban population among the Ossetes, Kabardians, Adygeis, Karachais, Balkars, Chechens, Ingushi, and the peoples of Dagestan, due to the tempestuous economic and cultural development of the autonomous entities of the North Caucasus. It is precisely during the Soviet years that the towns of the North Caucasus have become major industrial, administrative, and cultural centers. Higher educational institutions and research institutes have been founded in them, and a considerable corps of non-manual personnel of the local nationalities has come into being. In addition, having become important centers of the economy and cultures of the North Caucasian peoples, these towns are gaining ever greater significance in the inter-national contact between the peoples of the North Caucasus and other peoples of the Soviet Union in the process of the building of communism.

It is the purpose of the present article to demonstrate the fundamental changes that have occurred in the ethnic composition of the population of the towns of the North Caucasus in the Soviet period, as well as the reasons for these changes.

The data of the 1897, 1926, and 1959 censuses, as well as certain information from the 1920, 1923, and 1939 censuses, are the basic sources for treatment of the questions in which we are interested. In utilizing the data of a number of censuses, it has been necessary to take into consideration certain inaccuracies and shortcomings in them.

Thus, in the 1897 census, the question of

nationality was replaced by that of native tongue. (1) However, a number of languages were not recognized in the census: Balkarian was counted with Tatar, Abazin with Abkhaz, and Agulian, Rutulian, Tsakhur, and Tabasaran were listed among "other Lezgin dialects," etc.

The data of the 1920 census for the North Caucasus were not systematized, and are known from a very tiny number of documentary publications and records in the archives. (2) The most detailed information from that census is on the urban population of the Kuban-Black Sea and the Tersk oblasts, and on Stavropol' Guberniia.

The census of urban population of 1923 did not list certain nationalities of the North Caucasus: Chechens, Ingushi, Kabardians, and all the peoples of Dagestan were listed as "Caucasian mountaineers." The Balkars, Karachais, Azerbaijanis, Kazan' Tatars, and Nogais were listed under the headings "Tatars" and "Other Turks." Thus, this census is usable only for study of the urban population of the Slavic group, Armenians, Georgians, Greeks, Jews, and Ossetes. (3)

Only the censuses of 1926 (4) and 1959 (5) provide detailed data on the numbers and ethnic composition of the urban population of the North Caucasus.

* * *

The towns of the North Caucasus may be divided into three groups. The first includes Krasnodar, Maikop, Ordjonikidze, Grozny, Mozdok, Kizliar, Buinaksk, Makhachkala, and Derbent. Having been founded between the mid-18th and mid-19th centuries as Russian military posts, (6) some of these towns had become large administrative and economic centers even before the Revolution.

The second group comprises Nal'chik, Cherkessk, (7) Dokshukino, Beslan, Alagir, Gudermes, and Khasaviurt, which were comparatively small population centers before the Revolution, and which became towns only during the Soviet period.

Towns founded in the Soviet period comprise the third group: Karachaevsk, Malgobek, Tyrny-Auz, Kaspiisk, and Izberbash, plus a small group of industrial settlements. Some of them were built specifically as administrative centers for newly established autonomous entities (for example, Karachaevsk, the center of the Karachai Autonomous Oblast), and others as new industrial centers (Tyrny-Auz, Kaspiisk, Izberbash).

The special historical circumstances governing the founding of the first group of towns was responsible for their distinctive ethnic makeup in the past. At the outset, their population consisted primarily of Russians and Ukrainians. However, in the process of development of fortifications in these towns, settlements of Armenian, Georgian, Mountain-Jewish, Ossete, and Kabardian merchants and craftsmen rapidly developed alongside them.

There were certain differences in ethnic formation between the towns of the first group in the northwestern and the eastern Caucasus.

Thus, the northwestern Caucasus and its towns had been centers of extremely large migration of various peoples over a long period of time, but the bulk of the people were Ukrainians, Russians, Armenians, and Greeks. According to the 1897 census, it was precisely in the northwestern Caucasus that centers of Ukrainian population were to be found: 25,100 in Ekaterinodar and 10,700 in Maikop. (8) Of the other North Caucasian towns, only Vladikavkaz had any significant number of Ukrainians (1,300). The same census showed 1,500 Armenians and 600 Greeks in Ekaterinodar. The numbers of these peoples in the town increased considerably during World War I, and in 1920 there were over 12,000 Armenians and 2,300 Greeks. (9)

The dominant population in the towns of the Eastern Caucasus was Russian, Armenian (from various parts of Persia), and Georgian. Thus, we find many Armenians making an appearance in Mozdok and Kizliar (10) at the end of the 18th century, while 500 Armenian families from the khanates of Baku and Derbent had moved to the vicinity of Madzhar, where they were permitted to found the town of Sviatoi Krest. (11) Thus,

Table 1

Numbers and Proportion of Urban Population to Total Numbers in the Nationalities (1897 Census)

Nationality	Total number	Of which, in towns of North Caucasus	% urban
Circassian (Adygei)	42,991	188	0.4
Abazin	12,481	-	-
Ņogai	64,017	255	0.4
Karachai	27,093	6	0.0
Kabardian	98,464	638	0.6
Balkar	23,184	72	0.3
Ossete	98,707	4,084	4.1
Ingush	47,184	446	1.0
Chechen	224,139	764	0.3
Dagestani Nationalities			
Avar	174,398	895	0.5
Dargin	122,491	353	0.2
Kumyk	83,240	2,923	3.0
Lezgin	95,230	133	0.1
Lak	77,972	481*	0.6
Tabasaran	No data	-	-
Rutulian	No data	-	-
Agulian	No data	-	-
Tsakhur	No data	-	-
Tat	2,998	16	0.5

* The extreme predominance of men, as indicated by the census data, compels us to assume that this was a temporary population of seasonal laborers.

Kizliar, Mozdok, and Sviatoi Krest (now Prikumsk) are the oldest centers of Armenian migration in the North Caucasus, and virtually until the end of the 19th century remained just about the largest Armenian population-centers. According to the 1897 census, about half the population of Kizliar consisted of Armenians (3,500 persons). In Mozdok there were 2,300. In addition, at the end of the 19th century, a substantial number of Armenians lived in the towns of Dagestan (1,500) and in Vladikavkaz (2,000).

Starting in the 1760's, Ossete, Kabardian, and Ingush settlements began to appear near the Mozdok fortification. (12) Kabardian feudal chiefs and their ezden [members of the feudal nobility of Kabardia and Dagestan — Trans.] and runaway Ossete and Kabardian peasants (13) settled here as a consequence of feudal internecine warfare. For nearly a century, the Ossete urban population was concentrated in Mozdok, as the development of Vladikavkaz as a town began only in the 1860's. It was specifically in Mozdok that a substantial number of Kabardians lived until the end of the 19th century (1,133 persons in 1875, reduced to 447 in 1897), while in Nal'chik they numbered only 65 in 1897.

The absence of towns in Ingush territory and the fact that they lived immediately adjacent to the Ossetes facilitated the settlement of a portion of the Ingush in the towns of Ossetia. At Mozdok the so-called newly converted Ingushi made an appearance in the 1760's, and settled in a sloboda [a] of their own. (14) An Ossete and Ingush population made its appearance in Vladikavkaz at the beginning of the 19th century, (15) but was very small. In 1874 there were only 334 Ossetes in the town, whereas in Mozdok there were 1,226. (16) Only at the end of the 19th century did the number of Ossetes in Vladikavkaz increase to 2,900 persons. The Ingushi settled both in Vladikavkaz and in its outskirts. In 1897-1898 there were 378 Ingushi in the town, and 200 Ingushi from the Khamkhin, Metskhal, and Tsorin communities [b] of Ingushetia in the German "colony" of Mikhailovskoe. (17)

In the towns of Dagestan — Temir-Khan-Shure (now Buinaksk) and Petrovsk (now Makhachkala) — the indigenous peoples made an appearance as a permanent population only in the 1890's. At that time, the Kumyks and Avars constituted 1.3 and 0.1% of the population, respectively. (18) The number of Kumyks in Temir-Khan-Shure and Petrovsk in 1897 increased to 1,900 persons, in addition to which 800 individuals lived in Kizliar. The statistical data for 1875 showed no Kumyks — i.e., their settlement in Kizliar occurred only in the two decades following.

According to the 1897 census, there were, in addition to Kumyks, 800 Avars, 200 Dargins, 200 Laks, and 200 Lezgins in the towns of Dagestan (19) (see Table 1).

The ethnic composition of Derbent, unlike the towns previously named, was largely determined by the ethnic affiliation of the surrounding population of the Caucasus; a considerable percentage of its inhabitants were Azerbaidjanis. (20) By the 1860's and 1870's, the population of Derbent had been supplemented by Mountain Jews and Russians although, as before, Azerbaidjanis predominated (9,600 persons). (21) Residents of mountain Dagestan made an appearance in Derbent as seasonal laborers, but they were not yet present in the town as permanent residents as late as the period from the 1880's to the beginning of the 1890's. (22) It was not until the 1897 census that we find Avars, Darbins, and Lezgins there (totalling 600 persons altogether), and an increase in Mountain Jews to 2,200.

The Chechens, Balkars, Karachais, Adygeis,

and certain Dagestani peoples did not live in towns. An order of the Caucasian Administration in 1891 prohibiting Chechens not in government service to live within town limits played a role in this regard, particularly with respect to the Chechens. It was not until 1902 that they were again granted the right to settle in Groznyi. (23) However, even during the first decade of the 20th century the number of Chechens in the town did not exceed 200. (24)

Until the Revolution, towns in the second group comprised settlements of rather homogeneous ethnic composition (the Kabardin settlement of Dokshukino, the Russian stanitsa [Cossack town] of Batalpashinskaia, the Chechen settlement of Gudermes). The population of Alagir was comprised chiefly of Ossetes, as well as of Russians employed at the Alagir Works (25) and Rachin Georgians (about 1,500 persons) who moved there in 1877. (26) During the second half of the 19th and the first quarter of the 20th centuries, the ethnic composition of some of these towns changed somewhat: a Russian population came to predominate in Dokshukino, and Russians, Ukrainians, Armenians, and others appeared in Gudermes.

* * *

The towns in the third group were industrial centers built in Soviet times, where populations grew rapidly, chiefly core groups of workers and non-manual people of the indigenous nationalities. The ethnic composition of such towns took shape in the Soviet years and was determined not only by the ethnic affiliation of the population of the surrounding areas, but by the national composition of the migrating industrial population.

* * *

In analyzing the urban population of any given people, it is necessary to consider three factors: the change in the total numbers of the people, the percentage of urban population within it (Table 2), and the proportion of that people in the urban population (Table 3).

Table 2

Urban Population of North Caucasian Nationalities, and Urban Population as % of Whole

Censuses

| Nationality | 1926 | | | | | | 1959 | | | | | |
| | In autonomous entity | | | No. Caucasus as whole* | | | In autonomous entity | | | No. Caucasus as whole** | | |
	Total	Urban	%	Total	Urban	%	Total	Urban	%	Total	Urban	%
Adygei	50,821***	19	0.0	51,717	1,109	2.1	65,908	5,937	9.0	76,545	9,611	12.5
Circassian	12,314	54	0.4	12,314	54	0.4	24,145	1,446	5.9	24,918	1,845	7.4
Abazin	10,993	-	-	13,813	72	0.5	18,159	1,271	6.3	18,526	1,500	8.0
Karachai	52,503	-	-	55,068	1,709	3.1	67,830	4,839	7.1	69,255	4,839	8.7
Nogai	-****	-	-	36,034	93	0.2	-	-	-	36,657	2,372	6.5
Kabardian	122,402	866	0.6	139,689	1,633	1.1	190,284	22,987	12.1	192,545	24,092	12.5
Balkar	33,197	350	1.0	33,280	394	1.1	34,088	4,693	13.8	34,088	4,693	13.8
Ossete	139,120	11,186	8.7	155,936	13,766	8.8	215,463	68,451	31.7	228,676	74,206	32.4
Ingush	69,954	824	2.3	72,043	2,446	3.3	48,273	4,232	8.7	54,344	4,907	9.0
Chechen	293,190	2,001	0.7	318,133	2,902	0.9	243,974	22,318	9.1	257,111	25,683	9.9
Dagestani Nationalities												
Avar	177,341*****	2,013	1.1	178,219	2,172	1.2	239,373	22,529	9.4	244,961	23,128	9.4
Dargin	125,707	891	0.6	125,743	965	0.7	148,194	19,505	13.2	149,027	19,789	13.2
Kumyk	87,960	6,544	7.4	94,480	7,028	7.4	120,859	40,332	33.3	130,336	41,896	32.1
Lezgin	90,509	2,108	2.3	92,435	3,169	3.4	108,615	12,121	11.2	108,883	12,303	11.2
Lak	39,878	1,127	2.8	40,233	1,211	3.0	53,451	13,731	25.7	54,797	14,393	26.2
Tabasaran	31,915	34	0.1	31,915	34	0.1	33,548	2,284	6.8	33,548	2,284	6.8
Rutulian	10,333	-	-	10,333	-	-	6,566	15	0.2	6,566	15	0.2
Agulian	7,653	-	-	7,653	-	-	6,378	52	0.8	6,378	52	0.8
Tsakhur	3,531	-	-	3,531	-	-	4,278	14	0.3	4,278	14	0.3

*Data for North Caucasian Krai (excluding Donets, Don, Shakhtinsko-Donets and Sal'sk okrugs).

**Includes autonomous republics of the North Caucasus, and Stavropol' and Krasnodar krais.

***In the 1926 census, the Adygeis were recorded as Circassians, and the Adygei population of the Circassian Autonomous Oblast as Kabardian. We employ the designations utilized in the last census: Adygei and Circassian.

****Inasmuch as the Nogais are divided between the territories of two autonomous entities (the Karachaevo-Circassian Autonomous Oblast and the Dagestan ASSR), we adduce the totals for the North Caucasus.

*****Including the Ando-Tsezian group and the Archins.

Table 3

North Caucasian Nationalities as % of Urban Population (in Present Boundaries)

Territory; nationality	Censuses		
	1897, %	1926, %	1959, %
Adygei Autonomous Oblast			
Adygei	0.2	0.03	10.6
Karachaevo-Circassian Autonomous Oblast			
Karachai	0.0	-	7.3
Circassian	0.1	-	2.2
Abazin	-	-	1.9
Nogai	0.0	-	0.5
Kabardino-Balkar ASSR			
Kabardian	1.3	6.7	13.8
Balkar	-	2.7	2.8
North Ossetian ASSR			
Ossete	8.0	14.5	28.8
Checheno-Ingush ASSR			
Chechen	3.2	2.0	7.5
Ingush	-	0.8	1.4
Dagestan ASSR			
Avar	1.9	2.5	7.1
Darbin	0.44	1.09	6.1
Kumyk	4.3	8.0	13.1
Lezgin	0.3	2.4	3.8
Lak	0.4	1.3	4.3
Tabasaran	-	0.04	0.7
Mountain Jewish*	12.9*	12.0	4.9
Nogai	-	-	0.4
Rutulian	-	-	0.0
Agulian	-	-	0.0
Tsakhur	-	-	0.0

* Counted together with "European" Jewish.

Examination of the results of two of the censuses held in the Soviet period, in 1926 and 1959, shows that the process of establishment of the urban population of the peoples of the North Caucasus was not uniform, and that it led to diverse results which make it possible to distinguish a number of categories in terms of percentage of urban population (within the groups, the nationalities are arranged in order of declining percentage of urban population).

1. Kumyks, Ossetes, Laks. Except for the Laks, (27) these peoples also had some small urban population before the Revolution. Not less than 25% of each of these peoples live in towns.

2. Balkars, Dargins, Adygeis, Kabardians, Lezgins. The number of these in towns was small, even at the 1926 census. In 1959 the urban components of these peoples comprised not less than 10% of the whole.

3. Avars, Chechens, Ingushi, Karachais, Abazins, Tabasarans, Circassians. The urban components of these peoples comprise less than 10% of the total number of each.

4. Only individual Rutulians, Tsakhurs, and Agulians may be found in towns.

It is essential to note that the peoples of the North Caucasus may also be found in other parts of the Soviet Union, where they are predominantly urban. Thus, the percentage of town dwellers in the Ossete (35%), Lezgin (23.2%), Adygei (15.1%), and Kabardian (14.7%) populations is rising in the USSR as a whole.

Such an increase in the numbers of the urban population among the North Caucasian peoples was the result primarily of a substantial influx of their rural population into the towns of their republics. Thus, in 1952 alone, 3,100 people moved from the villages of North Ossetia to work and study in the towns. (28) Moreover, 12,000 persons were added to the urban population in 1959 by the reorganization of the villages of Buron, Verkhnii Zgid, Mizurskii, and Sadon as urban settlements. Since 1926 the percentage of urban population among the Ossetes has increased from 8.7 to 31.7%.

The Ossetes comprise 28.8% of the urban population of their republic.

The Kabardian urban population began to take shape at a rapid rate starting in the late 1930's. Whereas in 1926 only 866 Kabardians lived in the towns of their autonomous entity, 22,987 persons lived in the towns of the republic in 1959, an increase of more than 26 times. However, one notes a decline in the number of Kabardians in such old urban centers as Mozdok. (29)

According to the 1959 census, most of the urban Kabardian population lives in Nal'chik (about 16,000 persons) and Tyrny-Auz (about 3,000 persons).

There has also been a substantial increase in the Kumyk urban population. Among the Dagestani nationalities, the Kumyks have the highest percentage of townspeople (13.1%); in this respect they lag behind only the Ossetes and Kabardians, of all the North Caucasian nationalities.

According to the 1926 census, the Kumyks lived primarily in Buinaksk (2,700 persons) and Makhachkala (2,500 persons). By the early 1940's the proportion of members of this nationality had increased to 21.7% in Derbent and 43% in Khasaviurt. (30) According to the last census, most of the urban Kumyk population lives in Makhachkala (about 15,000), Buinaksk (over 8,000), and Khasaviurt (about 8,000). In the 1940's and 1950's, Kumyks made an appearance in the new towns of Kaspiisk and Izberbash, where their numbers exceeded 3,500 in 1959.

An Adygei urban population has also come into being in the Soviet period. No small role in this respect was played by the formation, in 1922, of the Adygei Circassian Autonomous Oblast by detaching territory populated by Adygeis from the Krasnodar and Maikop portions of the Kuban-Black Sea Oblast. The center of the autonomous region was in Krasnodar, and Maikop was placed in Maikop Okrug. In 1936 the oblast center was moved to Maikop where, according to the last census, the majority of the urban Adygeis (about 3,000 persons) live. In addition, some 3,000 Adygeis live in the cities of Krasnodar Krai.

The data of the 1939 census (31) show a substantial increase in the numbers of the Chechen urban population. From 1926 to 1939 the number of Chechens in the towns had multiplied 16-fold. Such a rapid increase in the numbers of the urban population in so brief a period was, of course, the result of a considerable influx of Chechens from the villages to the towns of their republic, as a consequence of the intensive economic and cultural development of Checheno-Ingushetia.

According to the 1959 census, the Chechens live chiefly in Grozny (about 17,000) and Gudermes (over 3,000).

Before the Revolution, the Karachais did not live in towns, but within the first years of Soviet authority they came to number 1,500 persons in Kislovodsk. (32) 1926-1927 saw the start of construction of the first Karachai town, Mikoyan-Shakhar (now Karachaevsk), which became the center of Karachai in the 1930's. In 1934 its population was about 4,000. (33)

Today there are two towns (Cherkessk and Karachaevsk) in the Karachaevo-Circassian Autonomous Oblast, and six urban-type settlements, inhabited by 4,800 Karachais.

The number of Avars in the towns of the Dagestan ASSR has increased almost 12-fold since 1926, and reached 22,500 in 1959, while their share in the urban population of the republic attained 7.1%. Whereas before the 1926 census the Avars lived chiefly in Buinaksk (1,100), and only 679 of them were to be found in Makhachkala and Khasaviurt, the 1959 census showed their numbers to have increased considerably, coming to about 9,000 in Buinaksk, some 7,000 in Makhachkala, and approximately 4,000 in Khasaviurt.

The number of Dargins in the towns of Dagestan increased by a factor of over 21. Centered, as before, chiefly in Makhachkala (about 6,500 persons), the Dargins have come to inhabit other towns of Dagestan in considerable numbers in recent years: over 2,000 in Buinaksk, over 1,500 in Khasaviurt, over 1,500 in Derbent, and about 3,500 and 3,000 in the new towns of Kaspiisk and Izberbash, respectively.

The urban Lak population has multiplied more than 12-fold since 1926, and constitutes 4.3% of the people in the towns of Dagestan. Whereas the 1926 census showed a small number of Laks

living in Buinaksk, Khasaviurt, and Makhachkala, in 1959 there were not only more than 6,000 in Makhachkala and over 2,500 in Buinaksk, but in excess of 2,500 in Kaspiisk and over 1,500 in Khasaviurt.

The number of Lezgins in the towns of Dagestan has increased nearly 6-fold since 1926 to constitute about 4% of the urban population of the republic. As before, the largest number of Lezgins continues to live in Derbent (some 5,000). However, their numbers have risen substantially in Makhachkala as well (about 4,000). According to the last census, nearly 9% of the population of Kaspiisk consists of Lezgins.

In 1926 there were only 350 urban Balkars, a figure that multiplied by a factor of 13.4 by 1959. However, they constitute only 2.8% of the urban population of their autonomous entity. The rapid growth of Nal'chik, and the building of the industrial town of Tyrny-Auz, have played a major role in shaping the Balkar urban population.

There were no towns in Ingushetia prior to the Great October Socialist Revolution, and the largest population center was Nazran', which was classed as an urban settlement in the 1920 and 1926 censuses. Until the 1940's, the bulk of the Ingush urban population was concentrated in Ordjonikidze. With the founding of the Checheno-Ingush ASSR, centered at Groznyi, the number of Ingushes in the towns of their republic began to increase. Today most of them live in Groznyi (over 2,500 persons) and Malgobek (over 1,500). (34)

The latest census shows small percentages of Circassians (2.2%), (35) Abazins (1.9%), Tabasarans (0.7%), and Nogais (0.4%) in the total urban population.

* * *

Russians, Ukrainians, and Armenians live in most of the towns of the North Caucasus. The percentages of Georgians and Greeks in the urban centers of various parts of the North Caucasus differ widely. Thus, the Greeks dominate in the northwestern Caucasus, and the Georgians

Table 4

Numbers and Share of Peoples in Total Urban Population of North Caucasus

Territory; nationality	1897		1926		1959	
	No.	% of total	No.	% of total	No.	% of total
Adygei Autonomous Oblast						
Russians	20,820	60.7	39,532	72.8	81,464	84.0
Ukrainians	10,722	31.2	8,096	15.7	3,964	4.0
Armenians	327	0.9	1,420	2.7	1,466	1.5
Karachaevo-Circassian Autonomous Oblast						
Russians	10,460	91.0	15,998	82.0	51,362	78.0
Ukrainians	521	4.5	1,743	9.0	2,012	3.0
Kabardino-Balkar ASSR						
Russians	2,679	55.7	5,968	46.0	115,197	68.0
Ukrainians	472	9.9	1,472	11.5	6,425	3.8
Belorussians	4	0.0	413	3.2	-	-
Armenians	65	1.3	217	1.6	1,200	0.7
Georgians	55	1.1	516	4.0	1,400	0.8
North Ossetian ASSR						
Russians	33,371	62.8	41,124	54.0	131,561	54.9
Ukrainians	1,638	3.0	4,083	5.3	7,370	3.1
Belorussians	63	0.1	1,123	1.4	937	0.3
Armenians	4,373	8.2	6,547	8.5	11,136	4.2
Georgians	2,861	5.3	5,062	6.5	5,802	2.4
Greeks	529	0.9	864	1.1	2,411	1.0
Checheno-Ingush ASSR						
Russians	10,349	66.4	68,328	68.8	227,676	77.0
Ukrainians	970	6.3	7,810	7.7	9,067	3.0
Belorussians	33	0.2	1,899	1.6	1,139	0.3
Armenians	352	2.2	5,844	5.7	11,782	4.0
Dagestan ASSR						
Russians	13,111	29.1	33,077	40.6	136,551	43.0
Ukrainians	1,448	3.2	2,350	2.8	7,071	2.2
Azerbaidjanis	9,767	21.8	8,129	9.9	15,752	5.0
Armenians	1,414	3.1	4,887	6.0	5,091	1.6

in the towns of the central portion of the North Caucasus (Table 4).

The census data show that the percentages of Russians, Ukrainians, Armenians, Georgians, and Greeks vary in the urban population of the North Caucasus. The Russians are the largest percentage, which is explained, as already stated, by the historical conditions under which the towns of the North Caucasus came into being. The percentages of other nationalities (Ukrainians, Belorussians, Armenians, Greeks, Georgians, and others) showed a decline in the 1959 census, although in certain cases their actual numbers in the urban population increased. Thus, in Groznyi, the number of Armenians rose from 5,843 to 11,533, and their percentage in the urban population dropped from 6 to 4.5%. In Ordjonikidze the number of Armenians rose from 6,529 to 9,093, while in percentage they declined from 8.6 to 5.4%, and so forth.

Ukrainians also showed a considerable diminution relative to the total population in most towns, in the period from 1926 to 1959. This was true primarily in Krasnodar (from 30.8 to 4.3%), Novorossiisk (from 23.6 to 5.1%), and Nal'chik (from 11.4 to 3.8%). Makhachkala is an exception, for there the percentage of Ukrainians rose from 1.7 to 2.4%, as it did in Ordjonikidze (5.2 to 5.4%).

Russians showed the greatest increase in the urban population in Krasnodar (from 51.3 to 89.8%) and in Novorosiisk (from 54.7 to 86.7%). In certain towns within autonomous ethnic areas, the percentage of increase in the Russian population was comparatively small, as in Makhachkala, where the rise was 1.4%, and in Ordjonikidze, where it was 4.8%.

The change in the numbers of these peoples in various towns shows certain peculiarities. Thus, the major center of Ukrainian population in the North Caucasus continues today, as before, to be Krasnodar, where in only six years, from 1920 to 1926, the number of Ukrainians rose from 30,000 to 48,000. The subsequent reduction in the number of Ukrainians, shown by the 1939 and 1959 censuses, is substantially explained by the continuing process of merger of the Ukrainians with the surrounding Russian population. The similarity of language and culture, and the community of historical destiny of these peoples, have always created conditions favoring this process.

The Ukrainian population of Grozny increased by only 100 persons in 33 years (from 7,800 in 1926 to 7,900 in 1959). Natural increase among the Ukrainians of Groznyi has averaged +130 persons per year — i.e., apparently here also the bulk of the natural increase has been absorbed by the process of mixing of Ukrainians and Russians. In Ordjonikidze, on the other hand, there has been a considerable influx of Ukrainians. Here the number of Ukrainians has increased by about 2,000 since 1926, and thus more than one-third of the total represents an influx from without.

The considerable increase in actual numbers of Russians in the towns cannot be explained solely in terms of the high rate of natural growth and strong influx from without. Apparently the share of the nationalities who have merged with the Russians (Ukrainians, Belorussians, Poles, "European" Jews) is also great here.

* * *

It is clear from these materials that the ethnic composition of the prerevolutionary towns of the North Caucasus consisted primarily of Russians, Ukrainians, and Armenians. A rapid influx of North Caucasian peoples into the urban population did not occur until the Soviet period, starting in the late 1930's and early 1940's. This was the period of socialist industrialization, when the founding of industrial centers in agrarian districts and the appearance of industrial personnel of the indigenous nationalities led to a substantial population movement from the villages to the towns and from one region to another, a movement that had a significant reflection upon their ethnic composition.

The establishment, during that period, of the autonomous republics of the North Caucasus and their rapid economic and cultural development also facilitated a rise in the urban population and a change in its ethnic composition.

The substantial increase in the numbers and percentage of the urban population among the nationalities of the North Caucasus has progressed with particular intensity since the late 1950's and early 1960's, during the period of the country's mighty economic and cultural rise to a new stage of transition from socialism to communism.

Let us pause to consider the factors influencing the dynamics of the numbers and ethnic composition of the population: births and deaths, migration, and ethnic processes. (36)

It goes without saying that natural increase is an important factor in enlarging the urban population but, in our times, processes of migration yield a larger percentage of this growth. Natural increase was responsible for a rise of 14,000 in the urban population of North Ossetia from 1958 to 1962, of which more than 6,000 were Ossetes. During the same period, the natural increase in the urban population of Checheno-Ingushetia was about 27,000 persons, of whom nearly 7,000 were Chechens. Processes of migration change the numbers and density of the population in given territories, and modify the long-established population distribution of peoples and the numerical ratios among them. These processes are due chiefly to economic causes. Both the causes and the character of migration processes have changed in our day.

Whereas before the Revolution agricultural population movements in the rural districts of the North Caucasus were dominant and the percentage of those migrating to the towns was small, today it is migration into town that is dominant, and the bulk of the migrating population consists of industrial workers and students. Thus, in 1952 the urban population of Mozdok rose by 8.93% as a consequence of the influx of workers for construction of the Terek-Kum Canal. (37)

Before the Revolution the participation of North Caucasian peoples in movements from the rural localities to the towns of the North Caucasus was negligible, and movement into other regions of the country was even smaller. However, certain nationalities comprised the bulk of seasonal migrants (particularly to jobs in town). Seasonal migration for jobs was particularly pronounced in Dagestan, due to the insufficiency of land convenient for farming in its mountain districts. (38)

Seasonal migrant labor has also disappeared in the Soviet years, as the economic basis for it has disappeared. Migrations have continued to be seasonal, but this is connected primarily with going to school, for the flow of people migrating to the cities has increased due to the large numbers of students.

Unfortunately, the statistics do not record the ethnic composition of the migrating population. However, even determination of points of departure, principal directions, and intensity during given periods is of no little importance to our subject.

There are a number of major directions of migration in the North Caucasus: from other regions of the USSR to the towns of the North Caucasus, from the rural areas of the North Caucasus to the towns of the same regions, from the mountains to the plains, and from the plains to mountains. (39)

Migration from rural districts to the towns and urban settlements of one's own republic, as well as from neighboring territories, autonomous and constituent republics, is dominant.

In 1952 alone, 1,900 persons moved to Ordjonikidze, (40) while in 1959 the number had risen to 3,200, of which 2,600 were from North Ossetia (including 2,000 from rural places). In 1962 nearly 5,000 persons moved, with the rural population of the republic again comprising the bulk of the migrants. The homogeneity of the ethnic composition of most of the rural districts of the republics of the North Caucasus provides a basis for assuming that the indigenous population is dominant among the migrants. (41)

The final factor — ethnic processes — also influences change in the numbers and ethnic composition of the population, although it does so considerably more slowly than does migration.

Present-day ethnic processes are expressed in convergence with the surrounding Russian population and the wide dissemination of the

Russian language, or in merger with an ethnic community similar in language and culture (for example, the Nogais of Dagestan with the Kumyks). Finally, remnants of tribal division and of local ethnographic groups of large ethnic communities are disappearing. In addition to these processes, the convergence of the peoples of the North Caucasus with the other peoples of the Soviet Union, and the establishment of common characteristics in the culture and mode of life of these peoples, are becoming increasingly intensified in the process of the building of communism. (42)

Many factors play a role in intensifying the mixing and mutual influence of ethnic communities: economic and cultural ties, mixed marriages, etc.

Processes of convergence of various nationalities are most rapid in the towns, whose multinational composition and high population mobility create considerably better conditions for mutual linguistic and cultural influences than are found in a rural population environment.

The data of the last census demonstrate a considerable intensification of processes of convergence in the urban population of the North Caucasus. (43) These processes are chiefly expressed in identification of Russian as the native tongue, and are most intensive among the Adygeis, Lezgins, and Ossetes. In the last census, 900 urban Adygeis listed Russian as their native tongue. Thus, for every 1,000 urban Adygeis, more than 93 regard Russian as their native language.

Whereas under the 1926 census 524 Ossetes listed Russian as their native tongue, this figure reached 3,446 in 1959 — i.e., 50 per 1,000 regard Russian as their language. Among the urban Kabardians, the 1926 census listed 18 who regarded Russian as their native language. In 1959 this number had risen to 863 — i.e., 37 per 1,000. Among the Lezgins there are more than 70 per 1,000 listing Russian as their native tongue.

Thus, the census data show not only a reduction in the numbers of urban people regarding the language of their nationality as their native tongue (this pertains to the Adygei-speaking,

Ossete-speaking, and Lezgin-speaking population), but a considerable rise in the role of Russian as native language. Processes of convergence among Ukrainians, Belorussians, Armenians, and other peoples are also expressed in the dissemination of the Russian language and its acceptance, in some instances, as native tongue. These processes are particularly intensive among the Slavic group of peoples and the "European" Jews. Thus, 650 urban Ukrainians per 1,000 in Krasnodar Krai regarded Russian as their native tongue at the 1959 census; 729 per 1,000 urban Belorussians in the same krai also gave Russian as native language. Of 2,000 "European" Jews in the North Ossetian ASSR, 1,500 regard Russian as their native tongue, etc. It is common that, in addition to change of language, peoples of the Slavic group and the "European" Jews also undergo a change in ethnic self-awareness, which is reflected in a reduction in their numbers.

As compared with the data of the 1926 census, there has been a considerable intensification of dissemination of the Russian language as native tongue among Armenians living in the towns of the North Caucasus. By the last census, over 29,000 Armenian townspeople of a total of 80,847 regard Russian as their native tongue, meaning that 358 of each 1,000 regard Russian as their language. These processes are also pronounced among the urban Greeks. Of every 1,000 urban Greeks in Krasnodar Krai, 670 gave Russian as their native language. Similar processes are under way at a slower rate among the Georgians of the North Caucasus. At the same time, recognition of another language as native (in this case, Russian) is not, among these peoples, the final step in the process of assimilation, as they continue to regard themselves as Armenians, Georgians, or Greeks — i.e., they retain their ethnic self-awareness. (44)

In these complex processes, statistical data do not always provide the answer to the questions that interest us. Thus, we get no information on the question of bilingualism or multilingualism, as the statistics record only the culminating stage in the development of bilingualism — transformation of the second language into a people's native tongue.

Study of these questions is very important to an understanding of processes of nationality development. It is precisely the broad and active dissemination of a second language among the people that points not only to the existence of ethnic processes in the given milieu, but to the direction they are taking.

Bilingualism and multilingualism are widespread among the population of multinational cities. In addition, for most of the peoples of the multilingual regions (Dagestan, for example), mastery of a second language in addition to Russian, and sometimes of several, is a vital necessity. (45) The so-called in-migrant peoples are also bilingual. Living surrounded by another, compact ethnic community, they are naturally subject to the active influence of the latter. These peoples learn a second language as a matter of necessity, and within a few generations it becomes their native tongue, but national consciousness of self is often retained considerably longer than the original tongue. (46)

* * *

Let us draw some conclusions.

During the Soviet years, vast changes have occurred in the urban population of the North Caucasus. There has been a considerable increase in the number of urban settlements (44 in 1959, of which 21 rank as towns), and the population has risen in number. Thus, in Kabardino-Balkaria it has almost doubled since 1939, reaching the figure of 166,100. In actual numbers, the urban population is most numerous in Dagestan (314,968 persons). However, in the total population of the republic, the percentage of urban people is somewhat lower here (30%) than in the other autonomous entities of the North Caucasus. In the Kabardino-Balkarian ASSR it is 40%, in the Chechen-Ingush — 41%, and in the North Ossetian ASSR — 53%.

The towns of the North Caucasus have undergone "nativization" in the Soviet years, as it was during this period that a process of formation of an urban population occurred among the peoples of the North Caucasus.

Statistical data demonstrate intensive increase in the urban population of most of the North Caucasian nationalities. By comparison to 1926, the figure has risen more than 26-fold among the Kabardians, 11-fold among the Chechens, 6-fold among the Ossetes, etc. The 1959 census shows the number of urban dwellers to be largest among the peoples of Dagestan (112,100), the Ossetes (68,500), the Kabardians (23,000), and the Chechens (22,300). However, the situation is not uniform among the various peoples of Dagestan. While the Kumyks now have 40,300 townspeople, the Avars — 22,500, and the Darbins — 19,500, the figure is still low among the Tabasarans and Nogais (2,300 and 1,500, respectively) while, as already stated, only individual Rutulians, Aguls, and Tsakhurs may be found in the towns. The numbers of Russians, Armenians, Greeks, and Azerbaidjanis in the cities have grown, albeit to varying degrees. Whereas the number of Armenians in Checheno-Ingushetia has risen from 5,800 in 1926 to 11,800 in 1959, and from 6,500 to 11,100 in North Ossetia, it has remained virtually stable in Adygeia and Dagestan, and in Krasnodar the number has dropped from 13,500 to 7,200.

The numbers of Ukrainians and Belorussians have not increased in all towns. Thus, in the towns of the Adygei Autonomous Oblast, the number of Ukrainians dropped from 8,100 in 1926 to 4,000 in 1959, and in Krasnodar from 48,600 to 14,100. As indicated above, the process of merger of the Ukrainians with the Russians has played a considerable role in reducing the numbers of this people. (47) Similar processes are occurring among the Belorussians, Poles, and Bulgarians of the North Caucasus.

It is clear from the data adduced in the article that it is precisely during the Soviet years that an urban population has taken shape among the peoples of the North Caucasus. In 1926 it was only among the Ossetes and Kumyks that the percentage of urban people attained 8 or 9%, while among other peoples it varied between 3 and 1%.

According to the most recent census, the percentage of townspeople is highest among the Kumyks (33.3%), Ossetes (31.7%), and Laks (25.7%). Among most of the other nationalities, the ratio of urban to rural population ranges between 10 and 15% (Kabardians, Adygeis, Balkars, Dargins, Lezgins, etc.). Less than 10% of the Karachais, Abazins, Tabasarans, and Nogais are urban.

The percentage of urban population among the nationalities of the North Caucasus would be considerably higher if one considered that the population of most raion centers in the North Caucasus, which in recent years have become urban settlements for all practical purposes, consists chiefly of the indigenous peoples.

The predominance of a given nationality in the urban population is subject to certain regularities. Thus, the ethnic composition and percentage of various nationalities in certain towns (Derbent, Buinaksk, Khasaviurt, and Alagir) are determined primarily by the national composition of the surrounding area. The ethnic composition of the administrative centers of the autonomous entities of the North Caucasus is determined chiefly by their administrative and economic-and-cultural role both with respect to the peoples of the given republic and to other peoples of the Soviet Union.

In connection with the growth of industry in the autonomous entities and the founding of a working class among the peoples of the North Caucasus during the Soviet period, the percentage of these peoples rose in the new industrial centers. Thus, in 1959, in Beslan, the Ossetes were 50% of the total population, while in Sadon, Buron, Zgid, and Mizurskoe they numbered 70%.

The numbers of people of the Dagestani nationalities have increased in its industrial centers (Kaspiisk, Izberbash, Dagestanskie Ogni), and they now comprise about 50% of the residents of these cities.

In the towns of their own republics, the Ossetes, Kabardians, and Kumyks number 28.8%, 13.8%, and 13.1%, respectively, while most of the other nationalities do not number as much as 10% of the urban population in their native republics.

By comparison to 1926, the percentage of Ukrainians, Armenians, Georgians, and other nationalities in the urban population of the North Caucasus has diminished. The Russians are an exception, as they constitute an increasing percentage in the populations of most of the towns of the North Caucasus. That percentage has diminished only in the towns of Karachaevo-Circassia (from 82 to 78%), while in North Ossetia and Dagestan its increase has been negligible (0.9 and 2.4%, respectively).

There has been a sharp reduction in the percentage of Ukrainians (from 15.7 to 4% in Adygeia, from 11.5 to 3.8% in Kabardino-Balkaria, from 7.7 to 3% in Checheno-Ingushetia), and of Armenians (from 6 to 1.6% in Dagestan, and from 8.5 to 4.2% in North Ossetia), etc.

Thus, at present, the processes occurring most rapidly in the urban population of the North Caucasus are the increase in percentage and absolute number of the Russian and North Caucasian nationalities. Despite some increase in their absolute numbers, the percentage of other nationalities is declining.

Since the 1926 census there has been something of a change in the geographical distribution of the urban population among certain nationalities. Thus, Krasnodar, which had the largest Armenian population in the 1920's and 1930's, is now third in this respect after Groznyi and Ordjonikidze.

The number of Georgians in towns such as Mozdok and Alagir, where the percentage of that nationality was high at the end of the 18th and 19th centuries, has diminished considerably. (48) This process was noticed as early as 1926 and was due to the migration of the Rachins to Georgia during the Civil War. (49)

In considering change in the number of members of various nationalities, it is necessary to consider not only migrations and natural increase but the processes of convergence and, in certain cases, assimilation of certain peoples under urban conditions. In some cases, processes of this order have led to real changes in the number of members of nationalities in the towns of the North Caucasus (Ukrainians and Belorussians), while in others a significant tendency to change in numbers is to be seen.

* * *

Editor's Notes

a) A large village with a non-serf population, often situated outside the walls of a city.

b) Russian: obshchestva, more often translated as "societies." In the Caucasus, these were self-governing endogamous villages — the largest native political unit.

Footnotes

1) Pervaia Vseobshchaia perepis' naseleniia Rossiiskoi imperii 1897 g., St. Petersburg, Vol. LXII, Dagestanskaia oblast, 1905; Vol. LXV, Kubanskaia oblast, 1905; Vol. LVIII, Terskaia oblast, 1904.

2) Central State Archive, North Ossetian ASSR (below —TsGA SO ASSR), Division R-97, File 1, Storage Unit 431, sheets 10, 11; Trudy Iugo-Vostochnoi planovoi komissii, No. II, Rostov-na-Donu, 1923, pp. 54-55; Kubanskii statisticheskii sbornik, Krasnodar, 1925, pp. 44, 45, 50; Zhizn' natsional'nostei, a journal, 1924, Vol. 1 (6), pp. 132-162.

3) Trudy Tsentral'nogo statisticheskogo upravleniia, Vol. XX, Part IV, Moscow, 1927, pp. 28-51.

4) Vsesoiuznaia perepis' naseleniia 1926 g., Vol. V: Krymskaia ASSR, Severo-kavkazskii krai, Dagestanskaia ASSR, Narodnost', rodnoi iazyk, gramotnost', Moscow, 1929.

5) Itogi Vsesoiuznoi perepisi naseleniia 1959 goda, RSFSR, Moscow, 1963.

6) Derbent, founded in the 6th century, is an exception.

7) Nal'chik and Cherkessk (formerly Batalpashinsk) were administrative centers of Nal'chik Okrug of Tersk Oblast and of the Batalpashinsk Otdel of Kuban Oblast.

8) The high percentage of Ukrainians in the towns of Kuban Oblast was due to the settlement here, in 1792-1794, of the Black Sea Cossack Troops, organized of Zaporozh'e Cossacks.

9) Terskie vedomosti, (newspaper), 1916, No. 181; Kubanskii statisticheskii sbornik, p. 45.

10) In 1802, 1,600 Armenians lived in Kizliar and 600 in Mozdok (see Vedomost' o chisle naroda Astrakhanskoi gub. i Kavkazskoi oblasti na 1802 god, Akty Kavkazskoi arkheograficheskoi komissii (cited below as AKAK), Vol. I, Tiflis, 1866, p. 765.

11) P. G. Butkov, Materialy dlia novoi istorii Kavkaza s 1722 po 1803 g., Part II, St. Petersburg, 1869, pp. 169, 265, 425; AKAK, Vol. I, p. 663; Vol. II, Tiflis, 1868, pp. 1154, 1156; Vol. VI (2), Tiflis, 1874, p. 602.

12) AKAK, Vol. II, pp. 964, 970.

13) AKAK, Vol. I, p. 81.

14) V. I. Larina, Ocherk istorii gorodov Severnoi Osetii (XVIII-XIX vv.), Ordjonikidze, 1960, p. 53.

15) Terskie vedomosti, 1876, No. 41.

16) Ibid.

17) TsGA SO ASSR, Division 24, File 1, Dossier 50, Sheet 46; Dossier 119, sheets 16-18.

18) Dagestanskaia oblast. Svod statisticheskikh dannykh, izvlechennykh iz posemeinykh spiskov naseleniia Zakavkaz'ia, Tiflis, 1890.

19) It should be noted that a considerable number of seasonal migratory workers from Dagestan comprised, for several months during the winter, a temporary population in the towns of Dagestan, the North Caucasus, and Transcaucasia. A particularly large number of them came to Kizliar and Derbent. However, with the onset of spring they returned to their villages (see "O narodakh Severnogo Kavkaza," Ms. section, Lenin Library, Division 169, Catalog 81, No. 7, sheets 30, 31; I. Przhetslavskii, "Dagestan, ego nravy i obychai," Vestnik Evropy, Vol. III, St. Petersburg, 1867, p. 178).

20) Armenians too lived in the town, but at the end of the 18th and the beginning of the 19th centuries most of them moved to the North Caucasus (see AKAK, Vol. II, p. 1154, 1156; F. F. Simonovich, "Opisanie Iuzhnogo Dagestana 1796," in Istoriia, geografiia i etnografiia Dagestana XVIII-XIX vv., Moscow, 1958, p. 143).

21) A. V. Komarov, "Narodonaselenie Dagestanskoi oblasti," Zapiski Kavkazskogo otd. RGO, Vol. VIII, Tiflis, 1873, p. 42.

22) Dagestanskaia oblast. Svod statisticheskikh dannykh, izvlechennykh iz posemeinykh

spiskov naseleniia Zakavkaz'ia, p. XIII.

23) Ves' Groznyi i ego okrestnosti, Vladi-kavkaz, 1914, p. 17.

24) Otchet nachal'nika Terskoi oblasti za 1904 g. (Vladikavkaz, 1905), za 1905 g. (Vladi-kavkaz, 1906), za 1906 g. (Vladikavkaz, 1907).

25) Kavkaz, (newspaper), 1914, No. 30.

26) TsGA SO ASSR, Division R-81, File 1, Dossier 106, Sheet 45; P. D-ko, "Cherez Glavnyi khrebet po Voenno-Osetinskoi doroge," Kavkaz, 1887, No. 286.

27) Prior to the Revolution, a considerable portion of the Lak craftsmen engaged in occupations taking them seasonally away from home, and comprised a temporary population in the towns. In the spring they returned to their villages.

28) TsGA SO ASSR, Division R-384, File 7, Dossier 134, Sheet 3.

29) According to the 1926 census, only 275 Kabardians lived in Mozdok.

30) Statistiko-ekonomicheskii spravochnik po Dagestanskoi ASSR, Rostov-na-Donu, 1933, pp. 204-205.

31) In 1939, in addition to Groznyi, there were four urban-type settlements in Checheno-Ingushetia (Gorskii, Malgobek, im. Kalinina, and Gudermes). The 1959 census listed three towns (Groznyi, Malgobek, Gudermes) and three urban-type settlements (Chernorech'e, Novogroznenskii, and Gora-Gorskii).

32) The Executive Committee of the Malo-Karachai Okrug was in Kislovodsk.

33) U. Aliev, Karachai, Rostov-na-Donu, 1927, p. 28.

34) Some 700 Ingushi live in the towns of North Ossetia.

35) Descendants of the Kabardians who settled in the Trans-Kuban during the first half of the 19th century. In the 1850's, their auls were moved to the Bol'shoi and Malyi Zelen-chuk and the right bank of the Kuban.

36) For the role of these factors, see V. I. Kozlov, "Kul'turno-istoricheskii protsess i chislennost' narodov," Vestnik istorii mirovoi kul'tury, 1959, No. 1. S. I. Bruk, V. I. Kozlov, M. G. Levin, "O predmete i zadachakh etnogeo-grafii," SE, 1963, No. 1 [see Soviet Sociology,

Vol. II, No. 1].

37) TsGA SO ASSR, Division R-384, File 7, Dossier 134, Sheet 3.

38) The number of Dagestani seasonal migrants reached 39,900 in 1892, 59,100 in 1899, and 83,300 in 1914. See G. Izakson and A. Nazarevich, Dagestan. Fakty i tsifry, Makhach-kala, 1929, p. 113.

39) For example, the appearance of Kabardians in the mountains as a result of the development of the industrial center of Tyrny-Auz, and the considerable increase in the number of Ossetes in industrial urban settlements of Os-setia: Buron, Sadon, Zgid, and Mizurskii.

40) TsGA SO ASSR, Division R-384, File 7, Dossier 134, Sheet 3.

41) Thus, Mozdok Raion is the only exception in North Ossetia, and Sunzha and Shelkovo raions in Checheno-Ingushetia. A Russian population predominates here.

42) V. K. Gardanov, B. O. Dolgikh, and T. A. Zhdanko, "Osnovnye napravleniia etnicheskikh protsessov u narodov SSSR," SE, 1961, No. 4 [See Soviet Anthropology and Archeology, Vol. I, No. 1].

43) Prior to the Revolution, considerable linguistic assimilation was recorded among certain of the North Caucasus peoples. Thus, the Kumyk language was found to be widespread in daily life among the Dagestani Nogais at the end of the 19th century, and the Azerbaidjan language spread rapidly among the Dagestani Tats (see Dagestanskaia oblast, Svod statisti-cheskikh dannykh...op. cit. supra, p. 110).

44) In studying processes of merger of ethnic communities it is, of course, necessary to consider not only changes in the sphere of language and self-awareness, but mutual influences in the area of daily life and the material and intellectual culture of the peoples. However, this is a separate subject for ethnographic research and cannot be dealt with in a brief article.

45) Certain regularities observable in the extent of bi- and multilingualism are dealt with in an article by L. I. Lavrov, "Nekotorye itogi Dagestanskoi ekspeditsii 1950-1952 gg.," KSIE, XIX, Moscow, 1953, p. 3.

46) For example, in the past the Adygei Armenians were Adygei by language, but regarded themselves as Armenians (see F. Shcherbina, Istoriia Armavira i cherkeso-gaev, Ekaterinodar, 1916, p. 155).

47) L. N. Chizhikova, "Zaselenie Kubani i sovremennye etnicheskie protsessy," SE, 1963, No. 6.

48) Thus, in Alagir, a total of only 40 Georgians were recorded at the last census.

49) TsGA SO ASSR, Division R-81, File 1, Dossier 106, Sheet 45; State Archive of Rostov Oblast, Division R-2607, File 1, Dossier 25, Sheet 8.

Sovetskaia etnografiia, 1963, No. 5

V. I. Naulko

THE PRESENT ETHNIC COMPOSITION OF THE POPULATION OF THE UKRAINIAN SSR

The Ukrainian SSR is one of the largest republics in our country, being second in population and third in territory. At the beginning of 1962, the Ukraine numbered 43,500,000 people, or about 20% of the entire population of the Soviet Union.

The overwhelming majority of the peoples of the Ukraine (see ethnic map on pages 194-195) belong to the Slavic group of the Indo-European linguistic family: Ukrainians, Russians, Belorussians, Poles, Czechs, Slovaks, Bulgarians. Jointly they constitute 98.8% of the population of the republic. Representatives of other groups in this same family are present in considerably smaller numbers. Jews (2% of the population) are conventionally placed in the Germanic language group (1) and Moldavians and Rumanians, who number 0.8%, fall into the Romance group. Armenians, Greeks, and Albanians living in the Ukraine belong to independent groups of the Indo-European family (they total 136,000 persons).

Peoples of the Uralic linguistic family (Hungarians, Estonians, Mordvins, and others), and of the Altaic (Tatars, Gagauz, Chuvashes, Karaims, Krymchaks, etc.), also live in the Ukraine. They total 309,000 persons (0.7% of the population). The number of members of other nationalities, not in the three families listed above, is quite small: 70,000 persons.

Table 1 (2) shows that the population of the republic is constantly rising, despite the vast human losses due to wars, particularly World War II.

Table 1			
Year	Population (millions)	Including (as % of whole)	
		Urban	Rural
1913	35.2	19	81
1939	40.5	34	66
1959	41.9	46	54
1962	43.5	49	51

This type of numerical change in population is explained by the high rates of natural increase in the Ukraine. The Ukraine currently stands ahead of all the largest capitalist countries of Europe in rate of natural population increase. In 1960, natural increase per 1,000 population was 13.6 (against 17.8 for the USSR as a whole), while in England the figure was 6.0, in West Germany — 6.4, in France — 6.6, in Italy — 8.8, etc. (3) The high rate of natural increase is a result of the sharp decline in the death rate, which was reduced by three-fourths during the Soviet years due to the rise in living standard and improvement in medical services to the population.

However, comparison of the Soviet censuses of 1926 and 1959 reveals significant changes in the numbers and distribution of the peoples inhabiting the Ukraine.

As the statistical data demonstrate, the unification of all Ukrainian lands within the Ukrainian SSR resulted, first, in an increase in the number of Ukrainians (from 23,200,000 to 32,200,000) and of the peoples dwelling interspersed with the Ukrainians within the ethnic borders of the

184

latter (Rumanians, Moldavians, Hungarians, Slovaks), and others.

Let us see how the ethnic population of the Ukrainian SSR changed, within its original boundaries. (4)

Our calculations show that in the period between the censuses of 1926 and 1959, which saw an overall population increase of over 10%, the number of Ukrainians rose by about that percentage, while the number of Russians increased by more than 100%, that of Belorussians 200%, that of Tatars 250%, etc. At the same time the number of Poles and Czechs dropped by half, and that of Moldavians by 60%. The number of Bulgarians, Greeks, and others changed little.

Let us pause for a brief consideration of certain factors influencing change in the ethnic composition of the republic.

One was socialist industrialization and the associated increase in urban population, which, of course, tends to be of more mixed ethnic composition.

In the cities of the Ukraine, as in the USSR as a whole, we find about one-half the total population (49% in 1962). The Soviet years have witnessed a fundamental change in the relative proportions of urban and rural population in the Ukraine (see Table 1). This was due to the rapid rates of socialist industrialization, particularly after World War II.

The growth of the cities of the Ukraine was accompanied by an influx of population from other Soviet republics. During the first years of Soviet government in the Ukraine, an increase in the numbers of male Russians was to be seen, particularly youth, as a consequence of the direct participation and help given by the Russian people in rebuilding the Ukrainian economy. For example, in the 20-24 age group, there were 37,000 more Russian men than women. (5)

In addition to the organized recruitment of workers from the villages for work in industry, the transformation of rural settlements into urban ones in the course of industrialization also exercised a major influence in determining the ethnic composition of the urban population. The expansion of towns often results in the incorporation of adjacent rural settlements. For example,

the town of Khmel'nitksii was enlarged to incorporate the large villages of Matskovtsy and Sharovechka, populated by Poles, while a number of rural settlements of Greeks came to be part of Zhdanov, etc.

The military operations and occupation for a period during World War II resulted in major population losses in the Ukraine.

In launching their war, the Hitlerite hangmen developed a number of plans for the extermination of Soviet people, containing instructions on the treatment of the local population of various nationalities of the "Eastern" regions. (6)

The influence of the war is reflected very noticeably in the sex ratio in the population of the Ukraine. The total number of women in the republic (see diagram) greatly exceeds the number of men. There are 1,252 women for every 1,000 men (in the USSR as a whole the figure is 1,222 women per 1,000 men). This is explained by the greater losses of male population during the war. In 1926, after World War I, when population losses were incomparably smaller, the number of men approximately equalled that of women, age group by age group. In 1959, particularly in the 35-70 age groups, which had been most actively involved in the war, one observes a marked predominance of women.

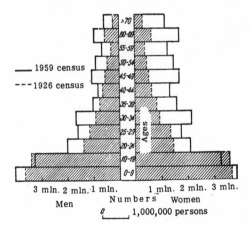

A similar ratio between the male and female population holds for the various peoples constituting the republic. Among the Ukrainians, for example, men number 36.6% of the whole in that age group, while among Russians the figure is 39.8%, Jews — 40.4%, Belorussians — 40.6%, etc.

The war brought not only high population losses, but significant migrations due to the transfer of industry and the evacuation of population to the eastern parts of the country.

The migrational processes are causing the Soviet republics to become increasingly multinational. This is one of the most important factors in bringing the Soviet peoples closer to each other. Whereas 82 nationalities were to be found represented in the Ukraine in 1926, today the figure is 120.

In addition to the increase, in the Ukraine, of the number of people of other Soviet nationalities, the dispersal of Ukrainians into other Soviet republics has become more generally observable. Let us examine this a bit more closely.

There are more than 5,100,000 Ukrainians living elsewhere in the Soviet Union. They constitute 2.9% of the population of the Russian Federation, 8.2% in Kazakhstan, 14.6% in Moldavia, 6.6% in Kirgizia, 1.6% in Belorussia, etc.

About 75% of all Ukrainians living outside the Ukraine dwell in the RSFSR. The number of Ukrainians in the RSFSR increased by 4.8% from 1939 to 1959, although their share in the total population of that republic diminished somewhat, due to ethnic assimilation. This becomes understandable when one considers that, at present, about 60% of the Ukrainians live in urban places. Thirty-seven oblasts and krais of the RSFSR have seen a substantial rise in the numbers of Ukrainians over the prewar period. This pertains primarily to the eastern and northern districts of the RSFSR (the Komi ASSR, Sakhalin Oblast, the Iakut ASSR, etc.).

The very nature of the population shifts has changed fundamentally. Differences in language and ethnic boundaries, which played no major role even in the past, under Soviet conditions today provide no obstacle whatever to the community of the peoples and fraternal collaboration among them. In actuality, the limits of ethnic dispersal merely record the historically-established distribution of peoples in a given territory.

"In the Soviet republics," we read in the CPSU Program, "people of many nationalities live together and work in friendly fashion. The boundaries between the constituent republics are in-creasingly losing their former significance, because all the nations hold equal rights and their lives are built on a single, socialist foundation." (7)

In the past, particularly at the turn of the century, hunger and landlessness resulting from the relative agrarian overpopulation in the Ukrainian guberniias drove hundreds of thousands of Ukrainians to the eastern parts of Russia. This was fundamentally an agricultural colonization. (8) We know that entire townships [volosts] and villages migrated. There were 223,200 Ukrainians in the Amur District and the Maritime Province alone, according to the 1897 census. During the same period, a large number of Ukrainians from the western oblasts emigrated abroad (primarily to Canada and the United States). In the later prerevolutionary years, migration of Ukrainians (and, in part, of Jews living in the Ukraine) became even more pronounced. For example, 1,305,000 persons left the Ukraine from 1897 to 1914. (9)

Population migrations today are not spontaneous but planned. In the summer of 1954, the Party and Komsomol sent over 150,000 volunteers to the eastern parts of the country, including more than 24,000 from the Ukraine. (10)

Today 52% of the Ukrainians in the Kazakh SSR dwell in the Virgin Soil Territory (Tselinnyi Krai), where they number 396,000.

Migration of other peoples from the Ukraine has also been quite considerable. For example, about 40% of the Poles resident in Kazakhstan speak Ukrainian.

Certain other factors have influenced the change in the ethnic composition of the Ukraine.

In the postwar period, under a treaty between the Soviet Union and the Polish People's Republic, the Polish population (788,000 persons) was repatriated from the Ukraine, as well as the Ukrainian population (518,000 persons together with the Lithuanians and Belorussians) from Poland. (11) The Ukrainians settled primarily in the L'vov, Ivan-Franko, and Nikolaev oblasts. After the repatriation of the Polish population from the Western Ukraine, the question of training personnel became quite acute in a number of places, particularly Borislav, where Poles had held most of the skilled posts in the oil fields. (12) This problem was resolved in part by sending expert personnel to Borislav from the Russian Federation and Azerbaidjan. Today Russians, Azerbaidjanis, Tatars and others work in Borislav, along with the Ukrainians. The majority of the Czechs also were repatriated after the war.

The following is the distribution of nationalities in the Ukraine. All the central and most of the western oblasts are populated solidly by Ukrainians. As one approaches the boundaries of the republic, the ethnic composition of the population becomes more mixed. Let us examine in fuller detail the distribution of peoples in the Ukraine.

The Ukrainians, the indigenous population of the republic, are one of the most numerous peoples in Europe, ranking second in the Soviet Union after the Russian socialist nation. The census of January 15, 1959, showed 32,158,000 Ukrainians in the Ukraine (the figure increased to about 33,500,000 at the end of 1962), constituting 76.8% of the total population of that republic.

The Ukrainian people and nation came into being along the middle reaches of the Dnieper (the areas around Kiev, Poltava, and Chernigov), where the term "Ukraina" — which gave the Ukrainian people their self-designation — first took root, later spreading to other Ukrainian territories.

In the 16th and 17th centuries, a considerable portion of the Slobodskaia Ukraina (today Khar'kov, Sumy and, in part, Belgorod and Voronezh oblasts) was populated chiefly by Ukrainians who had migrated from the Ukrainian lands under the control of the Polish military gentry (szlachta). In these regions, the yoke of feudal serfdom was weaker.

Colonization by Cossacks along the lower reaches of the Dnieper began in the 15th and 16th centuries. Later, this was the site of the Zaporozh'e camps, fortified settlements, and wintering stations. The Ukrainian steppes and the Black Sea coast were settled particularly quickly, starting in the second half of the 18th century, during which Ukrainian ethnic territory expanded considerably southward. Of exceptional importance to the further economic and cultural development of the Ukrainian people and acceleration of the processes of formation of the Ukrainian nation was the union with Russia in 1654.

However, the political fragmentation of the Ukrainian territories continued for a long time. As late as the early 20th century they were divided between Russia and Austria-Hungary (while after World War I the western regions became part of capitalist Poland, Rumania, and Czechoslovakia). The political fragmentation of the Ukrainian people hindered its consolidation. Lacking their own state, Ukrainians in various countries were called by a variety of names — Little Russians, and so forth.

Not infrequently, concepts of the ethnic affiliation of Ukrainians were supplanted by concepts based on religious faith, geographic origin, etc. As a consequence, even the census records for 1926 reveal self-designation by Ukrainians as "Catholics" (in Zhitomir and Nikolaev oblasts), "Galicians" (in Sumy Oblast), (13) etc.

Differences in history and natural conditions were responsible for considerable differences in the culture and mode of life of Ukrainians in various oblasts of the Ukrainian SSR. Even today a number of ethnographic groups are distinguished (Hutsul, Lemki, Boiki, and others).

Today, 86.1% of all the Ukrainians in the USSR live within the republic. The Ukrainians are settled solidly through virtually the entire territory of the republic, except for most of the Crimean Oblast and certain industrial raions in other — chiefly southern and eastern — oblasts. In most of the oblasts Ukrainians constitute 70-75% of the urban population. The figure goes higher in some cases — for example, in Cherkassy Oblast, where it attains 83% — and diminishes almost to 50% in the Donets Oblast, where there are many Russians. We note that one-fourth of the urban ethnic Ukrainians of the Donets Oblast give Russian as their native tongue. On the whole, however, the percentage of urban Ukrainians who regard Russian as their native tongue fluctuates between 5 and 15, diminishing to 2 or 3% in some oblasts.

The percentage of Ukrainians in the rural population is considerably higher than in the urban, attaining 95-98% in a number of oblasts (Kiev, Poltava, Cherkassy, Chernigov, Khmel'nitskii, Vinnitsa, L'vov, Rovno, Volhynia [Volynskaia], Ivan-Franko, Ternopol'). In these oblasts, Ukrainian is the native tongue of virtually the entire rural population. In the villages of Dnepropetrovsk, Zhitomir, Kirovograd, and Nikolaev oblasts, Ukrainians number up to 90-95%, and in the remaining oblasts they range from 75-90% (except in Odessa Oblast, where they constitute less than two-thirds of the rural population).

Russians, numbering 16.9% of the whole (7,091,000 persons), rank second in the population of the Ukraine.

Russians began to settle the present-day Ukraine in the 16th through 18th centuries: in the Slobodskaia Ukraina, the southern Ukraine (formerly Novorossiia), and to a lesser degree in Podolia and the Poles'e. Both government-sponsored and spontaneous colonization took place.

It should be noted that at the outset part of the Russian settlers were Raskolniks [Schismatics], Old Believers, sectarians and others fleeing religious persecution. A particularly large number of such settlements was founded by fugitives from the central and western guberniias of Russia during the 18th century in Ekaterinoslav Guberniia (Bol'shaia Znamenka, Kamenka, Zybkoe, Nikol'skoe, Tambovka, Spasskoe, and others) and in Khar'kov Guberniia (Staroverovka, etc.). In Bessarabia there were nearly 30,000 Russian Old Believers at the end of the 19th century, (14) chiefly in Budzhak and Khotin uezds. Nekrasovka Sloboda was founded in Southern Bessarabia by descendants of the Old Believer Don Cossacks, the Nekrasovtsy, who fled across the Danube after the Bulavin Uprising.

Many of the villages founded by Russians in Ekaterinoslav Guberniia later became part of the military settlements of Novorossiia and played an important role in protecting Russia's southern borders.

A number of Russian settlements in the Ukraine resulted from government-sponsored colonization, carried out by resettling Russian landowners with their peasants from the interior guberniias of Russia. This is the origin of the villages of Dneprovka, Liubitskoe, Novaia Nikolaevka, Alekseevskoe (Zaporozhskaia Oblast), Staroi Saltov and Andreevka (Khar'kov Oblast), and several settlements along the Sea of Azov.

The development of capitalism in the southern Ukraine during the second half of the 19th century brought about, along with the Ukrainian, a considerable influx of Russian population. According to the 1897 census, Russians constituted 67.8% of the personnel of the mining and metal industries in Ekaterinoslav Guberniia.

Today Russians constitute over 71% of the people of Crimea Oblast, where they are more heavily represented than anywhere else. In Lugansk, Donets, Khar'kov and Zaporozh'e oblasts they number between 25-38% of the population. In Kherson, Nikolaev, Odessa, Dnepropetrovsk and Sumy oblasts this figure diminishes to the 10-17% range.

In all other oblasts, Russians number less than 10%. About 80% of the Russians live in the cities of the Ukraine. It is in the Donets Oblast that the Russian urban population is greatest relative to the whole (over 40%).

Belorussians. There are 291,000 Belorussians in the Ukraine (0.7% of the population). They are chiefly (about three-fourths) city dwellers here. In villages with a Belorussian population, as a general rule, about 40% of them regard Belorussian as their native tongue, while the others speak Russian or Ukrainian. Many cases are known in which emigrants from Belorussia have come to call themselves Russians with the passage of time. Thus, for example, in the mid-19th century there were, in Khar'kov Guberniia alone, 27 places (15) — including such populous ones as Kamenetskoe, Soldatskoe, Nitsakha, and Protopopovka — which were regarded as Belorussian, as were a number in the south of the Ukraine. In later census data, specifically the censuses of 1926 and 1959, their residents were called Russians. And whereas, in a number of cases, tsarist statistics erroneously classified the Russian Old Believers from Belorussian guberniias as Belorussians, as has been noted by L. S. Berg (for example, the Russian Old Believers of Khotin Uezd, Bessarabia), (16) there is no question that in a number of cases the national self-identification among Belorussians changed. Thus, the village of Snegirevka (like the large Belorussian settlements of Barmashevo, Iavkino, and others, still existing) was founded by Belorussians from Bobyletskii Uezd, Mogilev Guberniia, from which they were resettled during the War of 1812 as a consequence of the establishment of the military settlements of the Elets Musketeer Regiment in their former homes. (17) In the census of 1926 the inhabitants of this village called themselves Russians.

In Rovno Oblast there are several thousand Belorussians listing Ukrainian as their native tongue. In a number of rural places in the Ukraine (for example, Sursko-Litovskoe village in Solonianskii Raion, Dnepropetrovsk Oblast), some of the Belorussians call themselves "Liatvin."

Poles. There are 363,000 Poles in the Ukraine, constituting 0.9% of the population.

The many centuries of oppression to which the Western Ukraine was subjected and the policies of feudal Poland directed toward the Polonization of the Ukrainian population and the weakening of its resistance to feudal enslavement — for example, the Union of Brest of 1596 — resulted in a considerable portion of the rural population west of the Dnieper, Ukrainian in origin, coming to consider itself Polish. This was noted by numerous investigators, including a number of Poles. For example, Czynski (18) wrote that in Volhynia Guberniia, which was annexed by Russia at the end of the 18th century, there were a large number of Catholic Ukrainians whom some writers wrongly classified as Poles. Therefore the so-called Poles employing Ukrainian as their native tongue are, to a considerable degree, Polonized Ukrainians.

Many Greek-rite Catholic Ukrainians in the Western Ukrainian oblasts (about 150,000 in the L'vov Wojewodstwo alone [19]) were classified as Poles by Polish official bourgeois statistics, although it is common knowledge that virtually all Poles belonged to the Roman Catholic [Latin-rite] Church.

At the same time it is known that, to reinforce its dominance over the ancient Ukrainian lands they had seized, feudal Poland intensified the settlement of Poles there. To this day there are two different groups of Poles, differing somewhat in culture and mode of life, in Khmel'nitskii and Zhitomir oblasts. There are the Mazury, whose forebears were poor peasant migrants, chiefly from Mazowsze, and the Shliakhta, descended from Polish petty szlachta on military duty, chiefly in the border districts. For example, the villages of Sharovechka and Grechana (near Khmel'nitskii) were settled by Mazury, while Bekhi, Khodaki, Kalenskoe, and Chopovichi near Korosten' were founded by Shliakhta. In a number of villages they are mixed together (Zelenoe, Volochisskoe Raion, Khmel'nitskii Oblast, and elsewhere).

A considerable number of Polish peasants came under the dominance of Polish landlords, who, after the acquisition of the land west of the Dnieper by Russia, acquired the same rights and privileges as the Russian nobility. A few small Polish villages in the southern regions of the Ukraine were founded in the mid-19th century by emigrants from Podol'sk Guberniia and the Vistula country.

The largest percentage of Poles in the cities is somewhat higher than the rural Polish population. Nearly half the Poles in the towns speak Ukrainian, while the rest speak Polish and Russian, and in the villages the majority speak Ukrainian (83%) and Polish (15%). The Ukrainian language is most widespread among the Poles in Zhitomir Oblast (up to 95% in the villages and 80% in the towns).

Czechs. 14,500 Czechs now dwell in the Ukraine. The development of capitalism in Bohemia in the mid-19th century, and the impoverishment and social stratification of the displaced peasantry resulting from this, led to mass emigration of Czechs to other countries. A considerable number of Czech emigrants appeared in Russia. The first Czech colonies appeared in the Ukraine after the abolition of serfdom. They were established in the mid-1860's in Volhynia (Liudgardovka), in the south of Podol'sk Guberniia (Chekhovka), in the Crimea (Tabor, Bogemka,

and Tsarevich), near Melitopol' (Chekhograd).
A particularly large number of Czech colonies
appeared in Rovno and Dubno uezds of Volhynia
Guberniia in the late '60's and early '70's.

Slovaks. The Slovaks (14,000) live chiefly in
the towns of Transcarpathia (particularly in
Uzhgorod). On the Czechoslovakian border there
are several mixed Ukrainian-Slovak villages, in
which Ukrainians are numerically predominant.
Some 200 Slovaks live in Kirovo settlement near
Muka'čevo. A portion of the urban Slovaks speak
Hungarian.

Bulgarians. There are 219,000 Bulgarians
(0.5% of the population of the Ukraine). The first
Bulgarian colonies appeared in the Ukraine during the second half of the 18th century. We know,
for example, that the large Bulgarian settlements
of Kirovograd Oblast (Ol'shania village and others), founded in 1774, were originally part of the
Bug Cossack District and later transferred to
the category of military settlements of Novorossiia.

Bulgarian colonization was particularly intensive, however, at the end of the 18th century
and during the first three decades of the 19th,
when, during the time of the Russo-Turkish wars,
Bulgarians fled to Russia en masse to protect
themselves against Turkish oppression. This
period saw the founding of their largest settlements in Southern Bessarabia (centered at the
town of Bolgrad) and in Kherson Guberniia,
particularly near Odessa, as well as in the
Crimea. By the end of the 19th century there
were 92 Bulgarian colonies here. (20)

At the beginning of the 1860's, Bulgarian
colonists began to settle in the Azov area,
founding a whole series of colonies, because of
the conquest of a considerable part of Bessarabia
by the Rumania of the boyars (as a result of
which the Bulgarians were deprived of any privileges). According to N. S. Derzhavin, as many
as 30,000 Bulgarians originally migrated here.
(21)

The Bulgarian colonization of the late 18th to
mid-19th centuries essentially shaped the present distribution of Bulgarians in the republic.
The majority of the Bulgarians live in villages
of Odessa Oblast, chiefly around Izmail, and in

Zaporozh'e Oblast. Small islands of Bulgarian
settlement exist in Kirovograd and Nikolaevsk
oblasts, too, where a considerable portion of the
Bulgarians live intermixed with Ukrainians.

Jews. There are 840,000 Jews in the Ukraine.

The Jewish population began to appear in what
is now the Ukraine as early as the period of
Kievan Rus'. A large number migrated from
Poland in the 15th and 16th centuries. The Pale
of Settlement introduced by the tsarist government (Jews were allowed to settle only in small
populated places west of the Dnieper) resulted
in the majority of the Jews coming to live in
small towns and villages in that area. Thus,
under the census of 1897, only 40% of the Jews
lived in towns and cities. At the end of the 18th
century, a large number of Jewish agricultural
colonies was founded in Novorossiia. However,
it was primarily Jews converted to Christianity
who were permitted to settle there. By the mid-
19th century there were twenty such settlements
in the southern Ukraine, with a total population
of about 12,000. (22) Their number increased
further thereafter. Many of these villages existed until World War II. Today Jewish rural
settlements have survived only in a few places
in Krasnogvardeisk Raion of the Crimea. These
were pioneered in the 1920's. Before the war,
Jews constituted twice as large a percentage of
the population of the Ukraine as today, but the
figure declined as a result of the barbarous
mass extermination of the Jews by the Fascist
conquerors.

Most of the Jews live in cities. In Kiev, Odessa, and Chernovitsy oblasts, Jews constitute 6-
7% of the population. In the other oblasts the
percentage of Jews is very much lower. In the
cities of Chernovitsy, Odessa, and Kiev, Jews
are highest in proportion to the population: 15-
17%. Only about 17% of the Jews regard the
Yiddish language as their native tongue.

Germans. Among the small number of German
settlements in the Ukraine there are a few mixed
Ukrainian and German villages in Transcarpathia.
They consist of migrants (chiefly in the mid-18th
century) from various parts of Austria-Hungary and Germany (Bavaria, Württemberg, the
Black Forest, etc.), so that even neighboring

German villages retain some differences in language, culture, and mode of life. Until World War II there were, in the southern and western oblasts of the Ukraine, a considerable number of descendants of German colonists who migrated from Germany in the late 18th and the first half of the 19th centuries.

Moldavians. There are about 242,000 Moldavians in the Ukraine (0.6% of the republic's population).

Starting in the 16th century, Moldavian serfs, seeking to escape feudal oppression, fled Bessarabia to the Ukraine, "to the land of the Cossacks" in whole villages. (23) Very often such settlements, particularly east of the Dniester and in Bukovina, were populated from the very beginning simultaneously by Ukrainians and Moldavians. As a consequence, these peoples became closer in culture and mode of life.

Toward the end of the 18th century there was a considerable increase in the number of Moldavian villages between the Dniester and the Bug, and also in the Ukraine west of the Dnieper. These consisted chiefly of Moldavians fleeing the oppression of the Turks and Phanariotes, under which Moldavian lands west of the Dniester remained. This was facilitated by the fact that the Moldavian boyers and officials acquired stupendous land grants in the areas freed from the Turks. Thus, in 1792 the Russian government granted them 260,000 desiatins of land in Tiraspol' and Anan'ev uezds alone. (24) As a consequence, numerous villages and farmsteads came into being in a few years' time, populated primarily by Ukrainian and Moldavian peasants.

The Moldavians participated actively on the Russian side in the Russo-Turkish wars. Many of the Moldavian settlers of the late 18th century became part of the military settlements of Southern Russia. This is how free Cossack settlements consisting of Moldavians and other peoples came into being. As is evident from the data of the 1926 census, a string of Moldavian settlements stretched from west to east, reaching from the Bug to the Northern Donets. These settlements were first called roty (companies): i.e., the village of Novo-Ukrainka — Perva [First] (rota); the village of Martonosha – Os'ma

[Eighth], etc. (in Kirovograd Oblast). This was also the designation used for several Moldavian villages in the Donbass.

It is interesting that in a number of Ukrainian villages (Voloshskoe in Soloniansk Raion, Dnepropetrovsk Oblast, and the Moldavian villages in the Donbass), the Moldavians call themselves Volokhi [Wallachians, Vlachs]. This is because the Eastern Romance population from the Carpathians to the Dniester had for centuries been termed "Volokhi" by the adjacent Slavs even after the formation of the Moldavian state in 1359 A.D. The term "Volokhi" struck such deep roots that the Moldavians in the Central and Eastern Ukraine began to call themselves by that name.

At the beginning of the 19th century, when Southern Bessarabia was liberated from the Turks, many Moldavians were settled there among the other colonists. More than 80% of the Moldavians live in rural areas. The largest numbers are in the eastern raions of Chernovitsy and Odessa oblasts. Some 10,000 live in Kirovograd and Nikolaev oblasts. There are also individual Moldavian settlements in the southern and eastern regions of the Ukraine.

Rumanians (101,000 persons) live in the southwestern portion of Chernovitsy Oblast, both mixed with the Ukrainians and in separate settlements (primarily in Gertsaevskii and Glybokskii raions and in the Transcarpathian Oblast); 85% of them are rural.

The earliest Rumanian settlements in the Ukraine (about the 14th century) were founded by emigrants from Wallachia (Maramureš) and southern Transylvania. They settled in what are now the Tiachev and Rakhov raions of Transcarpathia and in some places in present-day Chernovitsy Oblast.

From the time of the unification of the two principalities of Moldavia and Wallachia (mid-19th century), the Moldavians of the former principality of Moldavia gradually came, because Rumania had become sovereign, to consider themselves Rumanians. However, those Moldavians who were not incorporated into united Rumania (the bulk of Bessarabia at that time was part of Russia) continued to regard themselves as Moldavians. This is very clearly evident in

Chernovitsy Oblast, where the boundary ran between Austria-Hungary and Russia.

Tatars (61,500). These are chiefly emigrants from the Tatar ASSR and the Volga country. However, in the town of Ostrog and the village of Iuvkovtsy nearby (Khmel'nitskii Oblast) there remain a small number of Tatars descended from people moved out of the Crimea in the 14th century by the Lithuanian princes.

The majority of the Tatars who have come to the Ukraine in recent decades work in the industrial districts of the Donbass.

Gagauz (24,000). They settled in Odessa Oblast early in the 19th century, and later a very small number of them moved to the shores of the Sea of Azov, in the 1860's. More than 80% of the Gagauz are rural. They speak chiefly their own language, which falls into the Turkish group.

There are about 149,000 Hungarians in the Ukraine. Almost all live in the southwestern portion of the Transcarpathian Oblast, often mixed with the Ukrainians. They occupy most of Beregovskii Raion, about half of Vinogradovskii, and the smaller portions of Uzhgorod and Mukačevo raions. Seventy-five per cent of the Hungarians are rural.

Estonian settlements (in the Crimea) were established in 1861-1879 (25) by members of a sect founded by a peasant from Jarvamas, J. Leinberg ("the Prophet Maltsvet"). Despite its religious covering, this movement was essentially an expression of the class struggle of the peasantry against the Baltic landlords and clergy. Of the five colonies founded in the Crimea, all that now remains is a single village in Pervomaisk Raion. The inhabitants of the others have been assimilated. Half of the Estonians regard Russian as their native language.

Greeks in the Ukraine number 104,000. They live in the south of Donets Oblast and in some towns in the southern Ukraine. About half the Greeks in the Ukraine live in urban places.

The forebears of most of the Greeks now living in the republic were moved to the Azov country in the 1770's from the Crimea (some 18,000 persons), which had then been proclaimed an independent khanate. The resettlement of the Greeks was carried out by the tsarist government for the purpose of populating the empty southern lands. The pretext was the desire to settle these lands with people of "our faith," Crimean Christians — Greeks, Armenians, (26) Moldavians, etc.

From the very outset of their settlement in this area, the Greeks of the Azov Coast formed two linguistic groups: the "Hellene Greeks" (speaking a dialect of modern Greek) and the "Tatar Greeks" (whose language was of the Turkic group). This was a consequence of their many centuries in the Crimea. The first group founded the city of Mariupol' (now Zhdanov) along the Sea of Azov and 12 nearby villages, while the latter established 10 villages. Later other settlements appeared. The native languages have been retained primarily among people of the older generations. The majority speak Russian.

Albanians populate the village of Zhovtnevo near Izmail and two villages in Zaporozh'e Oblast. The language is retained, particularly in Zhovtnevo. They migrated from Albania first to Bulgaria, and then, early in the 19th century, to Bessarabia. In 1861 they moved, with the Bulgarians and Gagauz, to the Azov country, where at first they had three villages: Devnenskoe, Gamovka, and Georgievka.

Gypsies are most numerous in the Transcarpathian and Odessa oblasts. They established two villages in the latter: Faraonovka and Kair ["Pharoahville" and Cairo]. At the end of the 18th century these villages were part of the Danube Cossack settlements. Today the Gypsies of Faraonovka call themselves Cossacks and Moldavians. (27) In the Crimea (Dzhankoe Raion), Gypsies have lived settled lives also since the end of the 18th century. In addition, a considerable number of Gypsies are presently scattered among the Ukrainians, primarily in the western and southern oblasts.

The Karaims live in the Crimea (chiefly Feodosiia and Bakhchisarai). The majority speak Russian. A negligible number are found in Galich and Lutsk, and have largely retained the Karaim language.

Of other nationalities in the Ukraine, we note

the Armenians (some 28,000, in cities), the Chuvash, who founded small settlements in the Central Crimea in the mid-19th century, and the Krymchaks, who live in the towns of the Crimea. There is also a small number of Assyrians living chiefly in Nezhin, Kiev, and the cities of the Donbass.

The processes of ethnic development now under way in the Ukraine are proceeding primarily in two directions: 1) the continued consolidation of the Ukrainian Soviet socialist nation, and 2) processes of ever more intimate convergence of the peoples of the Ukraine both within that republic and in the USSR as a whole.

The Soviet years have seen an unprecedented rise in the level of culture and education of the peoples living in the republic. Today illiteracy has been virtually eliminated in the Ukraine, while during the first Soviet years, to cite the rural situation, only 39.2% of the Ukrainians were literate, 43.1% of the Russians, 42.5% of the Poles, and 26.7% of the Moldavians. (28)

Today people of a variety of nationalities are studying in one fraternal family in the educational institutions. Thus, in 1961/62, enrollment in the higher educational institutions and tekhnikums of the Ukraine included: some 603,000 Ukrainians, 252,000 Russians, 34,000 Jews, 8,500 Belorussians, 2,800 Poles, 2,200 Moldavians, 2,000 Bulgarians, 1,700 Greeks, and 1,000 Hungarians. (29)

The convergence of the various nationalities and their education in the spirit of internationalism are promoted by the rapid growth of the urban population and the joint labor of members of various ethnic groups in industry and on collective and state farms. Thus, for example, workers of fifteen nationalities are employed at the Khust Furniture Factory of the Transcarpathian Oblast.

The Ukrainian and Russian languages constitute important media for international communication, facilitating the convergence of the peoples of the republic.

More than 73% of the people of the republic speak Ukrainian. More than 93% of ethnic Ukrainians speak in their mother tongue. The percentage of persons who regard Ukrainian as

their native language is quite high among the other peoples. About 131,000 Russians, a majority of the Poles, and a considerable portion of the Czechs, Slovaks, Moldavians, Rumanians, etc., speak Ukrainian.

The Soviets made possible free development of the Ukrainian language. Today there are more than 33,000 schools in the republic in which teaching is in Ukrainian.

In addition to the Ukrainian schools, there are, in the Ukraine, over 6,000 schools in which instruction is in Russian; Moldavian is used in 218, and Hungarian in 140. There are Polish schools, as well as 586 in which education is conducted in more than one of the languages of the people resident in the republic. (30)

The Russian language, spoken by 24% of the population of the Ukraine, has come into wide use there. Nearly all the peoples of the Ukraine know both Ukrainian and Russian.

The wide dissemination of the Ukrainian and Russian languages in the Ukraine occurs alongside processes of development of the languages of other peoples in the republic. Among the Moldavians, for example, 83% use their native tongue, as do 80% of the Bulgarians, 84% of the Rumanians, 87% of the Gagauz, 98% of the Hungarians, etc. (see Table 2). (31) Naturally, those peoples who live in less compact groups, particularly in cities, abandon their native tongues considerably more rapidly.

In addition to the many thousands of publications in the Ukrainian and Russian languages, oblast and raion newspapers are published in the languages of peoples dwelling in the republic, as are papers at certain enterprises.

Certain peoples living in the Ukraine, particularly in the Odessa and Transcarpathian oblasts, are characteristically multilingual. They have a good grasp both of their native tongue and of two or three of the languages of neighboring peoples.

As a consequence of the all-round convergence of the peoples, some are acquiring the language and culture of others. (32) For example, in 1926, 95.8% of the Bulgarians along the Azov Coast gave their language as that of their nationality, while in 1959 the figure was

INDO-EUROPEAN FAMILY

Slavic Group

Ukrainians

Russians

Belorussians

Poles

Czechs

Slovaks

Bulgarians

Romance Group

Moldavians

Rumanians

Albanian Group

Albanians

Greek Group

Greeks

Indic Group

Gypsies

Germanic Group

Germans

Jews

URALIC FAMILY

Finnic Group

Estonians

Ugric Group

Hungarians

ALTAIC FAMILY

Turkic Group

Gagauz

Tatars

Chuvashes

Karaims

Krymchaks

Boundaries of ethnic territories consisting of a single nationality.

Boundaries of ethnic territories of mixed nationality.

ETHNIC RATIOS IN MIXED AREAS

Approximate equality.

One people predominates.

Borders

International

Soviet Socialist Republics of USSR

Oblasts

Cities

КИЕВ   Capitals of republics

Львов   Oblast' centers

Умань   Other cities

60   0   60   120км

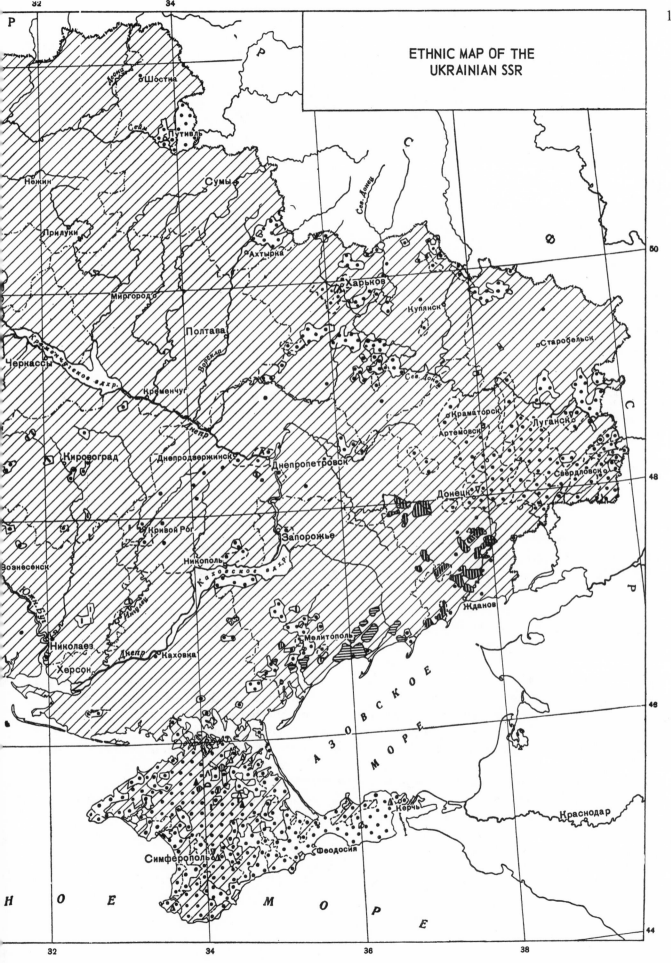

ETHNIC MAP OF THE
UKRAINIAN SSR

Table 2

Peoples	Number (thous.)	Of which, regard as their native language (thous.)		Ukrainian	Russian
		That of their nationality			
		Number	%		
Entire population of which:	41,869	38,136	91.1	490	3,213
Ukrainians	32,158	30,072	93.4	–	2,075
Russians	7,091	6,959	98.1	131	—
Jews	840	142	16.9	23	672
Poles	363	68	18.7	249	45
Belorussians	291	107	36.0	27	157
Moldavians	242	201	83.0	16	24
Bulgarians	219	177	80.8	5	36
Hungarians	149	147	98.6	1	1
Greeks	104	8	7.6	3	93
Rumanians	101	85	84.1	13	1
Tatars	62	38	62.9	1	22
Armenians	28	12	42.8	1	16
Gagauz	24	21	87.5	–	2
Germans	23	8	34.7	4	11
Gypsies	23	9	39.1	6	4

25.3% Similar processes are typical of other peoples, too. Unlike the situation in capitalist countries, in the USSR such processes are spontaneous in nature. "The working masses, freed from the yoke of the capitalists, are striving with all their strength toward unity and merger with the largest and most advanced socialist nations," wrote Lenin. (33)

There are many characteristics in common in the daily life, material and nonmaterial culture of the peoples living in the Ukraine. (34) Association in economic, cultural, and everyday life results in the enrichment of the various peoples. For example, the farm experience of leading Bulgarian grape and vegetable growers is widely employed by other peoples. In turn, Ukrainian wheat farmers and the Moldavian corn farmers help the Bulgarians.

At the same time, internationalist communist characteristics are developing ever more widely among the peoples of the republic: "they are all united by common vital interests into a single family and are marching jointly toward a single goal, communism." (35)

Footnotes

1) The 1959 census showed the majority of Jews indicating Russian as their native tongue.

2) Narodne gospodarstvo Ukrain'skoi RSR v 1961 r., Kiev, 1962, p. 8.

3) Radians'ka Ukraina (tsifri i diagrami), Kiev, 1962, p. 10.

4) Calculations are within the 1926 administrative boundaries of the Ukrainian SSR (excluding raions transferred to the Moldavian SSR), as it has not proved possible to compare indices of ethnic composition within the present boundaries of the Ukraine, due to the different approach to the question of ethnic affiliation, and to the falsification of statistical data for the West Ukrainian oblasts by the ruling circles of Poland, Rumania, and Czechoslovakia during the years of bourgeois rule.

5) Vsesoiuznaia perepis' naseleniia 1926 g., Vol. XI, Moscow, 1929, p. 41.

6) Voenno-istoricheskii zhurnal, 1960, No. 1, pp. 88-95.

7) Materially XXII s'ezda KPSS, Moscow, 1961,

p. 405.

8) Today, in the RSFSR alone, 80% of the Ukrainians are blue-collar and white-collar workers.

9) Statistika Ukrainy, No. 103, series Demografiia, X, 1927, p. 3.

10) E. M. Tiazhel'nikov, "K voprosu o migratsii naseleniia v sviazi s osvoeniem tselinnykh zemel'," Uchenye zapiski Cheliabinskogo otdela Geograficheskogo obshchestva SSSR, No. 2, Cheliabinsk, 1957, pp. 35-37.

11) Rocznik statyczny 1949. Glowny urzad Statystyczny Rzeczypospolitej Polskiej, Rok XIII, Warsaw, 1950, P. 26.

12) Five hundred fifty skilled petroleum industry personnel left Borislav for Poland after the war (Sambo Branch of the L'vov Regional Government Archives, Sect. 646, File 8, p. 39).

13) Archives of the USSR Acad. Sci., Sect. 135, File 3, # # 581, 600, 607.

14) L. S. Berg, Naselenie Bessarabii, Petrograd, 1923, pp. 18-19.

15) N. A. Cherliunchakevich, Natsional'nyi sostav Sovetskoi Ukrainy, Ob'iasnitel'naia zapiska k etnograficheskoi karte USSR, Khar'kov, 1925, p. 19.

16) L. S. Berg, op. cit., pp. 10-11.

17) N. Petrovich, "Prinuditel'noe pereselenie bobyletskikh krest'ian," Trud v Rossii, Vol. I, Leningrad, 1924, pp. 149-155.

18) E. Czynski, Etnografiaszno-statystyczny zaryz liczebności i rossiedlenia ludności Polskéj, Warsaw, 1887, p. 23.

19) Skorowidz miejscowości Rzeczypospolitej Polskiej, Opracowany na podstawie wyników pierwszego spisu ludności, Sept. 30, 1921, XII, Wojewodstwo Lwowskie, Warsaw, 1924, p. IX.

20) N. S. Derzhavin, "Bolgarskie kolonii v Rossii," Sofia, 1914, p. 10 (from collection Za narodnye umotvoreniia i narodopis, Vol.

XXIX, No. 1).

21) Ibid., p. 11

22) A. A. Skal'kovskii, Opyt statisticheskogo opisaniia Novorossiiskogo kraia, Part I, Odessa, 1850, p. 316.

23) Istoriia Moldavii, Vol. I, Kishinev, 1951, p. 198.

24) A. A. Skal'kovskii, op. cit., p. 255.

25) A. Nigol, Eesti asundused ja asupaigad Venemaal, Tartu, 1918, pp. 62-63.

26) The Armenians were settled on the Don, near Rostov.

27) Data collected by an expedition of the Institute of Art Research, Folklore and Ethnography of the Ukrainian Academy of Sciences, 1958.

28) Vsesoiznaia perepis' naseleniia 1926 g., Vol. XI, Ukrainskaia Sovetskaia Sotsialisticheskaia Respublika. Itogi po respublike, p. 21.

29) Data of Division of Culture, Central Statistical Office, Ukrainian SSR.

30) Data of Ministry of Education, Ukrainian SSR.

31) Narodne gospodarstvo URSR v 1959 r., Statistichnii shchorichnik, Kiev, 1960, p. 15.

32) However, only the appearance of a new national consciousness can be considered the culminating stage of the very complex problem of ethnic assimilation.

33) V. I. Lenin, Soch., Vol. 22, p. 324.

34) See V. S. Zelenchuk, "Skhidnoslov'ians'ki risi v moldavs'kii vesil'nii obriadovosti," Narodna tvorchist' ta etnografiia, 1959, No. 3; G. Iu. Stel'makh, "Deiaki pitaniia vivchennia narodnogo zhitla na Ukraini XIX-XX st.," Ukrains'ka etnografiia, Vid. AN URSR, Kiev, 1958, pp. 43-58 ff.

35) Materialy XXII s'ezda KPSS, Moscow, 1961, p. 405.

* * *

Empirical Studies of Worker Communities

Separate Paper. 7th International Congress of
Anthropology and Ethnography, Moscow, August
1964, "Nauka" Publishing House, Moscow, 1964

L. S. Efremova, A. A. Luts, and E. P. Chivkul'

CHANGES IN FISHING TECHNOLOGY AND IN THE CULTURE AND DAILY

LIFE OF THE FISHERMEN OF SOVIET LATVIA AND ESTONIA

The fact that the Baltic Sea is near at hand is the determining factor in the development of the fisheries of Latvia and Estonia, which occupy an important place in their economies. The long-established specialization of the various fisheries is retained to a considerable degree. The taking of herring is the major activity in the Gulf of Riga, cod is the most important object of open-sea fishing, and sprats are the chief catch off the shore of Estonia.

In the second half of the 19th century and the beginning of the 20th, fishing was second in importance to agriculture among the occupations of the coastal population. The development of the fisheries was inhibited by the feudal privileges of the landlords in fishing, the primitive means of transportation (rowboats and sailboats), and the low level of the equipment used in fishing. The traditional fishing implements of the Letts and Estonians were hand-hauled shore nets, off-shore nets, various fish-traps, and hooks. Until the end of the 19th century, the tackle was made by members of the fishermen's families. During the winter and autumn evenings the women spun and threw flaxen thread, and knotted it into nets. The men made the remaining tackle. Factory-made cotton thread came to be used in net-tying only at the end of the 19th century.

The nature of the fisherman's work determined the collective forms it took. The fishing cooperatives differed in character, depending upon concrete conditions. In fishing with hand-hauled shore nets, fishermen joined into groups of 10 or 12, and in Estonia hand-hauled shore-net fishing even of a communal nature remained, in spots, until the very end of the 19th century. When off-shore nets were used, four to six men worked a boat. Large-scale fish-trapping arose at the end of the 19th century. The large funnel-type stationary trap-nets used for herring usually belonged to capitalist entrepreneurs or groups of the more prosperous fishermen. Small eel nets of the same type were owned by individual fishermen.

In the years of capitalist dictatorship in Estonia and Latvia, fishing was a backward branch of the economy. A considerable portion of the coastal population engaged in fishing only in the spring and autumn, spending the rest of the year in farming, working as lumberjacks, etc.

Because of their low earnings, the number of professional fishermen tended to diminish. (1) The main reason for the stagnation of fishing was the limited market and the lack of a developed fish-processing industry.

The technical level of the fisheries remained low in capitalist Latvia and Estonia. Fishing continued to be a coastal enterprise, with the catch taken by passive means primarily. (2)

An improvement in technique occurred when motorboats came into general use in the late 1920's. Because of the high cost of motors, most of the fishermen bought them as part of a group or on credit. In Latvia, in 1938 there was one motor per 4.8 fishermen, on the average, (3) and one per 6.6 in Estonia in 1939. The motors were of low power: five to seven horsepower.

The primitive equipment was responsible for the low productivity of labor. In Latvia, in 1939, the average catch per fisherman was 4,519 kilograms, (4) and 4,121 in Estonia. The fishermen's position was substantially worsened by the fact that sale of the catch was dependent upon price-speculating middlemen. The fish was bought for next to nothing, while tackle was expensive. (5) Therefore most of the fishermen were enmeshed in debt. It was not uncommon for a fisherman's property to be sold off at auction. Because of poor technology, damage to tackle was common. The virtually complete lack of safety devices led to the death of many fishermen. The capitalist governments gave no help to the families of such men.

In their struggle against the pressure of the buyers, the fishermen united into cooperatives to buy tackle and, in part, to sell their catches. However, this did not lead to major changes in their status. In capitalist Latvia and Estonia, fishermen belonged to the least prosperous section of the population. Most of the fishery settlements — Kolka, Roia, Kuiviči and others — lay between the dunes and forests of the coastal strip, having no contact to speak of with the centers of culture. Small wooden houses pre-dominated, and smoke-houses and sheds for tackle and fish-drying stood on the dunes. Most of the fishing villages had no piers, and boats were lowered into the water and hauled ashore by hand. The fishermen usually had small pieces of land (two to three hectares). A fisherman's homestead lacked many of the structures characteristic of peasant farms (grain-drying floors, barns, etc.). Usually the center of the fisherman's house was a large room used for cooking and work, repairing and making tackle, drying clothes, and so forth. Many of the poorest had no homes of their own and took dwelling space at high rentals in the homes of peasant landholders. Some fishermen had no tackle and worked as laborers for prosperous fishermen or entrepreneurs (the "funnel-net laborers" in Estonia).

The private property relationships and competition gave rise to an atmosphere of mistrust, suspicion and competitiveness in the fishing villages. The fishermen concealed from each other their methods of fishing, improvements in tackle, and the best places to fish. The low level of culture and complete dependence upon chance and the caprice of the sea gave rise to a mass of superstitions among fishermen (lucky and unlucky days to go to sea, patron saints, etc.).

With the establishment of Soviet authority in the Baltic states, the position of the fishermen changed fundamentally. Fishing was transformed from a petty craft into a large-scale branch of the socialist economy.

The fishermen were united into collective "farms." There were 17 of these in Latvia in 1963, and 43 in Estonia. However, the Estonian collectives were smaller than the Latvian, as the topography of the Estonian coast and the types of scattered settlements that had come into being in the course of history prevent the establishment of large fishing enterprises. At present, two types of fishing collectives exist: those devoted purely to fishing and those in which agriculture is a secondary occupation. (6) Collective farms of the second type still predominate, but there is a tendency for them to decline in number. The process of separating fishing from farming has entered its final stage, and in Latvia it has gone farther than in Estonia.

The Soviet state is manifesting extraordinary concern for maximal mechanization of fishing, for easing the working conditions and improving the circumstances of life for the fishermen. Since the collective farms were first organized, fishermen have been receiving new equipment and ships from the state. Several stages may be traced in the mechanization of fishing in the Soviet Baltic: a) equipment of the collective farms with high-powered motorboats and stationary seines; b) mass-scale introduction of trawling, a progressive technique; and c) organization of fishing in the open Atlantic.

The use of trawlers came into general practice in Latvia from 1949 on; in Estonia – from 1952 on. At present it is the dominant technique in the Baltic Sea, and the fishermen of the Gulf of Finland and the Gulf of Riga are also changing over to it. The trawlers possessed by the collectives are increasing in number each year. (7) The extension of trawling has considerably expanded the area of the fisheries and reduced the seasonal nature of fishing.

The year 1956 marked the turning point in collective-farm fishing, for in that year the collective fishermen of Latvia equipped expeditions to the open Atlantic. In 1961 and 1962 they put in use new fisheries off North America and in the North Sea. The number of ships in the Latvian deep-sea fleet increased from 5 to 47 between 1956 and 1962. Estonian fishermen entered deep-sea fishing later, and had 6 ships in operation in 1962. (8)

Fishing techniques are constantly being improved. The catch is taken with identical trawlnets at different depths. The ships have radio-telephone communications, echo-sounders, net-selecting and net-shake-out machines, vibrators to fill containers to the fullest, and so forth. Fishing is taking on an ever more industrial character, and the work of a fisherman is becoming a variety of the work of a seaman. This is the second major change in the traditional forms of the economy of the coastal population of the Baltic states in the Soviet period, and has had a significant influence in changing the conditions of life and daily existence.

The introduction of modern fishing equipment resulted in a substantial improvement in labor productivity and in the catch.

The total catch in 1961 in Latvia was 133,000 tons, and in Estonia – 108,700, while the highest catch under capitalism in Latvia was 16,200 tons in 1939 (9) and 18,500 tons in Estonia. (10) Output per fisherman rose from 91 to 225.5 centners in Latvia between 1950 and 1962, and from 59 to 162 in Estonia. (11) The increase in labor productivity is leading to a constant rise in incomes of the collective farms and to an improvement in the well-being of the fishermen. The average annual earnings of a Lettish fisherman increased from 715.29 rubles in 1950 to 1,813 in 1962, while in Estonia the rise was from 431.6 to 1,324. (12) The high earnings of the Lettish and Estonian fishermen constitute the foundation of their prosperous and civilized lives.

Most of the fishermen of the coastal collectives are from families long settled there, primarily Letts and Estonians. The descendants of the Livonians engage in fishing on the north coast of Kurzeme. In the postwar years the make-up of the population of the fisheries has changed as a consequence of an influx of people from the farming areas of Latvia and Estonia. There are also settlers from other Soviet republics, chiefly Russians. They are primarily members of crews fishing the Atlantic. In the Latvian SSR the composition of the coastal population has changed less than in Estonia. In Estonia, during World War II, the Swedish population on Noarootsi Peninsula and Wormsi and Ruhnu islands left the country almost entirely, and a new population has taken its place. In the postwar years the open-sea fishermen of Estonia have been supplemented by men living along Lake Chud. (13)

The organization of the fisheries on socialist principles has fundamentally changed the consciousness of the fishermen, their mode of life and attitude toward their work. A new type of fisherman, who takes a creative and businesslike attitude toward his work, has emerged during the Soviet years.

The occupational and cultural connections between the Lettish and Estonian fishermen and those of other Soviet republics have grown stronger. Numerous Latvian, Estonian and Lithuanian collectives engage in systematic exchange of delegations and excursion parties. Among the fishermen there are many deputies to the local and Supreme Soviets of the republics and to the Supreme Soviet of the USSR.

The years of collective economic life have witnessed not only the rise of a new attitude toward work and an increase in the public activity of the fishermen, but a substantial broadening of their horizons and the level of their technical knowledge. The complex modern equipment demands that the fishermen be well trained. Navigators, marine engineers, and trawlmasters are now found among the fishermen, where there were none before. The training of men with specialized fishing skills and of officers for the fleet is conducted by the collectives through schools of seamanship and technical secondary schools. The collectives have periodic courses for upgrading, with the result that virtually every other fisherman is qualified as a motor operator. In the first years of the collectives there were no fishermen in either republic with master's licenses; yet by 1961 1,867 individuals were certificated captains, navigators and engineers trained for the Latvian collectively owned fleet, (14) while in Estonia some 3,400 persons of specialized skills have been trained since the war.

These people are trained primarily from among youth and persons in their middle years, having seven to eleven years of schooling, while older people, most of whom have had three or four years of education, are engaged in shore fishing.

The organization of fishing in large enterprises employing the last word in equipment has led to major changes in the forms of organization of the work. Instead of small boat crews, often consisting of members of a single family, and small cooperatives, new work collectives have appeared. The basic work unit in the collectives is the brigade, which consists in turn of teams. The brigade consists of persons living in the same place. Fishing with stationary seines is conducted by an entire brigade of 20

to 25, while fishing with offshore nets and funnel-type stationary trap-nets is by teams of 3 to 5. Ship's crews consist of 5 to 25 persons, depending upon tonnage.

Age, health, and experience are considered in the assignment of duties in coastal fishing. Elderly people are assigned to the use of funnel-type stationary trap-nets, which is lighter work but requires much experience. The youth work the stationary seines.

The women of these collectives do not participate in the heavy work at sea, although in the past it was not uncommon to find them going out. Today women work at auxiliary jobs: removing fish from nets and sorting them ashore. They also work in net-making workshops, fish-processing plants, and in offices of the collective "farms." As previously, most of the women work in agriculture. Thus, the traditional division of labor between the men and women of the coastal population has proved satisfactory under present conditions as well.

The fundamental change in the social and occupational lives of the fishermen has led to the appearance of a new mode of daily life. The face of the fishing villages has changed, and they have taken on the appearance of urban settlements. Major construction is under way. Modern docks and ports are being built, along with equipment-storage warehouses, mechanized fish-receiving shore stations and processing plants. The erection of civic and dwelling structures is also under way.

Many of the collectives have put up attractive community centers with spacious gymnasiums, movie auditoriums, libraries and recreation rooms. (15) Stores, barber shops, and bathhouses may be found in the villages. Secondary or eight-year schools, many of which were put up out of the funds of the collectives themselves, can be found in virtually all fishing villages. (16)

In the place of the ancient fisherman's hut one finds new houses with modern conveniences. (17) Fishermen's homes, like those of agricultural cooperatives, have radios and electric wiring; many of them possess television sets.

The house furnishings of the fishermen's homes combine elements of the traditional with others of modern material culture. A large portion of the apartments of the younger and middle generation of fishermen have modern furniture of urban type. In the families of elderly fishermen one finds furniture of the 1930's and earlier periods predominating. Much attention is given to the use of ethnic decorative fabrics in the homes: napkins, runners, rugs, pottery, and flowered materials.

The increase in the fishermen's earnings makes it possible not only to furnish their homes comfortably but to acquire good clothing and appliances to ease housework: washing machines, vacuum cleaners, and the like, and to eat a variety of tasty foods. The fishing collectives usually extend over considerable areas, and therefore each family has two or three bicycles. Every third family has a motorcycle, and many have cars. (18)

Fishermen living in farming areas have small private plots of 0.15 to 0.6 hectares, used for gardens and for keeping a cow, sheep, little pigs and fowl. Some of the fishermen (35% in Latvia, 14% in Estonia) live in towns or urban-type communities, and their mode of life does not differ in any way from that of other strata of the urban population. The increase in material well-being and the rise in the level of education and technical skill among the fishermen, as among all rural people, is making for a gradual integration of the ways of life of the rural and urban populations.

A cultural revolution has taken place in the fishing villages during the Soviet years. Libraries, movies, and television are generally accessible to the fishermen, as to the entire rural population. The collective farms are spending large sums on various cultural measures and on sports. In 1962, there were 70,000 books in the libraries of the collective farms of Latvia, and 40,000 in those of Estonia. (19)

The improvement in the prosperity of the fishermen and the increase in their free time as a consequence of the mechanization of fishing are making possible an improvement in their level of culture. The present-day collective fisherman is a man of broad interests and high cultural standards. In Latvia and Estonia

there is no such thing today as a family of fishermen that does not subscribe to two or three papers and magazines. Many fishermen have substantial home libraries. Much attention is being given to the development of amateur arts. Virtually all collectives have dramatic and dance groups, choirs and, in Latvia, children's ballet companies. (20) Participants in collective-farm amateur activities perform not only in neighboring collectives but beyond the frontiers of their native republics.

Movies are shown regularly in the fishing villages, and urban theater companies tour them. Expansion of the fishermen's horizons is promoted by excursions in their own republics and beyond them. Many fishermen spend their vacations touring, and go to vacation resorts and sanitaria. Sport is expanding. Many collectives have their own stadiums. Volleyball, soccer, bicycling, track-and-field, and heavy athletics are particularly popular. It has become the custom for fishermen to organize annual republic-wide Spartakiads to which fishermen of neighboring republics come.

A vivid reflection of the changes that have occurred in the minds of the fishermen is the appearance of new traditions in work and everyday life. Traditional among the Lettish fishermen is the Holiday of the Sea, which is celebrated jointly by several collectives. (21) At these solemnities, the work triumphs of the fishermen are publicized, experiences are exchanged, and awards are made to top performers. Rowing contests, tugs-of-war, net-weaving competitions, motorboat races, and the like, have become customary at the Holiday of the Sea. Estonian and Lithuanian fishermen come to the celebration.

The Day of the Young Fisherman is also widely celebrated. On this occasion, old fishermen transmit their knowledge and tell their experiences to the youth and, as it were, confirm the youngsters as fishermen, commending to them the preservation and furtherance of the best traditions of comradeship and mutual assistance.

It has also become the custom to celebrate public holidays, the anniversaries of the founding of the respective collectives, the departure of draftees into the army, and retirement on pension.

Major changes have occurred not only in the social lives of the fishermen but within the family. Family relationships and ways of life change more slowly than do the economy and public life, inasmuch as vestiges of the past, religion in particular, survive longer in the family. The old hangs on in family relationships by force of custom, habit, and tradition. Therefore certain holidays, particularly in families with elderly members, continue to be marked with religious ritual. However, the new customs and traditions, in which a certain continuity is observed in the form of retention of the best folk traditions, are dominant in the family lives of the fishermen. Such new traditions as the Holiday of Childhood, the Day of Reaching Maturity, the new marriage ritual, civil funerals, days of remembrance of the dead, and so forth, have become a firm part of the modern way of life of the fishermen.

The Holiday of Childhood is celebrated as a day on which a new young member is accepted into the collective. This solemnity retains the ancient custom of inviting godparents, who bear, jointly with the parents, the public responsibility for the upbringing of the infant.

On the Day of Reaching Maturity, young people are solemnly accepted into the ranks of full-fledged builders of Soviet society. Warm speeches of welcome are made by older comrades, teachers, parents and friends. Each confirmant is given presents and flowers. The celebration ends with an excursion to the country.

Funeral customs have changed noticeably of late. Church rituals are increasingly giving place to civil funerals. Elderly people are generally buried in church. The abandonment of observation of religious rituals in everyday life by the overwhelming majority of the population of the fishing settlements is testified to by the new custom of memorial repasts participated it by the personnel of the collective "farm." The memorial meetings note the work done by the departed, and their paths through life, and the memories of revolutionaries and those who died in World War II are honored.

The new customs find vivid response among the fishermen.

Footnotes

1) In Latvia the number of professional fishermen diminished from 2,887 to 2,547 between 1925 and 1938 (V. Miezis, Latvijas jūras zvejnieciba, 1939, Riga, p. 5), while in Estonia the decline from 1922 to 1939 was from 6,424 to 4,488 (Eesti Kalandus, 1939, p. 247).

2) Miezis, op. cit., 1925-1938, pp. 28-29, 36-38.

3) Ibid., p. 7.

4) Id.

5) The average annual earnings of a Lettish fisherman in 1926 came to 651 lats, and in 1936 to 761 (Meizis, op. cit., p. 5), while a funnel-type stationary trap-net for salmon cost about 1,500. The average annual earnings of an Estonian fisherman in 1938 came to 600 crowns (Eesti Kalandus, p. 247).

6) Three collective farms in Latvia do not have agricultural brigades, while the others have small field-crop brigades or cattle-farm teams. The incomes from agriculture do not exceed 15 to 20% of the whole.

7) Since the collectives were founded, the total power of the trawler fleet in Latvia has multiplied almost 14 times. The figure for Estonia is approximately the same (data from the associations of fishing collectives of Latvia and Estonia).

8) Ibid.

9) Razvitie narodnogo khoziaistva Latviiskoi SSR, Riga, 1962, p. 125.

10) Data from the Economics Institute of the Academy of Sciences of Estonia.

11) Data from the associations of fishing collectives of Latvia and Estonia.

12) Ibid.

13) A. Luts, "Novoe v bytu estonskikh rybakov i zadachi ego izucheniia," SE, 1960, No. 3, p. 160.

14) Zveiniecibas biletens, 1962, No. 1, p. 3.

15) The Salatsgriva collective "Brivais vilnis in Latvia" has built a community center with an

800-seat auditorium and the Engura "Padomju zvejnieks" built one with 600 seats. Thirty-seven Estonian fishing collectives have community centers; 22 have libraries. The others make use of the community centers and libraries of the village soviets.

16) Such schools exist in Skulta, Pavilosta, Engura and other settlements.

17) From 1958 to 1962 alone, Latvian fishing collectives put 19,000 square meters of housing space into use (data from the annual reports of collectives), and in 35 Estonian collectives, 28 dwelling structures with 120 apartments were erected, plus 580 private homes (survey data).

18) In the Estonian "Audrurand" and "Lakhta" collectives, and the Latvian "Bolshevik" and "Sarkana baka" collectives, every tenth fisherman owns a car.

19) Zveiniecibas biletens, 1962, No. 3, p. 3. For Estonia the data are from questionnaire surveys.

20) In 1962, the Latvian fishing collectives had 75 amateur performing-arts groups with a total of 1,200 members, meaning that every eighth resident of a fishing village took part.

21) The Holiday of the Sea is celebrated formally in Roe, Kolka, Salatsgriva and other villages.

***

Trudy Instituta etnografii XLVII
(Sredneaziatskii sbornik II), 1960

K. L. Zadykhina

ETHNOGRAPHIC DATA ON THE MODE OF LIFE OF THE UZBEK WORKERS

OF TASHKENT AND ANDIZHAN

During the second half of the 19th century, as a consequence of the annexation of Central Asia to Russia, vast changes occurred in the socio-economic and cultural lives of the Uzbek people. Annexation to Russia promoted the development of capitalist relations in Central Asia. Industry began to develop, class stratification in town and country intensified, and the establishment of a new and progressive social class — the industrial proletariat — began.

In conjunction with the building of railroads and the development of manufacturing industry, the need arose to bring skilled Russian workers to Turkestan. The establishment of the first groups of industrial workers from among the native population began. Conditions arose for direct association between the native and the Russian workers on the job, and in politics and culture. Subsequently their work side by side in manufacturing industry and transportation and the community of class interests promoted the progressive influence of the more advanced Russian workers upon the development of the work habits and class consciousness of the workers of the local nationalities. It created the prerequisites for the development of friendship between the Russian and local workers and for joint actions by all workers in Central Asia against exploitation and in the revolutionary movement against tsarism. They participated in the October Socialist Revolution under the leadership of the Russian proletariat and the Communist Party.

Under the conditions of the Soviet social system and the socialist economy, Uzbekistan witnessed a change in the class structure of society: a new, Soviet society arose, consisting of the working class, the collective farm peasantry, and the Soviet intelligentsia. The social life of the Uzbek people was now based on new, socialist relations, fundamentally changing the political system and the cultural life of the people. At present, the socio-political and intellectual cast of the Uzbek socialist nation is determined in many ways by the influence of the working class that developed in Uzbekistan during the Soviet period.

In view of the importance of a study of the development of the new Soviet conditions of social and working life and of the culture and home lives of the working class, the USSR Academy of Sciences' Institute of Ethnography has in recent years organized the collection of data on this theme. Studies have been made of the culture and mode of life of the workers of Moscow, the Urals and Baku, the workers of Kirgizia, and so forth. (1) In Uzbekistan, too, a study was set up of a number of industrial enterprises. This work was done by the present author.

It was conducted in 1951, 1952, and 1954 in Tashkent and Andizhan, primarily among Uzbek workers. The places studied were a small number of industrial enterprises in different fields, and their personnel.

In Tashkent the study made was of the conditions of life and work of the workers of the Integrated Textiles Mill and the Locomotive and Rolling Stock Repair Works, and in Andizhan the subjects were the workers of the Strommashina Diesel Works, which was the center around which an advanced workers' district arose within the limits of the "old" city of Andizhan. (2)

* * *

After the triumph of the Great October Revolution, the Uzbek people, upon completing the restoration of the economy of the republic, undertook the building of socialism. The broad scope of the brotherly assistance given by the Russian people, the constant attention and far-sighted decisions of the Communist Party and the government of the Union to the development of centers of industry in the East, facilitated the establishment in the Uzbek SSR of large industrial enterprises — the foundations of heavy industry — in the fields of power, metalworking, petroleum, chemicals, building materials, and the like. A textile industry was also established, and the cotton ginning industry of the republic was completely reequipped.

Along with the industrialization of Soviet Uzbekistan a numerous, literate, cultured and skilled working class developed, capable of furthering the cause of the building of socialism. This may be traced in the example of the enterprises studied in which, as in all industrial enterprises of the Uzbek SSR, the working class is multinational, consisting of Uzbeks, Russians, Kazakhs, Tadjiks, Tatars and others.

The supplementing and enlargement of the working class from among the Uzbeks took place by involving workers of both the towns and the kishlak villages in socialist production. In addition, a considerable percentage of the young workers consists of individuals who gained their trade schooling in the FZO and trade schools, which are constantly training personnel for industry from among the local nationalities.

Uzbek women are also being drawn into industry on a large scale, learning new skills as workers and working alongside men in the textile, silk-reeling, clothing, footwear and other branches of industry in Uzbekistan.

The new Uzbek working class has not only increased in numbers, but has also seen qualitative change, as is manifested in the rise in its cultural level and technical skill. In connection with the appearance of new branches of industry, a considerable number of Uzbek workers and workers of other nationalities are sent each year for job training in factories and mills in various industrial parts of the Soviet Union. As the production technology improves and the cultural and technical level of the Uzbek working class rises, there has been a considerable accompanying rise in the proportion of Uzbek workers who are skilled.

Today there are tens of thousands of skilled Uzbek workers who have mastered the complex trades of metal smelting and refining, power production, construction, erection, chemical skills, mining, the operation of spinning and weaving machinery, the mechanic's trade, etc.

The concern shown by the Communist Party and the Soviet government for improving the conditions of the workers' labor has been clearly manifested in the lives of the industrial enterprises of Uzbekistan. Lenin pointed out that under socialism the electrification of all factories and railroads "would make the conditions of work more hygienic, emancipate millions of workers from smoke, dust and dirt, and accelerate the transformation of dirty and repulsive workshops

into clean, bright laboratories, worthy of man."
(3)

The growth of industry in Uzbekistan has established the base needed for improving the conditions of life and the level of culture and technical skill of the workers. As in all Soviet enterprises, the workers of Uzbekistan have an eight- or seven-hour workday, weekly days off, and a three-shift system of operation. The arrangement of the workday gives consideration to the needs of women who are breast-feeding their children, young workers who are also studying, etc.

Public eating places are provided everywhere in industry, in the form of factory and shop cafeterias and snack bars.

To meet the national tastes of the Uzbek workers, teahouses have been established both on a factory and a shop basis. The menus of cafeterias, snack bars, and teahouses all list local dishes, which are very popular among the Russian workers as well. The workers are provided with medical care at health stations in their departments, and in factory-wide outpatient services, polyclinics and hospitals. Measures for improving working places and conditions of work, for planting greenery around the factories, and so forth, are in evidence everywhere.

Tens of millions of rubles are spent annually by the government and the unions upon the material and household needs of the workers, and for cultural services.

Thousands of workers and office personnel take cures and vacations, at the expense of the unions, at sanatoria and vacation resorts. Overnight sanatoria have been established at many factories and mills in Uzbekistan.

The factories are in new, bright structures and equipped with first-class, modern equipment. Simultaneously, large-scale introduction of mechanization and automation of technological processes is occurring. High-speed methods of work are being introduced in the metallurgical industry and high-speed techniques of drilling in the petroleum industry; all-round mechanization of all processes in coal mining is under way, and so forth. All this has the purpose of easing difficult and harmful trades, of making them health-

ier and of improving the conditions of labor in every possible way. As mechanization and automation of production processes are intensified, the duties of an ever-increasing number of workers will become more skilled and assume the nature of engineering and technical functions. The workers will begin more completely to combine physical with mental labor in their work, and will deepen their knowledge in the process of production.

The process of establishing groups of skilled workers of the native nationalities and of improving the conditions of labor, along with the general growth of the industrial culture of the Uzbek working class, may be demonstrated concretely with the aid of materials obtained as a consequence of study of the history of the development of particular enterprises and their personnel. As already stated, in 1952 we undertook a study of the culture and mode of life of the workers of the Tashkent Locomotive and Rolling Stock Repair Works.

This was one of the first industrial establishments in prerevolutionary Turkestan. It was originally organized as the main railway shops of the Trans-Caspian (Central Asian) Railroad, which was built and put into operation at the end of the 19th and the beginning of the 20th centuries.

After the Revolution, the main railway shops were renamed the Red Eastern. They became the Red Eastern Locomotive and Rolling Stock Repair Works.

Today Uzbeks are employed in all departments of this enterprise. They have various levels of skill and have mastered many trades. Among them one finds steel smelters, molders, rolling-mill operators, pattern makers, machinists and mechanics, boilermakers, blacksmiths and others. On the basis of incomplete data, 50% of the oldest Uzbek workers in the rolling-stock assembly department came to work at this establishment between 1920 and 1930. By social origin, the majority of the workers in this department and in the others were peasants or from the families of peasants and craftsmen. They came chiefly from the rural area around Tashkent, in part from the city of Tashkent itself, and also from other districts of Uzbekistan. They all entered the factory as unskilled laborers and acquired skills under Russian foremen.* (a)

A vivid picture of the lives of the first Uzbek workers may be compiled from the example of workers in the departments we studied. Thus Railway Technician-Lieutenant Lutfeddin Tadjiev, foreman of a rolling-stock crew consisting of both Russians and Uzbeks, was born in 1904 in the family of a dekhkan peasant (b) in the rural locality of Parkent, not far from Tashkent. After the death of his father, the 11-year-old Lutfeddin, oldest child in a family of nine, continued with his mother to farm the tiny piece of land they held. Speaking of those days, he says: "There were days when we hungered; it was hard to support the family; we didn't have clothing." With the establishment of the Soviets, the conditions of life changed, for no taxes were exacted from this poor family. In 1929 they joined a collective farm. Lutfeddin then began to work in Tashkent, first as a repairman and later at the Red Dawn Factory as an unskilled laborer. Here he gradually learned the work of a roofing tinsmith in the repair and construction department. During the Second World War Lutfeddin entered the factory's technical school, organized to train skilled workers. Finishing the course in 1944, he became a foreman; to this day he works in that capacity. Lutfeddin at first did not want to enter the school, and after enrolling felt like quitting because his level of literacy was low. But he was given moral support by the shop chief, V. M. Kudrin. Hearing that Lutfeddin wished to drop his studies, he said to him: "Tadjiev, I've been watching you work the last few days. Don't you worry. You do as well as the educated workers. You'll be a good foreman. Go ahead and learn." As a result, Lutfeddin decided not to quit school, and finished with distinction, for which he was given a prize.*

Umar Pulatov, born in 1906, son of an artisan-bootmaker of Besh-Agach (now the Stalin District of the city of Tashkent), works as a pattern-maker in the steel casting shop. He came to work at the Red Eastern Works in 1930 as an apprentice pattern-maker. A Russian foreman named Bogoslovskii helped him learn his trade.* Planer-operator Saidvali Akbarov, born in 1902, son of a peasant from the area near the town of Turkistan, runs a new slotter in Mechanical Shop No. 2. He came to the factory in 1929 and learned his trade from a Russian, Novikov.*

Whereas during the first years after the Revolution the Uzbeks acquired their skills and work habits from Russian master mechanics, later, Uzbek workers who had developed at this plant and acquired high levels of skill were involved in the training of fellow Uzbeks. By way of example we cite Khasan Muminov, whose father was a bullock-cart driver in old Tashkent. When his father died, Khasan was ten. He learned shoe-making from his foster-father and worked at this until 1930. Then he dropped this handicraft and came to work in the tool department of the works as an apprentice to Shcherbakov, a Russian. Having become a mechanic, he decided to transfer to the pressure gauge division, where he acquired his skill under the guidance of the Uzbek foreman Babakhanov. When the latter moved out into teaching, Muminov took his place.* Equal conditions of life and work, joint work and common interests brought the workers of various nationalities closer together, and created between them relations of comradely mutual assistance, friendship, respect and a feeling of responsibility to each other. Thus Muminov, a member of the CPSU since 1932, received his recommendation for party membership from his comrades on the job — one Uzbek and three Russians.*

The training of skilled personnel goes on constantly at this plant. Young workers, including Uzbeks, are regularly trained in the FZO school. (c) The term of instruction is 4-6 months, depending upon the skill to be learned. Upon completion of the term of education, the student has to produce a test job and pass an exam on safety theory and techniques. If he receives a positive evaluation, he is transferred to independent work and given a grade classification. He then masters his trade in practice and acquires production skills. According to the leader of production training on the job, A. N. Alekseev, a personnel-training engineer, the instruction is so successful in the majority of cases that the students gain a skilled-labor classification either within the time period planned or even before completing the course.

In addition, instruction in various skills is given on an individual basis by assigning apprentices to highly skilled workers — not only Russians but Uzbeks — as well as in schools of advanced methods of work, by the procedure of assigning 3-4 workers to advanced workers. Thus, the worker Iadgarov was attached for purposes of instruction to boilermaker Zhuravlev, Abdullaev in the car-assembly department to the carpenter Perekhodtsev, Iuldashev in the mechanical repairs department to machinist Tashmukhamedov, Davydov in the steel-casting shop to the gas-flame cutter Mirsagatov, etc.* It has become a matter of honor for the foreman and a good tradition for the experienced workers to train young workers quickly and in a highly skilled fashion, and to assist them in the transition to independent work and earnings. The relationship between the former apprentices and their teachers continues thereafter. Creative friendship arises among the workers in the course of the labor process. The foreman keeps an eye on his former apprentice, helps him with advice and example, and thereby assists him to gain in skill. There are technical production courses for apprentices in the mechanic trades and for machine-tool operators. At these courses they study the theory of their trade, materials technology, the reading of drawings, and tools and measuring instruments. In 1953, 1,387 persons were engaged in various types of technical schooling at the plant, of whom 171 were Uzbeks, among them 7 women.*

As of 1946, a school for working youth, operating in two shifts, has functioned at the Locomotive and Rolling Stock Repair Works. At this school the workers — Russians, Uzbeks and members of other nationalities — obtain seven-year or secondary education without leaving their jobs. For the youth of Uzbek nationality there is now a special seventh grade class conducted in the native tongue.*

The Strommashina Works, manufacturing diesel engines, has developed in another way. A cotton mill was built on the outskirts of the old city of Andizhan in 1924. When the war resulted in the evacuation of a number of plants to the East, an aircraft plant was assembled in what

had been the cotton mill. At the end of the war the aircraft plant was returned to the West, and in 1946 a new enterprise was established to build diesel engines, using a portion of the remaining equipment, buildings and installations. The sphere of employment of the diesels produced by this plant is extensive. They are utilized for irrigation in Central Asian agriculture, to actuate various construction mechanisms, in the mining industry, as small-capacity electric-power producers, etc. As it grew, the plant came to occupy a part of the bazaar in the old city. By 1951 its area had grown threefold over that of the former cotton mill.

The construction of the plant began with utilization of the buildings of the cotton mill. The erection of new shops started shortly thereafter. First a spacious and bright machine shop was built, an iron-casting shop, a central boiler room, a forge shop and a carpentry shop. Roads have been built on the plant site, and internal water and heat lines installed. A number of measures are under way to improve working conditions, mechanize particularly heavy and laborious jobs, and assure safety. The workers are issued working clothes: felt boots for metal-pourers, matted felt headgear, goggles, overalls and two-piece garments of densely woven fabric, canvas gloves, leather shoes, etc. Workers in occupations harmful to health — babbitt-metal pourers, mold-dryers, heat-treatment personnel working with lead baths and pickling baths — are issued milk daily. The grounds have been planted with greenery.

The personnel of the Strommashina Works is also multinational. The number of Uzbeks is quite large. About 6% of them are former employees of the cotton mill on this site. When the plant was converted to diesel construction they were retrained and taught new skills in accordance with the duties of the department in which they work. In addition, certain of the workers who had come to the plant from collective farms, craft cooperatives or from other establishments in Andizhan have mastered new skills here. In this category, for example, we find Sharabeddin Shamseddinov, born in 1902, the son of a craftsman of Andizhan. In 1925 he went to work as an unskilled laborer on the railroad; in 1942 he came to work at this factory and learned the trade of bronze smelter.* In the older generation of workers we find Azizkhodja Mekhmankhodjaev, born in 1901, son of a dekhkan, who worked at the cotton mill and then learned the trade of sandblast hardener;* Ibragim Igamberdyev, born in 1906, son of a dekhkan, working at the plant since 1933 at the water pumps;* Nurutdin Mukhammedov, born in 1902, son of a dekhkan of Andizhan, working as senior foreman in the wood-finishing department, and many others.*

There are many youth among the Uzbek workers. They are primarily men who have done their army service, and former pupils in the schools — children of collective farmers and handicraftsmen — who came to the factory as apprentices. Others are young workingmen who came to the factory from trade schools and FZO schools.

Most of the workers in this category had already acquired six, seven or eight years of schooling before coming to work at the plant and, upon entering the shop, rapidly mastered the knack of working in industry and gained skilled grade classifications both in the shops and in courses for foremen. In this group of workers we find, for example, Abdunabi Nishanov, son of a handicraftsman. In 1946, having completed the seven-year school, he came to work as an unskilled laborer. Becoming interested in the work of a diesel-engine operator, he became apprenticed to foreman A. D. Nuzhdin and, upon learning the trade, gradually went over to independent work as a diesel operator.* Khamid Azizov, also the son of a craftsman, came to work at the plant in 1942 after completing six years in a school taught in Russian. Beginning as apprentice to an assembler mechanic, Khamid rapidly learned a trade and in 1944 was transferred to the post of shift foreman in a repair group. In 1947 Khamid joined the Communist Party. Without leaving his job, he completed a three-month course for foremen at the plant, and then went to the evening school for working youth, planning, upon graduation, to continue his education in a higher educational institution.*

The training of skilled personnel and the upgrading of workers are also conducted system-atically and in a variety of forms here: by taking courses for the technical minimum, (d) in schools of advanced methods of work, at courses teaching particular second trades, and in technical job-related courses, etc.

An indicator of the rise in the technical level of knowledge of the Uzbek workers at this plant is the fact that, after becoming skilled workers in any field, one finds them alongside Russians and workers of other nationalities in all types of work in the plant and particularly in the most important and basic departments. Thus, for example, in the machine shop Uzbeks number 25% of the workers.* They have learned to be machine-tool operators, mechanics, assemblers, automatic-machine operators, grinders and workers in the cold working of metal. In the heat-treatment shop 45% of the workers are Uzbeks; their ratings are mechanics, brigadiers, and heat-treatment foremen, electricians and inspectors.* In the casting shop 95% of the workers are Uzbeks; among them are skilled metalworkers who have become masters of the casting trade.*

Many of these workers hold jobs as foremen and brigadiers. Thus, for example, there is Akbar Khaidarov, who went to work at the plant as a molder in 1942 when he finished trade school. Two years later he completed six-month courses for foremen of socialist labor, and passed the examination for expert melter and caster of ferrous metals; then he became senior foreman of molders. In order to further improve his skill, he was sent by the plant to a two-month course for foremen in the city of Shcherbakov, and upon his return again began to work as senior foreman in the department.*

Abdusalim Turgunov, working in the same department, entered the plant in 1943 as a molder with an 8th grade education. Within three years he had become shift foreman for molding, and then went to the foremen's courses in Shcherbakov. Returning to the plant, he completed the 10th grade at the evening school for working youth and then entered the Railway Transport Institute in Tashkent.* Abdunabi Mamadjanov works in the heat-treatment shop. He came to the plant after completing 9th grade. He soon became a highly skilled mechanic and then, having taken the courses for heat-treatment foremen, began to work as senior heat-treatment foreman. He is now second in command to the department chief.*

Abdukarim Abdullaev is a brigadier in the same shop. He too began to work at the plant, after nine years' schooling, as an apprentice annealer. Then, having completed the courses for foremen, he became a highly skilled worker.*

Instruction of workers newly arrived in the plant also proceeds by individual assignment of apprentices to the best foremen, experienced workers and instructors, and in a two-year trade school.

Thus, for example, in the machine shop A. L. Burlutskii, a turret lathe operator, taught his skill to the Uzbek Muidin Babakhodjaev; drill operator Mamadjan Ismailov, an Uzbek, taught V. A. Semenov, a milling-machine operator, a second skill. He also trained Gonidjan Kuzybaev, a new worker at the plant, and a Central Asian Liuli gypsy, while the Liuli machinist Nizamdin Abdullaev trained the Uzbek Iusupdjan Oripov.* The brotherly friendship of the peoples of the Soviet Union is manifested in concrete forms at work, as in all aspects of the life of Soviet people. The relationships among workers of various nationalities are built on mutual respect and a feeling of friendship.

The origin and development of a team of workers of the Tashkent Integrated Textile Mill, studied in 1951, were somewhat different. This mill was erected in the Soviet period.

Large-scale industrial construction got under way in Soviet Uzbekistan as early as the First Five-Year Plan. The erection of industrial enterprises, of which the Tashkent Integrated Textile Mill was one, proceeded at a rapid rate.

The decision to establish a base of the textile industry in Central Asia was taken in 1932 by the 17th Party Conference. The same year saw the issuance of a resolution of the Council of Labor and Defense of the USSR Council of People's Commissars on the time period for construction and launching of operations at the Tashkent Integrated Textile Mill.

The party and government gave major attention to this first enterprise of the textile industry in the east. The Soviet Union's textile equipment plants set about filling the orders of this mill in accordance with contracts. Skilled workers of long experience, engineers and technicians, from Moscow, Ivanovo, Serpukhov, Kalinin and other cities were sent to the construction project to assist with their knowledge and experience in building this new establishment. Long trains hauled the building materials and equipment to the site. Uzbeks, Russians, Tadjiks, Kazakhs, and workers of other nationalities participated in the work of construction. Communist Saturdays of donated labor, participated in by 32,000 working people of Tashkent, were of considerable assistance in speeding construction. The first machines went into operation in 1934, and in 1936 the plan of construction and assemblage was fulfilled and the first section of the spinning and weaving mill went onto the list of functioning Soviet establishments. The chintz printing mill went into operation at the same time.

The mills continued to expand during the war. Spinning and Weaving Mill No. 2 was built in 1942. Simultaneously, machine shops were constructed, out of which a machine works later developed to fill the orders of factories constituting the integrated mill. A thread factory and other enterprises were established on the territory of the plant. The factories of the integrated mills are equipped with the latest machinery of Soviet manufacture. All the work is mechanized, and safety equipment is well established. The shops themselves are light and spacious. The grounds of the integrated mill have been planted. Flowerbeds are everywhere, and a high fountain cascades in front of the main building.

The number of Uzbek workers in the Locomotive and Rolling Stock Repair Works, one of the oldest establishments in Uzbekistan, and those of the Strommashina Factory had increased by gradual involvement of workers of the local nationalities. But in developing the Tashkent Integrated Textile Mills, built rapidly and possessing complex modern equipment and the latest in machinery, it was necessary to carry out extensive and organized measures for mass training of skilled workers for this new giant of industry.

During the erection of the integrated mills, the installation of its complex equipment required a large number of skilled workers and specialists. Therefore, before Russian foremen and specialists were brought in, steps were taken to prepare experienced riggers and workers from among the local residents. A group of riggers, including the Uzbeks Nadjiev, Akhmedjanov, Iskhakov, Khakimov, Tiliakhodjaev, and others, were taught at courses in the Frunze Factory in Moscow; 40 were trained at FZU schools at the Khalturin Works in Leningrad, about 300 at the courses in general education of the integrated mills,* and so forth. In 1934 the erection of the integrated mills and the assembly of machines in the spinning and weaving shops were already being done by workers of the mills themselves, who had returned from their courses of study and were working under Russian foremen-instructors from the machine-manufacturing plants of the USSR.

In 1934, after the new spinning and weaving machinery had been installed, 40 women spinners and strippers from the central areas of the USSR and 100 spinners and weavers of local origin, who had undergone instruction at the Fergana Factory, and others,* went to work operating them. Subsequently employment rose to several thousand.

Today Uzbek men and women, who have become skilled workers of the various textile trades — foremen, assistant foremen, weavers, spinners, and so forth — are working in all the mills and shops alongside the Russians. They came to the integrated mills from various districts and towns of Uzbekistan. In the past, many of them had been craftsmen or dekhkans, or the children of craftsmen and collective farmers.

Thus, Pulat Babadjanov was born in 1903 in the family of a dekhkan near Samarkand. In 1916, when the native population of Central Asia was drafted for labor in the rear, Pulat, to avoid the draft, fled to Tashkent with the agreement of his father and on his advice. There he found work as an apprentice ("khal'pa") to the master bootmaker Markhamat-Kulu in the Mul'kun-kocha makhal' (district). After the Revolution, Pulat left to work at a leather works, became a trade

union member and, from 1920 to 1924, worked as instructor in bootmaking at a school and a boarding school. The year 1925 saw the beginning of training of native personnel for the Fergana Integrated Textile Mills, and he was among the 500 persons sent to study at a FZO to learn the trade of textile worker. Then, as one of the best students, he underwent a period of practice work at enterprises in the Ivanovo-Voznesensk region. In 1930 Pulat Babadjanov began work as an assistant foreman at the Dzerzhinskii Factory of the Fergana Integrated Mills and in 1933, having moved to Tashkent, went to work at the Integrated Mills there as instructor in training repairmen. Then he moved on to installation work in the scutching department, then to assistant foreman, and, as of 1937, to foreman of that department.

The work record of Sadyk Maradjabovich Uzakov, chief of the weaving department, born in Kokand in 1908, is somewhat different. In 1935, after graduating from the native-language school in the Fergana Textiles Trade School, he went to work at the Dzerzhinskii Works in Fergana, and then as teacher of special subjects for assistant foremen at the Tashkent Integrated Textile Mills. In 1942 he was transferred to the post of shift foreman of the weaving shop of the spinning and weaving mill, and since 1946 has worked there as chief of the department.*

Some of the Uzbek workers began as trainees in the shops. Working at the machines under foremen and assistant foremen, they learned the trades of spinner, stripper, calico printing doctor, engraver, etc. Thus, for example, Akmal Akhmetkhodjaev, born in 1919, the son of a craftsman of Tashkent, has worked at the Integrated Mills since 1935. He was assigned as trainee to engraver D. I. Kolokol'nikov; after seven months of training as a beginning engraver he was able to do simple drawings with the aid of his teacher, and then he gradually began to improve his skill. Returning from service in the Soviet army, he again went to work as an engraver in 1946, learning this skill thoroughly.*

Makhmadali Shukuraliev works at the chintz-printing works. He was born in 1914 in Tashkent in the family of a dekhkan. In 1929 he and his father joined the collective farm. In 1931 Makhmadali went to work as a molder trainee in the casting shop of the Sel'mash Works, where he put in two years. He then studied in a school for government and party functionaries and, upon graduating from it, worked for a while in government. In 1935 he returned to the Sel'mash but within a year transferred to the Integrated Textile Mills as assistant examiner. Successfully mastering this skill, he became shift foreman in 1939 and continues to this day to work at this post.*

At present, women constitute a majority of the workers at this enterprise. Uzbek women work in all departments on a par with Russians. Among the Uzbek women there are some who are elderly, but the majority are young women who received their training in the factory trade schools.

Among the older Uzbek women we find Zukhra Abdullaeva, born in 1896. Her husband was a handicraft saddle-maker in the old city of Tashkent. Zukhra discarded the veil as early as 1932. After the death of her husband, she was left alone with four children. In 1937, on the advice of her neighbors who were working women, she went as a ribbon-maker to the Integrated Textile Mills, where she worked for several years. But when her children grew up and went to work, Zukhra quit and returned to housekeeping.* Her daughter, Khabiba Israilova, is of the second generation of working women. She was born in 1924, went to secondary school and, upon graduation in 1940, went to work at Spinning Mill No. 1 of the Integrated Mills as a stripper-trainee. Then Khabiba, under the guidance of the experienced working woman Markhamat Iusupova, undertook to learn the trade of ring-spinning frame operator. After two years, having completely mastered this skill, she went to work on this complex machine, fulfilling her plan by 160 to 165% of the quota.*

At the Integrated Mills, work is constantly and systematically under way to improve the level of technical skill of the workers and to train new skilled personnel. Courses in the technical minimum have been opened, as have schools in progressive methods of work and special courses teaching operations that have been poorly

mastered and constitute bottlenecks, and courses to teach workers a second trade. On-the-job instruction is given systematically. At the same time "open lessons" are conducted regularly at the factories and in the shops, as well as conferences for exchange of work experience, at which Uzbek men and women innovators speak. These include the spinners Khadicha Salikhodjaeva, Tursun Ermukhamedova, assistant foremen Iskhakov, Akhmedov and Kadyrov, on-the-job training instructor Abdullaeva, and the leading workers Madjuda Abdurakhmanova, Mirsagatova and many others.*

Along with this variety of methods of improving the workers' level of technical skill, workers are able to acquire secondary education and spinning and weaving skills in the evening school for working youth and the textiles trade school on the grounds of the integrated mills.

New workers are also trained in a one-year FZU school and in a school of trades and technology. In the latter, which trains assistant foremen, the course of instruction is three years. The students of these schools are maintained by the state. They receive uniforms, three meals a day, and those who need housing live in well-set-up dormitories of the integrated mills, etc.*

The majority of the young workers and working women, who have the high job rating of textile worker, have at various times passed through the FZO school of the integrated mills. These include Tursun Ermukhamedova, who systematically overfulfills her quota. She was born in Tashkent in 1918, finished the FZO at 17, and is working as a spinner in the department of basic ring-spinning frames.* There is Nuriia Maksumova, born in 1922, the daughter of a Tashkent worker, who completed a FZO school and has become one of the best weavers in the mills.* Many such examples may be cited. At present, Uzbeks at these mills fall primarily in the category of highly skilled workers: foremen, assistant foremen, weavers, spinners, etc.

The management, party committees and trade union organizations of these enterprises engage in a variety of political and cultural undertakings among the workers at large, directed at elevating the general outlook and cultural level of the

214

workers. Lectures are given, political education clubs function, movies are shown, plays performed, amateur performances of various kinds put on, and other similar activities undertaken at the Textile Workers Palace of Culture and the clubhouses of the component mills.

Thanks to the rise in the cultural level and technical skill, an ever-increasing number of workers are drawn into the general and important work of rationalization and invention. Many inventions are introduced and improved in a process of creative collaboration between workers and engineering-and-technical personnel of the enterprises and the personnel of research institutions, the designing offices of plants of nationwide significance, individual scientists, etc. For example, the Strommashina Works and its personnel maintain a direct relationship with the Research Institute for Construction and Highway Machinery, and with certain scientists at the Bauman Higher Technical School in Moscow, the Diesel Research Institute in Leningrad, and others.* The Locomotive and Rolling Stock Repair Works maintains a relationship with the research staff of the Tashkent Institute of Railway Transport Engineers.*

The following fact alone permits a judgment of the economic effect of the work of rationalization and its role. In 1953 the plan for introduction of 265 rationalization proposals at the Locomotive and Rolling Stock Repair Works, with a projected saving of 1,255,000 rubles, was overfulfilled, inasmuch as 277 proposals, yielding a saving of 1,349,000 rubles, were applied. Here, in order to stimulate thinking in the direction of rationalization, the plant printing office publishes and displays in the departments what are called "Bottleneck Lists" in the form of small pamphlets. They list the operations and particular jobs that need thought so as to make improvements. Moreover, consultations, interviews, conferences and trade union meetings are held at the factory; rationalizers, their proposals and methods of work are written up in the wall newspapers, in the widely circulated factory paper Gudok Krasnovostochnika, etc.

In addition to individual inventors, this plant has entire teams of inventors consisting of several persons each, sometimes of the most diverse skills. The co-authors of new ideas include both workers and engineering-and-technical personnel. Relations between them are built on the principle of comradely mutual aid, which, in the process of work, undergoes transformation into real creative collaboration. The work of rationalization is participated in actively by skilled Uzbek workers: boiler-cleaner Radjapov, machinist Miradylov, core-makers Tuliaganov, Shadmanov and Mansurkhanov, forming-machine operator Bekbulatov, template-maker Kazakbaev, engineer Guliamov, and others. The rationalizing proposals of casting-foreman Umar Pulatov, a Communist Party member, have yielded a saving of 7,800 rubles, and his work jointly with engineer Zhizhemontov has resulted in a saving of about 75,000 rubles.*

All the enterprises have technical libraries which are regularly supplemented with the latest technical literature needed by workers and engineering-and-technical personnel. The Uzbek molder in the steel-casting shop, Shakhashim Shakasimov, the Uzbek machinist Irgash Iuldashev of the locomotive department, and many other Uzbeks are regular readers in the technical library of the Tashkent Locomotive and Rolling Stock Repair Works.*

In addition to the technical libraries, the general libraries are very popular with the workers and engineering-and-technical personnel. The Integrated Textile Mills have two such libraries — one attached to the party office, another in the Textile Workers Palace of Culture.* The factory library of the Tashkent Locomotive and Rolling Stock Repair Works has over 13,000 volumes of creative writing in the Russian and Uzbek languages.*

Active utilization of the technical and creative literature is one of many evidences of the rise, under Soviet conditions, of the technical and industrial knowledge and of the cultural demands of Uzbek workers as compared to prerevolutionary times.

These data demonstrate how the Soviet era has seen a continuous increase in the number of Uzbek skilled workers and engineering-and-technical personnel, and how, as a result of their active involvement in civic and industrial life and cultural progress, there has been an immeasurable rise in the technical and cultural level of Uzbek workers.

The growth of socialist industry in Uzbekistan on the basis of modern equipment and the systematic improvement of working conditions constitute the foundation for a continuous rise in man-hour output, which in turn results in an increase in the workers' wages, improvement in their material welfare, growth in their culture, and transformation of their mode of life. Socialist relationships have taken shape in the home lives of Uzbek workers and are continuing to develop. Fundamental changes are occurring in culture and home conditions, along with active elimination of vestiges of patriarchal-feudal and bourgeois modes of life, which were retained in the form of old customs adhered to by prerevolutionary peasants and craftsmen in some families to this very day.

We see from each of the enterprises described in this article that their growth processes are accompanied by major undertakings in the field of culture, way of life, and housing construction, for which special funds were appropriated by the state.

In Lenin Raion of the city of Tashkent, a large and well designed settlement has grown up around the locomotive and freight-car repair plant; it has its own Railwaymen's Park of Culture, the Udarnik and Uzbekistan movie theaters, the October Revolution Community Center, the Central Polyclinic of the Tashkent railway junction, the central railwaymen's hospital, and a bathhouse. Food and other stores and kiosks are found adjacent to the factory and in surrounding streets.

There are a number of cultural and personal service institutions directly on the plant territory: a community center, libraries with reading-rooms, a museum, a dispensary, medical offices, showers, a barber shop, a large restaurant, a teahouse, etc.

Housing construction increased with the growth of the factory. In 1930 the housing controlled by the plant measured only 720 square meters; by 1940 it was 9,518 square meters, by 1950, 15,536 square meters, and in 1953, 17,522 square meters. Starting in 1942, this area included

buildings used as dormitories for workers. In 1942, a three-story dormitory was built on Cherviakovskaia Ulitsa, and two more dormitories were built in 1948 and 1949 on Sary-Kul'skaia Ulitsa.* Young single working men and women live in the dormitories, but there are also some separate rooms for married couples.

All the necessary conditions for cultured life and personal service have been provided in the dormitories. They are wired for radio, have electric lighting, water supply, and plumbing. The workers' bedding is changed every ten days. All the dormitories have gymnasiums and well equipped and cozily arranged "red corners." Storage rooms, water-boiling devices for tea, kitchens for cooking one's own food, and buffets have been provided for the workers. Each dormitory has an isolation room for those who are ill.

The dormitories on Sary-Kul'skaia Ulitsa are side by side. The yard between them is fenced and planted. There are clumps of flowers, and asphalted paths. The yard has a stage for summer use, used for delivering lectures and reports, showing scientific and artistic films, and performances by amateur groups.*

Some of the Uzbek workers still live in the Old Town of Tashkent and in the raions of the suburbs, Iangi-Iul', Chinaz, etc. Prior to being hired at the factory, these workers were collective farmers. They continue to have private plots and their own homes. The factory assists them with housing repairs and provides coal for heating the homes.* In striving to satisfy the housing needs of all its workers, the factory has organized do-it-yourself homebuilding. This is under way in the Lenin Raion of the city, not far from the factory. The do-it-yourself homes now fill entire streets: Vesna, Svetlaia, and others.

Workers living far from the plant use the urban transport system, while those who live in the suburbs use summer commuter trains, in which two cars are reserved for them.*

As we have already stated, the Strommashina Diesel Works at Andizhan is located in the former "old" city inhabited primarily by local people of the native nationalities (Uzbeks, Tadjiks, and others). Therefore, a considerable number of the Uzbek workers live in their own homes in the vicinity of the factory and on adjacent collective farms. With the construction and expansion of the plant, considerable housing construction was started around it and in the center of town.

In 1950 the area of the workers' settlement already occupied 75 acres. The houses in the workers' settlement were arranged along streets, and its entire territory has been planted with greenery. A shady park has been established on the shore of the sai (rivulet) opposite the factory. Alongside it, stores, a restaurant, and a summer teahouse have been built. Winter and summer community centers, a day nursery and kindergarten have been built in the factory village.* A fruit orchard has been planted on the grounds of the day nursery. The day nursery building is in the factory park.*

The factory town has a polyclinic hospital, a pharmacy, a bathhouse, stores and kiosks. The factory town has electricity and wired radio. Water mains have been laid through it and standpipes for water have been set up. This factory, too, has a large do-it-yourself home-building movement, actively assisted by management and the organized public. In addition to the workers' settlement, the plant has three large apartment houses in the center of Andizhan. These houses have gas, radio, (e) and electric lights. The workers' settlement adjacent to the factory has a dormitory for young workers with all modern conveniences.*

The factory has provided a special bus for workers living in the central portions of the town, which makes scheduled trips along the route most convenient for these workers.

The Integrated Textile Mills in the Frunze Raion of Tashkent has become a major industrial and cultural center. The construction of dwelling houses, cultural and therapeutic institutions proceeded simultaneously with the building of the various mills of this enterprise, in order to create good living conditions and meet the cultural needs of the textile workers.

The textile workers' residential town was planned in the southern part of Tashkent on a large hilly and ravine-intersected area. A great deal of work had to be done to clear the territory and

prepare it for construction. Again, the working people of the city came to help the builders and took an active part in the Saturdays of contributed labor organized at construction sites.*

By the time the vertically integrated mill went into operation, a socialist town with all proper conveniences had been built around it. The Textile Workers Palace of Culture is a decorative feature of this town. Nearby a large park, named for Kirov, has been laid out.

Buildings specially designed for day nurseries and scenic gardens, a three-story trade school, two school buildings, a large building of the Textile Institute, a combined bathhouse and laundry, food and other stores, and the like, have been erected among the apartment houses of the textile workers' community.

The mill has its own hospital system. It includes a three-story polyclinic hospital, surgical and therapeutic hospitals, two children's hospitals (one general and one for infectious diseases) and a maternity hospital. Moreover, each mill in this extensive enterprise has its own medical offices with a physician and a nurse constantly on duty. Alongside the mill there is an overnight sanatorium for textile workers, the function of which is to prevent tuberculosis. Particularly favorable conditions have been established in this overnight sanatorium for improving the workers' vitality and health.

Assistance to working women who are nursing mothers is well organized. In accordance with Soviet law, provision is made during the working day for feeding children in the day nurseries at normal intervals. At the required time, nursing mothers working at the machines are driven to the nurseries and then driven back to the department.

A beautifully equipped stadium with swimming pool has been built alongside the mill. The mill also has its service industries enterprise, including shoe repairing and tailor shops, a clothing factory for making clothes from the workers' own goods on a large scale, etc.*

All streets in the textile town have been planted with greenery, and there are many trees in the yards of the apartment buildings. Small orchards have been planted near large apartment houses.

The apartment houses are wired for radio and electricity. There are telephones in many apartments. The apartments have water supply and plumbing. A new artesian well was sunk in 1950 in the socialist town to improve the water supply. An electrical substation has been built to increase power supply. Streets in the textile workers' town are asphalt-paved.

Housing construction goes on each year in the textile workers' town. In addition, the management and civic organizations of the integrated mill are highly active in assisting do-it-yourself home-building, and issue loans to individual home builders.*

A number of well-equipped dormitories have been built by the mills for single young men and women.

The majority of workers live in housing under the control of the mill. However, there are some Uzbek workers who live in their own homes in the former Old Town of Tashkent and other districts of the city.

Thus, the Uzbek workers and the workers of other nationalities live both in various parts of the city proper and compactly in the territory of the socialist towns and settlements that have grown up in the Soviet years around the enterprises.

The rise in economic well-being and the socialist transformation of the mode of life of the workers are reflected not only in the type of workers' settlements and towns, but also within the workers' dwellings today. Our data suggest three chief types of workers' homes. In the factory and other urban developments, they live in new large multi-story apartment houses, in which they have an apartment or one or two rooms. In the city proper they occupy new two- or three-room, one-story houses built either by the mills or by themselves, in which the typical characteristics of a modern dwelling are combined with certain elements and furnishing arrangements of the traditional Uzbek home. However, in some districts, chiefly within the confines of what used to be the Old Town, the workers still live in houses of the old Uzbek type, only partially rebuilt.

The modern multi-story or one-story house in a workers' town or development is a typical urban structure. Workers have apartments or single rooms in this type of structure in the Tashkent textile workers' town. Thus, Pulat Babadjanov, a foreman in the scutching shop of the spinning-and-weaving mill of this enterprise, lives in a house on Stakhanovskaia Ulitsa. His apartment consists of a vestibule, a kitchen, two rooms and a balcony. The apartment has running water and plumbing, electric lighting and radio, and is heated by a round Dutch stove. The floor is wooden, painted; the walls and ceiling are whitewashed. The apartment is very light: one room has a window on the street; the other two windows and door open onto an open balcony. The furnishings of the apartment display a combination of urban Russian-style furniture with individual items of furniture, furnishings and decorations in the national style. There are two beds in the first room along opposite walls. One of them is covered with an Uzbek embroidered bedcover, and the other with a white factory-made bedcover. The floor between the beds is covered with a pile-less rug. In the corner there is a chest of local handicraft workmanship with tinplate hoops. Neatly piled on it are blankets, also covered with embroidered Uzbek bolsters. The radio loudspeaker hangs over one bed, and a large mirror over the other. In the left corner, at the balcony wall, there is a night table on which stands a phonograph, and the phonograph records are kept in the drawers of the night table.

The second room has one bed and a bookcase, above which hang a mirror, a clock and a photograph. Alongside the bookcase is a table with bentwood chairs. In the corner is a small table for dishes. Along the wall to the right of the door is a native chest with a pile of folded blankets and pillows in white pillowcases. A rug hangs on the wall over the chest. To the left of the entry, on the wall, there is a clothes rack with curtains.*

The chief of the weaving department, Sadyk Maradjabovich Uzakov, has his apartment in another portion of the textile workers' town on Shota Rustavel' Ulitsa. The apartment contains two dwelling rooms, a vestibule, a kitchen, bath and shower, a toilet and washroom, and two verandas. The furniture is of the modern urban type: factory-made beds, a chiffonier with mirror, wardrobes, a buffet, a night table, tables and chairs. In addition, the furniture includes the traditional chest of local workmanship, and on top of it folded blankets covered with tulle blanket covers. There are rugs hanging on the wall above the bed. Runners are on the floor of one room, and an ornamented sheep's-wool felt on the other. The apartment has telephone, electric lighting, and radio.*

The family of shift foreman Khamid Azizov of the Strommashina Works lives in a large urban apartment house in Andizhan. One room has a stove with a flat cooking top and oven. This room also contains a table, chairs, a chest for kitchenware, and a small chest with books. A second room also has a table, covered with a tablecloth and, on top of that, an oilcloth; bent-wood chairs, and two beds. The bedclothes are covered with woolen blankets, and at the heads of the beds are piled pillows in white and colored pillowcases. There is a sideboard for tableware and a tea set, a bookshelf with books, a phonograph and records, an alarm clock and mirror. On the table there is a sewing machine and radio. The room also has a chest of local workmanship. Both rooms have clothes racks nailed to the walls, with white cheesecloth curtains. The floors are covered with patterned pile-less rugs of local manufacture.

In the courtyard there is a tandyr (a stove for baking native flat dough cakes).

A second common type of modern dwelling of Uzbek workers consists of new single-story houses on small plots. The plots are on both sides of a broad tree-planted street, along the edges of which there are aryks (irrigation ditches). The plot is from five to ten hundredths of a hectare in size. When a house is built on the plot, it is usually set back and the windows open onto a yard which one enters from the street through a gate. As an example of this arrangement, one might cite the home of a foreman in the Locomotive and Rolling Stock Repair Works, Lutfeddin Tadjiev, in Karasui Raion on Zelenaia Ulitsa, or that of Umar Pulatov, a molder at the same plant who lives in the Tashkent rural district, or of the embosser Abdulkhamid Akhmetkhodjaev on Karasuiskii Shosse, etc.*

Lutfeddin Tadjiev's plot of ground is about six hundredths of a hectare in area and is surrounded by an adobe wall. A small gate through the wall leads into the yard. Here there are a few fruit trees and a grapevine in front of the house. In the spring a small part of the yard is used as a vegetable garden where the family grows onions, tomatoes, carrots, peppers, and the like, for its own use. Flowers are planted in front of the house.

The house contains two rooms ("vi") and a vestibule ("dakhliz"). The ceiling and walls are plastered and whitewashed inside and out. The walls of both rooms contain several small recesses taking the place of shelves for dishes and small household items. The front room has one window, and the second has three. The windows look out into the yard. In winter, the house is heated in two ways. The first room contains a sandali (a depression in the floor in which is placed a brazier with coals and, above it, a low table), and in the hall there is a small iron stove. Side by side with the old-fashioned traditional sandali, which is harmful to health and heats the room poorly, one finds electric light and a radio receiver.

The house of Saadvali Akbarov on Sary-Kul'-skaia Ulitsa, built in 1942, is arranged somewhat differently. In accordance with the old Uzbek tradition, the front of this house, containing the windows, faces the yard, while its blank rear faces the broad street. However, despite its traditional planning, this is a completely modern urban house with all conveniences. The entry to the house from the yard is in the form of a small covered porch, while the entry door opens onto a hall, with the dwelling rooms to the right and left. All three rooms are connected by doors. The room to the left of the hall is larger than the others and has two windows, the one to the right is smaller and has one window. The ceiling of the large living room is covered with patterned squares of plywood, while in the other room the ceiling, like the walls, is plastered and whitewashed. There is no sandali in this room, which is heated by a small iron stove and range in the hall. The range is used for cooking in the winter. The house has electricity and radio. In the yard there is a shed and leanto, under which there are a hearth and a tandyr. This is where the cooking is done in summer. In front of the house several grapevines have been planted and an arbor has been arranged. The yard contains several fruit trees, and a small portion is used for a vegetable garden.

The interior arrangement is quite unique. Factory-made furniture and household goods are combined with ethnic furnishings. In the room to the right of the hall the floor is covered with a woolen felt on which are piled quilted cotton blankets for seating. On the woolen felt at the wall opposite the entry there is the "seat of honor" ("tor") where guests are seated. Here there is a low table for eating ("khan-takhta"), which one sits at on blankets. In the same room there is a small table covered with a tablecloth and oilcloth. On it there are books and a tea set, but it is apparently used rarely. By the left wall is a bed, covered with woolen blankets. Pillows in colored chintz pillowcases are piled at the head of it.

In the room to the left of the hall there is a bed against the wall opposite the entry. The bed is covered with a factory-made woolen blanket. The floor in front of the bed is covered with a pile-less rug, on top of which there is a patterned woolen felt. To the right of the bed, in the corner, there is a chiffonier wardrobe. In one of its compartments the tea-ware (native piala cups and teapot) is kept, along with dried fruits, while the other compartment contains clothing. On top of the wardrobe are two nickel samovars, an enameled coffee pot, a vase for fruit, a water pitcher, and glassware.

On the wall to the right of the entrance there is a row of three local hand-crafted chests ornamented and hooped with yellow tinplate. On two of the chests blankets are folded; they are covered with embroidered Uzbek bolsters. A sewing machine stands on the third. A large mirror hangs on the wall to the left of the entry, between the windows.

A rack for outerwear is nailed to the wall of the hallway near the entry. Near the range is space for kitchenware, which includes both enameled and aluminum factory-made ware and local hand-made ware: copper trays and kumgans,

painted clay ware, as well as painted trays of Russian manufacture.

The houses of Makhmadali Shukuraliev, shift foreman at the Tashkent Textile Mills, and of his father, Shukurali Mirzaliev, are similar in external appearance, technique of construction and material to the new homes widespread today in the Central Asian cities. Both houses were built between 1947 and 1950 in accordance with architect's plans. Both have foundations of burnt brick and walls of adobe brick, plastered and whitewashed inside and out. Contrary to the old Uzbek tradition, the windows of these homes face the street. Makhmadali's house faces the new broad Zavodskaia Ulitsa. Entry to the house is from the yard. The house contains two rooms and an open terrace. The floors of rooms and terrace are wooden, and the ceiling is covered with plywood. A door leads from the terrace to the first room, and in it is a door into the second. Thus, the floor plan is also not traditional. In the first room, two large windows face the street and one faces the terrace, while in the second, one window faces the street and another the terrace. A number of large and small niches are provided in the walls, and household furnishings are conveniently and attractively arranged in them.

The plot on which this house is built belongs to Makhmadali's father — Shukurali Mirzaliev. Until 1947, an Uzbek-type house with a bolokhon stood here. In 1947 the head of the family, Shukurali, apportioned part of the land to his married sons and himself remained in the house with his wife and youngest son. The whole house was taken down between 1947 and 1950, and Shukurali and his younger son built a new one with the front and windows facing the street. This house is similar to that of Makhmadali; it has two rooms. On the yard side two small steps lead to the first room, with one window. A door from it leads to the second and larger room. The first room has a broad built-in recess for a chest and another, smaller one, for dishes. A third of the room is occupied by a large "supa" (adobe platform), covered with closely woven bast matting and sheep's-wool felt. The second room has two windows in the wall facing the street and one in the opposite wall onto the yard.

220

Two recesses are provided to the right of the entry. One contains dishes and trays, the second a chest of local craftsmanship, with a sewing machine on top of it. Two large recesses are also provided in the wall opposite the door. In the right-hand one there is a dresser with glass doors. Blankets are folded into this dresser, and books stand on a shelf in it. Recesses are also built into the wall to the left of the entrance, with a cupboard holding various kinds of household goods in the central one. A bed stands by the wall to the left of the door.*

As already stated, some workers continue to live in houses of the old Uzbek type, which they have inherited. Thus, in Tashkent, in the "Old Town," the plot belonging to a woman textile worker, Zukhra Abdullaeva, stands in the former saddle-makers' ("igarchi") makhal (quarter). There were two such makhals in the city. The majority of their residents were related to each other. The house of Zukhra Abdullaeva was built over a hundred years ago. It has been remodeled repeatedly and has by now lost many of the characteristics of the old Uzbek dwelling. Formerly the house was divided into the "tashkari" (male half) and "ichkari" (female half) and had a second story in the form of a bolokhon, and shutters instead of windows. Today the dwelling rooms are no longer divided into those for men and women. The bolokhon has been removed and the shutters replaced by glass windows in frames. In accordance with the old Uzbek custom, this residence has a blank wall facing the street. The wall is continued as an adobe fence ("duval"). The entry to the yard from the narrow street is through a small door in the fence. The yard of the property ("khauli") now also contains the outbuildings of three related families. To the right of the entry door from the street is Zukhra's house, in which she lives with her eldest son. This house has two dwelling rooms, behind which there are out-buildings, one used as a washroom, the other for household purposes and as a store-room. The entries to the dwelling rooms are from the interior yard. The ceiling is of the ancient type: above the beams are thin rounded slabs ("vasa") with the protruding sides facing downward. The floor is of burnt brick. There

are six recesses in the first room, which is occupied by Zukhra and her daughter. Two large open recesses ("takhman") and one small one ("tokcha") have been provided in the wall opposite the entry. The large recesses are used to store colored quilts ("korpe") and pillows ("iastyk"). There are books and kitchenware in the tokcha. There are three small recesses for various miscellaneous household items on the wall to the right of the entry. Thus, the room furnishings are simple, in the national style. There is no furniture; instead there are rugs and recesses. The floor is covered with woven bast and, on top of it, a woven cotton pile-less rug ("alocha"). Members of the family who engage in housework spend a good part of their time in that room.

One goes from the first room to the second, which is the residence of Zukhra's son and his wife. Here, several recesses in the walls have been converted into wall closets with glass doors. One of them contains a heap of quilts and cushions, another contains dresses and books; two contain dishes and books. In the hall opposite the door there are two large recesses rising from floor level. One contains a bureau, the other a chest; quilts and cushions are piled on top of them. Dress racks are nailed to the wall to the right of the entry, and a radio loudspeaker hangs here as well. A large part of the floor is covered with two rugs. The house has electric lighting.

The windows of the second room open onto an open supa, with a pile-less rug on the floor. The house of Zukhra's brother-in-law is on the other side of the supa. It has the usual floor plan of an Uzbek house and consists of a large summer room ("aivan") and a dwelling room ("ui").

On the other side of the yard, to the left of the entry door in the fence from the street, is the summer kitchen, "ashkon." Here there is a large hearth with two openings for pots ("kazan") in which food is prepared. Some distance away is the toilet ("khalakhona") and a granary for the cow ("malakhona"). The house of Zukhra's younger son, consisting of two rooms, abuts on the granary wall. A door opens from the interior yard to the first room, an antechamber (dakhliz), from which one turns to the right into the dwelling room, ui. The dakhliz is divided in half by a curtain called a chimyldyk. On the other side of the curtain, in the wall opposite the door, is a large recess where dishes are stored. Here there is also a kerosene or gas-burning stove for cooking. Two windows from the dwelling room open onto the yard. There are recesses in all the walls. One contains a mirror and ewer, a second has been rebuilt as a wall cupboard in which kitchenware is placed on shelves, the third contains a radio, and the others also contain kitchenware and various other household items, as well as native chests, quilts and cushions. To the left of the door is a clothes rack for dresses and a bed with embroidered covers. Closer to the rear wall of the room is a metal child's bed. The floor of the first room is earthen and that of the second is wooden and covered with a rug. The house is electrically lighted. Sandali heating braziers are placed in the dwelling rooms in the winter.

The small yard of this property is exceedingly clean and is sprinkled each morning and evening from the irrigation aryk going through the yard. The edges of the aryk are planted with green bushes and flowers. A grapevine grows in front of Zukhra's house and an arbor, covered at the top and sides with the vine branches, has been built there. Three cages containing quail hang in the arbor. A bush and a tree have also been planted in front of the ashkhona.*

The properties of a number of workers of the Strommashina Works in Andizhan also provide examples of the old Uzbek type of dwelling. This is true of diesel-operator Abdunabi Nishanov, founders Shirabeddin Shamseddinov and Djurabai Rakhmanov, Ibragim Igamberdyev, and others. These old houses have a number of distinctive features characteristic of dwellings in the Fergana Valley, but they have been partially rebuilt so as to render them more convenient. Abdunabi Nishanov's house is in a fenced-in yard. The entry from the narrow street is through a small door. The house is old and belonged to his grandfather. It consists of an aivan (a raised porch in the front of the house), an entry-hall (dakhliz) and a dwelling room (ui). The ceiling of the room is of the old type, decoratively painted. The floor is earthen, packed down solid, and the walls are

plastered and whitewashed. Household furnishings and kitchenware are stored in the dakhliz, where there is also a cooking oven. Two large windows open from the room onto the porch.

In the wall opposite the entry are two large recesses — "mikhrab." (4) A painted Uzbek low wardrobe ("djavan") stands in one, and a chest ("sandyk"), on top of which quilts and cushions are piled, is in the other. Dishes are stored in a recess in a wall opposite the windows. The place of honor (tor), piled with rugs, is ready on the floor near the rear wall. The very small yard contains a grapevine, a few rosebushes and flowers.*

On the property of Njurabai Rakhmanov, an irrigation aryk flows through the small yard which one enters from the street. A grapevine and flowers are planted in the yard. The dwelling also consists of a summer sleeping-porch (aivan), an ante-chamber (dakhliz), and a dwelling room (ui). A very small chest ("kuty") stands in one of the wall recesses. On top of it is a phonograph, and in another recess there is a low Uzbek wardrobe ("djavan") containing various soft goods. Dishes and trays are found in the other recesses. To the left of the door is a fireplace.* This form of heating arrangement is characteristic of Fergana Oblast and is not encountered in Tashkent.

In winter many of the houses are heated with sandali. Illumination everywhere is by electricity. The planning of the houses, the furnishings and arrangement of persons living in the old Shamseddinov, Igamberdyev and other houses is analogous to that described above.*

It may be concluded from the detailed descriptions offered here that, despite the fact that the Uzbek workers, particularly those at the Strommashina plant, have a considerable number of old-type housing properties, their homes are gradually being modernized both by the remodeling of various architectural features and by the introduction of new Russian urban furniture and modern houseware, easing and improving the home conditions of the workers. The same process may be observed in the collective farm villages ("kishlak"), but it is naturally more intensive in urban conditions. An ever-increasing number of Uzbek workers are tearing down the old houses and building new ones of the type described above. As already observed, heating in the wintertime, particularly in the older houses, is with the aid of the traditional sandali. This is completely absent in modern homes. This unsatisfactory form of heating is gradually disappearing from the mode of life of the workers. In new houses, which the owners regard as incomplete, it is considered a temporary device. Space is provided, when these homes are planned, for a stove to be installed at a later date. In many workers' homes one finds sandali alongside of iron stoves and ranges. They are retained more as a matter of habit and are a gradually disappearing tradition.

At the same time, it should be noted that workers make more extensive use than do collective farmers of factory-made furniture: beds, chests, tables and chairs, and the universal use of factory-made kitchenware. Although the tandyr is retained for cooking the native flat cakes, as is the Uzbek hearth with its pot for cooking, the use of the range, the kerosene or kerosene-and-gas stove and, particularly, the electric hot plate and electric iron have become standard features in workers' families. Electric lighting is customary. Radio loudspeakers, radios and phonographs are quite common. Simultaneously with the introduction of new elements of urban culture into the lives of the workers, the Soviet period has made possible, as a consequence of the rise in the workers' living standards, decoration of dwellings in accordance with national tastes and rising standards. In all houses and apartments, without exception, the furnishing is decorative and in the national taste. Each home has many quilted chintz, satin and silk blankets, and a variety of dishes. These objects are an indication of the prosperity of the homeowner and are not only used by members of the family, but are essential when receiving guests. Each house has its embroidered bed covers ("suzani"), pile-less rugs, pile rugs, and sheep's-wool felts used to cover floors. Everywhere one encounters ornamented chests with heaps of quilts piled atop them, low native cupboards, low "khantakhta" tables, etc.

The home arrangement of today's Uzbek work-

ers clearly demonstrates the fundamental changes that have occurred during the Soviet years: they live in new housing conditions and are in a position to acquire new, modern furniture. They have learned to use it. They have adopted Russian culture to a considerable degree, but also retain the ethnic coloration of their way of life.

Until the October Revolution, the cut of workers' clothing did not differ from that of the rural population. The economic position of the worker determined both the quality and the quantity of clothing he and members of his family possessed. Clothing was sewn from hand-made cotton or cheap factory goods. It consisted of a single set, often incomplete.

During the Soviet years, major changes have taken place in the costumes of the entire population of the republic. A rise in prosperity has increased purchasing power, and the development of the domestic trade has made it possible to satisfy the rising demands of the population. Contact with the Russian population on the job and as neighbors has had the consequence that, among workers and members of their families, one sees, alongside of retention of ethnic items of clothing, considerable popularity of the Russian urban type of costume.

The process of introduction of urban costumes is particularly noticeable among the men. The overwhelming majority of Uzbek workers at the enterprises studied wear modern urban costume. However, in warm weather a great many wear black "tupi" skull-caps with white thread ornamentation in the form of a stylized almond or pepper; these skull-caps are also called "chusti" (i.e., because they have spread from Chust Village). Elderly workers often wear smooth black skull-caps, over which they wear hats with ear flaps in the winter. Younger workers wear the usual type of hats, traveling-peaked caps, or caps in the winter. Elderly workers shave their heads bare. Among the youth, many do not shave their heads, but have their hair cut in barber shops.

Among a number of workers of the older generation, particularly at the Strommashina Works in Andizhan, clothing of the national cut is still often encountered: the Uzbek kuinak blouse, the ishtan balloon trousers, the chapon robe of dark cotton fabric, quilted with wadding, and often belted with a twisted cotton or silk embroidered kerchief called the kars. The headgear is the skull-cap around which a colored kerchief is wound in winter. However, mixed costume is very often found. The traditional national clothing is combined with modern Russian urban clothing — a jacket or tee-shirt, or modern trousers, tucked into factory-made boots, etc. As an example, the male urban suit is often belted not with a belt but with a kerchief; an Uzbek robe may be worn over a suit; a skull-cap on the head, etc.

The male national costume is kept for weddings. By custom, the bride-to-be makes a gift of a colored silk robe, a skull-cap, and an embroidered silk belt-kerchief to her future husband.*

Some workers go to the plant in the robe, but remove it when they get there. The robe is still very popular among the workers as a convenient garment around the house.

In women's and children's clothing, what is new, as is the case with men, is the fact that the quantity of clothing owned has increased and the quality of the material of which it is made has improved. The textile and light industries of the republic satisfy the needs of the working population for cotton, woolens and silk fabrics, footwear and other objects of clothing. The Tashkent Integrated Textile Mills alone annually processes millions of yards of a great variety of fabrics of all colors. The working population makes great use of silk fabrics processed by local industrial cooperatives for women's dresses and for blankets. There is great demand for women's and children's footwear, including lacquered footwear made by shoemakers' cooperatives.

In the workers' families, local costumes with traditional identifying details of cut and color pattern are retained to a greater degree among the women and children. Dresses and underclothes in the national fashion are sewn at home from purchased fabrics on sewing machines. Dresses are often ordered from dressmakers. In addition, the purchase of ready-to-wear dresses in the Uzbek style (silk, satin, and cotton prints) is very widespread. The clothing industry in Uzbekistan manufactures these things with due consideration of the national tastes of the consumer.

The women's national costume includes a wide-yoked dress, the kuinak, with a turned-down collar, bloomers worn as underdrawers cut for ample motion (they reach to the ankles), and a vest, usually of black material, frequently velvet. Young women and girls wear dresses in bright colors, while the middle-aged and aged wear dark ones. The headgear of girls and young women is a quadrangular skull-cap, in bright colors and embroidered, or silk or cotton printed head-kerchiefs folded to triangular shape and knotted in back. The hair is usually combed straight and braided into two braids hanging in the back. Young women wrap their braids around their head. The footwear consists of kid and, for holidays, lacquered slippers and boots with low heels, made by local shoemakers' cooperatives. They are frequently ornamented with stitching in bright threads.

The national costume is preserved as the wedding gown.

As in the past, various small ornaments are very popular: rings, beads, bracelets, and earrings, partly of old fashioned local make and partly new, store-bought.

However, the national costumes of women, like that of the men, is today supplemented by urban clothing. Needless to say, working women and workers' wives have long since abandoned the parandja horsehair veil. Outerwear in winter and for going out in summer consists of purchased spring and winter coats with fur collars, as well as velvet coats. The house garment worn for work at home is a padded jacket. In winter the head is wrapped in a woolen or fur kerchief, the ends of which are tucked into the dress or tied in back.

Women's clothes often include a double-breasted jacket made of black material — satin, wool and especially velvet. The Uzbek-type undertrousers are gradually going out of use, being replaced by modern underwear and socks. Many women and working girls, as well as many workers' wives, wear bought clothes of the general urban type: silk, wool or rayon dresses, silk or batiste blouses, woolen skirts, knit jackets, suits, coats, stockings, high-heeled shoes, rubber overshoes, etc.*

The youth studying in the schools and colleges have played a major role in the change in dress. Most schoolchildren wear the pupils' uniforms or urban clothing, sometimes in combination with items of the national costume. Students wear urban clothes as a general rule, but the girls favor bright dresses, particularly the "shoiy-kuinak," made of silk in specifically Central Asian patterns. Young boys and girls normally wear a skull-cap.

The rise in living standards has also manifested itself in the diet of the working population. The variety of dishes known to the Uzbeks has become available to all workers both in urban restaurants and at home. The diet regularly includes meat, dairy and vegetable products bought in stores and at bazaars. Some workers supplement their table with fruits and vegetables from their own garden and orchards. Some workers, living in their own homes, have cows; some raise rams for meat.

Shopping for food is done by both the women and the men. On Sunday many married couples go out to shop together. In many workers' families the men stop in for food or goodies for their children on the way home from work. Some purchase flat native cakes and bread for their families at the factory restaurant or tea-house. Virtually every family possessing a tandyr will bake fresh flat cakes at home when needed, although the working population also makes wide use of bread baked Russian style.

Usually, the worker eats at home in the morning and evening with members of his family. The general custom is for the family to have three meals a day. Hot food is made for the evening, when the head of the family is expected home. In daytime, during the lunch break, the workers make use of the factory cafeteria or tea-house where they drink tea and eat some hot dish. To satisfy the national tastes of the Uzbek workers, the cafeterias and the tea-houses include on their menus plov (pilaf), shurpa, lagman, dumplings and other dishes in the Uzbek diet. At home, various types of dishes are also prepared: shurpa soups, mosh-khurda gruels, mosh-kichiri rice mush with butter and milk; plov, a main dish of

stewed meat and potatoes with onions and other vegetables; pirozhki [meat-turnovers] with meat and onions (samsa); chikvara dumplings, noodles with meat (lagman), and various items potted in butter, flat cakes, etc. With tea they eat sweets, sugar, candies, dried fruit. During the summer they eat fresh fruits, watermelons and other melons.

The Uzbeks eat at low tables — khantakhta — covered by pile-less or regular rugs and a tablecloth [dastarkhan]. If there is a sandali, a dastarkhan is placed on it in the winter, and all the members of the family seat themselves round it. If Russians come, they are offered food at an ordinary table, and everyone sits on chairs. Some families have stools around the table, and special bright quilted cushions are placed on top of the stools.*

We directed our major attention to determining the nature of the changes that have occurred in the material culture and household circumstances of the Uzbek workers, but we simultaneously collected some data on family life. Needless to say, these mere fragments, while of considerable interest, are inadequate for any synthesis of the fundamental changes that have occurred in marriage and family relationships among the working-class elements of the Uzbek population in the Soviet years. Soviet legislation has provided equality for women with men, and has repealed, in Uzbekistan as well as in other republics of the union, the demeaning and harmful customs of the bride-money payment, of child-marriage, etc. These measures, along with the reorganization of the entire lives of the workers, have introduced major changes into family relationships and into family life. They have done away with the causes that have a negative effect upon family relationships, increase the material difficulties faced by workers' families and bring discord into family life.

However, the change in living customs and family relationships has been gradual; the remaining vestiges still have vitality and there are some families in which old customs still remain. During the first decade after the Revolution, weddings in workers' families took place without payment of bride-money, but still entirely in accord with the old traditions characteristic of peasant and craft backgrounds. Very early marriages were still the general rule in the 1930s. Thus, when Lutfeddin Tadjhiev's father died in 1930, his mother, who was left with small children, insisted upon the marriage of her eldest son, Lutfeddin, when he was 16 years of age, and found him a 14-year-old bride. No bride-money was paid. The bride (kelin) brought a small trousseau (bisot), including bedclothes and dresses.

Before the Revolution, the payment of bride-money was a great burden upon working-class families when their sons were married. In order to avoid payment of bride-money and excessive wedding costs, it was common among workers, as in the villages, to attempt to marry a boy to a relative, usually a female first cousin. After the Revolution, this custom continued for a while. Thus, in 1932, at the demand of his parents, 24-year-old Makhmud Akhmedov married his amak-bacha — the daughter of his father's first cousin, 17-year-old Tadji.* In 1928, 18-year-old Abdurashid Kazakpaev also married his amak-bacha, 15-year-old Ogul'-Bibi,* daughter of his paternal uncle, also at his parents' demand. The wedding ceremony followed the general local custom; the marriage was not registered in the ZAGS [vital statistics office]. Workers of the older generation sometimes registered their marriage legally at the ZAGS when they were 40 years old or older, for various practical reasons.*

Despite the fact that the tradition of marriage to a relative is still observed in some cases, marriage based on the personal desire of the participants has become predominant among workers. The boy and girl generally get to know each other before they are married, which was not the case in the past, when the custom of seclusion of women was dominant. Thus, Akbarali Khaidarov, a worker of the Strommashina Works, married Sabira-Khon in 1950. She was the daughter of his kola, the younger sister of his maternal grandmother. However, although this marriage was between relatives, it was at the desire of the boy and girl themselves. They had known each other previously, and when they decided to get married, it was with the full approval of their parents and the marriage was registered at the

ZAGS. Another worker, Sadyk Isaev, married the daughter of his mother's sister in 1934, under the old custom. After his wife died, he married again in 1952. He had become acquainted with a girl working as a weaver in a cooperative and they agreed to get married. Through his mother, Sadyk obtained the girl's mother's approval of the marriage, and the marriage was recorded at the ZAGS.*

Workers who marry girls from artisan or collective farm families, particularly those in which elderly members are alive and traditional customs are observed, have a great positive influence toward eliminating old relationships in family life and changing the status of the woman in the family, her way of life, and behavior. In 1949 a worker of the Strommashina Works, Khadji Tadjiev, a Communist Party member, decided to get married. His wife-to-be, daughter of a craftsman of Andizhan, in whose family the patriarchal traditions were observed, had left school after finishing sixth grade, did not work at a job and lived with her parents. Obedient to their will, the girl put on the veil when she left the house. Tadjiev became acquainted with her when he visited his brother, a neighbor of the girl's family. They became fond of each other, agreed to get married, and asked the girl's parents' permission. The parents gave their agreement to the marriage and to a wedding without observance of the old customs. The young couple first recorded their marriage at the ZAGS and then arranged a wedding feast, tui, at which the new young bride appeared without her veil. After marrying Tadjiev, this young woman never wore a veil again.*

In accord with present-day viewpoints, young Uzbek workers and Uzbek girls persistently reject attempts of parents to influence them to a marriage they themselves do not wish to make. In cases where parents oppose their will, they attempt to overcome the backward views of the latter. Shakhashim Sh., a worker of the locomotive and rolling-stock repair works, upon seeing the girl, Napiza, who appealed to him, went to her mother, told the latter who he was, where he worked and lived, and asked for permission to get to know the girl better. Napiza, after meeting Shakhashim several times, told her mother that he appealed to her and she would like to marry him. But the mother refused, because she had already promised to give Napiza in marriage to a relative. Napiza strongly protested and said that she would marry no one but Shakhashim. Shakhashim, too persistently asked the mother for permission. Finally, yielding to persuasion and out of sympathy for her daughter, the mother gave her permission for this marriage.*

In a case in which parents absolutely refuse to give their agreement to their daughter's marriage to the man she has chosen, the young people take matters into their own hands and defend their rights, relying on Soviet law. This was the situation in which Shukur Kh., a worker of the Strommashina Plant, found himself. On a collective farm, he became familiar with a girl working as secretary of a village soviet and living with her parents. When they got to know each other better, the young people decided to get married and asked the girl's parents' permission. The latter refused, stating firmly that they would not give their daughter in marriage to a worker in Andizhan. Then, with the girl's agreement, Shukur "stole" her. They went to the city without the parents' knowledge and got married, recording their marriage in the ZAGS. The parents guessed that the daughter had left with Shukur. The father left for town to take his daughter home. When Shukur's friends told him that the father had come, he asked a police deputy to come. The latter explained to the young woman's father that he had no right to take the girl, inasmuch as she was adult and had, of her own free will, become the wife of the man she had chosen. The father had no choice but to return home alone. Only after three months had passed did the parents agree to recognize her marriage to Shukur. However, when the young people decided to celebrate their marriage with a tui wedding feast, no one came from the wife's side. This was the manner in which the parents expressed their dissatisfaction with the failure of the young to subordinate themselves to their will.*

Working youth — young boys and girls, working together, and meeting at community centers,

at movies, meetings, etc. — have greater chances for personal socializing and for getting to know each other. As a consequence, many vestiges and conventions of the old way of life are rapidly uprooted.

The attitude toward marriage between Uzbeks and people of other nationalities has also changed. A fair number of Uzbek workers are married to Tatar and Russian women.

The foundations of contemporary marriage in Uzbekistan are the legal equality of parties, mutual respect for each other, and personal affection.

The wedding feast itself (tui) often follows the traditional customs accepted in the given locality. Thus, for example, when one of the workers, Umar I., whose elderly parents were still alive, was married, he decided not to violate the traditional procedure of the wedding tui. However, Umar invited to the tui not only his relatives and those of his bride, but his Uzbek and Russian comrades at work. The dastarkhany were spread on the rugs in the courtyard, while tables were set with food and drink, for the Russian guests. His fellow workers brought presents and wine. The guests celebrated until evening, when the bridegroom brought his bride to the house. In accordance with the old custom, she was wearing the veil. Umar, who always wore urban clothing, was now wearing the costume normally presented by the bride to the bridegroom. He had on a silken robe belted with a kerchief, and a skull-cap. Upon meeting his bride, he took her by the hand and took her through a small fire set before the entrance to the yard and into the room prepared for the young people, decorated with rugs and embroidery. Then the guests were invited into this room. In accordance with established custom, the guests were treated to boiled mutton and to presents prepared for this purpose in advance (dresses, skull-caps, etc.). At the close of the tui, each was given a flat cake wrapped in a kerchief; at this point the guests departed.*

Today, the most important factor in the wedding ceremony is the feast, which may take place either in the bride's or bridegroom's house. Thus, the contemporary wedding tui is essentially merely an evening with supper at which everyone makes merry to mark the happy event in the young people's lives. The feast arranged by Shukur, to whom we have referred, was attended by the relatives of the groom, his comrades at work, and his neighbors. The bride, wearing the parandja, was in a circle of elderly women seated apart. After a while the bridegroom's guests asked him to bring the bride to them. She and Shukur's mother approached the guests, sat among them, whereupon the bride removed the veil and remained with the guests to the end of the evening.*

The birth of a child is marked solemnly and with celebration. People prepare for the arrival of guests not only with foodstuffs, but very carefully clean the house, decorating the walls with rugs and embroideries.

The old Muslim custom of sunnet (circumcision of boys) is gradually disappearing. True, the older generations still seek to have this custom observed. In some families, circumcision is arranged by the women in secrecy from their husbands, or else the husbands make believe that they are unaware of what is happening. Nevertheless, sunnet is gradually going out of use.

The changes in the workers' family lives are particularly pronounced with respect to the position that the woman has come to occupy in the life of the worker today. In Uzbekistan, where the seclusion of women in the past took on particularly warped forms, especially among the urban population, women now occupy a position of equality with men. She is the boss at home and decides family matters jointly with her husband. The family is a unified and friendly unit welded by common interests.

The new relationships in the family of Uzbek workers are particularly clearly reflected in the use of the dwelling rooms of the house or apartment. In our study of home conditions, we paid attention to a number of interesting facts testifying to the fundamental change in the relationship between members of the family as compared to old patriarchal relationships. Usually, in families where there are grown children, the husband, his wife and young children occupy one room, while the grown children, working or studying, occupy the second. The second room

may often be reserved for a married son, who later builds a house for his own family, as we witnessed earlier in the cases of Shukurali Mirzaliev and Zukhra Abdullaeva.*

We may also cite the example of the family of Saidvali Akbarov, consisting of five persons. In the Akbarov home, all the members of the family gather regularly for breakfast, lunch and dinner. This same room serves as the sleeping room for the parents and the youngest daughter, who studies in a school where instruction is in Russian. The two grown sons live in a second room.* In the family of Umar Pulatov, the grown daughter, a student, studies and sleeps in a room of her own. All other members of the family live in two other rooms.*

The Soviet worker's family is characterized by the effort to educate the children. All the children go to school; many, both boys and girls, have secondary and higher educations. In the home, as we have just seen, all the conditions necessary for study are established. They have their study corner, sometimes a separate room. The parents try to dress them as well as possible, buy them school uniforms, purchase books and other study aids. Many parents persistently advise their children to continue education in higher institutions.* Thus, for example, in the family of Abdurashid Kazakpaev, a worker in the locomotive and rolling stock repair plant, the daughter graduated from the seven-year Russian-language school and then entered technical secondary school, while the son, by decision of the family, aimed for entrance to a higher institution after completing the ten-year school.*

In the family of Nurutdin Mukhammedov, a worker of the Strommashina Works, his older son, at the time we knew this family in 1951, was studying at a teacher training institute, the second son was in the 7th grade, the daughter in the 6th grade of an Uzbek-language school, and a third son in 3rd grade in a class in which Russian was the language of instruction.* Saidvali Akbarov gave all possible support to his son's desire to get a higher education. The same is true for other workers who have children studying in secondary schools.

One observes in workers' families an effort to

have their children educated in the Russian language. Sometimes parents enroll their children in Russian-language schools. Nor is it uncommon for parents to transfer children from the elementary grades of Uzbek to Russian-language schools. A considerable number of such examples may be cited. We have already observed that Khamid Azizov, a worker of the Strommashina Works, had graduated from a Russian-language secondary school.* Saidvali Akbarov transferred his daughter Railia from an Uzbek-language to a Russian-language school after the 1st grade.* Nasyr Azizov did the same with respect to his son.* The daughter of Abdurashid Kazakpaev completed seven grades in the Russian-language school; the children of the textile worker Pulat Babadjanov are studying in a Russian-language school, etc.* Here we see manifested the desire to strengthen ties and contact with Russians and an understanding of the fact that knowledge of the Russian language enlarges the general horizons of young people and permits them to make broader use of all the achievements of culture and science. It opens the door to study in higher institutions not only in one's own republic, but to those in other cities of the Soviet Union. The friendly relationships with the Russian population are characterized by the following very widespread phenomenon. Children and young workers, in addition to the Uzbek name in their passport, actually acquire in daily life similar-sounding Russian names that are used at home by parents and other members of the family and at work in their relations with each other. Thus, in the Akbarov family, the daughter Railia is called Raia, in Umar Pulatov's family the four-year-old son Kamildjan is called Mitia, the young worker Shakhashim Shakasimov is called Zhora by his friends, the textile worker Zul'fia Radjabova is called Zoya, etc.*

As they obtain education or begin to hold jobs, young people organize their lives in the family in accordance with their own desires and cultural needs, in which they usually find support on the part of their parents.

The presence of schoolchildren and students at technical secondary schools and higher educational institutions in all families is a factor playing a vast role in transforming the mode of life and raising the level of culture of the workers. They bring new, modern views of life into the family, struggle with prejudices, and introduce sanitary and hygienic habits into the family.

The effectuation by the Communist Party and the Soviet government of socialist construction in Uzbekistan on an enormous scale has served as the basis for fundamental reorganization of the lives of the Uzbek people and, as a consequence of this reorganization, for establishment of a new, advanced class — the working class. The Uzbek worker, male or female, is a Soviet worker. And like all workers of the republic and of the entire Soviet Union, regardless of nationality or sex, he works under job and social conditions equal for all Soviet workers, constantly engages in improvement in his skill, his knowledge of technology, and his culture, both technical and general.

The lives of these workers are being lived, on the one hand, under the conditions of socialist and highly organized production, and on the other hand, under new and modern conditions of residence and mode of life. Together, these are the factors which, in the final analysis, determine the nature and content both of the social and family lives of the workers and of the transformation of their culture and life on new socialist principles.

Editor's Notes

a) Asterisks represent references to the author's manuscript field notes, which have been omitted.

b) Dekhkan: a peasant in prerevolutionary Central Asia holding land under feudal conditions.

c) FZO and FZU both represent various forms of schools offering elementary, secondary and technical education in the factory.

d) The minimum knowledge necessary for holding a particular job.

e) That is, equipped with a public address system.

Footnotes

1) See, for example, N. N. Cheboksarov, "Etnograficheskoe izuchenie kul'tury i byta moskovskikh rabochikh," SE, 1950, No. 3; V. Iu. Krupianskaia, "Opyt etnograficheskogo izucheniia ural'-
skikh rabochikh vtoroi poloviny XIX veka," SE,
1953, No. 1; S. M. Abramzon, "Proshloe i nastoiashchee kirgizskikh shakhterov Kyzyl-Kiia," SE,
1954, No. 4; A. G. Trofimova, "Bakinskie rabo-
chie-neftianiki (opyt etnograficheskogo izucheniia
Ordjonikidzevskogo raiona g. Baku)," manuscript
of Candidate's dissertation, Moscow, 1954, Archives of Institute of Ethnography, USSR Academy
of Sciences.

2) After the annexation of Central Asia to Russia there grew up, beside the existing cities,
new parts of the city settled by Russians, which
received the name of "new" cities. The territory
of the original city began to be called the "old"
city.

3) V. I. Lenin, Soch., Vol. 19, p. 42.

4) The term mikhrab is characteristic of
Fergana. It is employed to denote the wide recesses in the west-facing wall. The term takh-
mon is employed both in Fergana and Tashkent
for large recesses in the side walls.

* * *

Sovetskaia etnografiia, 1962, No. 5

A. Daniliauskas

A CONTRIBUTION TO THE STUDY OF THE CULTURE AND MODE OF LIFE

OF LITHUANIAN WORKERS

(Based on Data from the Niamunas Factory in Rokish Raion)

One of the objects of investigation by expeditions of the ethnographic sector of the Lithuanian Academy of Sciences' Institute of History in the summer of 1961 was the Niamunas Woolen Mill. It is in the settlement of Iuodupe in the northeast of the republic, at the Latvian border, and is an industrial enterprise in a rural locality remote from other industrial centers.

The Niamunas Mill was founded in 1907 when a steam boiler, carding equipment, spinning machines, and machinery for dyeing and finishing fabrics were installed adjacent to a water mill. Some time later looms were installed. In 1914 thirty workers were employed at this factory, which belonged to a local miller and businessman. These workers were engaged primarily in combing and spinning wool for the local peasantry, and in dyeing and finishing home-woven fabric.

During the years of the bourgeois regime in Lithuania, the weaving of imported raw material was introduced into Iuodupe. In 1939 the factory had only 281 regular workers. When the German fascist troops retreated in 1944, it was half destroyed. In the postwar period the Niamunas Mill has been rebuilt and expanded, with an increase in the number of workers. In the summer of 1961 it employed 1,041 people. The workers' settlement of Iuodupe arose near the factory.

The workers employed at the mill are chiefly local people — former peasants and the children of peasants of nearby villages. People from other raions of the republic are 18.2% of the total; those from other republics constitute 2.2% of the total number of workers and office personnel. Through other members of the family 11.9% of the workers are still associated with agriculture. Of the remaining families, 24.7% have domestic livestock (cows, pigs); 51.7% have truck gardens (ranging from .06 to .15 hectare).

By ethnic composition, 85% of the plant's workers are Lithuanians and 14% are old Russian settlers in this area. Latvians, Belorussians and Germans total only 1%. Women constitute 52.5% of the employees. The age of the majority of workers (56%) is between 25 and 40.

There are few workers with high seniority or of working class parentage. Persons who have worked here 20 years or more are 7% of the total; 32.6% have worked here for five to ten years. More than one-third of the total number of workers and office personnel has less than five years of industrial experience. This is a general picture of the subject of our investigation.

The object we chose to investigate enables us to deal with the following topics:

a) establishment of a working class from a peasant environment in capitalist and socialist societies; b) interaction of urban culture and way of life with the traditional peasant culture and way of life in capitalist and socialist societies; c) mutual influence of two (or even several) nationalities in a process of joint life and labor; d) establishment of characteristics of communist society in a working class environment that retains substantial ties to agriculture.

The survey of the Niamunas Mill, which lasted a total of five weeks, was one of the first efforts to study the culture and way of life of workers in the Lithuanian SSR. The method of investigation was based on techniques employed in the study of the culture and life of collective farmers. We also took into consideration similar researches by ethnographers of the RSFSR and the Ukraine.

What proved to be most laborious was filling out the family questionnaires developed by the ethnographic sector of the Lithuanian Academy's Institute of History, which was intended to obtain data on the work, mode of life and culture of the workers and office personnel of the Niamunas Mill. The questionnaire survey covered 721 workers' families. In addition, questions were put to individual workers in the factory, residents of the community, and pensioners (the information provided by the latter constitutes 58% of the total quantity of records obtained): personal observations were also recorded. Photographs were taken of typical architectural structures and interiors, and a number of drawings of furniture made. In the plant records we familiarized ourselves with a small number of documents, with respect to this mill, remaining from the days of bourgeois Lithuania. In view of the fact that we

had not previously investigated this mill, the survey party's study in the summer of 1961 was directed merely toward a general preliminary familiarization with the present and past of our subjects, to be subjected to subsequent study by a resident field party.

After the founding of the Niamunas Mill, the local peasantry no longer had to carry out certain operations essential in the home manufacture of woolens (combing, spinning, dyeing, and finishing the fabric).

During the initial period of the mill's existence, when it belonged to miller Oscar Trei, whose father was a volost' clerk, the workers had the status of farm laborers and had what amounted to an unlimited working day. They were used for agricultural work on land rented by this same Trei. The system of payment included meals, a bed, and dwelling space provided by the boss. The boss refused to hire married workers. The only exception he made was for married foremen and highly skilled workers indispensable to the mill. Trei gave them land for a truck garden, and pasture rights and hay for their cows.

At the same time, Trei obviously attempted to divide the workers by creating a peculiar kind of "labor aristocracy." For example, the meals provided by the boss were divided into three "tables." The first was set for the boss himself and his foreign foreman (Germans and Czechs), the second for skilled workers, and the third for unskilled workers, apprentices, servants, and farm laborers. A considerable difference in the way of life between the foremen and rank-and-file workers was preserved for a long time.

In 1933 Trei was pushed out by more enterprising businessmen. The position of the workers of Iuodupe was distinctive in that many of them held from five to twenty-five hectares of land and combined factory work with operation of their own farms. This naturally affected their way of life and thinking. In this respect one may observe certain analogies to the position of the proletariat of the old mills in the Urals at the beginning of the 20th century: the influence of landownership upon the type of home, the clothing of the workers, their wages, and the retarded development of class struggle. (1) Naturally, in the proletariat of Iuodupe, which came into being under conditions of mature capitalism, the archaic characteristics were less pronounced.

In general, the data on changes in the mode of life and culture related to the establishment of the Iuodupe proletariat provide a picture similar to that observed by Lenin in his writings on the development of Russian capitalism (of course, there are certain local peculiarities).

With respect to the mutual influence of the capitalist town and the countryside in the process of establishment of the proletariat, criticism must be directed against the views on this matter by personnel of the Chamber of Agriculture of capitalist Lithuania. Their idealization of the old rural culture, the general talk of the corruption of tastes under the influence of city and factory production, their attempts to preserve household industry as something to fall back on in the small private enterprise (2) — all had no foundation in reality.

The development of capitalist relationships was accompanied, as data from Iuodupe confirmed, by the breakdown of the traditional rural way of life. While evaluating this phenomenon as inevitable and progressive, it must be observed that it had a dual influence in the field of culture and mode of life. On the one hand, progressive achievements of science and urban culture and advanced revolutionary ideas gradually spread into the countryside. On the other hand, the peasantry was influenced by the philistine petty bourgeois environment. As a consequence, achievements created by many centuries of folk experience disappeared: folklore and folk decorative weaving decayed; folk games, dances and the like disappeared.

One task facing ethnographers is that of making a clear-cut distinction between the influence of urban culture and that of the petty bourgeois environment upon the peasantry.

The summer 1961 field study of the Niamunas Mill provided a certain amount of data on change in customs in Lithuania under the dominance of the bourgeoisie (weddings, etc.), on the relationships between mill workers and peasants of adjacent villages, and on the gradual growth in class consciousness and the development of class struggle by the local working people.

The experience of Soviet ethnographers who have investigated similar objects demonstrates that a study of the culture and mode of life of the workers must be closely interwoven with a study of the peasantry of the same period, inasmuch as the latter often constituted the basis out of which a local working class developed.

* * *

A large part of the material collected in 1961 describes the current position of the Niamunas Mill workers. In studying the questionnaire data, we discovered phenomena which, on the one hand, confirmed the general laws of development of society and, on the other, demonstrated certain local peculiarities in these processes.

The statistical data we collected revealed a very rapid rise in the workers' demands and prosperity. A rather high family budget was found. The families of workers and office personnel with incomes of more than 30 rubles per member per month comprise 75% of the total.

Moreover, small families are dominant in Iuodupe, that is, families of up to four members, plus single workers. In the majority of workers' families (71.9%), consisting of mother, father and their under-age children, the mother as well as the father holds a job in the mill.

A considerable rise in the level of general education of the workers was observed. Among young workers and office personnel born after 1936, 33.3% have secondary educations, while of those born prior to 1936 only 6.7% do. Among those taken on in 1961, people with secondary educations comprise 43.9%.

The overall data on the level of education of workers and office personnel in the Niamunas Mill are as follows: the proportion of people who had taught themselves to read and write is 2.5%, that of people who did not finish elementary school is 6.7%; people with elementary school education number 55.5%, those with incomplete secondary education number 20.6%, those with secondary education number 13.6%, and those with higher or incomplete higher education are 1.1%.

Among women working in the mill, 16.7% have

secondary education and 21.6% have incomplete secondary education; among men the corresponding figures are 9 and 19%. Among secondary school graduates born between 1936 and 1943 taken on by the Niamunas Mill, 82.9% are girls (we note that girls made up 72% of the secondary school graduates in Iuodupe in 1961).

However, the percentage of women lacking elementary education is higher than the corresponding figure for men (10.2% as against 8%). There is only one woman among the ten individuals who have higher or incomplete higher education. This is explained by the fact that until World War I most girls in Lithuania did not receive even elementary education. Men also outnumber women among those who obtained secondary education during the years of the bourgeois regime in Lithuania.

A definite interrelationship may be seen between wages and level of education among both men and women working at the Niamunas Mill. Among women with secondary education, 28.2% have wages of over 80 rubles a month; 17.3% of the women with incomplete secondary education are in that earning category; 17.7% of those with elementary education, and 8% of those lacking elementary education. However, there are cases in which earnings are not determined by level of education. For example, the largest percentage of persons earning less than 60 rubles a month is found among women who are secondary school graduates. This is because they lack experience. Among men having elementary education, those earning 80 rubles a month and more are 46.6%, while among those having incomplete secondary school education only 27.3% have such earnings. In this case as well, the explanation is to be found in the relative experience of these workers.

The technical equipment now in use at the Niamunas Mill is adequate to enable workers having the required know-how and skill to achieve relatively high earnings independent of their level of general education. Nevertheless, in 12 comparisons of earnings for working men and women by educational groups, we found in nine cases confirmation of the principle that the higher the education, the higher the earnings; only three cases deviated from this principle.

Upon analysis of the questionnaire data on earnings we note that, in general, the earnings of men employed at the Niamunas Mill are higher than those of the women; 8.3% of the men and 22.1% of the women earn less than 60 rubles a month. On the other hand, 42.5% of the men and 21.4% of the women earn more than 80 rubles. Finally, 14% of the men earn over 100 rubles, and only 2.5% of the women earn as much.

This is explained by the fact that the men are generally engaged in highly skilled operations requiring the use of the technical equipment of the enterprise, or in work requiring great physical strength. The engineering and technical personnel are chiefly men. On the other hand, the women, both in production work and in the administration, do lighter and less skilled work and, consequently, work that is paid at a lower rate. When the men and women do identical work, for example, work at the looms, there is no difference in earning rate and, therefore, none in earnings.

The survey of the Niamunas Mill workers in the summer of 1961 provided rather interesting material on the appearance of a new urban type of culture. This is expressed primarily in the continuing process of abandonment of the old rural way of life. The following are examples from the area of material culture.

As recently as twenty years ago, home weaving met most of the local population needs for fabrics. Young Niamunas working women of peasant families no longer wear home-woven clothing, although 30 to 40% of their bedclothes (sheets, pillowcases, blankets and bedcovers) are of home manufacture. Most of them no longer know how to operate the hand loom and those who can do not do this work. The ability to operate the hand loom quickly and with attractive results is no longer regarded as the sign of a good housewife. Fabrics are now purchased in the stores, except for certain decorative types.

Likewise, traditional home-cooked dishes are disappearing from the diet of the young working women. Eating habits now depend entirely upon factory hours and the operation of the factory cafeteria. In families that have close ties to agriculture, with gardens and domestic livestock,

234

the traditional dishes have remained a greater part of the diet.

The planning of new homes by individual builders in Iuodupe village shows nothing at all in common with the old traditional types of Lithuanian dwelling houses. Only in rare cases does one see provision for a bread-oven, and then only in the simplified form that appeared in Lithuania after World War I.

The interior is changing accordingly. The arrangement of the furniture frequently depends upon the size and features of the dwelling space and upon the dimensions of the furniture. Observations show clearly that modern factory-made furniture and style changes will largely determine future alterations in dwelling interiors in Iuodupe village.

Major changes have taken place in family relationships. All inequality between men and women in the worker's family has disappeared. In certain cases (up to 20%), the earnings of the women doing production work exceed those brought home by their husbands. It is curious that the younger workers who were instructed by the factory administration to fill out our questionnaires often did not fill in the space for "head of family" and merely listed the members of the family: "husband," "wife," "son," etc., without singling out any particular individual. Moreover, one frequently found the names of women or younger members of the family listed first.

The equality of girls and women with men is also manifested in the descriptions of workers' weddings which we have recorded. There were no cases at all of the girl being "given in marriage." She "married." Families are established on the basis of the mutual sentiments of the individuals getting married, regardless of the desires of their parents, and sometimes despite them. No matter how complex family relationships may sometimes be, one may observe with satisfaction that material considerations and calculations play virtually no role whatever in the founding of families among the workers.

There has been a further advance in eliminating harmful survivals of the past. The workers' intellectual demands have risen; there is a steady disappearance of religious prejudices and customs related to religious concepts or social inequality. However, the presence of the vestiges of philistinism referred to earlier is still observed today. For example, along with highly artistic specimens of Lithuanian or Russian folk art, one still sees in workers' homes tasteless bazaar art, embroidery patterns displaying no talent whatever, and banal decorative industrial products.

The esthetic tastes of the former peasants who are now lifetime workers in the Niamunas Mill are currently at a critical stage in which the old traditional standards and tastes are dying off, and new ones have not yet actually been defined.

In socialist society the process of development of folk art and its relationship to urban culture takes on the nature of mutual enrichment. This may be traced in the work of a former weaver of Iuodupe, I. Bitinas, today a People's Artist, whose rugs and decorative fabrics are further developing the traditional folk patterns.

The factory recreation center includes a folk dance group, and the chorus sings traditional songs, among others.

The mutual influence of the urban culture and the traditional folk culture is also expressed in the employment, in the republic's industry, of the best elements of folk art. The products of local folk craftsmen are sold through the raion cooperative. Work of real quality is finding an increasing market in people's homes, and aids in fighting against philistine "esthetics." Interiors in which folk tradition exists in combination with the products of modern industry may be found in Iuodupe in families where cultural standards demand and material circumstances permit the purchase of modern furniture and decorative fabrics manufactured by the enterprises of the republic.

Family and calendar holidays are celebrated with considerable solemnity in Iuodupe. One observes rather marked preservation, and sometimes even a revival, of certain of the more theatrical aspects of the wedding ceremony, in particular those of a carnival and comic nature.

Thus, the custom of matchmaking has disappeared completely, and along with it the real and meaningful functions of the matchmaker. However, the "execution of the matchmaker" is played out at every wedding feast. Someone known for his quick wit is usually chosen to play the role of matchmaker, and his function is to amuse and entertain the company. The "execution of the matchmaker" is also found at all Komsomol wedding ceremonies today. In general, one sees a growing modernization of the traditional wedding custom, with a retention of certain of its elements. Note should also be taken of the attempt by the Rokish ZAGS [vital statistics bureau] to establish its own forms of wedding ceremony.

Turning now to the relationships among workers of different nationalities, they are progressing in the direction of closer mutual influence. Thus, for example, there is evidence of mutual influences in the sphere of material culture, manifested in the process of disappearance of the traditional way of life both among Lithuanians and Russians. Clothing, diet and home interiors in the families of young Lithuanian workers differ little from those of the Russians, and vice versa. A new mode of life, common to all and having a common foundation, conditioned by uniform laws of development, is coming into being. A new culture is being established that is absorbing the best to be found in the old traditional cultures of the interacting nationalities. Mixed marriages are becoming more frequent. There is also a mixture in language development. In the daily speech of the local Lithuanian workers one finds a certain number of Russian words, expressions and technical terms. The opposite process is also observed, although to a lesser degree (for example, this is seen among the old Russian settlers in this area). Many workers know some language in addition to their native tongue. The majority (62%) of the workers in the factory know both Lithuanian and Russian. Among workers born between 1941 and 1943, this percentage is 90.2%; this is simultaneously a confirmation of the general growth of culture among the young workers. In filling out the answer to the question "What foreign languages do you know?", Lithuanians did not enter the word "Russian," or Russians "Lithuanian." They considered "foreign"

languages to mean German, English, Polish, etc.

It is also necessary to emphasize the significant changes that have occurred in the production activities of workers. A number of brigades have gained the designation of "teams of communist labor." The Niamunas Mill is engaged in competition for the designation "enterprise of communist labor." The associated personnel are giving considerable voluntary aid as patrons, primarily in the form of physical work, to the nearby collective farm. In the summer of 1961 alone, workers at this mill put in 26,000 manhours in the fields of the collective farm. The mill has its court of public opinion ("comradely court"), and workers are no longer searched when they leave the mill.

The students of the local secondary school receive on-the-job training at the mill. The kindergarten has an excellent reputation. In 1962 it is planned to complete the construction of a day nursery.

In the recent past, the mill has gotten rather large-scale housing construction under way, the completion of which will substantially ease housing conditions for the workers. At present 11.6% of the workers have less than five square meters of dwelling space per member of the family; 33.1% of the workers rent rooms in private homes.

Successful fulfillment of the assignments set by the Seven-Year Plan will ensure a further rise in the welfare of the workers of Iuodupe and create the material conditions for further changing the mode of life and improving the culture of the workers of this factory.

Footnotes

1) D. L. Kasitskaia, N. R. Levinson, and T. A. Lobanova, "Polozhenie i byt rabochikh metallurgicheskoi promyshlennosti Urala," Trudy Gos. Istoricheskogo muzeia, No. XXIII, Moscow, 1953.
2) See Sodziaus Menas, Kaunas, 1931, Vol. I, pp. 3-10; Vol. II, pp. 3-16.

* * *

Sovetskaia etnografiia, 1963, No. 4

V. V. Pimenov

LIFE OF KARELIAN LUMBERJACKS ON THE JOB

The worker's life on the job is one of the least explored aspects of ethnography. The first attempt to describe the workaday life of workers is due to N. N. Cheboksarov, who succeeded in making a number of important first-hand observations in disclosing certain aspects of the question which deserved investigation, and also in directing the attention of ethnographers to this entire problem. (1) However, shortcomings in his work, of a type that was entirely natural in the initial stage of research, were interpreted by a number of ethnographers as an argument against any study of the lives of workers on the job. They preferred for a long time not to touch the problem.

Yet, if ethnographic studies were made of workers' lives, embracing all aspects of life in their interrelationship, the treatment of life on the job would be of major importance, as it would help us to identify traces of continuity and useful folk working traditions in modern industry, to demonstrate the degree of progress achieved in that field to the present day, and perhaps to offer practical suggestions for improving life on the job.

Below we attempt, on the basis of the concrete example afforded by description of the on-the-job life of the lumberjacks of Karelia, to demonstrate that it is both possible and useful to study this aspect of workers' lives.

By life on the job we mean: 1) typical work skills essential to the workers in the employment of their tools and the exploitation of the means of production, as well as the manner in which these skills are acquired; 2) forms of organization of the work-force (producing cooperative, brigade, etc.); 3) working conditions (work and safety clothing, safety methods, provision of food, etc.); and 4) stable forms of workers' habits on the job (customs, traditions, etc.).

In investigating all these components of the life of the workers of Karelia on the job we must take into consideration the historical peculiarities of the development of the lumbering industry in this area, the structure of the enterprises in the field, as well as the unique nature of the labor process itself, which takes place right in the north woods and which, as a result, cannot be centered at a single place for a long time. The major type of production unit is the mechanized felling unit. (2) Immediately adjacent is the logging camp. These camps are in wooded places, often near a river or lake. They consist of standard frame and log houses and are usually marked by orderly street-type or block-type planning. There are now more than 300 such camps in Karelia.

The lumbermen of Karelia include members of many nationalities. About half the workers are Karelians. In addition there are Ingerman-land Finns from near Leningrad (and also Finns, some of whom have immigrated from Finland and Canada), Russians, Belorussians, Ukrainians, Lithuanians, Estonians, Vepsy, and others. This ethnic composition came into being over a period of time, as seasonal lumbering was eliminated and permanent staffs formed. (Until the mid-1930's, approximately, lumbering was conducted only during the winter.)

In the postwar years the equipment of the industry with large quantities of new and complex mechanisms, the constant improvement of procedures and forms of labor have led to a genuine technological revolution in the lumbering industry. The very word "woodcutter" is employed today only by force of tradition and indicates merely that one is engaged in a particular industry. Today's lumberjacks are equipped not only with aces, but with gasoline-powered saws, skidding tractors, powerful lumber trucks, etc.

* * *

The felling and rafting of lumber is a traditional pursuit in Karelia. "The cutting of wood and the primary processing of it for their own use," wrote Lenin, "is an ancient occupation of the peasants, and is almost everywhere part of the overall range of jobs performed by the tiller of the soil." (3) The trees were felled by axe (kirves [4]), and cut into log lengths right at the stump. The felling of trees by cross-cut saws came into wide use during the final third of the past century, when good steel saws came on the market. Only later, in Soviet times, was the two-man saw replaced by the buck saw. The felled trees had to be barked. Rough barking was done with the hatchet, while special two-handed chip axes (kabli) were employed for more careful work. Then the teamster used a

special "tipper," with a special grab-hook, or more often an ordinary crowbar (kangi) as a lever to roll the log onto his sledge (regi), with a small trailing sledge to support the ends of the log (taga regi), and hauled it to the bank of the stream or lake, where the logs were stacked. (5)

During the spring high-water, special lumber-jacks rolled the logs from the stacks into the water. The tools of these men consisted of crowbar and gaff (bagru). The logs were floated loose down the rivers, while on lakes they were transported in "bags." A bag was a closed chain of connected logs, within which a large number of individual logs were collected. The "bag" was moved by means of a raft or large boat with a capstan.

The lumbermen did not bother to improve lumbering techniques. The workers, employed on contract, were required to provide their own implements and horses. When he lacked them, the worker had to rent what he needed at usurious rates from the contractors who usually belonged to the kulak top stratum in the countryside.

During the Soviet years the loggers' work has been substantially mechanized in all its many aspects. Truck roads or narrow-gauge logging railroads and spur roads are laid to the area to be logged, and measures are taken to assure the safety of the men (removal of trees that have not fallen all the way to the ground and of dead standing trees). More recently, the logging crews themselves have undertaken, with increasing frequency, to prepare the area to be logged. Only after this is the section of forest to be felled divided by the foreman into cutting areas, large and small, which are assigned to the individual crews.

Then the felling begins. This is done by a logger using a gasoline-power saw. When he has accumulated enough trees for the capacity of a skidding tractor, he signals the skidder that it is safe to approach.

The tractor operator pays out cable with a winch, which has special cable grabs with flat steel hooks at their ends—chokers. (6) The feller, the choker-man and the tractor driver attach the chokers to the tips or butts of the trees, the tractor man starts his winch and "collects" them into a bundle, which is pulled up onto the platform of the tractor. He then skids them to the "log landing," which is a few meters from the spur of the logging road, and here the branches are trimmed off. When the log landing is full, a loading unit comes up. This may be an Anderson crane, (7) which is served by three workers, a tractor-craneman and two loaders. In 1959, the first large-packet loading installations were built in Karelia. (8) This method has come into large-scale use in the Padan Lumbering Enterprise, for one.

Lumber trucks or trains pulled by gasoline or steam engines on narrow-gauge lines transport the trimmed trunks to concentration points. A measurer and bucker then approach the unloaded tree trunks. The measurer, using a five-meter stick with a scale, decides the lengths into which the trunk should be cut, and the bucker uses an electric saw to cut it into logs which are then stacked. At some lumbering enterprises, the Shuiskii-Vidan for example, the concentration points have mechanized and partially automated lines for sizing the lumber. But there are as yet few of these, and they are regarded as experimental.

The concentration points (which the floating loggers call the top of the wine glass) mark the start of the log rafting. (9) The logs are still floated loose, but the method is now one in which loggers are stationed at fixed distances, depending upon the configuration of the stream bed and the current, and move the logs along their sections, which they patrol. The logs are moved across lakes in "bags" propelled by motorboat. Raft building machines have been installed at the mouths of rivers to propel the logs across lakes Onega and Ladoga. (10)

Thus, the forms of labor, equipment, and techniques used in the Karelian lumber industry have changed radically in a comparatively brief period. This was a significant factor contributing to change in the life of the workers on the job.

Conditions causing the workers to wish to master specialized jobs, and providing an understanding of the need to master certain work techniques and skills, result from the nature of the work, which includes the need to be able to operate machines. Other factors having this effect include the improvement of the forms of organization of the labor force, the fact that work is done in a crew, socialist competition and, finally, cash incentive (the skilled work of the machine-operating logger is more highly paid, and careful operation of equipment is also rewarded by bonuses). Skilled workers are trained at special courses and schools. Today, since there are highly skilled men in the logging industry, with the capacity to serve as instructors, training courses for tractor operators, truckers, and fellers are often set up right at the camp. They are organized on the volunteer principle, and are conducted after hours. Attendance at these classes is not at all obligatory, but the loggers attend willingly, so great is the desire to acquire technical knowledge. This is one of the reasons for the success of the small crews of men with diverse skills. Their essential principle — mutual aid, support, and assistance — could not be carried out if the members of these crews had not acquired the knowledge and habits required by operations abutting on their own.

A most important means of mastering associated skills is mutual instruction in the course of work side by side, supplemented by independent study of theory, equipment, and the rules of operation of particular mechanisms from textbooks and instruction manuals. A considerable number of workers have acquired second and even third skills.

*　*　*

In the past, the organization of the work force was not complicated. According to available information, the old income-sharing cooperative (artel') played no part to speak of in Karelia. Temporary associations of workers from two or three closely related families, or "family cooperatives," were more common.

In the 1920's, the so-called "nucleus" type of organization became very popular. A nucleus consisted of three persons — two loggers and one teamster with his horse. The nucleus performed the entire cycle of logging operations: cut roads, built a dwelling shack, felled the logs, etc. In practice, therefore, the nucleus organization of the work was a continuation of the traditional cooperation based on the family. (11)

It was only in the early 1930's that the more advanced crew type of organization of the workers was introduced. The establishment of crews, no matter how imperfect at the outset, played a most important role in improving not only the man-hour output, but the entire level of management of the operation, and also promoted the development of a feeling of collectivism among the workers.

From the moment the first crews were established, their structure underwent significant changes. In the prewar years, when manual labor was still dominant in the logging industry, so-called functional single-operation crews became popular. Crews of saw-men felled the trees, workers of the next team trimmed and bucked the trees into log lengths, etc. This division of labor was in accord with the level of equipment available at the time and with the seasonal nature of the work, as well as with the composition of the labor force, for a considerable portion of whom lumbering was a form of seasonal migrant labor, albeit on a new social foundation. (12)

The use of machinery soon revealed that this system of organization of the crews was inappropriate. The auxiliary workers were unable to keep up with the fellers, and much lumber was never hauled away. Therefore large "flow of production" crews, numbering some dozens of men, were organized, within which an effort was made, by the establishment of single-operation gangs, to maintain the necessary coordination between mechanized and manual functions. However, here again the crews failed to merge into integral organisms, all of whose members would have an equal interest in smooth functioning and the final results. The machine operators were concerned only with increasing their own earnings. It took a considerable number of auxiliary workers to make it possible for the mechanized equipment to function. Man-hour output rose but slowly. This did not make it possible to raise the over-all earnings, inhibited

the development of competition, interfered with any feeling of collectivism, and so forth.

Nor were matters improved by an attempt to apply to the logging industry the "cycle method" of the coal industry. Only with the elimination of seasonal operation in the industry and the establishment of a permanent labor force in the lumbering field, and with the introduction of modern machinery, including the gasoline saw, was a form of organization found that corresponds to the present level of mechanization. This is the small multi-operation crew. Since 1957 it has become the main form of labor organization in Karelia.

The scope and nature of the operations (felling, choking, skidding, trimming, and clearing the area) determined the composition of the small crew — a power-saw feller, a choker-man, a tractor operator and three trimmers. Sometimes (in winter, if the snow is deep), a woman is added to dig the snow away from the base of the trees. One of the skilled workers, a feller or tractor operator, with the capacity to lead the crew, is named as leader. When a crew is formed, the tractor driver chooses the choker, and the crew leader chooses the trimmers. Thus, the small multi-operation crew is formed by the workers themselves, who know one another and keep tabs on each other's work.

The small integrated crew is an extremely flexible, convenient, and effective form of organization of the labor force. Its members all have an incentive for increasing labor productivity. They work together with a will, and are concerned not with earnings from some single operation, but with the over-all indices. They help each other. This is facilitated by the established method of payment for labor. The loggers are still paid on a piece-work basis, but the pay is calculated not on the output of the individual worker, but on that of the team as a whole. The crew then divides the earnings among its members in accordance with their classifications and the efforts of each. In addition to the small integrated crew, recent years have seen a further improvement in the arrangement, with the formation of the "full" crew, to which a truckdriver has been added, so that the

240

delivery of the trunks to the concentration point is regarded as the final stage in the work of the crew. Crews of this type engage in large-packet loading of trunks.

* * *

In the pre-Revolutionary period the loggers' working conditions took shape spontaneously. (13) The lumbering entrepreneurs were not interested in improving conditions for the lumberjacks, and the workers looked after themselves as well as they were able. The need to spend several months in the woods in the cold season required the building of temporary dwellings. Upon arrival at the area to be logged, the lumberjacks immediately set to the building of a semi-dugout (muaperti) which was sunk up to one meter into the ground, or a woodman's shack (meččuperti), which was used in the lowlands, where the semi-dugout was impractical.

The floaters and rafters worked under even more difficult conditions. The fact that they had to be on the move continually behind the floated lumber made it almost completely impossible to establish housing of any decent sort. If it was impossible to spend the night in a village on the way, the rafters built a lean-to, and a fire (nuodöj) of two logs, one atop the other, supported by four props. On cold nights they sometimes lay down to sleep over the burnt-out fire, upon which they first spread pine branches.

Considerable improvements in the life of the loggers were made in the first years of Soviet power, but the fundamental changes came with the conversion of logging from a seasonal occupation to a branch of modern industry functioning the year round. With the formation of a permanent labor force living in logging towns, the need to build temporary structures in the woods disappeared. At the same time, there arose the need for portable structures at the logging area and the concentration point, where it would be possible to take shelter from bad weather (particularly in winter), to eat, to dry out, or to spend the lunch break in a warm place. In addition, the need arose for a shop structure on the spot, where equipment could be repaired. Caboose-type railway cars came into use for

this, modified for use as temporary housing, cafeterias and mobile repair shops. What was decisive here was the fixing of the length of the workday and the use of a shift system for the crews. The floaters and rafters of Karelia live in the villages, and in special settlements at the head of navigation on the lakes. Bunkhouses are also set up for them.

Before the Revolution there was no fixed workday in logging and, particularly, in floating and rafting. Piecework, which was, moreover, very low-paid, made for an increase in the length of the working day. Its duration fluctuated in accordance with the time of year. In winter, the workday was shorter, and lasted ten to twelve hours. It began and ended in the dark. Fires were built to light the work site. In spring and fall, the workday was stretched out to fifteen or sixteen hours, to take advantage of the period of light. The floaters in income-sharing cooperatives sometimes did not sleep for three days on end while following the lumber.

Lumberjacks reached the logging area on foot or behind horses, on sleighs. They used skis (sukset) to move through the roadless country in winter. (14) There was no attempt to enforce even the simplest safety measures in logging and floating. Injuries were very common in the industry, which was based on manual work.

The situation changed sharply under the Soviets. Now, as is the case in all enterprises of our country, the loggers have changed over from the eight-hour to the seven-hour workday. Only one shift is worked in felling the trees. It has been necessary to organize a two-shift system to load, haul, and do the work at the concentration points so as to remove, buck, and stack all the lumber felled.

All the workers engaged in the basic jobs in a logging area receive protective work clothing free of charge. In summer they are given two-piece cotton outfits and gloves, with tarpaulin boots. In the rainy autumn, workers (chiefly the loaders) put on canvas raincoats and jackets with hoods reaching down over the shoulders (krylyshki). In winter, as well as in early spring and in the fall, the set of work clothes and footgear includes wadded, quilted, cotton fabric-covered, padded jackets and trousers, plus felt, or tarpaulin, or rubber boots, which are worn with warm foot wrappings. The feller's head is protected by a helmet.

The work clothes constitute an important achievement for the logging industry. At the same time it must be recognized that the problem of providing protective work clothing for loggers has not been entirely solved. For example, the workers have a low opinion of the winter set. Both the padded trousers and jackets wet easily, but dry and wash poorly. The wadding quickly develops lumps, and the clothing becomes cold and constricts movement.

The task, consequently, lies in making work clothes of higher-quality material. In this connection it would be very useful to study the experience of the Karelians themselves for whom logging and rafting are traditional occupations. For work in the forest the Karelians use a long coat (kouhtan) and very full trousers allowing easy motion (kuad'd'ät), made of 50% wool (linen warp, woolen weft). Of course, we are not proposing a return to homespun clothing, which is a thing of the past. What is needed is to design clothes made of factory-made fabrics, which would not constrict movements and would be lightweight, warm, and capable of protecting the worker from the dampness.

Proper consideration of the on-the-job experience of the local population and its rational employment would also make it possible to perfect certain other pieces of equipment and thereby to improve working conditions in the logging areas and the rafting. Let us cite examples. Under the conditions of the snowy Karelian winter, the feller and choker-man have to spend much effort on moving through the deep snow. Some fellers employ skis to move more easily around the logging area. However, the usual sport or even hunters' skis are not particularly useful. In 1952, two Karelian workers of the Upper-Olonets Logging Center (subordinate to the Olonets Lumber Enterprise) — D. Vorob'ev and N. Pekkoev — made snowshoes of plywood, and thereby perhaps pointed the way to the most probable solution. The fact is that racquet-shaped snowshoes, which are known to many

Northern peoples, also used to be common in Northern Karelia and certain adjacent areas. It is curious to note that two types of walking "skis" were in use here: the marsh type (suo-sukset) among the Northern Karelians, Finns, and Estonians (15), and snowshoes as among, for example, the Saami [Lapps] of Kola Peninsula. The design principle of these walking devices, whether for use over marshlands during the haying season, or for moving over deep snow, is identical. Anyone can make them, so that to organize their manufacture would not be difficult. It would be considerably easier for the feller and choker-man to do their work if they had them.

As a consequence of the increasing amount of lumber moved by water, the problem of getting it onto the ice before the spring break-up becomes increasingly important. It is difficult to work on ice in ordinary footwear. Here and in stacking, it would be useful to use caulks (krap-pi, künnet), which have long been known both to the Karelian and the Russian population of Karelia. It is interesting to note that this simple device was recently "invented" anew under the name of "knife caulks," and is used at the Limand Water-to-Land Lumber Transshipment Depot, Arkhangel'sk Oblast for walking over wet and slippery logs. (16)

* * *

The participation of many generations of Karelians in logging and rafting has made for the development of stable forms or manners of behavior at work. It seems to us that certain purely functional habits have gradually become elements of an ethnic tradition. Particularly characteristic in this regard are certain aspects of the work of the floaters: the ability to run across a river or bay over floating logs, and the ability to navigate on one log or two logs side-by-side, with the aid of the gaff. (17)

On-the-job habits are, in general, very stable and exercise a powerful influence upon the selection of the branch of the industry in which one works. All our informants agreed that the vast majority of the Belorussians, Russians, and Ukrainians who came to work at logging in

Karelia had had some connection at home with that industry. "Every Belorussian peasant had done logging," they said. And one is able to see, at the logging areas themselves, which skills are preferred by particular national groups. Thus, the Olonets Karelians have a tradition as carpenters and builders. Today virtually every Karelian is a good carpenter. When large-scale construction of frame houses began in the logging towns, the Karelians showed their skill at this. Today, they also work successfully in the building of houses, log roads, bridges, etc. At the same time one must not exaggerate the power of tradition. For example, it is particularly among the Karelians, who are carpenters from way back, that one sees the most pronounced tendency to master machinery and acquire some mechanical classification. Thus, many of the power-saw fellers are Karelians. They are real masters at it, and bring their skill to the level of virtuosity. This was particularly pronounced in the first postwar years, when the newly arriving Belorussians, Ukrainians, and Russians often regarded their stay in the area as temporary. Today there is a gradual process of equalization of skills, and no predominance of any particular nationality is to be seen any longer among tractor-operators, boom-men or choker-men.

The workers' jobs and their mode of life on the job exercise a pronounced influence upon other aspects of their lives. This influence may be seen in the sphere of material culture. A new type of settlement has arisen — the logging camp. A new daily schedule has come into being, not characteristic of the former Karelian countryside and the seasonal loggers. A new type of lumberjack, familiar with machinery, has appeared. The speech of the logger is becoming technically precise and full of terms of that nature as soon as conversation turns to his work.

Many aspects of the non-material culture of the loggers show a relationship to their lives on the job. Modern chastushki [a chastushki is a brief topical song, consisting of a four-line stanza — usually humorous or satirical, but sometimes romantic — Editor.], heard in clubhouses and on the logging site, reveal the log-gers' work to be high on the list of themes. Even children's games reflect life in the forest to some degree. Work at the logging sites and at rafting and the features of life on the job serve as the source and foundation for the creativity of amateur poets, and influence the structure of their poetic thought.

At the same time the minds of some loggers retain certain vestiges originating in conditions of life on the job in the remote past. We have in mind the retention of certain old folk superstitions of the deep woods. They exist only among the Karelians. Many Karelian workers still remember the superstition of the wood-sprite, master of the forest (mečăn ižăndü). Of course, the young no longer believe in it. However, in some places taboos associated with the old beliefs persist. For example, when taking a break at work, the axe must not be left embedded in a tree: it will be dulled and become heavy because the forest devils (karut) will "work" on it. One must not sleep across a trail in the forest (or raise a shelter or build a fire on it): one might smother, and so forth.

On the whole, life on the job is overcoming rather quickly all that is backward and outlived. The forest shack and campfire, the old tools (bucksaw, sleigh, etc.) are gone, and the outlook of the past is also disappearing. The intellectual and moral outlook of the Karelian loggers is changing.

* * *

It appears to us that the foregoing provides the basis for the following conclusions.

To begin with it is clear that the life of workers on the job is subject to study by the standard techniques of ethnography. The greater rate of change in this aspect of life relative to other aspects of the life and culture of the loggers urgently demands a consistent application of the historical approach to a study of them.

The life of Karelian loggers on the job, which took shape in conjunction with the basic direction of their economic activity, is distinguished by a number of special traits arising out of the specific character of the work itself. However, even in this most mobile field of production, we see revealed features associated with the national traditions of the Karelians, Russians, Belorussian and other peoples found in the logging enterprises of Karelia.

It is to be expected that the introduction of the very latest equipment (felling and skidding machines, automated bucking and trimming lines), new methods (complete uprooting), etc., will result in a further improvement of the lives of loggers on the job.

Footnotes

1) N. N. Cheboksarov, "Etnograficheskoe izuchenie kul'tury i byta moskovskikh rabochikh," Sov. etnografiia, 1950, No. 3.

2) The logging camp is organizationally a department of a larger undertaking, the lumbering enterprise, which controls several logging camps, floating and rafting areas, as well as patrolling and replanting organizations. The lumbering enterprise as thus organized dates from 1929-1930, while the logging camp in its present form dates from 1934.

3) V. I. Lenin, Soch., 4th ed., Vol. 3, p. 460.

4) All local terms are given in the Livvik dialect of the Karelian language.

5) For a detailed description of the lumbering procedure, see B. I. Seliber, Lesa i lesnaia promyshlennost' SSSR, Vol. I, Lesa SSSR i ikh ekspluatatsiia, Leningrad, 1930, pp. 245-288 and 374-404.

6) The term "choker" is from the English. The term was introduced by Finnish lumberjacks from Canada in the 1930's. It is curious that the term gradually came to be regarded as a local one, from the Karelian čokki, meaning clamp or grasper.

7) This derrick is a local Karelian invention. Its inventor was chief mechanic of the Kover Logging Camp of the Olonets Lumbering Enterprise. See K. Beliaev, "Pogruzochnyi kran Andersona," Sbornik po nauchno-tekhnicheskomu i peredovomu opytu v lesnoi promyshlennosti Karelii, Petrozavodsk, 1958, No. 1, p. 27.

8) A large-packet installation is a device for loading packs of trunks making one complete load for a lumber truck. The skidding tractor is used to provide the power.

9) At many enterprises the lumber is not floated, but is immediately loaded onto standard-gauge railway cars.

10) We disregard other forms of productive activity. Specifically, we shall not describe the production of pine resin by tapping, as this would take us far afield.

11) Compare G. Vlas'ev, Lesozagotovki v Karelii, Moscow and Leningrad, 1932, p. 65.

12) In winter, collective-farm members from the nearest villages came to the logging areas to work on the basis of contracts concluded between the collective farms and the logging enterprises.

13) Lack of space makes it impossible for us to provide a detailed description of the working conditions. Therefore we shall confine ourselves to a general description, hoping to return to this major and important subject at a later time.

14) With respect to sleighs and skis among the Karelians, see R. F. Taroeva, "Sredstva i sposoby peredvizheniia u karel v dorevoliutsionnoe vremia (konets XIX-nachalo XX v.)," Trudy karel'skogo filiala AN SSSR, No. XXII, 1959, pp. 45-46 and 49-50.

15) Compare Suoman suku, osa III, Helsinki, 1934, pp. 209 ff.

16) See Lesnaia promyshlennost', 1951, No. 2, p. 19.

17) Compare M. A. Krukovskii, Olonetskii krai, St. Petersburg, 1944, pp. 75-76.

Rural Sociology and Agriculture

Komsomol'skaia Pravda, September 29, 1965

THE ARITHMETIC OF SOCIALISM ON THE LAND:

A LENINIST CLASS SESSION

A Few Words Before the "Bell"

This six-hour discussion bore hardly any resemblance to an ordinary class session, with the
teacher clothed with authority on the one hand,
and attentive pupils on the other. Here, all in attendance were simultaneously pupils and teachers, from the collective-farm team leader to the
academician from Moscow. However, this was a
class session even in the literal sense of the
word, describing time devoted to study of a concrete matter, a discussion with book in hand. It
was also a class session in the sense of a lesson
for the future, inasmuch as it provided food for
serious thought.

People prepared for it, of course. Everyone
prepared. Not for half an hour before, hurriedly
burrowing through the assigned reading, nor by
a month of learning indisputable truths by rote.

V. Kokashinskii, V. Onishchenko, V. Stepanov,
V. Chikin, and Iu. Shakutin, special correspon-
dents of Komsomol'skaia Pravda, prepared the
materials for this article.

They prepared by years of their lives, verifying
each thought by the experience of "the real movement," their practical work.

One might say that this class session was begun several years ago by the farmers along the
Amur River and in the Altai Mountains, when
they set up mechanized teams functioning as business units on a cost-accounting basis. The teams
of the by now well-known farm-equipment operators, Vladimir Pervitskii and Vladimir Svetlichnyi, in the Kuban were set up at the same
time as those and on the same principle.

Each year thereafter saw the appearance, in
the Altai and the Kuban, in Siberia and Kazakhstan,
in the Amur Oblast and other regions, of increasing numbers of followers of the squad-and-team
system, in which land and the needed equipment
are assigned to a specified group of equipment
operators, and earnings are made dependent upon the final product, i.e., upon the harvest obtained.

From the very birth of these basic units of production, Komsomol'skaia Pravda has carefully
followed their growth, regularly reporting to its

244

readers on how the introduction of cost accounting — the basic technique of socialist management in the new production unit — had a decisive and favorable influence upon the nature of the collective farmer's work, his concrete results, and even upon various aspects of the life of village society.

In their numerous responses to the articles "Does the Village Need the Peasant?", "Let's Look at the Land," "It Is the Force of the Ruble That Yields the Centner of Grain," and others published in Komsomol'skaia Pravda, practical workers, leaders of collective and state farms, upholding the propriety of the new organization and payment for work, were unanimous in warning that one must not try to make what had arisen fit artificially into old concepts. It was essential to arm oneself with the patience of the researcher and study all aspects of the operation of the squads and teams working in this new way.

This was how the idea arose of conducting a session based on Lenin's theory of cooperatives and of holding it in the Kuban, where the new system has long been firmly established in many farms and has gained the support of the Krai Committee of the Party and the state agencies for agriculture. The choice fell upon the "Lenin's Path" Collective Farm of Novokuban Raion. This farm has already accumulated rich practical experience both for analysis and for drawing general conclusions.

Eighty-six persons took part in the Leninist class session. They were secretaries of raion committees of the Party, active members of the Komsomol in the raion, researchers at the Kuban Agricultural College and the Kuban Research Institute for Tractor and Farm-Machine Testing, managers of state farms and chairmen of collective farms, professional people, equipment operators, livestock farmers, brigade and team leaders. The gathering was not limited to confirmed believers in the new system, but included people who were dubious about it. This was very useful because their questions and doubts deepened the channel of discussion, made it impossible to dodge troublesome questions, and made it possible to discover problems as yet unresolved. At our request, the Leninist class session was led

by I. M. Iudin, First Secretary of the Novokuban Raion Committee of the Party, F. I. Mamontov, Chairman of the "Lenin's Path" Collective Farm, and S. G. Kolesnev, Member of the Lenin Academy of Agriculture and Chairman of the Department of Organization of Socialist Farm Enterprises at the Timiriazev Farming Academy. A. M. Birman, Doctor of Economic Sciences and Chairman of the Department of Finance and Credits at the Plekhanov College of Economics, Moscow, served as consultant.

A Collective Farm Run by the Whole Collective Farm

"For the Soviet government, the most basic and burning question of the entire life of society is precisely the mode of organization of labor in the very largest individual enterprises and the individual rural communes."

These words of Lenin became the leitmotif of the entire discussion of the organization of the work force in the modern countryside. But talk centered not on the narrowly managerial, technological aspect of the matter to which people often limit themselves — assignment of people to work stations, methods and techniques of carrying out particular farm operations and seasonal campaigns. Rather, it centered on the organization of labor in the social meaning of the term, that is, how "to build new forms of social ties among people, to build new forms and techniques for involving people in work."

Taking this precise understanding as our point of departure, let us listen to the report of F. I. Mamontov, Chairman of the "Lenin's Path" Collective Farm, which opened the class session. Let us find out whether what is being done in that collective farm in the sense of organization and payment of the labor force is the building of new forms of social ties among people in the process of work. Does this arrangement correspond to our concepts of production relationships under socialism? And what is new in this?

F. I. Mamontov: "A few years ago, following the example of the prominent Kuban farm-machine operators, Vladimir Pervitskii and Vladimir

Svetlichnii, who work in our raion, we established small teams of three to five persons each. They were assigned to raise a single crop, sugar beets or corn, by the use of machinery. These teams were made independent units for purposes of cost accounting. That's how we took our first step."

V. L. Zemtsev (manager of the Khutorok State Beet Farm): "But small teams suffer from a major shortcoming. To assign a particular crop to such a team does not mean assignment of the land. The result is that the responsibility is divided between those who raise that crop and those who prepare the soil for it. We are convinced that mechanized squads of larger size should be established, and a complete crop rotation assigned to them. Then the same group of people will be responsible for the entire cycle of land use. . . ."

Mamontov: "Absolutely right. That's exactly what we did as our second step. In each brigade (we call them departments), two teams were set up. The equipment was divided between them, and they were assigned specific pieces of land (3,000 to 3,250 acres each). Each squad (or team) is given its own procedures chart, by which it raises all the crops — from wheat to perennial fodder grasses.

"The main question now is: how is work paid for in the team?

"The group of equipment operators has a strict plan for, say, grain production. It is not sucked out of our thumbs. We set the yield-per-acre goal each year on the basis of the level achieved on our farm during the preceding five years. But, you know, we had plans in the past as well. However, experience showed that previously the equipment operators had no incentive to produce the highest possible harvest. They were paid not for the final product, the crop, but for the fulfillment of each day's work quota. What this led to I'll get around to. But right now I want to say that the equipment operators get, year round, a monthly advance with bonuses for grade classification. However, the final settlement at the end of the year is per centner of output. Let me offer a table:

Question: "Your payments to collective farmers for their work rose more than threefold. Do you consider this proper? Isn't there a conflict here with the principles of the socialist economy?

Mamontov: "You have directed attention to only one side of the table. But compare the rise in the payments to members with the overall money income of the collective farm. Remember, during all the years under consideration we operated with the identical quantity of land and with, so to speak, identical production capacities. You have observed that our payments to members increased more than threefold in 12 years. That's true. But consider the fact that the overall income of the collective farm rose more than fourfold during the same period. Now look further. The ratio of payments to members to gross income was 34% in 1957, 30% in 1960, 30% in 1964, and is planned at 29% in 1965. Do you see the trend? In our collective farm, the increase in labor productivity is running ahead of the rise in payments to members. This means that the principles of socialist management are triumphant. Both the collective farm and society are the gainers."

Mamontov then described how the new system functions in various fields of the farm's operations — livestock, construction, the workshops, the garage. It is justifying itself everywhere. It is stimulating every collective farmer to regard himself as a true owner of the cooperative, responsible for both his own work and the common undertaking. In this connection, he described one very instructive incident.

Mamontov: "We had two tractor drivers named Ivanovich and Petr. Ivanovich was a farmer down to his marrow. An honest man. To shallow-up his plow or to make the soil look difficult were things he would never do. But Petr regarded himself as a visitor on the land. He never stirred a finger for free. Petr wasn't worth Ivanovich's little finger; yet he was honored. The reason was that there was only a single standard for the worker on the land: if you overfulfilled your quota, you were out in front. A pennant flew from his tractor and his picture was on the honor board.

Year	1957	1960	1964	1965
Money income of farm (new rubles)	909,300	2,541,500	3,402,500	3,850,500
Payments to members (new rubles)	306,600	766,600	1,030,700	1,114,500

Everybody knew how he managed to exceed the quota. Sometimes Ivanovich and Petr would be plowing side by side. The tractors were identical. The soil too. If you checked up, you found that Ivanovich barely made the quota, and sometimes didn't quite, while Petr always showed overfulfillment. He earned twice as much. Petr figured like this: whether there's a crop or not is in the lap of the gods, but if I do a quota and a half, I collect mine right now. For him, the quota was the bird in hand, while the promise of the year's-end settlement was two in the bush. So he wanted the former to be as fat as possible. Later, when the new system was introduced, it became clear immediately who was the real master of his work. Petr now had to look to improving his skill, but he had gotten used to sloppy work, which had been covered up until then by the piecework system. So he left the collective farm."

Retort from the audience: "So you think that a man's morality is shaped by his earnings?"

Mamontov: "That's not quite it. A man's morality is shaped in the course of his work. The most important thing is to create conditions favoring conscientious work, which gives both moral and material satisfaction. By assigning a field or another aspect of the work to a specific work group, and by making the payment for work dependent upon the end results of what it does, we create real opportunity for people to be managers on the land; we give full freedom for creative efforts, for developing their best powers. Our collective farmer is by nature a collectivist. But, working in a group and on collectively controlled land, he wants to know the true measure, the contribution, and the results of his personal labor. He wants to be able to see his personal authorship in work. Work must not be made impersonal. We have arranged a payment system such that, the more our collective farmer earns for himself, the greater his contribution to the common fund from which he also obtains a share. We used the money we obtained in common to build dormitories, health resorts, a vacation resort, a palace of culture, clubhouses, day nurseries; we give paid vacations, and so forth.

"On the other hand, when a man puts out effort for the sake of the collective farm, this is beneficial to the country as a whole. We are selling the government about a million bushels of grain, hundreds of tons of milk, meat, vegetables, and our contribution is increasing every single year. This is how the connection between personal interest, group interest, and the interests of society becomes firmer."

Thus, it is clear from the remarks of Mamontov alone that what the Kuban people modestly term a progressive system of organization and payment for labor is by no means a mere improvement in ledger-keeping, or simply a more orderly system of financial accounting. Comrade Mamontov connected a large range of social and moral problems with this system. It was this by which he explained both the qualitatively new attitude people manifested to their work, the psychological changes they had undergone, and the fact that each now perceived himself as master of the land and its fruits. This might be illustrated by dozens of examples from the life of the "Lenin's Way" Collective Farm. We note in passing that the participants in the Leninist class session had visited the departments and livestock ranches of the farm "before the bell rang" and had had numerous opportunities to convince themselves of the truth of Mamontov's winged words: "We have 1,800 people in our collective farm, and they are 1,800 chairmen. . . ."

Unfortunately, we lack space here to cite every figure and fact. But one thing that might be termed symbolic is worthy of mention. In the "Lenin's Way" Farm, the watchmen and the time-and-work-checkers taken for granted everywhere else no longer exist — i.e., those occupations have disappeared which by their nature, generally speaking, exemplify lack of trust in the individual.

Doubtless some of our readers will regard this, to put it mildly, as a far-fetched conclusion. Certainly cases of stealing, money-grubbing, and self-seeking have not disappeared from all our collective farms, or nearly all, by any means. We have to impose fines upon sloppy workers and hold people to responsibility for negligent and sometimes barbarous treatment of machinery and the soil. Why? And why is there no need for such sanctions in the "Lenin's Way" Collective Farm? Is the new system really a panacea?

248

"It Isn't Sweat That Deserves a Good Price. . . ."

The participants in the Leninist lesson undertook their proof of this theorem by "working from the other end" — by a unanimous and comprehensive criticism of the prior system of piecework for volume of work done. After Mamontov, Vladimir Pervitskii, the renowned Kuban equipment operator, who came in directly from the fields, took the floor.

V. Ia. Pervitskii (team leader, Hero of Socialist Labor, Deputy to the Supreme Soviet of the USSR): "A lot has been said about the work of our team. But most of it has been technical: how we plow, cultivate, plant. But can you explain our crop yields by procedures alone? Progressive use of equipment and modern husbandry are available to everyone. Why do we, and not others, get the desired results? Vladimir Svetlichnyi and I have visited lots of farms around the country and have shared our experience with them. We found over and over again that people cannot accomplish what is natural and simple for us as long as they remain individualists, pieceworkers on the job. Piecework compels a man to look upon every procedure, even the most progressive, merely from the quantitative side: 'Give me easy acres!' "

I. M. Iudin: "You can't weigh-in easy acres at the grain elevator."

V. Ia. Pervitskii: "And that's no lie! You've got to give them bushels. So here's a situation in which quantity does not convert directly into quality. On the contrary, piecework on the land most often kills quality in the work. I remember how, at the beginning, we squeezed in seven cultivations only to find that two are all that is necessary for a good harvest. Today every step we take is subordinated to just one goal — the harvest yield. There's no need for us to chase after numbers of acres worked. Nobody pays for that. As the saying goes: 'It isn't sweat that deserves a good price, but quality.' "

Question: "So your earnings don't depend upon the amount of work you've done?"

Pervitskii: "That's right."

Question to Mamontov: "And the same thing on your collective farm?"

Mamontov: "Right. We have no work quotas at all."

Question: "And there is no inspection of how the work is going at any time during the season?"

A. A. Chaiun (brigade leader of the "Motherland" Collective Farm, Novokuban Raion): "It's no accident that the question of inspectors arouses such strong feelings. Where people work to a quota and do not themselves manage the land, inspectors are needed left and right to supervise. But the equipment operator can fool any inspector. Lack of confidence in people yields no results, no matter how much you inspect! Today, everyone on our farm is his own inspector. Previously the equipment operator regarded the agronomist as some sort of a foreman. But now he's happy when he shows up on his field. We consult with him on the best things to do to get a good crop; we use his knowledge. For the last two years there hasn't been a single reprimand from the chief agronomist, and nobody has had a word to say against us on the score of quality. But previously our brigade was notorious for its sloppy workers. Am I telling the truth, Galina Antonovna?"

G. A. Dozortseva (Chief Agronomist, "Motherland" Collective Farm): "Right!"

A. D. Erkaev (economist at the Kuban Research Institute for Testing Tractor and Farm Equipment): "It's been clear to a lot of people for a long time that the principle of payment by the acre didn't meet the need, even from the viewpoint of output pure and simple. The nature of agricultural production is such that the volume of work done is not directly proportional to the product yield. Very often, lower volumes of labor will yield a greater crop. Piecework by the acre, as a rule, conflicts with the requirements of rational production technology."

Pervitskii: "It should be added that it is precisely the individual quota and the chase after greater earnings through these quotas that lead to selfish, money-grubbing interest. I don't recall exactly how he put it, but Vladimir Il'ich Lenin said somewhere that the striving to snatch a bigger piece for oneself is a carry-over from the unfree man, produced by the petty property owner's attitude: so long as I get more, I don't care if even grass won't grow elsewhere."

Erkaev: "I think it's no accident that Comrade Pervitskii brought up this matter. The question of quotas of work just isn't purely a matter of production. Pervitskii, does somebody pay you a wage?"

Pervitskii (smiling): "The crop is my paymaster. The accounting office issues us advances from our own team's distribution fund, which is part of the estimated value of the gross product the team will have produced — so that, in the usual sense of the word, we don't receive a wage."

Erkaev: "In essence, you don't."

At this point, the participants in the Leninist lesson, who had hitherto been attentively following the conversation, exploded in comment. Inasmuch as the usual strict presidium was lacking, as was the authoritative chairman's bell, and everyone was seated elbow-to-elbow at tables set out in a large square, the discussion temporarily became impossible for the stenographers to take down. This reaction on the part of the body was natural, because this was the critical point of the discussion.

Yes, Associated Labor!

Erkaev (resuming): "It seems that the new things we find in the 'Lenin's Way' Collective Farm, in the Pervitskii and Svetlichnyi teams, in Cherepova's and Chaiun's brigades, and in hundreds of similar production units that have sunk their roots in the soil of the Kuban, are to be regarded not merely as a change in the forms of payment for labor, but as a step forward in relationships of production, in the mechanisms of social ties among men.

"We practical workers, who are introducing the new organization of labor in the collective and state farms, stand in need right now of a theoretical analysis of the forms discovered. We have begun entirely too serious a matter to go ahead with it blindly. It was no accident that Marx ascribed enormous significance to the very form of labor. He stated that the form of labor is of decisive importance in characterizing the par-

ticular mode of production itself. He emphasized that change in forms of property does not automatically change the form of labor, but that, on the contrary, a single form of property may exist under different modes of production. It isn't hard to see that the slaveholding, feudal, and capitalist social systems differed not at all in form of property (private property was dominant in all), but in the forms of labor, the nature of the relationships of production, 'the immediate relationship of the owners of the means of production to the direct producers.' It is in this, said Marx, that we always discover the deepest secret, the innermost foundation of the entire social system.

"In our socialist society, this primary, fundamental relationship of production is expressed in the fact that the actual producers are the co-owners of the means of production — that is, we are talking about relationships of production in which each individual is simultaneously worker and manager. Socialization of the means of production presumes precisely such relationships. But this does not mean that they take shape of their own accord and that it is not necessary to seek a more perfect mechanism under which co-ownership and co-management become possible and visible in every branch of agriculture and in every production unit. Can the individual piece-work system, in which the wage is determined in its entirety by the individual's participation in production, be this mechanism? For in this situation, the actual producer continues to be an individualist in his relationship to production conducted socially. His direct interest lies in doing more work relative to his quota, in earning more, but what the result of this work will be, how well the work is done, is something with which he has no real concern. None — because he is hired to do a particular volume of work at a particular rate of pay, and that's all. It is in the very form, hired labor, that I see a serious flaw, creating a situation psychologically absurd for our society — one in which the managers of the labor process and its direct participants are placed at loggerheads. How often we find that, in the minds of those doing the work, it is only the board of the collective farm, the directors of the state farm, and the higher agencies of administration who are conceived of as engaged in managing."

G. N. Kolesnikov (economist of the "Sunrise" State Farm): "Isn't this the explanation for the fact that a portion of the peasantry has lost interest, to some degree, in socialist production; we see this fact expressed in money-grubbing, sloppy work, non-participation in the democratic collective institutions of management: in poor attendance at plenary meetings of the collective farm or production conferences at the state farms, and passivity at such meetings on the part of the rank-and-file toilers? And hasn't this, on the other hand, made possible the existence, for a long terms of years, of subjectivist, 'strong-willed,' order-giving methods of leadership, that have discredited themselves? Understanding the ridiculousness of some of the 'wise counsel' he has been given, the peasant, laughing, has said: 'So the bosses (read — the management) will get more glory.' "

Question: "Is it valid to identify piecework with hired labor?"

Erkaev: "Of course not. Hired labor is a form of relationship in production that defines a capitalist and not a socialist social order. But Lenin emphasized that the elimination of hired labor is a gradual and extended process. 'The abolition of private property in the land,' he said, 'is an enormous transformation, undoubtedly progressive, undoubtedly in the interest of economic development and in the interests of the proletariat, a change that every hired laborer will support with all his soul and every effort, but one that in itself does not in any way abolish hired labor. . . .'

"Lenin's thought was that the path to elimination of hired labor in agriculture lay through cooperatives. Why through cooperatives? Because cooperatives, aside from everything else, make it possible in the most tangible, concrete form to provide 'each member of society with the opportunity to participate not only in production but in distribution.' The more economically independent the production group, the closer it is to actual co-possession of the means of production and the mechanism of distribution. Isn't this why Lenin said that 'each cooperative and farming enterprise, each village converting to the new form

of agriculture with the adoption of the law on socialization of the land, is today, within the meaning of the democratic foundations of Soviet government, an independent commune with an internal organization of labor.' Yet some of our economists speak today of the 'economic individualization' of separate enterprises as virtually a defect from which we have to free ourselves as quickly as possible. Isn't this running ahead? Is it desirable to rush so to transform work into 'direct social labor' on the scale of society as a whole, something that looks, in the eyes of producers not yet prepared for this, as alienation of both the means of production and the mechanism of distribution from them?

"It is in this sense that I ask: is a wage capable of providing complete and comprehensive incentive for the worker as far as the ultimate results of his labor are concerned? The important thing is not the name given it, but the principles of distribution: receipt of a portion of the product for one's labor or the establishment of payment for labor 'from above,' independent of the quantity of product resulting."

There was a stir in the hall among the representatives of the "state farm sector." How's this? Isn't it accepted, and established in textbooks of political economy, that state farms are socialist enterprises of a higher type, and collective farms — i.e., cooperatives of producers — are not consistently socialist? And it is in the state farms that that form of labor has been most openly asserted under which wages comprise a fixed sum independent of the results of the economic functioning of the enterprise. Here it is truly impossible to avoid posing the question: what actually is the basic criterion for evaluating an enterprise as of a consistently socialist type — differences in form of property (the state farms being public and belonging to the state, while the collective farms are non-governmental, and belong to a group) or primarily the form of labor, the principles of distribution? All this needs serious study by our scholars.

What interests us now is the meaning of that form of labor which the founders of scientific communism called associated labor. Doesn't all that has gone before mean that under socialism, when the means of production are in the hands of the laboring population, it is this kind of labor that should score greater and greater triumphs, regardless of the form in which the working population possesses property? For it was no accident that Vladimir Il'ich Lenin stated that a system of civilized cooperative members, given public ownership of the means of production and class victory of the working class over the capitalist class, is a socialist system. And this widely known definition of Lenin is a continuation of Marx's idea to the effect that the significance of the cooperative movement cannot be overestimated. "Workers have proved not in words but in deeds," said Marx, "that like slave and serf labor, hired labor is merely a transient and lower form that must yield to associated labor. . . ."

Yes, for the participants in the Leninist class session, it is already quite obvious that the question under discussion goes far beyond the confines of bookkeeping and accounting. It is equally obvious that it was futile to expect answers here at this lesson that would deal with these theoretical problems in full. So the practical experience of each team, of each crew working in the new way, was gone over again, detail by detail. Now, however, the center of interest lay not only in quantitative accumulations but in qualitative changes.

Preference for Conscience and Preference for the Ruble

The crux of the discussion now flamed over what might be called antitheses: material incentive and communist conscientiousness. It was ignited by a sharp critical comment from Vladimir Pervitskii.

Pervitskii: "We don't need any agitators to tell us about 'one for all and all for one.' With us, that happens automatically. The conscientiousness of each individual rests on a firm economic foundation: the group interest of each in the course of our productive efforts and the results obtained."

Question: "Tell us, Vladimir Iakovlevich, how much do you make a month?"

V. Ia. Pervitskii: "Over 200 rubles, on the average."

Question: "And your equipment operators, Fedor Ivanovich?"

F. I. Mamontov: "About the same."

Rejoinder: "So isn't it true that you comrades lash your consciences pretty thoroughly with the whip of the ruble? What is there communist in this sort of conscientiousness?"

Pervitskii: "You can't put it that simply, as though conscience meant giving up what you have earned. We are not money-grubbers; we don't chase after the ruble, but we get our due share. We operate on the principles of cost accounting, on a self-liquidating basis: the more we produce for society, the more we get ourselves. This is the socialist principle of payment for work done. And the time has not yet come to abandon it. This principle doesn't contradict communist conscience at all. Just the reverse: it prepares the way for it. Remember what Lenin said about combining moral and material stimuli for the forward-looking Soviet worker. 'To be regarded as a shock-worker,' he said, 'is recognition, and recognition without consumption isn't worth a thing. If people give me the kind of recognition that means that I get a ration of two ounces of bread a day, you can keep that kind of recognition. [This was the entire food ration in Petrograd during the Civil War, in 1918, to which Lenin was referring; also in 1941-42, when Leningrad was surrounded by the Germans and Finns — Trans.] Recognition for shock-work is recognition expressed in consumption. Lacking this, shock-work is a dream, a cloud, and we, after all, are materialists. And the workers are materialists; if you say shock-work, then give them bread, and clothing, and meat. . . .' I repeat, there's no contradiction here. But the standard for measuring work must be correct. The standard for measuring useful work, and not all work whatever, whether it helps or hurts the crop yield. When you do this, you get a harmonious work group."

Rejoinder: "That's a little too simple. Where's the proof that this is a regularity? That your harmonious work group is the result of the new system of payment? Maybe you just chose your people well."

A. A. Chaiun: "You can choose five people to suit each other in character — but 28, as in our team? Here there's no question but that you'll get different kinds of characters. Yet in our brigade people are conscientious in their work and trust each other."

Erkaev: "Of course, it's not all that easy. And again it's hard for me to restrain myself and not direct another complaint at our scholars. From the writings of our philosophers and sociologists it's hard to form a tangible picture of what constitutes a production group in its social, economic, moral, and psychological aspects. They say that in a socialist society work makes collectivists. That's true. But what is the mechanism by which characters undergo this change? What is a group, really; how does it take shape; what is the foundation on which it becomes a unity; what is the dialectic of its development, based, of course, on the overcoming of internal contradictions? It seems to me that the machine-equipped teams and crews make for just that merger of personal and social interests essential to the functioning of a socialist group. To work collectively, in a group, does not in itself necessarily mean that you constitute a collective.

"Let the scholars not think that our complaints against them are abstract or purposeless. There are absolutely concrete, urgent questions that we find ourselves unable to solve. For example, the problem of the optimal size of a work group in agriculture is, in my opinion, one of fundamental significance precisely with respect to relationships of production. Wouldn't the answer to that question be found in developing a comprehension of the following dialectic? We have experienced constant mergers of farms, and this was called forth by the increase in available equipment, the needs for specialization, and many other considerations of production and economics. The policy of merging farms yielded major advantages and benefits. But at the same time it tended to disarm the peasant psychologically to a certain degree. His initial concept of collective property became less tangible. And if collective, cooperative work disappears, collective concern and collective responsibility will also disappear. As a matter of fact, the costs of gigantomania were

obvious over 30 years ago, when Stalin said that certain giant farms 'had degenerated into cumbersome paper commands lacking economic roots.' The enlargement of the collective or state farm should, it would seem, presuppose that within them economic self-reliance and independence would exist for a work group of a size optimal in terms of recognizing itself to be a cooperative."

A. V. Cherepova (brigade leader of "Caucasus" Collective Farm of Kurganinskii Raion): "Isn't this the reason why past attempts to eliminate consequences without touching causes had disillusioning results: organizational conclusions didn't work, swarms of officials proved unable to change anything, threatening directives 'to obligate' in fact failed to obligate anybody to do anything. Then it became clear that the reshuffling and reorganization of administration also failed to justify the hopes placed in it. Finally, the sober analysis of the situation in agriculture at the March Plenum of the Central Committee of the Communist Party of the Soviet Union put an end to one-man solutions and improvisations."

G. A. Romanenko (Chairman of "Spark" Collective Farm, Timashevskii Raion, and graduate student at an agricultural institute) [In the USSR, it is possible to do graduate as well as undergraduate work by correspondence, taking exams in person — Trans.]: "Let's get back to our experiments. I listened with great interest to the speeches of the team leaders, the brigade leaders, and Comrade Mamontov. It is clear that the new system is justifying itself wonderfully. Fifty-four bushels of grain to the acre is the best of proofs. But I am also troubled by the moral and social aspect of the new practice — not from the point of view that has been discussed here, not that of using the ruble to whip one's conscience, but exactly the opposite. I am afraid of egalitarianism. That this method of working the land contains the possibility of equal pay regardless of work contributed is a fact."

Chaiun: "In a small group, in which people have become friends with one another, trust one another, and are capable of keeping an eye on each other, of building each other's characters — in such a collective, internal honesty and conscientiousness become more effective means of discipline than petty calculations of who did a kopeck's worth more work than another. Let me go further. If one of our equipment operators asks that he be released for a day for personal reasons, we let him go, pay him anyhow, and jointly do the work he was supposed to. Once we sent one equipment operator to Sochi for a month for treatment and kept up his pay. We got everything necessary done without him. People like these friendly relationships of helping each other out. And each individual responds to this mutual concern by working well."

Romanenko: "But people's abilities differ; we aren't all Pervitskiis or Svetlichnyis. And if each is to give in accordance with his abilities, then each should receive in accordance with his work. Thus, it seems. . . ."

Mamontov: "I don't know how things are handled at Comrade Chaiun's, but we keep a record of the days people come to work. [On a collective farm, the individual is required to put in a given minimum of days per year to retain his membership, but beyond that is free to spend his time in his private garden, and otherwise come and go as he pleases — Trans.] And at the final sharing of earnings in the team, this is taken into consideration. We have also retained grade classifications for our equipment operators and this, too, affects the earnings of each individual. We haven't introduced egalitarianism but have merely abandoned piecework by the acre."

S. G. Kolesnev, Member of the Lenin Academy of Agriculture: "We must not allow egalitarianism. It's dangerous to depend upon emotions alone. Thus far this isn't a particularly acute problem with you, but as time passes antagonisms can develop within teams and crews. After all, one man is more skilled, another has less experience; one works creatively and shows initiative, another in stereotyped fashion. . . ."

Mamontov: "If conflicts arise among us because of this, it will be no problem to introduce a scale of wages. But we will not re-introduce piecework by the acre. However, so long as we have no conflicts, why go backward? It's good that in our teams, both in crop-raising and in stock-farming, the more experienced regard it as their moral duty to help the less experienced — to help

not because they'll make a kopeck that way, but because of conscious ideas about collectivist labor. I want to remind our guests that this collective farm is a collective of communist labor [a title awarded in recent years that in many cases represents nothing more than efficient operation (see Soviet Sociology, Vol. I, No. 4, article by Grushin and Chikin), but that in this instance clearly has deeper meaning — Trans.]. And we did not accept that honorable designation because we wanted to make a nice sign at the entrance to our stanitsa [the term stanitsa instead of selo (village) indicates that these are Cossacks — Trans.] but because we wish (and I think we are able) to work in communist fashion. And how did Lenin understand communist labor? This is labor done not to work off a fixed duty, not to obtain the right to particular products, not in accordance with predetermined quotas having the force of law, but voluntary labor, work done from the habit of working for the common good, work as a need of a healthy organism."

Of Course, All Questions Have Not Been Answered

The participants in the session scrupulously analyzed the finest nuances of the new organization of labor and discussed the sharpest questions this posed, but not with the purpose of seeking to discredit this system as such, when particular unresolved problems were discovered. If one poses the question "does a tractor have advantages over a horse?" the very placing of the question immediately strikes one as hopelessly stupid. But if one asks whether a tractor has shortcomings when compared with a horse, we find that it does: it is more difficult to operate, it has to be repaired, and so forth. But he who would, for this reason, today propose to abandon the tractor and return agriculture to horse traction would be the ultimate reactionary. The participants in the Leninist class session were thinking not of return to the old but of how to improve the progressive, the advanced.

Consider that problem of egalitarianism. In the "Lenin's Path" Collective Farm, as we have seen, it is no serious problem. But it may safely be predicted that in one group or another where the effort will be made to arrange the organization and payment of labor in the new way, this may arise in a more or less acute form, depending upon its peculiarities. Thus, if we wish egalitarianism not to become a frightening bogeyman, we must immediately develop all possible techniques for counteracting it — a system of grade classification, a scale of wages — and to think up other, adequately flexible methods for keeping books on the quantity and quality of individual labor.

The participants in the Leninist lesson faced one more problem, the answer to which has thus far been found only in approximate, problematical form. E. I. Garnaga, economist of the Bureau of Collective Farm Organization of the Krasnodar Krai Agricultural Administration, asked Mamontov how many able-bodied people there are on his farm.

Mamontov: "1,800."

Garnaga: "And how many of them are engaged in regular jobs under the team system of association, and are paid for their labor in terms of the final product?"

Mamontov: "As I have already stated, this system functions in all the fields of our operation. Nevertheless, the number doing regular jobs is 600 to 700. The others are employed on seasonal jobs and are paid by the piece."

The same picture is to be seen in other farms of Krasnodar Krai. The earnings of the seasonal workers, who are still the majority, are still only one-half to two-thirds of those of the skilled personnel: equipment operators, livestock breeders, builders. It is natural that skilled labor is paid more, particularly when it is made dependent upon the final product. But it is not possible for all to become equipment operators. How are equal conditions for all to be established? The

paths to the solution of this undoubtedly most complex problem, as the participants in the lesson made clear, lie, in particular, in reducing the amount of manual unskilled work, in further mechanization of all branches of agricultural production, in training and raising the qualifications of all those who work. These processes will naturally lead to completely freeing a large number of hands from basic agricultural employment. However, further development of cooperatives and cooperative labor through carrying out production and processing in one and the same place, and through establishing agro-industrial complexes, could provide year-round employment for the vast bulk of rural people. Moreover, the service industries, material and cultural, still have to be built in the countryside from the ground up. What opportunities open here for the employment of skilled hands!

And so the lesson reached its final hour. Academician S. G. Kolesnev and Party Raion Committee Secretary I. M. Iudin take the floor. Their speeches summarize the Lenin lesson.

"The experiences of the Kuban people constitute a social experiment deserving of the closest study."

"Material incentive is not to be understood in the naive phrase, 'to pay more,' but, when work has been properly organized, to pay justly."

"The team system of organization and payment without specific operating orders from above is not a step backward, but a legitimate development of socialist relationships of production. The essence of this development is the triumph of collectivism in the consciousness of the peasant cooperator."

"Our discussion is not immune to dispute." The village awaits social scientists, and Novokubanka invites them to pursue this debate.

* * *

Religion

Voprosy istorii religii i ateizma,
No. IX, 1961, Sovremennoe Sektanstvo

A. I. Klibanov

THE DISSIDENT DENOMINATIONS* IN THE PAST AND TODAY

Problems of ideological struggle with the dissident denominations, representing sophisticated and subtle forms of religion, occupy a prominent place in the propagation of scientific atheist knowledge. Lenin's words, "One must know how to combat religion, and this requires a materialist explanation for the source of faith and religion among the masses," (1) are particularly applicable to this facet of the activity of scientific atheism.

However, questions pertaining to the ideological struggle with the dissident denominations, a most dangerous vestige of capitalism in the minds of men, have not had adequate treatment in the scholarly literature. Thus far there have been no special studies devoted to the histories of the various dissident denominations, a description of their teachings, and revelation of the socio-

political role of these denominations at various stages in the struggle of the laboring classes for liberation.

This lacuna has been filled only in part by the first volume of the selected writings of V. D. Bonch-Bruevich, published in 1959, containing his report to the Second Congress of the Russian Social-Democratic Labor Party, "The Schismatics [i.e., Old Believers — Ed.] and the Religious Dissidents in Russia" [Raskol i sektantstvo v Rossii], which is of major and fundamental significance. Written some 60 years ago, it was the first attempt at a Marxist investigation of the social essence, history, and ideology of the dissident denominations in Russia.

The 1930's saw the publication of F. M. Putintsev's detailed work, The Political Role and Tactics of the Dissident Denominations [Politicheskaia rol' i taktika sekt], as well as a number of brief monographs by other writers on particular denominations. Generally speaking, these writings have not lost their significance as good reference sources, but they have become bibliographical rarities. However, what is most important is the fact that in the intervening years the development of Marxist-Leninist historical

---

*This term (Russian: sektantstvo) takes in all religious bodies not belonging to the Orthodox communion, but specifically excludes the various groups of Old Believers. It is rendered in this translation either as in the title or by "religious dissidents" or, in an abstract sense, "religious dissidence." — Editor, Soviet Sociology.

science has advanced greatly, and the experience accumulated in ideological struggle with the religious dissidents, as well as data on their status in the 1940's and 1950's, have not been synthesized.

I

The Orthodox Church, true to the interests of the serf-owners and reactionary capitalists, slighted and persecuted the dissidents as religious renegades and apostates. The concept "religious dissidence" had no other meaning to the men of the church. The church did not wish to — and could not — recognize religious dissidence as a phenomenon legitimate in the exploitative structure of tsarist Russia, as this would have been equivalent to recognizing the legitimacy of protest by the masses of the people against the established church.

However, religious dissidence is by no means an inclusive concept applicable to all organizations and groups of religious persons outside the so-called ecumenical churches and their religions. Religious dissidence is a specific socio-historical phenomenon, possessed of significant distinctive features.

In his Draft of a Platform for Our Party [Proekt programmy nashei partii], Lenin wrote: "We know that religious dissidence and rationalism have grown among the peasants, and the appearance of political protest in a religious covering is a phenomenon characteristic of all peoples at a given stage of their development, and not of Russia alone." (2) The appearance of political protest in a religious shell is a phenomenon characteristic of all peoples under the conditions of dominance of the system of feudalism and serfdom. "Revolutionary opposition to feudalism," wrote Engels, "existed throughout the Middle Ages. Depending upon the conditions of the time, it appeared either in the form of mysticism, that of open heresy, or that of armed rebellion." (3)

Lenin, in the work cited above, classifies "the appearance of political protest in a religious covering" among facts testifying to the presence "of revolutionary elements in the Russian peas-antry." Lenin further writes: "We do not at all exaggerate the strength of these elements and do not forget the political underdevelopment and ignorance of the peasants...." (4)

In Lenin's words — "Whether these revolutionary elements in the Russian peasantry will be able to manifest themselves at least as did the West European peasantry in the overthrow of absolutism is a question to which history has not yet provided an answer" (5) — it is decisively clear that by that "given stage" in the development of peoples when political protest by the peasantry may express itself in a religious shell, Lenin understood precisely the system of feudalism and serfdom.

Russian religious dissidence falls into that category of socio-historical movements which it is customary to term those of religious reformation. It possesses features differentiating it from the movements of religious reformation which had taken place in Western and Central Europe in the 15th-17th centuries. A reformational movement in Russia, in the form of anti-feudal heresies, developed at the same time as the Reformation in the West. But at that time the Russian movements of reformation were, if not exclusively, then predominantly urban in character.

It was a consequence of Russia's socio-economic backwardness that in the 15th-17th centuries, the peasantry, living under patriarchal conditions, responded only to a negligible degree to the urban movements of reformation, while in Germany, for example, it was precisely the peasantry that constituted the most active force in the Reformation. Russian reformational movements — heretical movements — did not overflow into a struggle of national dimensions, did not break the spiritual dictatorship of the Orthodox Church, and did not deprive it of its material wealth.

In 18th-century Russia, as a consequence of the ever-increasing exploitation of the peasantry, changes in the forms of feudal dues, and the onset of capitalist stratification of the peasantry, religious dissidence appeared as a kind of "second edition" of the reformational movements. Their principal base was in the villages. But at that point, this "political protest in religious form" failed to find a broad response in the towns. For the urban strata the religious form of social protest was by that date already to a considerable degree a bygone stage. Moreover, religious dissidence offered no prospects of ever becoming a universal form of peasant movement. Having developed at a rather late stage in socio-historical development, denominationalism made its appearance from the very outset not on the highroad of class struggle as it was developing in the 18th century, but on one of its side-roads. During the second helf of the 18th century, the main direction of struggle against serfdom was pointed by the peasant disturbances and uprisings of the '50's through '70's, the Peasant War of 1773-1775 led by Pugachev, and by the men of the Russian Enlightenment of that day, whose outstanding representative was Radishchev.

In its world view, early religious dissidence expressed a sharp protest against the church, the clergy, and the entire organization and system of Orthodoxy, which gave its blessing to the system of serfdom. Reverence for ikons, belief in miracle workers, reverence for the letter of Holy Writ, and the luxurious church ceremonial and ritual were condemned by the dissidents as worship of the "God of the dead," as a superficial, false faith for purposes of display. Contrasted to all this was a faith based on "internal conviction" and service to "God in spirit and truth." In contrast to the established, ruling church, there developed the formula: a man is his own church. This ideology of antifeudal protest contained a positive ideological element.

The religious dissidents' appeal to individual freedom, to a man's inner convictions, and their expressed confidence in man's intellectual and moral strength, enabling them to proclaim man "the living temple" — all represented the founding in the peasant environment of the ideology of bourgeois individualism, clothed in a religious form.

Serfdom and the church serving it were condemned by the peasant in the concept of the "God of the dead," while the striving of the peasant for economic autonomy and independence, for the status of free self-employed commodity-pro-

ducer, found a vague expression in the formulas of religious individualism.

The ideology of the movements of the West European Reformation was also marked by religious individualism. It is precisely because, despite all the uniqueness of Russian religious dissidence, it does fall into the category of reformational movements, that its world view is covered, to a pronounced degree, by the definition given by Marx to the ideology of German Protestantism. Marx wrote: "For in its theoretical aspect the revolutionary past of Germany was the Reformation. Just as then the revolution began in the brain of a monk, today it begins in the brain of a philosopher.

"True, Luther conquered enslavement to piety only by replacing it by slavery to conviction. He routed faith in authority by restoring the authority of faith. He converted priests into laymen by transforming laymen into priests. He freed man from external religiosity by making religiosity the internal world of man. He emancipated the flesh from fetters only by placing fetters upon the heart of man.

"But if Protestantism did not provide a correct solution to the problem, at least it posed it correctly." (6)

Even in the early stages of its development, the world view of religious dissidence expressed the peasant's unconscious striving for the bourgeois order of things, in which the peasants hoped to take their place as free commodity-producers. This is why the world view of the modern religious dissidents is a bourgeois ideological survival in the most exact sense of those words. The world view of religious dissidence thus differs from that of Orthodoxy which, while it paid its tribute to bourgeois ideology, also bore and still bears an enormous burden of ideological carry-overs from feudalism. It must not be forgotten that the Orthodox Church made its appearance in Russia many centuries before religious dissidence and unswervingly served the feudal lords and serf-owners throughout its history.

Initially (in the 18th and, in part, even in the 19th centuries) the religious individualism that distinguished the world view of religious

258

dissidence had not driven social concerns and collective action from its midst. The critique of the authoritarian church and the demand that it be democratized found support in religious individualism, which the dissidents themselves proclaimed the "soul" of primitive Christianity. Such sects as the Dukhobors and the Molokans, beginning with a critique of the authoritarianism of the church, then proceeded to criticism of authoritarian principles in the life of society, and attempted to embody their concept of the "kingdom of God" on earth in the communes they established during the first half of the 19th century.

But while religious dissidence was born out of the contradictions in the life of society, it was itself a profoundly contradictory phenomenon. As the class struggle between peasants and serf-owners became more acute and as class contradictions in the villages developed, the political protest of the peasants had either to burst its religious shell or suffocate in it. Mere comparison with the militant antifeudal outbursts of the masses during the second half of the 18th century reveals the limited and constrained nature of religious dissident social protest.

During the first half of the 19th century this comparison displays even sharper contrasts. The mass peasant movement, which grew progressively from the 1820's onward, was rich in examples of armed struggle and demanded freedom from the oppression of serfdom directly, without religious trimmings. In the 1830's and 1840's there began the formation of the democratic-revolutionary movement which increasingly grasped the idea of overthrow of the monarchy and elimination of the system of serfdom by the forces of popular revolution.

The religious dissidence of that day was the least mature and simplest form of democratic movement. It is significant that the fact that the folk religious movements were not adapted to active participation in the social struggle was remarked upon even by Herzen and Petrashevskii.

From the day that the workers' movement opened a new epoch in the development of the class struggle in Russia, the independent role of religious dissidence as a form of expression of democratic interests vanished.

Marx's words on the sectarianism of the labor movement help one understand the decline in the democratic significance of religious dissidence as the class struggle developed: "The development of socialist sectarianism and the development of a genuine workers' movement are always in inverse ratio to each other. Sects have their (historical) justification so long as the working class has not yet matured to independent historical movement. As soon as it attains this maturity, all sects become essentially reactionary."(7)

II

The vast variety of forms in the history of religious dissidence in Russia testifies to nothing other than the unceasing efforts, up to the very beginning of the 20th century, of elements representing the rank-and-file of the people to escape from the limited nature of these religious teachings and movements.

When they became convinced of the invalidity of particular religious teachings and encountered efforts by leaders to monopolize authority in the congregations and to employ them for purposes of exploitation, elements in the dissident denominations representing the rank-and-file of the people broke first with one denomination and then with another, but only to replace a set of "untrue" teachings by "true" ones, "false" and "unjust" ideas by "just" ones. This showed the effects of the depth of ignorance and lack of consciousness of the rank-and-file members of dissident movements, their detachment from the advanced social movements of their day, the strength of patriarchal traditions, and the constraints placed upon these elements by their belief in God.

The multiplicity of forms of religious dissidence was a unique expression of class struggle arising within the dissident denominations themselves and becoming stronger as social contradictions developed.

As early as 1903, Bonch-Bruevich had written: "The fundamental cause of all these schisms within the denominations is something we should seek in the differentiation taking place in the peasant movement as a whole and consequently in the forms of the religious dissidents as well. ...It is on this basis that new social concepts and strivings arise which, as they continue to develop, exercise a powerful influence and pressure upon the entire way of life of the congregation and thereby further stimulate its cleavage and subsequent decay." (8)

The principal dissident denominations in Russia consisted of the Khristovshchina (Khlysty) [whips — i.e., flagellants], Skoptsy [castrates], Dukhobors [spirit-wrestlers], Molokans (milk-drinkers), so-called Shtundizm [from German Stunde, hour (of prayer)], and, finally, Baptism, Evangelical Christianity, and Adventism. Parallel to these currents, which were dominant in religious dissidence at particular stages in its development, there were other varieties. Moreover, various schools of thought existed in the major denominations.

Capitalist historiography found itself at a dead end in the face of the diversity of denominations. Powerless to understand this further fragmentation into sects and dissident persuasions as a manifestation of the class struggle within the dissident denominations, it classified them by secondary criteria — dominance of the "mystical principle" or the "rationalist principle" in their teachings — or on geographical lines, involving a differentiation between denominations of "western origin" and those of "eastern origin," etc. This classification led away from the principal questions of the roots of religious dissidence in the life of Russian society itself, and of the contradictions within it which expressed contradictions in society.

The earliest forms of religious dissidence in Russia — Khristovshchina and, somewhat later, the Skoptsy — appeared during the period when capitalist relationships were coming into being, and expressed social protest on the part of the serfs, chiefly those paying quitrent. These movements, headed by "prophets" laying down "the spirit of God," declared the entire world to be sinful. The idleness and luxury of the dominant classes were countered by a teaching of strict asceticism, carried to extremes in the theory and practice of emasculation.

By this asceticism the desperate serf peasants wished to express and demonstrate their complete abandonment of the hated world of serf-owners and their irreconcilability to this world. While serfs to their landlords, they now called themselves "men of God," and during gatherings for so-called rejoicings brought themselves to a state of mystical ecstasy in which they believed they sensed the presence of God in themselves.

This was the course of illusory denial of the surrounding world. When in the second half of the 18th century the development of capitalist relationships began to manifest itself more strongly in the countryside, and when prosperous peasants — possessing craft enterprises and in some cases manufactories, and buying and selling grain, hemp, etc. — began to appear among the very Khlysty and Skoptsy themselves, the congregations ("ships") of these faiths began to be transformed into organizations for the exploitation of the "people of God" by their own leaders, and the "Khlysty"-Skoptsy asceticism was gradually corrupted into bourgeois stinginess. But as the congregations of Khristovtsy and Skoptsy were transformed into organizations of exploitation and accumulation, their rank-and-file participants were liberated from asceticism and mysticism.

Out of the ranks of the Khlystovtsy came the heralds of a new doctrine — Siluan Kolesnikov and Illarion Pobirokhin, who preached "spiritual Christianity."

This doctrine laid the basis for the Dukhobor and Molokan movements. The new teaching called not for abandonment of the world, but for the creation of the "kingdom of God" on earth, based on equality and the holding of property in common. The doctrine of "spiritual Christianity" enjoyed great popularity among the odnodvortsy (a) category of state peasants.

However, the development of social contradictions, inequality of property, and the gradual emergence of capitalist and hired-laborer categories in the peasant milieu — those very processes that had, at an earlier stage, brought Khristovshchina and the Skoptsy to a dead end — inexorably led to the same results for the congregations of Dukhobors and Molokans. As early as the beginning of the 19th century, an élite of leaders (the councils of elders), which grossly infringed upon the democratic principles of the movement, took shape among the Dukhobors. In the communes of Dukhobors and Molokans established in the first half of the 19th century, the joint property gradually came into the hands of the elders. In the 1880's the social contradictions among the Dukhobors led to a schism into the "large party" and the "small party."

The latter constituted an organization of prosperous rural property-owners who exploited the rank-and-file Dukhobors remaining under their influence, as well as the peasants in the vicinity, and who established a "mutual understanding" with the tsarist administration.

The Molokans underwent fission even earlier. On the basis of protest against pressures from the elders, the so-called Jumper sect came into being, headed by Lukian Sokolov and later by Maksim Rudometkin.

The period subsequent to the freeing of the serfs in 1861 saw the appearance, among both Russian and Ukrainian peasants, of a new movement against the established church, which attracted many followers of the Dukhobors and Molokans and which the authorities called the "Shtunda." This movement was not homogeneous either as to its participants, its social ideals, or the religious teachings developed in it.

Peasants having little or no land, in areas where the statute labor (b) system had dominated, or farms combining characteristics of capitalism and corvée labor, constituted the bulk of the so-called "Great Russian "Shtunda."

Farm laborers, elements of the peasantry undergoing proletarianization, and the rural poor in districts where capitalist forms of agriculture predominated, constituted the bulk of the so-called "South Russian Shtunda." It is natural that the pressing daily social interests of its followers were reflected to a considerable degree in the teachings of the "South Russian Shtunda." Personal labor was elevated to the status of a law; "common" ownership of land and the wealth of nature was proclaimed; property-owners and exploiters were damned. The teachings of the "Great Russian Shtunda" were considerably more moderate. They envisaged only the limita-

tion of exploitation, while on the positive plane the social creativity of the "Great Russian Shtunda" did not go beyond the idea of establishing communal treasuries. However, an important place in the teachings of this trend was occupied by matters of religious dogma, interpreted in the spirit of Protestantism. But just as the "Great Russian Shtunda" included the sect led by the Tver' peasant, Siutaev, whose teachings coincided in their main points with the social ideals of the "South Russian Shtunda," so did the latter find room for the moderate trend led by Riaboshapka, which confined itself to teaching philanthropy and allotted a major place to problems of religious dogma.

Moderate tendencies, in which religious interests were in the foreground, were clearly predominant in the development of the religious dissident form of the peasant movement. This is explained by the fact that the conditions of the revolutionary situation at the end of the 1870's in themselves enabled those elements of the dissident denominations who made social demands to find a better outlet for their efforts in direct resistance to the landlords, seizure of landowners' lands, burning of manors, unauthorized felling of trees, etc.

As the farm-laborer, the semi-proletarian and the poorest peasant elements left the "Shtunda," elements of the rural capitalist class and the petty-bourgeois and artisan segments of the urban population came to predominate in it. During the 1870's the "Shtunda" began to be absorbed into Baptism, whose preachers were active in Russia as early as the previous decade.

In the West, Baptism had, by the 1870's, become one of the world-wide Protestant (reformational) churches, with its chief stronghold in the United States and with powerful organizations in England and Germany. It was financed by large-scale capitalists. Firm ties existed among the national organizations of Baptists in America, England, Germany, Holland, Sweden, Denmark, Switzerland, France, and Italy. The leaders of Russian Baptism brought to the "moderate" trends in the "Shtunda" an elaborate dogma, ritual, organizational forms, a body of trained preachers, literature, and funds.

Parallel to the organization of the "South Russian Shtunda" into the Baptist Church, the "Great Russian Shtunda" experienced the analogous influence of one of the schools of Baptism: Evangelism (Pashkovshchina, Redstokovshchina). Evangelism first developed under the aegis of a firm, the Society for Promotion of Spiritual and Moral Reading, whose book peddlers distributed in town and country many thousands of pamphlets on religious and hortatory subjects. Note must be taken of the interest manifested by the Evangelicals in publicizing their teachings among workers. For a twelve-year period (1875-1886) they published a journal, The Russian Worker [Russkii rabochii]. The content of the preachings of the Evangelists among the workers and urban lower middle class in many respects anticipated the propaganda of the followers of Zubatov. From the middle 1880's, Evangelism spread to the gubernias of St. Petersburg, Moscow, Tula, Iaroslavl', Tver', and others in central and northern Russia.

Adventism, which appeared in Russia in the 1880's (Tavricheskaia Gubernia) is a distinctive bourgeois Protestant denomination, although it bears resemblance to Baptism and Evangelism.

These sects no longer had anything in common with the interests of the people and, by the end of the 19th century, merged their socio-political standpoint with those of the liberal bourgeoisie.

Thus, during the entire history of religious dissidence, the struggle of its popular elements for their democratic interests led to its cleavage into ever smaller sects and the appearance of new forms. However, the old contradictions very rapidly developed with new strength in the new forms of religious movements, inasmuch as each and every "philosopher's stone" of the religious dissidents was an illusion and fiction, and could not bring them beyond the confines of social relationships.

In order to help the popular elements among the dissidents break loose from their religious limitations and prevent capitalist reaction from capturing these elements, the Second Congress of the Russian Social-Democratic Labor Party adopted the following resolution, at Lenin's suggestion: "Taking into consideration the fact that the religious dissident movement in Russia is, in many of its manifestations, one of the democratic trends directed against the existing order of things, the Second Congress directs the attention of all members of the Party to work among the religious dissidents for the purpose of winning them to Social Democracy.

"The Congress instructs the Central Committee to deal with the proposals in the report by Comrade Bonch-Bruevich." (9)

III

The Revolution of 1905 was of decisive importance in the historical fate of the dissident religious denominations. An exodus from them occurred during the revolution. Certain elements of the stratum of working people among the religious dissidents merged with the revolutionary movement, while others, disillusioned with the dissident movement, broke with it but remained aside from the revolutionary struggle. Although, even after the Revolution of 1905, the hard core of religious dissidence continued to consist basically of people from the peasantry and the non-aristocratic elements of the urban population, democratic currents no longer existed among them. The religious form of the democratic movement had outlived its time in history. "There was a time in history," wrote Lenin in 1913, "when...the struggle of the non-aristocratic elements and of the proletariat took the form of a struggle of one religious idea against another.

"But that period is long since past.

"Today, both in Europe and Russia, any, even the most sophisticated, most well-intended defense or justification of the idea of God is a justification of reaction." (10)

Capitalist elements were dominant in all the sects. The Molokans, who at one time were distinguished for the most democratic traditions, hastened in 1905, through their congress and leaders, to assure the tsar of their deep loyalty. The liberal bourgeois wing of the dissident denominations, which took shape long before 1905, consisted of the Baptists, the Evangelical Christians, the Mennonites, and Adventists. Now, at the very height of the revolution, they united to support the monarchy on the basis of their Political Platform of the Union for Freedom, Truth, and Peaceableness. It declared: "We do not want a Constituent Assembly, inasmuch as, for us, the question of the form of supreme governmental authority was resolved irrevocably by the Great All-Russian Zemskii Sobor (c) of February 13, 1613, and amended by the sovereign of our country on October 17, 1905." (11)

Parallel to the elimination of the democratic content of the dissident movement, which continued after the 1905 Revolution, a tendency took shape in that movement that began, after 1905, to manifest itself in the forming, on the basis of the denominations, of Christian political parties committed to capitalism. The Political Platform of the Union for Freedom, Truth and Peaceableness was supported by an organization, the Bureau of the Union for Freedom, Truth, and Peaceableness, and a founding convention of a new party was planned. The effectuation of this plan dragged out until the Revolution of February 1917, when one of the initiators of the Union, Prokhanov, established the Christian Democratic Party of Resurrection, based on the Evangelicals, and published a party platform that advocated the capitalist and landlord forms of property. (12)

The socio-political evolution of the dissident denominations was in accord with changes in their world view. The political slogans deriving from the capitalist upper ranks of the religious dissidents during and after the Revolution of 1905 are now primarily of historical interest. That which has remained in modern religious dissidence, however, is its religious philosophy, which, with the passage of time, has increasingly revealed itself to be militant reactionary bourgeois individualism.

During the second half of the 18th century, when the principle of religious individualism was developed in the sectarian milieu, it served the cause of struggle against the ideology of feudal authoritarianism, which depersonalized human beings, trampled upon human dignity, and elevated a slavish self-abasement of man to the status of a norm.

In the most recent religious-dissident movements, parallel to the transition to a bourgeois-

reactionary orientation, the principle of religious individualism has taken on a directly antisocial meaning.

From that point on, the followers of these movements called for the building of "the kingdom of God" within themselves. The concept of the social duty and the social goal of man and even the very concept of social man were ruled out.

The counterposing of the "inner man" to social man is what is distinctive in the "philosophy" of late religious dissidence. According to this idealist conception, the triumph of virtue in each individual automatically leads to the uprooting of "evil" in the outside world and thus eliminates all need for social struggle.

By contrast to the social essence of man, the term "spirituality" came to be applied to that which is fundamental in man, and this "philosophy" had a consequence which was far from abstract: the idea of revolution of the spirit was counterposed to that of social revolution. It is quite significant that the formula was framed and further developed in the dissident denominations in opposition to the revolutionary struggle of the working class for liberation.

In the late 1890's, in response to the activity of the St. Petersburg Union of Struggle for the Liberation of the Working Class, leaders of the Tolstoyan wing of the religious-dissident movement declared in their journal Svobodnaia mysl' [Free Thought]: "The economic basis of struggle is not the only one and not the most appropriate. ...Struggle on the basis of development of the spirit elevates a man over his opponent and in the final analysis always conquers the latter." (13)

Ten years later, in an article under the revealing headline "Socialism and Individualism" [Sotsializm i individualizm], published in the magazine Baptist, we read: "No equalization of economic conditions will ever equalize men's characters or achievements. Standing in opposition to Karl Marx, Friedrich Engels, and their appeal to self-interest we find Plato, Campanella, Leo Tolstoy, Burns and many others.... The change that socialism needs is a transfer of attention from the material to the highest good of man." (14)

In 1917 an ideologist of Baptism, Pavlov, wrote

in the magazine, Slovo istiny [The Word of Truth]: "Socio-economic problems are also close to the hearts of the Baptists, but their solution, in accordance with the teachings of the Gospels, must pass through a preliminary stage: revolution of the spirit. 'Seek thou first the kingdom of God, and all else will be given thee.' " (15)

The socio-political and ideological development of religious dissidence came to its end even before the triumph of the socialist revolution in Russia.

This was the distorted course of a popular movement that had separated itself from the common struggle of the laboring classes, was suffocating in its religious shell and — in the forms of Baptism, Evangelism, and Adventism — had been transformed into reactionary capitalist-oriented churches.

IV

The socialist revolution, which gave authority to the Soviets, expropriated capitalist property, abolished landlord property, and nationalized the land, dealt a decisive blow to the social roots of all religion.

Profound changes occurred in the state of religious dissidence.

Two stages may be seen in the development of the dissident denominations in the post-October period. During approximately the first 15 years of the history of Soviet society, a significant regrouping took place. This was a period of decay and decomposition of denominations of Russian origin — i.e., those which had come into being under Russian conditions as a unique form of social protest against serfdom (the "Khlysty," Skoptsy, Dukhobors, Subbotniki, [Sabbatarian], Molokans, and the last sects arising from these: the Old Israelites, the New Israelites, the Malevantsy, etc.).

At the same time, this was a period when, on the basis of the decay of the Orthodox Church and of the decomposition of the old forms of Russian religious dissidence, there was a considerable growth of denominations of Western origin; Baptism with its mystical offshoot, Pentecostalism, Evangelicalism (which is a form of Baptism), and Adventism.

As distinct from the old forms of Russian religious dissidence, which had arisen on the basis of the contradictions within the system of feudalism and serfdom, the Western denominations were a product of the contradictions of capitalism. In Russia, from the very outset, they were centered in areas distinguished for the scale and rates of development of capitalism: the South Russian and Baltic gubernias. The years of reorganization of the village in a capitalist direction on the basis of Stolypin's agrarian legislation — which staked its hopes on the "strong · muzhik" [peasant] — were also those of the greatest growth of these denominations in tsarist Russia.

The socialist revolution, which carried out the tasks of the bourgeois-democratic revolution as it proceeded, transformed into a historical anachronism the denominations that had developed at one time as democratic movements in a religious shell.

With respect to the teachings of the denominations deriving from the contradictions of capitalism, a basis for these continued to exist for a period under Soviet conditions — to wit, as long as the millions of toiling folk of the countryside functioned in fragmented individual forms; as long as a numerous exploiting class of kulaks existed, and as long as private capital retained certain positions in industry and trade.

This is why the next landmark to constitute a turning point in religious dissidence, subsequent to the socialist revolution, was the period of collectivization of agriculture and the elimination, on this basis, of the kulaks as a class — the period of attack of socialism against the capitalist elements all along the line.

The triumphant building of communism, the growth in the material well-being of the people, the mass dissemination of political and scientific knowledge, and the great achievements of Soviet science and technology are leading to increasing detachment of the working people from those sophisticated sects which succeeded in outliving old Russian religious dissidence.

Deviations in both directions are possible in the declining curve of the denominations presently existing. For example, during World War II, and particularly in the immediate postwar years, there was a certain revival of religious dissidence. This fact is deserving of close study and demands the most businesslike systematic and thoroughgoing work in the dissemination of scientific atheist knowledge. But this fact cannot conceal the overall regularity in the development of contemporary religious dissidence, which is manifested in a broad exodus of working people from it.

A survey even of the data that the dissident leaders have published in their own press demonstrates that, by comparison with 1928, i.e., the eve of collectivization, the number of followers of Evangelical Christianity and Baptism has declined by a factor of approximately 4.5 to the present. Great as is the significance of this fact, it does not in itself reveal the full scope of decay of modern religious dissidence.

The fact is that in the past the great bulk of its followers consisted of working people of village and town. According to a scientific study, in 1924, working peasants — "middle" (independent) and "poor" (requiring additional sources of livelihood) — constituted 89% of the membership of the dissident congregations in 47 rural okrugs of the Ukraine.

According to data obtained by an expedition of the History Institute of the USSR Academy of Sciences, which studied the state of the dissident denominations in Tambov Oblast in 1959, persons working on jobs and in agriculture constitute an average of about 30%, both in the Evangelical Christian-Baptist congregations and in those of the other dissident denominations.

Analogous data are characteristic of the Voronezh congregation of Evangelical-Christian Baptists. In the Moscow congregations of Seventh-Day Adventists, person working in industry and offices constitute 20%.

The overwhelming majority of Evangelical Christian Baptists, Seventh-Day Adventists, and Pentecostals are dependents, people retired on pension, and housewives. With respect to that portion of the religious dissidents who are directly engaged in socially useful labor, in the cities they are chiefly in semi-skilled or un-skilled occupations — cleaning-women, watchmen, practical nurses, janitors, and yard-men.

Thus, it was the working people of town and country, the direct builders of communist society, who were the first to abandon the dissident denominations.

A sharp rise in average age is also characteristic of the members of contemporary dissident denominations. The Baptists and Evangelicals had youth organizations even in the prerevolutionary period. In the 1920's these had mass membership. The leaders of Baptism and Evangelicalism placed their bets on the youth in all their work. The prominent Evangelical leader, Prokhanov, wrote in 1922: "... the hand of the Almighty has endowed the young generation, the Christian youth, with a happy, a great role." (16)

Let us turn our attention to the age composition of the Evangelical-Christian Baptists and the Seventh-Day Adventists of today.

According to the expedition which studied religious dissidence in Tambov Oblast, the ECB (Evangelical-Christian Baptist) congregation in the town of Michurinsk consisted 67% of persons of 60 and more, 31% of persons between 40 and 60, and only 2% of persons under 40.

The ECB congregation of Rasskazovo, Tambov Oblast, does not have one member under 40.

Age ratios similar to the foregoing apply in the Moscow congregations of Evangelical-Christian Baptists and of Seventh-Day Adventists, in which persons 40 and over number 85-90%.

The ageing of the membership is evidence of the fact that the dissident denominations have been abandoned above all by the youth, raised in Soviet society in the spirit of the world view of scientific communism and usually untouchable by the alien influences of these ideologies. It is therefore all the more necessary to struggle for those young men and girls — sometimes pupils in the upper grades of schools and special educational institutions — who by force of family tradition or for some other reason have come under the influence of the dissident denominations.

Changes in the sex composition of modern religious dissidence are also highly revealing.

True, as early as the mid-1930's, a preponderance of women was observed. Today this has reached an extraordinary level. Among the ECB in Michurinsk, Tambov Oblast, women number 70%, while the figure is 87% in that denomination in the town of Rasskazovo, in the same oblast, and 88% among the Moscow Seventh-Day Adventists.

Scientific study of the status of religious dissidence today has certainly not been developed on the scale needed. Facts which we have gathered from periodicals published in the Urals, western and eastern Siberia, and the Ukraine, fragmentary as they are, permit us to apply the conclusions we have drawn to those areas as well, of course, more or less with variation.

V

The history of the decay of the earlier religious dissidence and the gradual degeneration of the dissident denominations presently existing and functioning have been accompanied by revealing changes in their tactics and ideologies.

The religious dissidents, who had as early as the Revolution of 1905 become agencies of capitalist reaction, stood as one with the counter-revolutionary capitalist class during the October Revolution. "They wanted freedom," raged the Baptist journal Slovo istiny in November 1917, "but one party (the Bolsheviks), having gathered the bayonets on its side, continues to perpetrate horrors and repressions.... A repetition of the Paris Commune is occurring, and it will cause Russia to perish." (17) The same journal appealed: "... enough of blood, come to your senses! Let us overthrow the idols of partisan thoughtlessness and extend to each other the hand of brotherly communion on the basis of unity in spirit." (18)

The dissident denominations, to the degree that their reactionary hierarchy succeeded in imposing its will upon the rank-and-file, took a stand of nonrecognition, boycott, and resistance to Soviet authority during the entire Civil War period and during the first years of the period of reconstruction that followed. Even in 1920 the Baptist journal Istochnik iz kamnia [The

Spring from the Rock] published an article, "The Builders of Babylon" [Vavilonskie stroiteli], whose author uttered the screaming prophecy: "The fate of the godless builders is dispersal; the fate of their structures — ruin, destruction ...." (19) The Evangelical leader, Prokhanov, appealed in 1921 from the podium of a congress of his denomination to the Soviet "men of state": "... we are compelled to point out that all your reforms have crumbled before our very eyes, and will continue to collapse until you provide the proper foundation — man, who bears the image and shape of God." (20)

During 1920-1922 the leaders of the dissident denominations took steps to unite their organizations and also to establish, under specific conditions, a unified bloc with groups in the Russian Orthodox Church who sought to appeal to the people in the name of a religious reformation in opposition to the socialist revolution. Late in 1919 and early in 1920, the leaders of the Baptists and Evangelists agreed to form a joint center, called the "Temporary All-Russian Joint Council of Evangelical Christians and Baptists."

In 1922 Prokhanov issued a call, "The Evangelical Appeal" [Evangel'skii klich] to the old-style and reformed Orthodox groups; in it he agreed "to forgive the sins" of the Church for its centuries-long persecution of the dissident denominations, and declared: "... nothing could so rejoice the Evangelical Church as that the 'dead' Orthodox Church is coming 'alive.'" Prokhanov advised the Church to make a number of changes: "to remove the shroud of all vestiges of its former dead condition." He offered aid and alliance and boastfully closed his Appeal: "The united forces of renewal will prove so great that all obstacles will be overcome and the Galileean will triumph once again, and his triumph will be complete." (21)

The plans for unification of the dissident and Orthodox "forces of renewal," as well as the disloyal stand of the dissident leadership as a whole, broke down primarily because of the military and economic triumphs of the Soviet people. Nor were the dissident leaders capable of overcoming conflicts in their relations with each other, or competition in their relations with the Orthodox groups. They were all the more incapable of dealing with the fact of the increasing resistance to their policies by their own followers, chiefly from among the middle and poor peasantry.

The fact is that while Wrangel's troops included a unit of Mennonites noted for their prosperity, there were instances such as that in which poor-peasant Molokans took to arms and drove Nationalist Mensheviks out of Novyi Baiazet.

The Baptist leaders became persuaded of the insecurity of their influence over the rank-and-file: "And what is most terrible," wrote V. V. Ivanov in the magazine Slovo istiny, "is that many poor brethren wish to obtain land and all blessings from the hands of socialists who do not grant the existence of God and say with pride: none other but only we ourselves shall create a new life in Russia! One said to me in so many words that he had long since rejected God and settled all accounts with Him. Another declared outright that 'a revolutionary Social Democrat knows neither pity nor God nor the other concepts of the old world.' " (22)

The pressure of the lower ranks upon their leaders, under conditions in which the stability and durability of the Soviet government were no longer doubted even by its enemies, caused the élite of the religious dissident movement to declare that they would take a loyal attitude toward the Soviet government. Such declarations were made by the Baptist, Evangelical, Adventist, and Pentecostal leaders at the conventions held by their denominations in 1924-1926. It is significant that the "recognition" of the Soviet government by the dissident denominational leaders coincided in point of time with the period of "recognition" of our country and the establishment of diplomatic relations with it by such capitalist states as England, France, Japan, Italy, etc.

However, during those years this was merely a forced tactical maneuver, changing nothing in the fundamental attitude of the dissident leaders to the foundations of the Soviet governmental and social system.

The fact that the dissident leaders engaged in conscious deception in declaring from the platforms of their conventions political loyalty and even "entire sympathy for all the slogans of Soviet authority" is clear from the actions of a number of some dissident activists and fanatics who agitated against the internal loans to which the Soviet government asked the people to subscribe, and called for refusal to pay agricultural and other taxes, refusal to be counted in the census, interference in some places against grain procurement, etc., etc.

In a special composition titled "A Letter to a Friend and Brother" [Pis'mo k odnomu drugu i bratu], circulating among agents of the Adventists, it was admitted outright that the policy of loyalty proclaimed at the Adventist Convention of 1924 was merely a "shrewd diplomatic maneuver" and "an agile and astute way out of the difficult situation which had arisen." (23)

The new tactic of the dissident leaders was practiced particularly widely between 1924 and 1928, and was expressed both in formal acceptance of the Soviet regime and in a policy for a peculiar sort of "reconciliation" with Soviet reality. This was an adaptive device, rich in Christian socialist demagogy designed to deceive the working people, including rank-and-file religious dissidents, but secretly inspired by hopes for a gradual degeneration of the Soviet system to capitalism.

This was the essence of the "Smenovekhovstvo" (d) (change-of-landmarks movement) that occurred in the dissident denominations between 1924 and 1926. A typical product of this was an open letter published in 1925, signed by the leading Evangelicals, Baptists, Adventists, Dukhobors, Molokans, and Tolstoyans, under the flaunting title The Social-Revolutionary Role of the Dissident Denominations [Sotsial'no-revoliutsionnaia rol' sektantstva].

The tactic of adaptation and ideological speculation on slogans of Christian socialism was practiced by the religious dissidents for many years. However, the period of collectivization and abolition of the kulaks as a class provided a clear demonstration of the hypocrisy of this tactic. The dissident activists spoke out in support of the kulaks and against collectivization. Cases are known in which they wormed their way into leadership in collective farms and then acted so as to discredit the collective-farm movement. Often they established their own collective associations based on community of religion, attempting to separate the rank-and-file religious dissidents from the general movement of the peasantry and to guide their associations along the line of the capitalist cooperative movement. In the course of collectivization, the hidden mainspring of the denominational tactic of conformity — their hope for the restoration of capitalism — broke down.

We have already pointed to the exceptionally important consequences of the triumph of socialism in the countryside for the process of overcoming religion among the broad masses of the peasantry.

In general, these were more or less remote consequences. But it is necessary to take into consideration that, in the Ukraine for example, on the eve of collectivization, the rural dissident congregations included an average of 11% kulaks among their members, while in Novosibirsk Okrug, according to data of 1926, kulaks were 8% of the Evangelicals, 6% of the Adventists, and 4.4% of the Baptists. In individual instances, as in Odessa Okrug, for example, kulaks and merchants constituted over 30% of the gross membership of dissident congregations in 1925-1927.

The elimination of the kulaks as a class on the basis of the collectivization of agriculture weakened the denominational congregations, primarily because it was the kulak who was the leading force in the dissident denominations.

The collectivization of agriculture opened the eyes of many rank-and-file denominationals to the hypocrisy of the "left" tactic of their leaders and to the exploitative essence of the religious-dissident cooperative associations.

Of very great importance in the struggle against dissident influences were the educational consequences of working in a group, the public opinion of the collective farmers. This was well understood by the denominational leaders, who therefore attempted to isolate their following in economic units limited to them.

Even on the eve of collectivization, the denominational leaders were full of hopes for the flourishing of their communions. Even Voronaev,

leader of the comparatively small Pentecostal denomination, solemnly announced at the end of 1927: "We await a great spiritual awakening of our people, a people that seek God; we expect a broad and deep reformational movement in our vast country, with its great opportunities." (24)

However, in view of the reasons indicated, a decline of the dissident denominations, a reduction in numbers and breakup of many congregations, were observed even in the course of collectivization. Thus, in Western Siberia the number of Baptist congregations dropped by 10.9% from 1929 to 1932 and by more than three-fourths in the Far Eastern Krai, while the number of Evangelical congregations fell by nearly two-thirds. The ranks of the Baptists and Evangelicals in the Ukraine and Belorussia also became substantially thinner.

Whereas in the period preceding the building of the foundations of the socialist economy it was the old forms of Russian religious dissidence that fell apart, to be replaced by others of Western origin, now it was the Western denominations, originating under capitalist conditions, that began to decline, with the difference that no new forms of religious dissidence arose to take their place. (25)

During the 1930's the phenomenon of decline of the dissident denominations increased. The Baptists, at one time the largest among them, distinguished by strict centralization, fragmented into a number of weakly associated congregations of reduced membership, spontaneously forming alliances with and often uniting locally with congregations of Evangelicals and groups of Pentecostals.

A turning point in the politics of the dissident denominations occurred during the second half of the 1930's.

Openly hostile statements against the dictatorship of the proletariat, such as were made during the Civil War and the very beginning of the period of reconstruction, proved futile, as did the subsequent tactic of conformity, and masked disloyalty and opposition, to the building of socialism. This was a bitter lesson for the laboring element among the religious dissidents who had been deceived by their leaders. (26) In the face of the ever growing and increasingly firm moral and political unity of the Soviet people — the entire people, regardless of division into religious and irreligious — a politically loyal line became a prerequisite if the faithful themselves were to participate in denominationalism, i.e., it was a condition for its very existence.

The revival of religious dissidence in individual places, particularly noticeable between 1943 and 1952, was due to factors which had nothing at all in common with the reasons for the growth of these communions during the 1920's.

During the war years, the dissident denominations fed parasitically upon the people's sorrow, upon the sufferings caused by the invasion of the German Fascists and the consequent German Fascist occupation of a number of the country's territories. At that time, the denominations grew artificially as a consequence of the temporary reduction in the people's living standard. The growth of religious dissidence was stimulated by the activity of its preachers, operating under conditions in which the propaganda of scientific atheism in many places had been abandoned or was conducted unskillfully and sporadically. Often the preachers of these denominations acted (and act) in violation of and in evasion of Soviet law, which prohibits organizing of private charity, conducting religious propaganda (in homes), holding meetings without registering them with the Soviet authorities, and so forth.

The revival of religious dissidence brought with it a renewal of the organized activity of the Baptists, this time not independent however, but in alliance with the Evangelicals and the Pentecostals. This unification took place officially in 1944-1945, and was given the title Evangelical Christian-Baptism.

At present, under conditions of a new and mighty upsurge of the productive forces and the culture of the Soviet people, the growth of the dissident denominations has slowed down everywhere, and in a number of places ceased. But we have already spoken of the major trends in the development of modern religious dissidence.

VI

The religious ideology of the dissident denominations is irreconcilably hostile to the world view of scientific communism. In the philosophical sense, this ideology is the purest idealism, as is every other religious ideology. In its view of society, the denominationals' ideology is just as idealist as are their views of the universe as a whole. Typical of this ideology is denial of the very concept of society. Central to this ideology is the concept of man entirely absorbed by his relationship to God and, on that basis, condemnatory of any active attitude toward society.

All religion is antisocial, but its reactionary essence is manifested differently in accordance with the specific character of one or another church or denomination. Thus, the reactionary essence of Baptism consists, among other things, in denial of the very possibility of exerting planned and purposeful influence upon society and nature. The leading religious idea of Baptism is the so-called dogma of predestination.

Baptism proceeds, as is set forth in the Confession of Faith of the Baptist Christians [Ispovedanie very khristian-baptisov], from the idea that people "are children of wrath, completely incapable of and not inclined to all that is good, but capable of and inclined to all that is evil." (27) Possessing no positive characteristics, man, according to the Baptist belief, lacks free will and the capacity to engage in purposeful activity.

"From the beginning of time" and to "the end of time," Baptism teaches, God had determined who, in the succession of human generations, was "chosen" and "saved," and who was "condemned" and "lost." This divine predestination is immutable and unknowable. The religious fatalism of Baptist teachings is a typical product of capitalism, a society in which "success or bankruptcy depends not upon the activity or skill of particular individuals but upon circumstances beyond their control." (28)

This ideology of despair, helplessness, and blind submission to "fate," produced by the capitalist system, is sown by today's preachers of Baptism among Soviet people — builders of communism, proud transformers of nature, conquerors of the cosmos.

"Man: how proud that sounds," says socialist

humanism as expressed in Gorky's words. "Man is a lie," says Baptism. (29)

The preachers of Baptism try to persuade Soviet people, armed with the world-transforming theory of scientific communism: "The world is tired of theory. The world needs practicality." (30) Thus are the basic principles of Baptism rendered concrete in contemporary Baptist preaching.

Intimately associated with Baptism by history and ideology is what is called Pentecostalism (the Christian Evangelical Faith), also known as the "Jumping" religion [Prygunstvo], which was close to the Baptists from the 1880's on. (31) Reiterating the fatalistic teaching of Baptism — "Man himself cannot save himself either by his own piety or by works of any kind..." (32) — the Pentecostals preach "baptism with the Holy Ghost and with fire," reviving the mystical teachings of the Khlyst movement in their own manner.

The Pentecostals ascribe special significance to the third figure in the Christian trinity, the "Holy Ghost," of which their catechism says: "In him the faithful have joy and peace. He speaks mysteries, prays and sings. He comes into and is in people." (33)

At one time Pentecostalism (34) indirectly expressed protest against orthodox Baptism and its formality, its rigorously regulated religious, church, and congregational procedures, and its teaching of the utter inviolability of "divine predestination." To this the Pentecostals counterposed the theory of the "Holy Ghost" who "comes and is in people" and "speaks mysteries."

The religious self-deception of the Pentecostals has its roots in the history of capitalism, when people oppressed by poverty and exploitation, feeling themselves lost, sought special means of "forgetting" the world around them. Pentecostalism is a profoundly reactionary theory, one of the most poisonous forms of "spiritual rotgut."

Adventism is also a typical product of capitalist society. While fatalism typifies Baptism, and mysticism is typical of Pentecostalism, eschatology is characteristic of Adventism. This is the "doctrine" that man's life on earth will soon come to an end, with a divine trial held "upon the living and the dead" and the subsequent triumph of the "righteous" in the "heavenly kingdom." The despair of the middle classes, transformed by the course of capitalist development into proletarians, into paupers — this is what was expressed in Adventism, when it developed in the mid-19th century among American farmers impoverished by large-scale capital.

The eschatology of Adventism takes its origins primarily from the mystical fantasies of the Biblical prophecies of Daniel and the Apocalypse, within the framework of which Adventism seeks to define its attitude toward the outside world. A characteristic feature of this sect is a fraudulent acceptance of the achievements of the social and natural sciences, false claims to culture, education, modernity of its concepts, designed to win the confidence of the faithful and to undermine a scientific world view from within.

Adventists willingly "condemn" the men of the established church who slandered Copernicus, but their purpose is to reduce the work of this scientist of genius to nought on the "basis" that it was allegedly clear from the Bible that the earth rotates on its axis and around the sun.

Moreover, clearly lacking in any sense of humor, they cite the prophet Isaiah: "It is He who supervises the orbiting of the earth." (35)

They willingly "accept" Newton's law of universal attraction so as to say that Newton was impelled to this law by... the Biblical Book of Job, in which we read: "The earth hung from nothing." (36)

With a most scholarly mien, the Adventists record the events of world history, listing facts and names, and pedantically reckon up dates, but only so as to say: "In his prophetic word, God sketched out for man, as on a clock-face, the entire course of world history and, if we master this clock, we will know what period in world history we are living through and what we may expect in the nearest future." (37)

From this Adventist Biblical "sociology" the following conclusion is drawn: "The prophetic divine clock's stated time will soon run out, and His court will be held. Are you ready, albeit in your last hour, to become a citizen of the kingdom of God?" (38)

We note that in a number of its characteristics, Adventism is similar to that most reactionary of ideologies, so-called Jehovism (the "Jehovah's Witnesses").

We shall not cite here the numerous facts, familiar to us, testifying to the immoral acts or antisocial activity of individual representatives of religious dissidence.

These facts are indicative primarily with respect to the fact that no religion is able, despite the assertions of its apologists, to be of significance as either an absolute or a relative moral force. But regardless of these facts — and this is vastly more important — the ideology of religious dissidence is profoundly reactionary in itself. It is, as we have shown, a distorted survival of capitalist society, and this holds whether we are speaking of the ideology of the Baptists, the Pentecostals, the Adventists or any other denomination whatever.

Fatalism, mysticism, eschatology — these are all the products of the fantasy of a helpless man, lost and condemned to destruction by capitalism. This ideology of intellectual poverty and narrowness is what the modern preachers of the dissident denominations are trying to impose upon Soviet people. It is just as hostile and irreconcilable to the scientific world view of Marxism-Leninism as capitalism is hostile and irreconcilable to communism.

The history of religious dissidence shows how and why it made its followers the captives of capitalist reaction and how today it is a disseminator of antisocial and unscientific ideas. The ideological struggle with religious dissidence is a pressing task of the propaganda of scientific atheism and a component of our entire struggle for the cultivation of conscious and inspired builders of communism.

Editor's Notes

a) These were descendants of petty service gentry, who held land directly from the tsar on condition of military or civil service.

b) A special form of sharecropping, in which the peasant provided equipment and draft animals and was credited for this against a previous debt or loan.

c) This body, which is roughly translatable as "national assembly," elected the first tsar of the Romanov line.

d) A political movement of the time of the 1917 Revolution which looked forward to the transformation of the Soviet Union, after a period of socialism, into a capitalist state of Western European type. By extension, the term is applied in the Soviet literature to any movement espousing such an idea.

Footnotes

1) V. I. Lenin, Soch., Vol. 15, p. 374.
2) Ibid., Vol. 4, p. 223.
3) Marx and Engels, Soch., Vol. 7, p. 361.
4) V. I. Lenin, Soch., Vol. 4, p. 223.
5) Ibid.
6) Marx and Engels, Soch., Vol. I, pp. 422-423.
7) Ibid., Vol. XXVI, p. 174.
8) V. D. Bonch-Bruevich, Izbr. soch., Moscow, 1959, Vol. 1, p. 167.
9) KPSS v rezoliutsiiakh i resheniiakh s'ezdov, konferentsii i plenumov TsK, 7th ed., Part 1, 1954, p. 48. V. D. Bonch-Bruevich proposed the issuance of a Social Democratic publication for the religious dissidents. As a consequence, a magazine titled Rassvet appeared in 1904. See our article, "V. D. Bonch-Bruevich i problemy religiozno-obshchestvennykh dvizhenii v Rossii," in Vol. I of Bonch-Bruevich's Izbrannye sochineniia, Moscow, 1959.
10) V. I. Lenin, Soch., Vol. 35, p. 93.
11) F. M. Putintsev, Politicheskaia rol' i taktika sekt, Moscow, 1935, p. 48.
12) Utrenniaia zvezda, 1917, No. 1, p. 6.
13) Svobodnaia mysl', 1899, No. 3, p. 326.
14) Baptist, 1909, No. 18.
15) Slovo istiny, 1917, No. 1, p. 3.
16) Utrenniaia zvezda, 1922, No. 1-2.
17) Slovo istiny, 1917, No. 13-14, p. 180.
18) Ibid., p. 162.
19) Istochnik iz kamnia, 1920, No. 11-14, p. 2.
20) Utrenniaia zvezda, 1922, No. 1-2, p. 2.

21) Evangel'skii klich. Poslanie Vysshemu tserkovnomu upravleniiu pravoslavnoi tserkvi i gruppe "Zhivoi tserkvi" ot svobodnoi narodnoi evangel'skoi tserkvi (Vserossisskogo soiuza evangel'skikh khristian), 1922.

22) Slovo istiny, 1918, No. 9-12, p. 94.

23) I encountered this document among Seventh-Day Adventists in Novgorod in 1926 or 1927 and published excerpts from it in my pamphlet Adventisty, Priboi, 1931, pp. 24, 26, and 27.

24) Protokoly vtorogo vseukrainskogo i pervogo vsesoiuznogo s'ezdov khristian evangel'skoi very..., Odessa, 1928, p. 34.

25) Sects such as the Fedorovshchina, True Orthodox Christianity (IPKh), and the True Orthodox Church (IPTs) did not differ from Orthodox Christianity in any significant aspect of their dogma. They comprise one page in the history of the monarchist-Orthodox counterrevolution.

26) Among the few small dissident denominations noted for their disloyalty, the Jehovah's Witnesses and Reformed Adventists are outstanding. But even among rank-and-file members of these denominations there are no few individuals who take the religious phraseology of their leaders on faith and do not understand their real intentions.

27) Izpovedanie very khristian-baptistov, Moscow, 1928, p. 12.

28) Marx and Engels, Soch., Vol. XVI, Part II, p. 297.

29) Division of Manuscript Collections (hereafter ORF) of the Institute of History, Academy of Sciences, USSR, Folder for Tambov Expedition of 1959. From sermons of the Baptist presbyter of the town of Rasskazovo, Tambov Oblast, June 1959.

30) Ibid.

31) As early as 1884, at their conference in Novo-Vasil'evka, the Baptists considered the problem "Vopros o dukhe prygunstva, kak priznat' ego: dukhom zabluzhdeniia ili dukhom bozhiim" (see Bishop Aleksii, Materialy dlia istorii religiozno-ratsionalisticheskogo dvizheniia na iuge Rossii vo 2 pol. XIX st., Kazan', 1908, p. 577).

32) Kratkoe verouchenie khristian evangel'skoi very, Odessa, 1926, p. 6.

33) Ibid., p. 5.

34) It is not impossible that the genesis of the Pentecostals represents a product of mutual influence between the so-called spiritual Christian "Jumpers" (a Molokan sect) and Baptism. The most prominent ideologists of the Jumper Molokans, Sokolov and Rudometkin, started in Tambov Gubernia.

35) Blagovestnik, 1926, No. 1, p. 7

36) Ibid.

37) Blagovestnik, 1926, No. 3, p. 6.

38) Ibid., p. 8.

* * *

Local Government and Administration

Sovety deputatov trudiashchikhsia, 1965, No. 8

V. Chkhikvadze, I. Pavlov, and I. Azovkin

INCREASING THE ROLE OF THE SOVIETS: AN IMMEDIATE TASK

A large group of scholars of the Institute of Government and Law, USSR Academy of Sciences, jointly with personnel of the Institute of Philosophy and Law of the Academy of Sciences, Kazakh SSR, have familiarized themselves with the practices of the Soviets of Kazakhstan.

A great deal of factual material was accumulated as a result of this research. In this number we publish the first article written on the basis of the data obtained on this trip. — Editors, Sovety deputatov trudiashchikhsia.

* * *

The CPSU Program provides that the rights of the local Soviets (of local self-government) will be enlarged in the course of the building of communism. They will become the final authority in all matters of local importance. An increas-

Mr. Chkhikvadze is a corresponding member of the USSR Academy of Sciences; Mr. Pavlov holds the degree of Doctor of Jurisprudence, and Mr. Azovkin the degree of Candidate of Jurisprudence.

ing number of questions within the jurisdiction of the bureaus and departments of the executive is gradually to be turned over to the standing committees of the local Soviets. The strengthening of agencies on the raion level deserves special attention.

This was stated, as we see, clearly, flatly, and with sober consideration of the needs of the day and the tasks facing the country during the new stage of its development, in complete accord with Lenin's anticipations and with the experience and practices of the development of the state structure.

In this connection, it is not superfluous to recall that, during Lenin's lifetime and in the first years after his death, the organs of local government and their executive committees played an exceptionally important role in all branches of the economy, and bore on their shoulders a vast proportion of the work of government administration. They regularly discussed questions of Union-wide and republic-wide significance, and essentially decided all matters of a local nature — questions of planning, finances and taxation, the land, etc. They directed the work of the overwhelming majority of industrial enterprises, inasmuch as these were subordinate to bureaus of the gubernia executive committees.

Unfortunately, in subsequent years, for diverse reasons, the role of the local Soviets in political, economic, and cultural development began gradually to decline. It was particularly diminished as a result of the excessive centralization of government administration, and various bureaucratic distortions of the principle of democratic centralism in the development of Party and government. The range of questions decided by the agencies of local government was sharply narrowed and did not remotely include even those most important from the viewpoint of patently local interests. Local initiative was often artificially constrained by the need for endless "agreements to," even "confirmations of," their decisions by central agencies. This established favorable soil for stereotyped and paper-pushing modes of operation in both the formation and the functioning of agencies of the Soviets at the krai, oblast, city, raion, and village level. The local Soviets were reduced essentially, for the most part, to consultative organs subordinate to the administrative machinery, and ceased to function as "corporate working bodies," which is what Lenin wished them to be.

Naturally, this situation could not but disturb the Party and its Central Committee. In improving the administration of the country, reestablishing Lenin's standards in the functioning of government and developing them further in the light of the specific historical situation, the Party took measures to increase the role of the Soviets of Working People's Deputies in general, and of the local Soviets in particular.

The 20th Congress of the CPSU directed the attention of Party bodies to the need to revivify the functioning of the Soviets so as to increase their role in economic and cultural development, in satisfying the needs and demands of the population, and in educating the working people toward communism. This demand of the congress was subsequently embodied in the Jan. 22, 1957, resolution of the Central Committee of the CPSU "On Improving the Functioning of the Soviets of Working People's Deputies and Strengthening

Their Ties with the Masses" [Ob uluchshenii deiatel'nosti Sovetov deputatov trudiashchikhsia i usilenii ikh sviazei s massami], which contained a comprehensive plan of action toward that end. The resolution envisaged the strengthening of the responsibility of the local Soviets and their executive committees for the work of industry and agriculture, and for the fulfillment of production plans and assignments by every factory, mill, construction project, collective farm, and state farm. It was specified that the local Soviets should engage consistently in the building and repair of dwelling houses, schools, hospitals, children's institutions, urban and consumer service facilities, and should organize these to assure that they function normally. The Central Committee of the CPSU stated that Party committees must not interfere in the administrative-dispositive functions of agencies of government, and directed Party organizations to put an end to petty tutelage and unnecessary interference in the work of the Soviets and their executive committees, and to assure the development of their initiative and independence.

The 22nd Party Congress and the Program it adopted outlined an even broader sphere of activity for local agencies of government.

In other words, Lenin's line of strengthening the Soviets as representative and fully empowered agencies of the people's power, and of strengthening their role in economic, political, and socio-cultural progress has been expressed with ultimate precision and consistency in the major Party decisions of recent years, and remains unchanged. The Communist Party is working daily and tirelessly to carry them into life.

It would be false to disregard the colossal work done in the country in recent years to strengthen the financing and material position of local government agencies, to broaden their functions, strengthen their staffs, and increase the numbers of citizens voluntarily assisting in their work. Such measures as the transfer of a number of questions of economic and cultural development from republican agencies to local ones (conducted intensively in the republics from 1955 to 1959), the transfer of some housing to the local Soviets, along with consumer service enterprises, retail trade, children's preschool institutions, and schools, which had all been in the hands of a variety of bureaus, the introduction of consistent rotation of the membership of the Soviets, regular reporting by the Soviets and their staffs to the population — these and many other measures not only stimulated the work of the local organs of government, but created the preconditions for further intensifying their influence on all aspects of the life of society.

But it would be equally false and harmful to remain silent about the mistakes made in this field, particularly between 1960 and 1964. Above all, we must note that objective conditions and possibilities were underestimated or ignored, that there was a subjective approach to decision of questions of organization of the Soviets, and frequent and unfounded reorganizations of the government machinery occurring until the October (1964) Plenum of the Central Committee of the CPSU. Measures of this order essentially denigrated the role of the Soviets. The artificial narrowing of the sphere of activity of the organs of local government in the realm of production, and the clearly seen effort to concentrate their attention solely on housing, consumer, and socio-cultural services, became pregnant with the danger that their role might be reduced to fulfilling these tasks alone and that they might be converted into something resembling municipal governments in the West. The hasty and occasionally excessive enlargement of territorial-administrative units, accompanied, moreover, by a mechanical reduction in the paid staffs of the local Soviets and by the retention of an unjustifiably low salary scale for personnel at the bottom rung, threatened to make the Soviets remote from the population and to weaken their personnel. The division of oblast (krai) Soviets into industrial and rural, the establishment of the so-called "industrial" zones, centers, and raions, led to violation of the unity of the Soviet system of representative government, and complicated and confused the administration of government.

As we know, all this has now been condemned by the Party and the people. The organization of the Soviets on a basis of territorial economic units has been restored. A portion of the raions have been divided into smaller units and measures taken to make them easier to administer. The salaries of the large army of employees of the Soviets have been increased. Their attention has been redirected to include problems of production as well, including those of agriculture. Other measures, too, have been taken to increase the role of the local Soviets as organizers of the masses in town and country. Thus, much has already been done. Serious obstacles in the path of development of the Soviets have been eliminated.

But this does not mean that we have already done all that is needed, and may now rest on our laurels. The Party demands further improvement of the leadership of government, and search for new, effective devices for further activating the Soviets, so as to proceed further in carrying out the tasks set forth in the Program of the CPSU. And measures cannot be confined merely to reestablishing the situation that existed a few years ago, for that would mean marking time.

The essence of the measures elaborated by the Plenums of the Central Committee of the CPSU in October and November of 1964, and March 1965, including those having to do with the local Soviets, consists of a sharp turn by Party and government in the direction of a scientifically based economic policy. It is necessary to look upon things more broadly, viewing them from the standpoint of the truly scientific principles of government administration developed by Lenin, verified by many years of experience, and approved and creatively developed by the Party. The job is to analyze both plusses and minuses in the work, and to take as point of departure the actual and not the imagined needs of social development, to evaluate soberly all that has already been done and that which remains to be done, to study the opinions of the personnel on the spot, and the judgments arrived at by the population itself.

Rather recently, the Institute of Government and Law of the USSR Academy of Sciences, together with the Institute of Philosophy and Law of the Academy of Sciences, Kazakh SSR, undertook to study the experience of the local Soviets of Kazakhstan, toward which end a large group of personnel of our institute traveled there. With the active cooperation of Party and local government agencies of the republic, much factual material was collected, rich and highly instructive positive experiences were synthesized, and current problems in the organization and functioning of the Soviets and their executive apparatus were uncovered and discussed. Recommendations of Party and local government agencies were prepared on many of these matters. Some of the questions pertaining to the organization of the work of the Soviets, the executive committees, and the standing committees, and of primarily local nature, have been or will be solved locally, within the republic. Another group of questions, more general in nature, and associated with the formulation of conclusions and proposals important from a theoretical and practical point of view, are in need of further collective discussion, and comparison with data from other republics, krais and oblasts. We should like to direct the attention of our readers to some of these.

We will try to demonstrate the essence of these matters primarily with the aid of examples drawn from the Kazakh SSR, but not at all because they are typical of and limited to the latter alone. Examples of this order are typical of all the republics. And if, nonetheless, we deal primarily with Kazakhstan, it is merely because data pertaining to that area are freshest in our memories.

We would like to discuss the definition of the character of local Soviets, their nature and place in the political organization of society, inasmuch as, lacking this, it is impossible to evaluate correctly either their practical activity today or the prospects of their development.

Lenin called the Soviets the permanent and sole foundation of all government authority, of the government machinery as a whole. He emphasized that the Soviets are "agencies of state power, fully empowered deciding bodies." Their function is not merely to express and shape the will of the people on matters of significance to society, but to place behind it the power of the state — i.e., make it binding upon all. "Only elected persons may speak with the legislative authority of the state." This is Lenin's formula, defining the distinctive place of the Soviets in the system of organizations of socialist society, their supremacy. That all power, centrally and locally, belongs to the Soviets, was stated in the very first article of the Declaration of Rights of the Laboring and Exploited People, drafted by Lenin and adopted by the 3rd All-Russian Congress of Soviets in January 1918. The successive Soviet constitutions all carry this formulation. This means that the Soviets, which are of the same social nature as the other organizations of our society — the Komsomol, trade unions, cooperatives, unions of creative artists, working "in harness" with them and engaged in a common cause, developing increasingly in themselves many characteristics typical of volunteer organizations — are, unlike the others, agencies of government. The power of the state in the USSR is personified by the Soviets and effectuated through them. Only the Soviets have the right and duty to embody full state power, to issue decisions binding upon all, and to supervise their execution. Only the Soviets and their agencies possess the authority characteristic of government and can, when necessary, apply compulsion through the power of the state. This holds for the entire system of Soviets, both central and local.

Does not the posing of the question in this manner under today's conditions signify denigration of other organizations of Soviet society? Does it not reduce the leading role of the Party? No. The reason for the existence of various organizations in our society is that each of them has its own specific field of activity, important to society and essential to it specifically in its unique quality. Only with the disappearance of this specific property and as this disappearance progresses will all organizations merge into a single system of self-administration of society. Until then, each of them is required to pursue its particular affairs and to perform the tasks assigned it by the means characteristic of it. The Communist Party has been and remains the political leader in society, and its role as political leader, including its role in relation to the Soviets, is constantly growing. But its role is specifically that of political leader, developing a scientifically grounded policy, deciding the fundamental questions of organization of the leadership of society, selecting and training personnel, and carrying out the work of organization among the masses. In so doing, the Party by no means supplants the Soviets or other organizations.

The foregoing is common knowledge and comprises the ABC of Leninist administration of government. Nonetheless, it is necessary to repeat these truths, because in practice deviations from them are still committed, and one finds efforts to justify this in theory. The principle of the Program of the CPSU to the effect that, "combining in themselves the characteristics of governmental and volunteer organizations, the Soviets act increasingly as volunteer organizations with broad and direct participation of the masses in their activity," is often interpreted in the literature, for some reason, with the stress solely on the second portion. The impression is created that the governmental aspect in the organization and functioning of the Soviets is already something residual, secondary, and the quicker it withers away the better. In some writings on the local Soviets, the authors seem to be ashamed to use the term "organs of power," avoid this, and give preference to "local self-government." They center virtually all attention on demonstrating the absence of fundamental differences between the Soviets and volunteer organizations. There is clearly inadequate presentation of that which is specific to the Soviets and the governmental machinery subordinate to them, and of the characteristics of the forms of state powers which they alone possess, along with governmental forms and methods of applying those powers. And there is no stress at all on the fact that without the development and reinforcement of that which is specific, distinctive, and inherent only in agencies of government, our society cannot carry out its tasks. As we see, there is a clear, if unconscious, denigration of the role of the Soviets and hence a danger of blunting the implement that we justly term the major one in the struggle for communism.

We might have refrained from discussing this shortcoming of certain sources in the literature if they did not reflect particular phenomena in practice and, in turn, did not influence them. Unfortunately, the data of the investigations made by the institutes show that this is precisely the situation. The concept of the Soviets as solely volunteer organizations is quite widespread at the local level and in some places is leading to violation of the proper relationships between government and voluntary organizations: this is doing damage. For example, last year, in a number of raions and oblasts of the Kazakh SSR, where violations of the Model Charter and other legislation pertaining to the collective farms were common, it was impossible to find a case in which the rural Soviet had intervened and prevented the violation. One of the reasons was the position taken by the personnel of the rural Soviets: inasmuch as the collective farm is a voluntary association, the Soviet has no right to intervene in a situation existing there. Here is an example of another type. Upon study of the agendas of meetings of the executive committees of the Oblast Committees of the Komsomol and the Oblast Councils of Trade Unions of Kazakhstan, it was impossible not to see that, both in form and substance, they were duplicating many matters dealt with by the Oblast Soviets of Working People's Deputies and their executive committees. Moreover, in the records of the Karaganda and Alma-Ata Oblast Councils of Trade Unions there had been instances in which they had checked up on the work of certain bureaus of the Oblast Executive Committees of the Soviets, had called the latter to appear before them, had heard reports and issued binding instructions to their heads.

Particularly widespread is the practice of supplanting the Soviets and their machinery by the Krai, Oblast, City, and Raion Committees of the Party and the Committees of Party and State Control. The Party Committees and their bureaus decide the essence of many questions, not only economic but organizational, and often even procedural, and regulate the work of the local Soviets in detail. The bureaus of Party agencies for branches of the economy, and the personnel of the Party machinery, very often issue instructions to personnel of the bureaus of the executive committees of the Soviets over the heads of the executive committees themselves. They function, for example, as experts with respect to the lists of structures to be erected, as planners, supply men, and as "expediters" in purely economic affairs.

The practice is widespread of issuing joint decisions by Party Committees and executive committees of local Soviets on matters which the law places directly within the sole jurisdiction of the latter. This, too, diminishes the independence of the Soviets and their executive committees. Thus, in the Sary-Agach and Sairam raions of Chimkent Oblast, joint decisions of the Raion Executive Committees and Raion Party Committees regulate the registration of citizens of particular years of birth at particular draft offices, although the law places this duty upon agencies of government. In these same raions, joint decisions were taken on the functioning of post offices, including detailed instructions on how and with what communications offices were to be supplied, where mailboxes were to be placed, the rules for package acceptance, etc. It is characteristic that even monitoring of fulfillment of such decisions was assigned to the Ideological Bureau of the Raion Committee of the Party.

Instances of supplanting of the Soviets by Party agencies are numerous in other places, too. Wherever this practice exists, it leads to an abundance of decisions taken on the basis of "will," ignoring knowledge, experience, and exact accounting; the initiative and independence of governmental agencies is extinguished; their personnel become accustomed to confidence not in the specifications of the law and their Party conscience, but to phone calls and instructions "from above," even if they are plainly wrong, not motivated by the interests of the matter at hand, and originate with an individual who has a distorted understanding of his functions.

On Feb. 17, 1965, the Sairam Raion Executive Committee of Chimkent Oblast, acting on the recommendation of the Raion Committee of the Party, took a decision to assign 78 hectares of land, including 67 hectares of flood-irrigated ploughland of the Lenin Collective Farm, for construction of the Chimkent Tire Works, although the members of the executive committee were clearly aware of the irrationality of that decision. When the question was discussed at a meeting of the members of the collective farm, without whose agreement such condemnation is impossible under the law, the collective farmers began to object. They pointed out that there was much empty land in the oblast and raion suitable for new construction, and that under those circumstances to take irrigated, highly fertile lands planted to cotton — land into which the collective farm had put much labor and funds — was bad management. But the representatives from the raion insisted, and after a long discussion the meeting agreed, by a slight majority. There were doubts in both the Raion Executive Committee of the Soviets and the Raion Party Committee about the validity of taking the lands of the collective farm. Yet it was insisted that this decision be taken. Why? It turned out that there had been telephoned instructions from oblast agencies to the effect that the drawings for the building of the plant on this land had already been made (before the agreement of the collective farm to take its land had been obtained!), that the planning organization had already spent a lot of money, and therefore this particular piece of land had to be taken. This resulted because the local government agency had not been bold enough to resolve on its own a problem directly within its jurisdiction.

Insufficient clarity with respect to the nature of the local Soviets, the notion that they are primarily agencies for self-government in local affairs alone and comprise a particular form of voluntary organization or department — all this leads to artificial narrowing of the range of matters subject to their actual management, and sometimes interferes with the fullest utilization of their opportunities actively to influence the functioning of enterprises, institutions and organizations serving USSR-wide and republic-wide needs.

There is no need to prove that dwelling houses, urban and consumer service enterprises, schools, stores, hospitals, clubs, movie theatres, and pre-school institutions fall into the category of institutions of local significance and should consequently function under the direct guidance of the local Soviets. This is taken for granted, as it were, and is leading to the gradual concentration of such institutions in the hands of agencies of the local Soviets. This may be seen simply from the increase in local budgets. In 1956 they comprised (including the budgets of autonomous Soviet socialist republics) 8,800,000,000 rubles, and they are planned at about 20,000,000,000 for 1965. In Moscow, Leningrad, and many other cities of the RSFSR, in Moldavia and certain other republics, virtually all publicly owned housing, most retail trade enterprises, urban and consumer services, and socio-cultural institutions are now in the hands of the local Soviets.

Nevertheless, the process of transferring housing, consumer service, and socio-cultural units to the local Soviets is going exceedingly slowly. The notion that the local Soviets are some sort of separate, "foreign" agency, with a limited clientele to serve, has clearly become firmly established in the hands of the directors of certain enterprises, construction projects, government committees, ministries, and voluntary organizations. Therefore they do not wish under any circumstances to part with "their" bath-houses, barbershops, stores, made-to-order clothing stores, movie houses, and much else, although all this "business" is clearly not within the confines of their primary function.

In Kazakhstan a positive effect was obtained as the result of concentration of urban business in the hands of the local Soviets in Alma-Ata and Karaganda. But these are, thus far, individual cases. For the most part, the local Soviets are generals without troops. They hold only 6% of the republic's housing space, 27% of the pre-school institutions, 38% of the movie projectors, and a little more than half of the urban and consumer service enterprises. The remainder are in the hands of numerous ministries, agencies,

and the industrial enterprises and construction organizations subordinate to them. Only one-third of the funds expended in the republic for building dwellings and urban service facilities each year is allotted to the local Soviets. Therefore it is not surprising that in many cities, including large ones, everything — dwellings, water supply, bath-houses, laundries, and passenger transport — is in the hands of agencies of various sorts other than the local Soviets. To assert that in such conditions the Soviet is the "master of the city" is frivolous, to say the least. But this is not the whole story. The departmental approach to management of the local economy interferes with the execution of a unified urban development policy, complicates services to the population, divides them into "ours" and "somebody else's" and leads to ballooning of the administrative machinery. To push the process of concentrating housing, consumer, and socio-cultural services into a single set of hands is advantageous both to the people and to the state.

The role of the Soviets in the field of industrial and agricultural production has been diminished to the same degree. In the course of transferring industrial enterprises to the regional economic councils from the local Soviets, a considerable number of small, poorly equipped undertakings were taken from the latter. They operated, however, with local raw materials of which there was no shortage, gave work to unoccupied hands, and supplied the population with quite ordinary but essential products. Inasmuch as these enterprises added virtually nothing to the output volume of the economic councils, while they involved a great deal of bother, they were either shut down entirely or put in mothballs. The same thing happened to a number of enterprises transferred from the local Soviets to agencies of the Government Committee on Construction (Gosstroi). As a result, Semipalatinsk Oblast of Kazakhstan began to haul in from the RSFSR garden tools, saddleware, washstands, and many other things that had been successfully produced locally only a short while earlier. In this very place, the Glavvostokstroi of the Construction Ministry of the Kazakh SSR mothballed brickworks that had previously been part of the system of local industry, with a total annual output of some 8,000,000 bricks each, and limeworks with a capacity ranging up to 4,500 tons each. All told, little more than half the oblast's needs for brick and lime were subsequently met locally, and many raions had to haul these products from 500 or 600 kilometers away, which naturally runs into money. The conclusion is clear: to take out of the hands of the Soviets enterprises of obvious local significance not only reduced the attention these Soviets gave to industrial production, but in a number of cases had a negative influence upon the production of consumer goods.

Does this mean that the role of the local Soviets in the development of industry and construction can be increased solely by increasing the number of enterprises under their direct administration, and that it is now necessary to return to them everything that was taken out of their hands at one time or another? By no means. Certainly there are some things which it would be desirable to return to them. But what is most important is to intensify the influence brought to bear by the Soviets upon the functioning of enterprises not under their direct management, to enlarge their monitoring authority. As agencies of political power whose function it is to protect the interests of the state within the territory under their jurisdiction, the local Soviets cannot occupy the status of bystanders with respect to such undertakings, and pass by in silence shortcomings in their functioning. Things must be so organized that the local Soviet and its executive committee are kept current in the affairs of enterprises and organizations not under their direct management, assist in their operations, and that the views of the Soviets are considered by these enterprises as a matter of course in drafting plans for producing consumer goods and satisfying the socio-cultural needs of the people.

It is also important that the local Soviets make fuller use of their supervisory powers in the field of land condemnation and utilization, adherence to the rules and standards of building on the land, labor protection, and safety equip-

ment. Thought should be given to the desirability of enlarging these powers of the Soviets, and also that they have the actual opportunity to utilize them. We particularly desire to emphasize this in connection with the fact that the confines of this type of action on the part of the local Soviets have been narrowed to some degree in recent years. Thus, for example, the 1957 Statute on the Regional Economic Council granted oblast and krai government organs the right to hear reports by heads of regional economic councils on the work of these organizations and the enterprises subordinate to them, and thus to monitor this work to a certain degree from the viewpoint of combining the interests of the country as a whole and local concerns. The Statute on the Economic Council of an Economic District, adopted September 17, 1964, no longer contained even this timid formulation and thereby deprived the oblast and krai Soviets of the legal basis for fulfilling their constitutional duty to assure protection of public order, obedience to the laws and protection of citizens' rights, where enterprises and institutions under the control of the regional economic council are concerned.

The raion level has been particularly unfortunate in this connection. Contrary to the instructions of the CPSU Program on the need to strengthen this level, it was markedly weakened, and unfortunately remains in that state to this day. The raion Soviets, two-thirds of which are specialists and experienced production personnel of the collective and state farms, having an intimate concern with improving the operations of both collective and state farms and a thorough knowledge of the weak and strong sides of specific farms, found themselves deprived of the right to intervene in their affairs, to maintain order, to determine their prospects of development, the directions in which they should specialize and how they should divide the work. All this was given over entirely to the raion production administrations, which is an ordinary administrative apparatus, directly subordinate to the oblast or krai, and, where no oblast division existed, to the republic. The executive committees of the raion Soviets, to which the law entrusts the execution of the most important governmental functions in guidance of agriculture — registering the charters [of collective farms] and monitoring adherence to them, control over utilization of croplands for the proper purposes, proper maintenance and protection of equipment and plantings — are in practice unable to perform these functions, again because the experts in these fields are under the chief of the raion production administration, and not of the raion Soviet.

The raion administrations, directly subordinate to the regional or republic center, must naturally concern themselves above all with executing its directives, recommendations, or desires, even if they do not correspond entirely to the specific features of the raion, the collective or state farm. This is not due to ill will on the part of their personnel, but to the structure of these agencies, whose legal status is such that they have no legal obligation to consider that which is specific to the locality. As a consequence, stereotyped methods of operation, administration by fiat, and bureaucratism often ensue, and this has a negative influence upon collective farm and state farm production.

How can this be corrected? Lenin pointed out that, in agriculture, where one must "know how to consider the inevitability of differences that exists in reality," administrative agencies must be responsible to two different sets of authorities. This was the situation in our country for many years. And it would be desirable to reinstitute this Leninist principle, making the raion production administrations subordinate simultaneously to the raion Soviets and the oblast or krai agricultural administrations. There would probably be greater responsibility and order in their work.

Lastly, significant shortcomings in the forms and methods of work of the local Soviets are, in our opinion, connected with common mistaken notions of the real nature of the local Soviets as agencies of political authority and, consequently, as the bodies enjoying full powers in their territories. We refer, on the one hand, to the fact that most local Soviets feel a lack of authority, and on the other hand, that they make weak use of the powers they already enjoy, that the combination of methods of persuasion and compulsion is not always correct in their work, and that the measures they issue are far from being unconditionally and undeviatingly executed.

Consider the decisions taken by local Soviets, and you will note how few concrete instructions and binding orders they contain, and how many general declarations, slogans, and exhortations there are. We witnessed how the personnel of certain rural Soviets tortured themselves to find acceptable formulations in drafting decisions pertaining to conditions in the departments of collective farms, and how the personnel of the Alma-Ata City Executive Committee broke their heads over the same matter as they prepared a report on the state of legality and protection of citizens' rights at enterprises in the city to be presented at a meeting. We saw the verbal balancing act to which the Karaganda oblast executive committee had recourse in its efforts to obtain from the regional economic council and Glavtsentrostroi fulfillment of the government plan for construction of housing and cultural and social facilities. "Request," "recommend," "direct attention," "seek out possibilities," "consider desirable," were the terms used, when in each instance the matter at issue was elimination of outrageous situations discovered by the deputies, and the natural thing would have been to demand from the responsible authorities that they be eliminated within a fixed period of time. But this was impossible, inasmuch as the Statutes on Local Soviets adopted in 1957-1959 had omitted a considerable proportion of the formulations of the prior legislation with respect to the governmental powers of local state organs, replacing them by terms like "cooperates in," "assists," etc. During the last few years, these errors have not only not been corrected, but in some cases were even worsened. Let us be specific. Formerly the raion Soviets and their executive committees possessed and utilized the right to set aside any illegal decision of the management or general meeting of a collective farm. That is in their power as organs of government. But an exception is now made to these rules. In cases when the matter at issue is expulsion of citizens from membership in the collective farm, the raion government is deprived of authority and is reduced to the role of no more than an advisor to the collective farms.

The erroneous notion that the role of administrative orders and measures of compulsion is already reduced to zero in the present period and that it is dishonorable to employ these powers fully has also had the consequence that it has become a rarity for local Soviets to hold officials to responsibility for violation of the laws with respect to protection of the rights of citizens, conservation, observance of sanitation rules and safety procedures. This sort of connivance reduces the force of the documents issued by the local Soviets and diminishes their authority. Here is a typical instance. On June 9, 1964, the Sary-Agach Raion Executive Committee of Chimkent Oblast issued, in conjunction with condemnation of some of the lands of the "Red East" Collective Farm for construction of elements of the Poltoratsk Gas Storage Facilities, an order to reimburse the collective farm for the losses suffered in this connection. Simultaneously the Executive Committee forbade the Tashkent Administration of Major Gas Pipelines from undertaking construction where crops were standing, until they had been completely harvested. Upon receiving the land, the administration took these instructions as obligatory. But latter construction proceeded in such fashion that considerably more land was occupied than had been assigned for the purpose, and, in addition, the irrigation canals to the cotton fields of the collective farm were cut in April 1965. Nearly 350 acres of cotton were threatened. And the demands made by the Raion Executive Committee produced no action. The chief of the administration was not called to account by any of the personnel of the republic's machinery, although, as we see, he deliberately violated the orders of the organ of power. The reasoning was, in all probability, quite simple: the government here is local, on the raion level, while the organization involved is on the republic level.

We do not hold that the local authorities should shift from an undue emphasis upon persuasion to measures of administrative punishment, with orders and punishments one upon the other. But we are against their engaging solely in wheedling and appeals. It is necessary that, when required, they function as organs of power and perform functions of power. We know how sharply Lenin ridiculed flabby, jelly-like authorities, and how persistently he strove toward the end that our governmental bodies of authority, being the most democratic and humane, be firm at the same time. It is precisely these qualities — democracy, sensitivity, humaneness, along with firmness and decisiveness, that our government of all the people — the Soviets of Working People's Deputies — should possess.

* * *